PUTTING THE LOCAL IN GLOBAL EDUCATION

PUTTING THE LOCAL IN GLOBAL EDUCATION

Models for Transformative Learning Through Domestic Off-Campus Programs

EDITED BY

Neal W. Sobania

Foreword by

Adam Weinberg

STERLING, VIRGINIA

Published by Stylus Publishing, LLC
22883 Quicksilver Drive
Sterling, Virginia 20166-2102

Library of Congress Cataloging-in-Publication Data
Putting the local in global education: models for transformative
learning through domestic off-campus programs / edited by Neal
W. Sobania ; foreword by Adam Weinberg. – First edition.
    pages cm
Includes bibliographical references and index.
ISBN 978-1-62036-167-2 (cloth : alk. paper)
ISBN 978-1-62036-168-9 (pbk. : alk. paper)
ISBN 978-1-62036-169-6 (library networkable e-edition)
ISBN 978-1-62036-170-2 (consumer e-edition)
1. University extension–United States. 2. Service learning–United
States. 3. Community and college–United States 4. Education and
globalization. I. Sobania, N. W., editor of compilation.
LC6251.P87 2015
370.11'5–dc23
                                                            2014044191
13-digit ISBN: 978-1-62036-167-2 (cloth)
13-digit ISBN: 978-1-62036-168-9 (paperback)
13-digit ISBN: 978-1-62036-169-6 (library networkable e-edition)
13-digit ISBN: 978-1-62036-170-2 (consumer e-edition)

Printed in the United States of America

All first editions printed on acid-free paper
that meets the American National Standards Institute
Z39-48 Standard.

Bulk Purchases

Quantity discounts are available for use in workshops and for
staff development.
Call 1-800-232-0223

First Edition, 2015

10   9   8   7   6   5   4   3   2   1

For all our mentors on whose legacy we continue to build and innovate.

CONTENTS

PART THREE: FACULTY-LED SHORT-TERM PROGRAMS

PART FOUR: CONSORTIUM PROGRAMS

PART FIVE: COMMUNITY ENGAGEMENT AND DOMESTIC STUDY AWAY

FOREWORD

As a new college president, I am struck by the wide range of challenges faced by colleges and universities. Among the most pressing are financial models that no longer seem to be working, the difficulty of taking good ideas to scale, the globalization of higher education, the loss of public confidence in who we are and what we do, and the need to make certain we are using high-impact pedagogies to ensure that our students realize the learning outcomes they need to adapt to a changing and increasingly competitive world.

In this context, domestic study away is an important and understudied part of the higher education landscape. Prior to coming to Denison University, I spent eight years working in the international education space as president and CEO of World Learning. There, I saw daily the power of overseas study abroad through World Learning's SIT Study Abroad programs. It became clear to me that well-run international experiential programs transform students by increasing their intellectual engagement, opening their minds to new views and thoughts, and helping students develop important attributes, from language skills to humility, persistence, and grit.

However, I also came away from that experience frustrated by the dominant study abroad model. First, as many of the chapters in this volume note, too many students go on study abroad programs in places that are not challenging in part because they look and feel too much like U.S. campuses. Students are effectively having the U.S. college experience abroad, but with less academic work. Second, most programs are expensive. This means that too often they are open only to wealthier students or to students from wealthier colleges. In total, fewer than 5% of U.S. students have a study abroad experience. And while the numbers are increasing, they are doing so at a glacial pace.

Given the need to shift where students are studying, the models used, and the scale of participation, we safely can say that traditional study abroad is not likely to have a dramatic impact across higher education anytime soon. In this context, domestic study away is intriguing. The magic of off-campus study rests on the following pillars: (a) getting students outside of their comfort zones and into new spaces and places that challenge their assumptions and world views; (b) using active pedagogies that weave theory and practice together through reflection; (c) creating opportunities for students to inter-act with a wide range of people, encountering difference and a larger set of views than they typically will bump into on their home campuses; (d) cre-ating a total learning environment, where a set of courses and cocurricular experiences are woven together to explore a tight set of intellectual themes in depth; and (e) exposing students to the global dimensions of the world in which they will live.

Critics claim that students need to leave the country to experience pro-grams that meet these principles, especially via programs that expose them to new cultures and languages. This argument does not hold up under exami-nation. In fact, many of our students continue to go to places in Western Europe that likely feel much more similar to their home campuses than some neighboring U.S. cities. Having spent years in central New York State with students from the East Coast, I submit that they would be challenged by both the urban and rural parts of Texas, Arkansas, and Tennessee that formed a large part of my youth.

The chapters in this volume suggest that domestic study away may do a better job of delivering on the promises that study abroad too often fails to keep. The chapters also suggest intriguing aspects of domestic study away that cannot be met by traditional study abroad.

First, we can imagine these experiences happening earlier in a student's college career. Study abroad has been mostly relegated to a semester-long project for juniors. This comes too late in the college career and is discon-nected from the rest of the college experience. We could imagine domestic study away taking place earlier and perhaps effected in a way that would allow for multiple experiences.

Second, we can imagine domestic study away as an equalizer. I worry that wealthier colleges are quickly creating two colleges within one. As they have diversified their student populations, they have struggled to make all the educational experiences equally open to every student. Traditional study abroad is expensive. Domestic study away should allow us to craft programs that are more open to the broad range of students who populate our cam-puses.

Third, we also can imagine an important political dimension to this work. Many of the early proponents of study abroad were driven by a belief that cross-cultural understanding was crucial to creating a better world. We still face daunting international cross-cultural challenges. But we also face domestic cross-cultural challenges. Domestic study away can overcome both challanges. It can expose students to a broad array of global cultures, reli-gions, languages, and practices as they exist in many parts of the United States, while also creating the kinds of cross-cultural understanding that we need domestically to help this generation of students learn to work across difference.

Simply put, the chapters in this volume are interesting and important. They are grounded in existing programs, giving us real examples of what is possible. They are theoretically challenging, raising questions about the construction of key concepts in ways that could and should encourage us to examine institutional practices. As a volume, there is clearly a call to embrace domestic study away as a legitimate practice and strategy that should be more central to higher education, especially our efforts at internationalization. Count me in as one college president who is ready to shift his thinking.

Adam Weinberg
President
Denison University

ACKNOWLEDGMENTS

Particular thanks are due to Larry Braskamp for his guidance, encouragement, and unwavering support of this project. Our collaboration around the concept of study away that has shaped this book began innocently enough when I mentioned after moving to Pacific Lutheran University (PLU) that we did not talk about study abroad here, but study away. As the logic of this notion got hold of him and he began to think more deeply about it, as he is wont to do with interesting ideas, we began to toss around and spin off other implications of the concept. After I returned to the faculty at PLU and was finally able to accept the challenge of editing a book on domestic off-campus study, he was generous with his time, providing clear and insightful advice that has been invaluable in my thinking and writing, although responsibility for the final product is mine.

Over the past few years and now in preparing this book I have benefited from productive conversations with many colleagues, but I want to particularly acknowledge Joe Brockington, Andy Law, Jim Pellow, Rich Slimbach, and of course my many colleagues at PLU, especially those from the Wang Center for Global Education, who actively promote, offer, and lead study away programs at home and across the world.

I am also indebted to many mentors, friends, and colleagues in the field of study abroad from whom I have learned so much and with whom I have journeyed these many years, from a time when we could once actually name all the programs offered by the major third-party providers, to the dozens upon dozens that are now offered. Although these folks are simply too numerous to mention, the fact that one can call upon any one of them for advice or consultation is what so many of us enjoy about this field. And call upon many I did to help identify the programs that are featured in this volume. In the end this turned out to be a labor of love, providing an opportunity to speak with friends and colleagues in international education offices across the country, who offered suggestions or shared my frustration at how hard these domestic programs can be to identify. Some I would never have found on my own, and so I owe a special word of gratitude to Susan Holme, Irene Burgess, and Jacqueline McLeod.

Unlike study abroad, there are no national organizations or association meetings that bring together directors of off-campus programs that operate wholly or partly in the United States. National organizations exist for community-based education programs (and service-learning); for example, the National Society for Experiential Education, the National Youth Leadership Council, and the International Association for Research on Service and Service-Learning and Community Engagement. Rarely are these programs, even when students earn academic credit, thought of as off-campus study in the way study abroad is. Further, this seems somewhat ironic when the latter programs increasingly struggle to add meaningful program components that include community-based learning. It is hoped that one day a national group will step forward to give voice to the important role that domestic off-campus programs are playing in transforming global learners.

I also want to thank John von Knorring for his patience and encouragement, which have finally resulted in this volume seeing the light of day, and the terrific staff at Stylus, especially Alexandra Hartnett who made editing it such a positive experience. Most importantly, I am grateful to my wife, Liz, for her love, understanding, and forbearance as I keep finding new projects to tackle.

Neal Sobania
Lakewood, WA
October 2014

INTRODUCTION
The Local–Global Nexus

Neal W. Sobania

This and future generations of students are and will increasingly be interacting with a larger, more globalized community. It must then follow that they need to become even more competent in understanding, talking with, relating to, and working with persons who differ from themselves. Among others, these differences may manifest themselves politically, socioeconomically, racially, ethnically, and religiously. To become comfortable with such differences, students must have the opportunity—but not just any opportunity—to experience difference. This opportunity needs to be well-planned and structured to take a student beyond a mere experience, to confront what they believe they know and how they think and act.

For some time now colleges and universities have addressed this academically, in the classroom, through the promotion of study abroad, and cocurricularly, with volunteer activities through student life. The more recent acknowledgment of globalization as a factor in our everyday lives, even when not particularly well-defined, has given support to this approach, while recognizing that such efforts are not sufficient.

The reality with regard to study abroad is that it still involves sending the vast majority of students to study in Europe, where they expect to be comfortable among people they assume are "like us" and who will also "like us." However, when these students hang out together overseas, expect facilities similar to their home campus, want the bells and whistles of organized activities arranged for them, and spend their weekends traveling with each other, how much encounter is there with difference, and what is learned from it? What students learn—academically and interculturally—depends to a large degree on the program and the dedication of its leadership. Recognition of this has led to the establishment and promotion of best practices (The Forum on Education Abroad, 2011) and discussions of "high impact practices" (Kuh, 2008). The most recent cause du jour is "global learning," but what does this mean and must a student always go overseas to be a global learner (AAC&U, 2014; Hovland, 2014)?

This was our motivation to write the article "Study Abroad or Study Away: It's Not Merely Semantics" (Sobania & Braskamp, 2009). In this and a presentation entitled "Educating Students to Live Locally as Global Citizens" the following year at the AAC&U Annual Meeting, we made the case for domestic off-campus study to be given as serious consideration for meeting many of the same learning goals as study abroad. This was put forward as an expansion of opportunities, either/or or both, not instead of. And we went further, suggesting the term *study away* was a more inclusive way to label all academic credit-earning off-campus study programs, whether they took place overseas or here in the United States.

Study away is not a term we created. During 20-plus years in study abroad, I had not encountered the term until 2005 when I became the executive director of the Wang Center for International Education at Pacific Lutheran University in Tacoma, Washington. At PLU everyone speaks about study away when referring to academic off-campus study, regardless of program location. Although this feature was not originally reflected in the Center's name, this was corrected in 2010 to reflect what was already understood to be the case across campus, and the center was rebranded as the Wang Center for Global Education. (The only other concerted effort I made to change terminology—to ban the word *trip* as a four-letter word, especially for short-term study away programs—was futile. But the word *trip* is largely avoided in this book.) Although not familiar with the term *study away*, I was well aware of domestically based programs. As a faculty member (indeed, I have always approached off-campus study as an academic) and the director of international education at Hope College for many years, I had been a regular participant in the Great Lakes Colleges Association's "International and Off-Campus Education Committee" (see http://glca.org/groups/iocec), which, under this and earlier names, had for more than 30 years brought together the on-campus international education directors of the 12 colleges and the 4 directors of consortia-sponsored programs, 3 of which were exclusively domestic. But the term *study away* never surfaced.

Following conversations with John von Knorring of Stylus Publishing, two factors came into focus that suggested the need for a publication that would pull together a number of case studies of successful domestic off-campus programs in a kind of "how-to" volume. The first factor was the realization that domestic off-campus programs existed, albeit few and far between, but rarely as part of the purview of programs for which study abroad offices had responsibility. The second factor was recognition that some of the programs were not only hugely successful but also meeting many of the same learning outcomes as overseas programs. Further, some of these U.S.-focused programs were as old as the oldest study abroad programs. The more thoroughly these programs were considered, the clearer it became that the models and the essential characteristics of quality off-campus programs are the same (The Forum, 2011), wherever they are offered.[1] This was further driven home to me while I was reading essays of the PLU students who had participated in the January term class among the Makah Indian Tribe only 200 miles from campus (see chapter 14 in this volume). A first-year student, disappointed that all the overseas January term (J-term) courses were full, wrote:

> Studying abroad was something I always wanted to do. As an incoming first-year I knew that learning in a global environment was something I wanted to participate in, but I never expected that it would happen so quickly. Similarly, I never knew that I could interact with a distinct culture without ever having to leave my home state of Washington. . . . Though I did learn a lot about the Makah culture's past, I feel like I gained more from being a part of their present. . . . They WANTED us to experience their culture, not to study it . . . but the reason to take this course is the same reason you take any other study abroad course; to experience a new culture that is different from your own. I hear people say "Oh, you stayed in Washington" when I explain where Neah Bay is, and I can't help but feel sorry for those who do not understand the learning opportunities that are in our own backyard. (Aaron S., program participant, 2011)

It is not about location; it's about learning.

The particular challenge in making the case that global learning can happen in the United States is not in convincing college faculty or administrators that they and their students can encounter difference around the corner. Today, even in many rural locations, the United States has become so richly diverse that a student does not need to travel more than a few blocks from campus to encounter other facets of the world (after all, the world has been coming to the United States for decades and continues to come) or to have a cross-cultural experience, hear other languages spoken, meet people from different cultural traditions, and discover religious practices different from one's own. Rather, the first challenge was to identify rigorous academic programs offered by various colleges, universities, and consortia that are globally minded and locally focused. Such "local" programs are not generally accessed through a study abroad office; in fact, they are rarely found in any single office on a college or university campus. However, with advice from friends and colleagues who share this passion of providing students with high-quality, global experiential educational learning opportunities, I was able to identify many such programs, indeed more than we have been able to include in this volume. The second challenge was to demonstrate not only the potential range of opportunities possible in domestic off-campus programming, and that these need to be understood as an experience as valid as one undertaken overseas, but also the way in which these fit well with topics that are today front and center in higher education, including curriculum integration, intercultural learning, social justice, community engagement, access, and diversity. Responding to these challenges is what this volume is about.

An immersive, place-based learning experience is basic to all the programs described in the chapters that follow. In each of the case studies, the program is tied to a particular U.S. location, from Hawai'i to Maine and multiple places in between, and yet what they demonstrate is the delivery of learning experiences that support the creation of a globally competent, engaged, and informed citizenry and workforce.

Interestingly, in marketing overseas study opportunities, the case is often made that it is excellent preparation for living and working in the twenty-first century, yet the vast majority of alumni from such programs will work in the United States and not overseas. In reality, with an expanded knowledge base of strong and transferable intellectual and practical skills, regardless of where these are acquired, students who participate in off-campus study are better prepared to navigate an increasingly complex, diverse, and ever-changing world. Finally, if the case for study away needs any further reinforcement, it is that versatility, adaptability, cultural sensitivity, critical thinking, and a tolerance for ambiguity are among the same learning goals we have for all university graduates whether they study abroad or not—learning skills, self-identity formation, and appropriate interactions with others.

The book is organized in five parts. Before delving into the actual case studies, the book opens with a part titled, "Framing Study Away." In the first chapter, "The Faraway Nearby: Putting the Local in Global Education," Neal Sobania provides an in-depth rationale, only touched on briefly in this introduction, for both why and how domestic off-campus programs, when part of a rich set of off-campus offerings, can increase the opportunities for ever larger numbers of students to have broader global learning experiences. The next four chapters address issues with which every off-campus program must wrestle, but do so in the context of study away. While it is assumed that every off-campus program begins with a set of learning outcomes that drive the program's goals, organization, and structure, we know this is not always the case. But when drafting these learning outcomes, how conscious are we of the multiple variables (i.e., factors or influences) that can impact student learning on study away? Using a step-by-step explanation as he might when leading a faculty workshop on the subject, Mark Salisbury (Augustana College) in "Matching Program and Student Characteristics With Learning Outcomes: A Framework for Study Away Curriculum Development" (chapter 2) lays out these variables from program duration to pedagogical approaches that impact learning.

In "Where Experience Meets Transformation: Pedagogy and Study Away" (chapter 3), Amanda E. Feller (Pacific Lutheran University) uses communication theory to provide a valuable and thought-provoking distinction of the difference between experiential learning and transformational learning, a distinction she notes is too little taken into account when planning or leading a study away program. Recognizing that experience does not necessarily relate to experiential learning, Feller builds off the teacher–learner relationship to note that experiential learning, unless carefully guided, is not always transformative. Where experiential learning focuses on the student's whole sensory experience in a particular place, transformational learning is about an experience that prompts the collapse of the way the student once saw the world—shifting from an old paradigm to a new one. The premise is that assuming no one's identity is permanently fixed, then the goal of study away is at least in part about decentering a student—intellectually and personally, with the former being the experiential part, and the latter the transformational aspect.

In "Evaluative Approaches to Domestic Off-Campus Programs" (chapter 4), Mark E. Engberg and Lisa M. Davidson (Loyola University Chicago) tackle assessment, stressing that assessment is about design, implementation, and continuous improvement. It includes collecting evidence about characteristics of students, environmental conditions, and indicators of student learning and development. Today, with campuses everywhere engaged in assessment, and the hopes dashed of those who thought it might just go away, Engberg and Davidson offer an accessible guide for practitioners to consider when determining how they will gauge success. They carefully lay out the scrupulous planning required in the preliminary stages of an evaluative process, present the methodological considerations that need to be taken into account, and conclude with a set of recommendations to weigh when serious about connecting a study away experience with global learning.

In the last chapter of this part, "No Common Ground: The Spectrum of Policies Related to Domestic Off-Campus Programs" (chapter 5), Michael Edmondson (Augustana College) draws on his survey of college and university presidents and off-campus administrators, taken while he was part of The Philadelphia Center, to describe the differences of opinion, policies, and support that college and university campuses have toward domestic off-campus programs. From these institutional policies and levels of support, it is apparent that great disparity exists. Unlike the generally universal support for study abroad programs, support for off-campus programs in the United States ranges from actively embracing them as a way to expand student learning opportunities, to outright discouragement of student participation, and many points in between.

The chapters in the four parts that follow introduce and detail programs that are well-established and one that is in the final stages of development. The takeaways from these chapters include not only how programs treat a locale or region as a global learning environment, the pedagogies they employ, and the critical role played by reflection in the learning process, but also how the development of trusting personal and community relationships is the foundation of a successful program, how to utilize local voices as effective teachers, and how to assist students in confronting uncomfortable ideas and situations. Thoughtful student reflections are included in many of the chapters. These programs are not presented to be replicated, but rather to serve as models of programs from which one can draw ideas, knowledge, and encouragement to develop new programs that can push students outside their comfort zone and encourage them to see the world through different lenses and learn from these different perspectives. And in the process, I suspect that many readers will be introduced to, and perhaps derive inspiration from, some little-known aspects of the United States, from the "shout" of the Sea Islands and seizure of sacred lands in Hawai'i to our disconnect with the land and natural systems in the West and elsewhere that we unthinkingly assume are stable and will continue to sustain us.

The second part, as the title makes clear, focuses on "Semester-Long Faculty-Led Programs." Those featured are of course not the only colleges and universities that offer such opportunities.[2] This part includes three very different programs that are all focused in the western region of the United States, one in the Southeast, and another with offerings on each coast. These chapters illustrate how such programs can not only transform the way students look at our country but also provide the tools students need to begin to understand how global issues impact individuals and communities. "Global Issues Manifested in a Local Setting: The Arizona Borderlands" (chapter 6), by Patty Lamson and Riley Merline (Earlham College), offers a detailed look at a program that focuses students' study on an issue that has been part of this region's history for decades: immigration and the U.S.-Mexico border.

"Seeing Things Whole: Immersion in the West" (chapter 7) is an environmental studies program designed and led by Phil Brick, a political scientist (Whitman College). Taking full advantage of different regions across the Far West, the program immerses students in a range of issues, including ones that have evolved over the 10 years the program has been offered, such as the challenge of climate disruption and practices in land management. Throughout the program, using a unique model of directed reflection, students develop narratives that they then share with a broader public.

In "Sojourns in the Lowcountry: Gateway to Africa in the Americas" (chapter 8), Jacquelyn Benton (Metropolitan State University of Denver) charts her development of a fall semester program that focuses on the Sea Islands off the coasts of Georgia and South Carolina. This unique program examines the influences of African traditions that remain part of this region's celebration of cultural memory, and how the program grew from a student program to one that now encompasses alumni and community members.

Rob Pyatt (University of Colorado Boulder), an instructor in architecture and a practicing architect, with Jennifer L. Benning, Nick Tilsen, Charles Jason Tinant, and Leonard Lone Hill, detail a program that brings together students of architecture and engineering design from the University of Colorado, the Oglala Lakota College, and the South Dakota School of Mines and Technology to research and design appropriate and sustainable housing for the Pine Ridge Reservation. "Pedagogy Into Practice: Teaching Environmental Design Through the Native American Sustainable Housing Initiative" (chapter 9) begins with collaboration during the academic year, which includes learning about and taking into account Oglala Lakota beliefs and practices and culminates in a summer construction experience that includes teams of students from all three institutions.

This second part closes with "Study USA: Preparing Students to Enter the Most Diverse Workforce in the World" (chapter 10), in which Connie Ledoux Book and two program directors, J. McMerty and William Webb (Elon University), address how the university expanded two short-term programs in Los Angeles and New York City into semester-long programs. Elon, an institution that regularly ranks high in Open Doors, then established a Study USA program office within its Global Education Center. The Los Angeles and New York City programs have not only provided unique learning opportunities for Elon students, but also have created professional development opportunities for faculty, provided a means for meaningful interactions with the university's alumni in these cities, and in turn created a bridge to new internship opportunities and potential employment of Elon students.

Part three, "Faculty-Led Short-Term Programs," highlights five such programs. Just as in the second part, each program includes an immersive study away experience in which students are embedded in a local community and able to acquire a real sense of people's daily lives. The section begins with three intensive programs, one offered in the January term and two in the summer, followed by two chapters, both focused on Native Americans, that look closely at how an intensive study away experience of 7 to 10 days can be effectively embedded into a regular course taught on campus. One is part of a regular spring semester course and the other is a January term course.

In "From Immersion With Farmers and Autoworkers to Refugees and Immigrants: 40 Years of Transformational Learning" (chapter 11), Jeff Thaler recounts how a Williams College program begun 40 years ago, and in which he was a participant, has been renewed to allow students to experience the lives of refugees and immigrants in Portland, Maine. Focusing on the irony that as diversity in the United States has increased we know less about our neighbors, coworkers, and communities, he details how students are pushed outside their comfort zone to actively and considerately question, listen to, and learn from people whom they do not know and would not normally encounter. Oumatie Marajh and Esther Onaga (Michigan State University) in "Beyond Waikīkī: Discovering the *Aloha* Spirit in Hawai'i" (chapter 12), write about how they immerse students in aspects of the islands that are still vital to the indigenous population, but are rarely seen or experienced by the islands' many tourists. They also include a discussion of the different teaching models they employ in a rural community and the one used in a large urban setting cohosted by local university faculty. In "GO Long or GO Short, but GO: Study Away as Curricular Requirement" (chapter 13), Scott Manning and Christina Dinges (Susquehanna University) use two short-term programs, one in New Orleans and the other in Hawai'i, to address how their university made study away a curricular requirement and at the same time introduced a set of common learning outcomes that a study away program must meet whether it is offered overseas or in the United States.

The chapters on the First Nations of the Makah, "'It's So Good to See You Back in Town': Participating in Makah Culture" (chapter 14), and the Oglala Lakota, "Practicing Lifelong Learning and Global Citizenship on the Pine Ridge Indian Reservation" (chapter 15) are about programs embedded in on-campus courses. Both courses have pre- and postimmersion experiences of differing durations and include the examination of a facet of community-based learning (CBL)—service-learning, which is a feature of both these and a number of other programs. David R. Huelsbeck (Pacific Lutheran University) does so as an anthropologist immersing students in a Northwest Coast Salish community. Kathryn Burleson (Warren Wilson College) does so among the Lakota as part of a cultural psychology course. Yet both see service-learning as an embedded cultural practice that requires students to get beyond what they expect this "service" to be and what the communities want. Burleson explicitly frames her chapter around the practice of lifelong learning and Huelsbeck around service, trust, and respect, yet in both programs the overriding theme is about interacting and learning with community members outside a structured classroom environment and acknowledging and appreciating the significance of what the community is doing for the students.

The fourth part, titled "Consortium Programs," introduces five programs that are either sponsored by a college that makes its program available to consortium members and nonmembers or is offered by an independent not-for-profit to which institutions send their students. In "Is Place the Thing? Integrative Learning at The Philadelphia Center" (chapter 16), Rosina S. Miller argues that the most important criterion for determining the depth and nature of the learning is the program model and not the place. Then using The Philadelphia Center, an offering of the Great Lakes Colleges Association (GLCA), she demonstrates how this program's model and the programmatic requirements provide the structure of an intentional pedagogy to engage with place, wherever place may be located, to engender global learning.

The New York Arts program, another GLCA program offering, is the subject of "Learning to Stand on Shifting Ground: The New York Arts Program" (chapter 17). Linda Earle, the program's director, shows how the city's art scene, from artists, designers, and filmmakers to choreographers, museum curators, and theater administrators, serve as mentors and resources to offer students engaged learning opportunities. After seminars, internships, and deep reflection, each student emerges at semester's end with a finely honed independent project.

"Library and Museum Collections as Labs for Student Learning: The ACM Newberry Research Seminar in the Humanities" (chapter 18) discusses a Chicago-based program's structure and individualized learning plans, which are the agents for the acquisition of knowledge and growth. Museums, archives, heritage societies, and historical homes, as well as research libraries such as the Newberry, are found across the country. Whether in small towns, medium-sized cities, or large urban centers, each presents a unique learning environment in which opportunities exist for establishing creative off-campus study programs. Using the special collections of the Newberry, which provide the academic core of this program, Joan Gillespie, vice president and director of Off-Campus Study Programs at the Associated Colleges of the Midwest (ACM), addresses how the institution, its staff, and college faculty fellows who accompany the students lead seminars and enjoy a unique faculty development opportunity, taking advantage of both the place of learning (the library) and the place in which it is located (Chicago) to "introduce undergraduates to the library and to the rigors and excitement of scholarship" (personal communication, D. Dillon, 2014)

"Immersing Students in Conservation and Community: Northwest Connections" (chapter 19) offers its expertise to colleges and universities through long- and short-term educational programs. Melanie Parker, Northwest Connections' executive director, demonstrates how through field courses that integrate educational and conservation programs, homestays, and data collection, Northwest Connections' programs immerse students in real-world learning situations, all the while working hard not to promote one particular perspective. Throughout their time in Montana, students are challenged to integrate their knowledge from science with what they learn from local residents.

This fourth part concludes with Sarah Pradt, the director of programs of the Higher Education Consortium for Urban Affairs (HECUA), noting how HECUA's nearly 50-year history began with the offering of programs in the United States, particularly in Minneapolis, and their discovery as expressed in the chapter's title, "'No Such Thing as Away': Urban Immersion in the Upper Midwest—and Around the World" (chapter 20). Pradt illustrates the way HECUA's programs use theory and practice to assist students in understanding the constructed nature of knowledge and the learning that comes from students experiencing transformative encounters that can lead to imagining and building alternatives to the status quo.

The final part, "Community Engagement and Domestic Study Away," consists of four chapters that address the place of community-based education in global learning. These are academic programs that employ service-learning as a tool for collaborative learning, not volunteer activities that are sometimes framed as service-learning.[3] Clearly such programs play off the ever-increasing number of students who have participated in activities from mission trips to Habitat for Humanity projects. However, while these are all worthy enterprises, when young people believe they are the ones who are personally bringing needed knowledge to share with communities they understand as poverty-stricken and downtrodden, whether locally or overseas, what is the learning takeaway from these encounters with difference? What the authors and professional community-based education practitioners do in these chapters is strip away any ambiguity about who are the teachers and who are the students.

In "Liberal Education and Service-Learning as a High-Impact Practice" (chapter 21), Rachel Tomas Morgan and Paul Kollman (University of Notre Dame) open this fifth part by asking the challenging question, What matters in U.S. higher education today? and by connecting the Association of American Colleges and Universities's (AAC&U) LEAP vision for college learning and high-impact practices to CBL programs. After outlining the various types of CBL (service-learning) programs available to students at Notre Dame—seminars, summer service-learning programs, and community-based research projects—they address the practices and pedagogies these programs employ. In all these cases there is a focus on developing a sense of social responsibility and applying knowledge and learned practical skills in real-world settings.

Then drawing on assessment results from these programs, they make the case for combining global learning with civic engagement through CBL and service-learning to "restore the vibrancy of liberal education in the twenty-first century." They also demonstrate how the for-credit academic programs they offer both during the academic year and in the summer are structured in such a way so as to be flexible enough to enable the development of new seminar programs that are responsive both to emerging social issues and to student interests and can take advantage of the university's extensive alumni network.

The next two chapters focus directly on the critical role of faculty development in being able to offer academic programs that focus on community-based education. Celestina Castillo, Regina Freer, Felisa Guillén, and Donna Maeda (Occidental College), in "Faculty Development and Ownership of Community-Engaged Teaching and Learning" (chapter 22), and Kent Koth (Seattle University), in "The World Is at the Campus Doorstep for Putting the Local in Global Education" (chapter 23), are involved in community-based education through centers whose mission is to engage the local communities in which their institutions are located. Castillo and her coauthors note the significant shift in CBL, from volunteerism to development of long-term reciprocal relationships, and how through those relationships opportunities to share and create knowledge are enabled. They go on to demonstrate how this type of learning in community simply cannot be duplicated within the classroom, and how necessary faculty workshops are to enable faculty to successfully incorporate CBL into their teaching.

Koth picks up the theme of faculty development, noting the benefits that accrue from developing local community-based teaching and research and how this can also complement the international interests, expertise, and knowledge of faculty. Through a Faculty Fellows Program, faculty members are immersed in local neighborhoods and learn pedagogical tools to enable them to effectively use academic service-learning in their classes. Noting the additional benefits of CBL for students, for the university, and for the local community(ies), he offers a set of recommendations for universities that want to connect their classrooms with local communities near their campus.

In the last chapter, "The Power of Place: University–Community Partnership in the Development of an Urban Immersion Semester" (chapter 24), JoDee Keller, Rose McKenney, Kathy Russell, and Joel Zylstra (Pacific Lutheran University) detail all that they have gone through in planning and developing a soon-to-be-opening, deeply immersive urban semester in the Puget Sound. They document how they have gone about building trusting relationships and partnerships locally, developing program components and appropriate pedagogies to meet shared learning outcomes, and organizing for the faculty development necessary to sustain the program. Building on local diversity, students will be guided in acquiring the abilities to better understand and engage with cultural differences so they can one day be comfortable with diverse populations whether at home or abroad.

The value of putting not just human faces into the learning environment, but named individuals with whom the students have an opportunity to interact cannot be underestimated. A couple of years ago, I began to remark that increasingly my goals for students participating in global education seemed to boil down to two things: First, that they meet people during study away whose names they learn and recognize that these individuals have aspirations similar to their own, or those their parents have for them; second, that when they hear in the media that something has happened in the location where they studied—be it an election, an earthquake, an uprising, famine, whatever—they will think first about these named individuals and wonder how they are doing.

If one were to try to summarize the core characteristics that stand out as critical to the success of the programs featured in this volume, they would certainly include (a) the significance of a firsthand encounter with difference that makes a difference and that facilitates a student experiencing the complexity of the world's communities to challenge what they know, how they think, and how they act; (b) the importance of building a trusting relationship with local communities based on reciprocity, understanding, and respect in order for such encounters to occur; (c) the critical role of having a focused intellectual theme with appropriate learning outcomes and pedagogies to meet those outcomes; and (d) the necessity of directed reflection for students to make meaning out of their experience.

Putting the Local in Global Education concludes with an afterword by Larry Braskamp, with whom I first began this project some years back. Drawing on the multiplicity of programs detailed in this volume, and the pedagogies and strategies the contributors describe for ensuring their students encounter difference, he offers five suggestions that can be adopted by those who are already committed, or are willing to commit, to making global learning a goal of a twenty-first-century college education, a goal that can be enhanced significantly by expanding opportunities for students through the broader definition of what constitutes *study away*.

Notes

1. Interestingly, an early study (Hull, Lemke, & Houang, 1977) assessing the change in American undergraduates participating in overseas off-campus programs and off-campus domestic programs concluded that "no clear or general superiority of off-campus overseas programs was demonstrated over off-campus domestic programs on variables long considered to be in the semiexclusive domain of international programs."

2. Along with the semester internship programs that many individual institutions run in Washington, DC, and increasingly in New York City, are programs that range from the well-known Azusa Pacific University Los Angeles Term (www.apu.edu/losangeles), founded by Richard Slimbach, to the American and Global Mosaics program of Dickinson College (PA) (www.dickinson.edu/academics/programs/american-studies/content/Mosaic-Projects/).

3. Whether to talk about community-based education or service-learning presents a challenge, in part because the term *service-learning* is so deeply embedded in the literature of what has increasingly come to be identified as community-based learning, or CBL. Adding to this confusion is the use of "community service" to describe what students are assigned to do as punishment when busted for infraction of campus rules.

References

Association of American Colleges and Universities (AAC&U). (2014). Global learning in college: Cross-cutting capacities for 21st century college students. Retrieved from http://www.aacu.org/meetings/global/14/call

The Forum on Education Abroad. (2011). *Standards of good practice for education abroad* (4th ed.). Retrieved from http://www.forumea.org/wp-content/uploads/2014/10/ForumEA-StandardsGoodPractice2011-4thEdition.pdf

Hovland, K. (2014, Spring). What can global learners do? *Diversity and Democracy, 17*(2), 8–11.

Hull, F. W., IV, Lemke, W. H., Jr., & Houang, R. T. (1977). *The American undergraduate, off-campus and overseas: A study of the education validity of such programs.* Retrieved from http://www.ciee.org/images/uploaded/pdf/occasional20.pdf

Kuh, G. D. (2008). *High-impact educational practices: What they are, who has access to them, and why they matter.* Washington, DC: Association of American Colleges and Universities.

Sobania, N., & Braskamp, L. A. (2009). Study abroad or study away: It's not merely semantics. *Peer Review, 11*(4), 17–20.

PART ONE

FRAMING STUDY AWAY

I

THE FARAWAY NEARBY

Putting the Local in Global Education

Neal W. Sobania

The inclusion of an off-campus experience as a part of a twenty-first-century undergraduate education is a recognized and firmly established principle on the campuses of most U.S. colleges and universities. This is almost exclusively understood to be an overseas experience, or study abroad. However, off-campus study need not be exclusively an overseas experience. Many undergraduates have been participating in a range of lesser-known but just as significant off-campus programs offered here in the United States. Still others have been earning academic credit on well-established, community-based education programs that also offer students a similar off-campus experience. The position taken in this volume is that domestic off-campus study can be just as powerful a transformative learning experience as overseas study. Including such globally minded and locally focused programs as part of a rich set of off-campus offerings will result in many new potential opportunities, which had been previously overlooked. Domestic programs can also expand students' horizons, their knowledge of global issues and processes, their familiarity and experience with cultural diversity, their intercultural skills, and their sense of citizenship.

Further, when the impact of globalization,[1] a process that has and will only continue to shape the world economically, politically, and culturally, is coupled with the makeup of the United States—regionally, demographically, culturally, socioeconomically—it is our contention that all students, regardless of where they study off campus, are engaged in global learning.

At the same time it is important to recognize that off-campus study is but one component in a set of educational experiences that leads to students becoming increasingly globally competent. Students also learn on campus to be global learners—in class, through cocurriculum programs and activities, and from interacting with international, multicultural, and multilingual student peers.

However, in focusing on the role of off-campus programs in the preparation of globally competent citizens, today's raison d'être of these endeavors, it is helpful to recognize that off-campus study has two equal aspects: one overseas (study abroad) and one domestic. With both broadly meeting similar educational goals, this complementarity is most advantageously expressed as "study away" (Sobania & Braskamp, 2009). Further, when one recognizes that this same goal of effectively preparing students to be globally competent citizens can also be met through academic community-based education programs (including academic service-learning and internships), and that community-based education can also take place either overseas or in the United States, then "study away" becomes an inclusive concept as well as an educational strategy that integrates a broad range of off-campus programs. As Engberg asserts, "Despite the resource challenges and other barriers to implementation institutions may face, it is essential to think about an integrated approach to global learning that encompasses the full range of domestic and international off-campus experiences embodied in the terminology of *study away*" (2013, p. 478).

To demonstrate this, Figure 1.1 illustrates the way in which community-based education programs overlap with both domestic and overseas off-campus programs and together constitute the inclusivity found in study away programs.

In the very near future, if not already, it may be instructive to add a fourth overlapping circle within the larger study away sphere to represent online education and the many variations this is likely to take. It is in this arena, the world of online connectivity, that classrooms and community groups in different parts of the world are learning collaboratively from lectures and presentations, group discussions, and research, albeit, so far, without the daily encounters, sounds, and smells that come with being on-site. This point is recognized in Figure 1.2, with each sphere connecting to at least some degree with each of the others. Further, as institutions connect with institutions in other countries in collaborative courses and even degrees, it is the expertise U.S. faculty members have about the multiculturalism and pluralism of the United States that these overseas partners will want for their students.[2]

The new paradigm of study away challenges the privileged position study abroad has had on campuses across the country. Historically, however,

Figure 1.1 An integrated model of high-impact off-campus curricular experiences

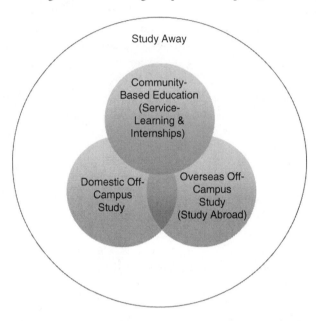

Figure 1.2 An integrated model of high-impact off-campus curricular experiences: The next iteration

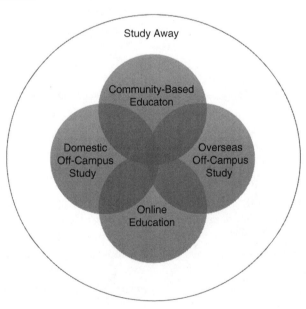

this has not always been the case. Not all that long ago an overseas experience was thought of as an "add on"—something of value to a student's education acknowledged by only a minority of committed faculty and administrators. Today, however, study abroad can be said to have come of age; it has been professionalized—from national and international organizations with meetings and annual conferences and journals reporting on the latest research, to the promoting of a set of standardized best practices and the availability of MA programs in international education. At the same time, campuses are full of initiatives designed to increase global learning by internationalizing both campus and curriculum. These efforts have been further supported by the federal government through commissions and most recently with initiatives to significantly increase the numbers of students studying overseas in China and Latin America.[3]

From the ship–aerogramme–poste restante era, when students typically studied overseas for at least a semester—and often a full year—to focus on language learning and taking courses with international content in hope of meeting general education and major course requirements, study abroad has evolved to today's 850-plus-seat airplanes, digital–social media era. One outcome has been an ever-increasing number of students studying overseas, albeit with the majority of today's sojourners traveling on short-term programs of as few as 7 to 10 days. In fact, many of today's students arrive on campus having already been overseas on one or more service projects with their local church or organizations such as Habitat for Humanity. Another outcome has been that even though the actual time students spend overseas has lessened, the expectations of what they are to acquire from such experiences have evolved to include the almost contradictory expectations that they will learn increasingly complex skills and dispositions to operate more effectively in a globally interdependent world. But again, these expectations are not unique to overseas study programs and also apply to domestic ones.

Thus, the next stage in this evolutionary development is study away, a position that embraces all off-campus study opportunities, or what Richard Slimbach has characterized as "doorstep to planet" (2012). By seeking points of complementarity from learning goals to program design, students can be provided with the most appropriate opportunity(ies) that best match their individual academic objectives and needs.

There are also a number of advantages to be gained from expanding off-campus study opportunities to include domestic programs. These programs can make an off-campus opportunity available to greater numbers of students who might not otherwise consider such an option, whether due to real or perceived obstacles. This is particularly relevant for the increasing number of today's students who are first generation and nontraditional. Domestic study away programs can also expand the range of on-campus partners in support of off-campus programming by creating opportunities for faculty whose teaching and research focus is in the United States; who have not lived, worked, or done research in overseas locations; and who have therefore not thought of themselves as being particularly relevant to campus internationalization efforts. Further, there is the potential for building bridges to better integrate professionals in multicultural life and community-based learning/service-learning[4] who share many of the same commitments as study abroad professionals and who also have extensive knowledge about programming that these same professionals ignore to their own detriment.

The title of this chapter, "The Faraway Nearby," is taken from the letter closing used by Georgia O'Keefe when she wrote to her friends in New York from New Mexico, where she moved in 1929. O'Keefe also produced a painting in 1938 with the title *From the Faraway, Nearby*[5] in which she juxtaposed images that were very close with others very far away, asking viewers, as Jennifer Sinor (2013) has written in *The American Scholar*, "to see, really see, what would normally be passed over—a flower, a broken skull, a shell from the shore—and to frame that attention with the possibilities of the horizon." With the principal focus on study abroad, students are looking at what is very far away to the neglect of what is so very close and are thus missing the possibilities inherent in both. Although "from the faraway nearby" has been characterized as a "striking oxymoron" (Warner, 2013), one has to question such a label in light of how easy it is, even in many rural locations, to travel only a few blocks from home or campus and have a cross-cultural experience—hear another language spoken, meet people from different cultural traditions, or discover religious practices different from one's own. That there is value in "really seeing" what is in one's own backyard, and considering it more closely, seems beyond doubt.

With the United States increasingly no longer a majority population with historic minorities, but a nation inclusive of diverse minorities and significant numbers of "new" Americans, as well as immigrant and refugee populations, what constitutes a majority is rapidly changing.[6] In this the United States is, like so many other countries around the world, a multicultural country made up of many different nations, each with its own history and languages that have shaped and continue to shape its cultural traditions and values (Blatt, 2014). The national narrative of a melting pot continues to find expression, yet our reality is much more that of a salad bowl. In the same way, the belief that there is anything like a single culture, even within a single state, is long past. As Woodard (2012) delineates in *American Nations*, since the United States is a country with mostly arbitrary state borders, it is more helpful to consider the United States as consisting of 11 rival regional cultures, the development of which has been driven by each region's diverse historical circumstances. Since there are few countries made up of a single ethnic group of people,[7] the United States is in fact like most other countries in terms of its demographic makeup, cultural traditions, and values. Thus, placing a premium on study overseas suggests our vision is too narrow and we are limiting our students' opportunities to also learn locally and region-ally. Just as overseas programs can provide important educational experiences and be an effective means of fostering the development of desired learn-ing outcomes and developmental skills, mind-sets, and behaviors, so too can domestic off-campus programs.

It has often been noted that you can live in another culture all your life and never completely understand it, but you will come to understand your own. Or as Paul Theroux (1967/1997) neatly summarized in the title of one of his earliest musings on travel, "Tarzan is an expatriate." But what part of your own culture will you understand? As the contributions to this volume will make clear, the multicultural diversity in the United States, which few students understand, appreciate, or are even acquainted with (really no dif-ferent from what they actually know and understand of societies and cultures overseas), is wide open for the development of domestic study away pro-grams that can meet, and in some instances even exceed, the global learning opportunities available through study overseas. The vast majority of students who participate in study away are not disadvantaged, do not consider or think much about themselves being privileged, and regard their place in soci-ety as normal. They may understand race and class as theoretical perspec-tives with textbook examples, but their lived experience is with people who resemble themselves. If they don't even know the names of these neighbors across town or in nearby locales or have not heard them express firsthand the challenges they face or their aspirations for the future, much less know any-thing of their traditions, history, or language, how can students come to fully appreciate that class and race are different dimensions of disadvantage, or begin to understand the stark divides that economic inequality, housing, and material goods impose on others' lives? How do students begin to understand or appreciate the complexity and heterogeneity of the group called "Lati-nos"; to comprehend the resonance that continues to exist in the memory of Chinese Americans or Japanese Americans and their historical experiences in America; to understand that African American and African immigrants who are now Americans have different understandings of slavery, Jim Crow, and the civil rights movement; or to appreciate the significant value Native Americans attach in their daily lives to traditional knowledge and how they rightfully view themselves as members of two nations—their tribe and the United States?[8]

The representations of people different from one's self are often framed as "the other." Typically "the other" is thought to be geographically distant—especially, for example, in Africa or Asia (think *National Geographic* or coffee table books by persons such as Carol Beckwith and Angela Fisher). As a result we do not talk about those who live in the United States and are different from ourselves as "the other." A recent study of social networks in America (Jones, 2014) found that the social networks of White Americans demonstrate a significantly higher degree of homogeneity (91%) than those of Black Americans (65%) or Hispanic Americans (46%). What this suggests is that Americans don't know each other outside of the relatively narrow confines of racial boundaries, and that we have a long way to go in recognizing people as individuals even when, in the broadest sense of the word, they are *neighbors*. Clearly there are borders that divide here from there and self from other, and these can prevent recognizing that even with different histories, religions, and values, others are not so different after all. If there is any positive in this, it is that the 2013 American Values Survey, from which these statistics are taken, does not distinguish age. Positive because there is evidence that Millennials—and especially the post-Millennials, also sometimes referred to as the Plurals—have broader social circles than those older than themselves, circles that are much more inclusive of individuals of diverse ethnicities, religions, and races (Hais & Winograd, 2012). It is this trend and the knowledge, skills, and dispositions that come from global learning that can move students toward a better understanding and appreciation of the multicultural world in which they will live and work.

Braskamp and Engberg (2011) speak of this desired transformation as the acquiring of a global perspective. This perspective draws on decades of research on holistic learning that categorize student learning as consisting of three dimensions: cognitive, intrapersonal/affective, and interpersonal/behavior (e.g., see Chen & Storosta, 1994; Kegan, 1994). My own preference is to characterize these three dimensions of global learning as awareness or disposition, knowledge, and skills, suggesting a learning process in which students must first become *aware* of difference, then become acquainted with the background *knowledge* (cultural, geopolitical, economic) that clarifies the implications of such historically embedded difference to the point that they can move *skillfully* from the new knowledge they have acquired to positive interactions across difference(s). Looked at this way, global learning becomes a journey.[9]

Managing the Global Learning Journey

Global learning constitutes a number of knowledge areas, and exactly what this includes will undoubtedly continue to be contested on campuses, at conferences, and in publications. What should be obvious is that one does not acquire global knowledge (that one should have or needs) through a single experience, whether that experience is in the United States or overseas. Hovland (2014) defines *global learning* in five domains of overlapping capacities. These capacities are skills that students "will need to thrive in the world as we understand it today and imagine it in the future" (AAC&U, 2014):

1. *Global Knowledge*: Students understand multiple worldviews, experiences, histories, and power structures.
2. *Global Challenges*: Students apply knowledge and skills gained through general education, the major, and cocurricular experiences that address complex, contemporary global issues (problems and opportunities).
3. *Global Systems and Organizations*: Students gain and apply deep knowledge of the differential effects of human organizations and actions on global systems.
4. *Global Civic Engagement*: Students initiate meaningful interaction with people from other cultures and take informed and responsible action to address ethical, social, and environmental challenges.
5. *Global Identities*: Students articulate their own values as global citizens in the context of personal identities and recognize diverse and potentially conflicting positions vis-à-vis complex social and civic problems.

What are encapsulated in these five domains are the knowledge and the complex skills and dispositions that we desire for all graduates. They are not acquired from a single experience on or off campus, but rather over the journey we call the undergraduate experience. One could in fact go so far as to suggest that global learning is just the latest way of talking about the education that needs to be imparted to all students as part of the undergraduate experience, and soon, as the globalization of the world takes further root, global learning will be simply learning.

None of this is about the place, it is about the journey. It is less about London, Prague, Buenos Aires, Santiago, Accra, Cape Town, Delhi, Beijing, Tokyo, New York, or Los Angeles, than it is about the expectation that students will change through the experience of studying away. Thus, the emphasis ought to be on the themes around which learning can focus, themes such as the environment, urbanization, refugees and immigrants, treaties, survival of traditional ways, and so on. Aspects of each of these themes can be found in the United States and overseas.

Thus, place can be seen as a contact zone where one crosses not just a geographic border, but physical, social, mental, intellectual, and emotional borders as well. Decentering a student is one way to think about this, but I also find useful the anthropological concept of "liminality" (Turner, 1969). Liminality (from the Latin word *limen*, meaning a threshold) is a transitional state of ambiguity or disorientation that occurs in the middle stage of rituals and rites of passage. It is at this point in time that participants no longer hold their preritual status, but have not yet assumed the status they will hold when the ritual is complete; think christening, bar or bat mitzvah, quinceañera, or wedding. During a ritual's liminal stage, participants stand in between their previous way of knowing and structuring their identity, time, or community, and the new status that they assume when the ritual is concluded. In terms of meeting learning outcomes, off-campus study is the liminal state from which the sojourner emerges as a more globally aware and engaged learner. (In the same way, one could also consider a student's entire time at college as being in a liminal state.)

In other words, students must be placed in contexts that enable them to experience the complexity of the world's communities, and thus foster greater understanding of the interrelationship that exists between what they know (knowledge) and how they think (awareness or disposition) and act (skills). In this way study away is also an educational strategy, a high-impact practice (Kuh, 2008) designed in part to create opportunities for students to experience and encounter difference. Domestic study away programs have been engaged in creating such encounters for some time; some have been around for as long as some of the oldest study abroad programs, which only began to develop significantly in terms of program and student participation in the early 1960s (Hoffa, 2007). Four of the consortia featured in this volume have been in existence and educating students off campus for nearly 50 years (Chicago, 1965; Philadelphia, 1986; New York, 1967; Higher Education Consortium for Urban Affairs in Minneapolis, 1968); one of the short-term programs was first offered in the 1970s (Williams). Also in existence for many years have been off-campus programs associated with community-based education and service-learning. Additionally, campuses have dramatically expanded their emphasis on multicultural learning. To respond to the student constituencies of these programs, professional staff have been hired and campus centers created. Study abroad too was growing and maturing, but over the years there has been too little contact between these professional fields, and each has grown and developed largely independent of the others. No doubt a number of factors played into this separation and distinctive growth, but a significant one would seem to be that from early on study abroad was characterized as academic, and these other areas were considered part of the domain of student affairs, now student development (Olson, Evans, & Shoenberg, 2007; Slimbach, 2012). Yet if one examines the overall outcomes of such programs, including offering students integrated learning experiences in a cross-cultural context, the separation appears increasingly artificial. This seems especially so as diversity and cross-cultural course requirements have been added to the curriculum and academic credit has been awarded for service-learning and internships. The continued separation also makes less sense when, as Chickering and Braskamp (2009) argue, developing and internalizing a global perspective is an essential part of a holistic development paradigm well-grounded in sound student development theory.

It is assumed that every study away program or course has its own learning outcomes. A further presumption is that these learning outcomes must be different if the program is offered domestically or overseas, yet there is often considerable similarity and overlap. More importantly to the argument being made here, it is not always obvious which is a learning outcome for an overseas study away program or one in the United States. Consider a few examples from my campus, Pacific Lutheran University: "to identify similarities and differences in cultural values," "to recognize ethnocentric reactions that inhibit the cultivation of cross-cultural understanding," and "to challenge one's own stereotypes and myths about people" are not all that dissimilar. Or the following: "to understand the complexities of changing patterns of urban and rural life, environmental challenges and the minority experience"; "to be able to distinguish cultural myths from cultural content"; "to broaden students' knowledge of approaches to and strategies for social change, and the values placed on the processes by diverse groups." The first set are learning outcomes from intensive, month-long study away programs that range from Makah Culture: Past and Present at Neah Bay, among a Northwest Coast Native American community some 120 miles from the PLU campus, to The Hilltop in Tacoma, which explores issues of poverty and homelessness only 15 minutes from campus. In the latter group, the first is from Continuity and Change in a New World Power in Sichuan, China; the second from Contemporary Global Issues: The Norwegian Approach to Development, Conflict Mediation and Peace Building in Norway, and the third from Development, Change and Social Development in Oaxaca, Mexico. Each of these programs, regardless of duration, has additional learning outcomes specific to its location, including important language learning outcomes for the last three. However, when global learning outcomes are looked at in their broadest sense and without country or regional specificity, they contain many overlapping goals that do not require great leaps of faith or academic gyrations to identify points of commonality that can be met either internationally or locally. In fact, the faculty at Susquehanna University has recently adopted an agreed set of learning outcomes that must be met by a program regardless of whether it is offered overseas or in the United States.[10]

Expressed another way, where once there was a focus on the local and the global, with each being distinctive, it is increasingly clear that this is a false dichotomy: local is global. As Cornwall and Stoddard (1999) already noted, "The nature of the world is such that national and global realities, whether economic, cultural, political, environmental or social, interpenetrate and mutually define each other to the degree that isolating U.S. studies from international studies is increasingly impractical"(viii).

When programs overseas address issues surrounding resettlement of immigrants and refugees or diaspora communities, how is this different from a local program that examines these same issues? Whether in the United States or overseas, immigrants or refugees are not the "same" as members of the same ethnic group or nationality of people in their own country or region of origin, but then how representative of the "people" of country X, Y, or Z are those students they study with, if they indeed actually study with the students of the country? How are the conditions under which American students live while studying overseas representative of the way the majority of the people in the country live? The list of subject matter that has a global context is nearly endless. Why are people hungry, why are people sick, how are international treaties observed and enforced, what is the impact of geographic boundaries on national identity, what are possible solutions to the shortage of water? All of these involve global issues that can be addressed either overseas or here. If students are engaged in globally contextualized learning, the location may be less a critical factor than with whom they are learning and from whom, and how they integrate what they learn in their own life.

Does a premed student or one in nursing, pharmacy, public health, or physical therapy need to go abroad to examine the impact of global health issues on populations in so-called developing countries? Or can they, as University of Wisconsin students do through the global certificate program, take a short-term course titled Communicable Diseases & Environmental Health in Humans: Detection, Monitoring and Control right in Madison, Wisconsin? By working with local partner agencies in the Madison area, students are introduced to and become familiar with methods of detecting, monitoring, and controlling communicable diseases. And as a result of international travel coupled with immigrant and refugee communities in and around urban centers, the nature of the communicable diseases that appear in our neighborhoods goes far beyond the flu, mumps, and chickenpox, but can also include malaria, TB, and typhoid (personal communication, Robin Mittenthal, September 9, 2013; Lori DiPrete Brown, October 2, 2013). Similarly, one can go overseas to observe the impact of international treaties on communities' rights and obligations, for example, in Northern Ireland, Rwanda, or the former Yugoslavia, but these same issues can be studied in the United States among Native Americans, on the border with Mexico, or even between individual states and Canada over water usage and other natural resources.

By recognizing that students can also engage in diverse cultures in the United States, a new set of off-campus opportunities and experiences is unlocked that can also foster global learning. As with study overseas, these can also enable students to develop holistically, including their cognitive development, their disposition, and their relationships with others unlike them. Moreover, study away greatly expands the range of opportunities that can assist students in working and living effectively in multicultural and intercultural situations, as well as learning about who they are and what they want to be. Such an expanded range of options provides students with multiple entry points to such learning. For some students the entry point will be an on-campus course and an internship or volunteer activity; for others it will be a short- or long-term study away program. For some that program will be overseas; for others it will be here in the United States. At the same time, domestic program options can provide opportunities for students returning from overseas study away programs to use knowledge they acquired in a comparative way, or try out what they learned abroad in a different cultural setting that happens to be local.[11] Again, this is not about substituting domestic programs for programs overseas—it's about offering both types to expand student opportunity and global learning.

Expanding Global Learning Through Study Away

Once we recognize and accept that the expansion of study away options through the creation and development of domestic off-campus study programs can also be a valuable tool for expanding students' understanding of the global world, we may well discover that there are other advantages as well. A more robust study away program, with an expanded range of domestic off-campus study programs, may also be helpful in addressing issues of access, finance, participation, health and safety, and faculty and staff support.

Access

Making study away more widely available involves financial concerns (for students and the institution), as well as expanding the number of participants. Since study away in the United States is generally less expensive than study overseas, it can prove more cost-effective for more students. Even when a student wants to take advantage of an institution that treats the cost of study abroad the same as if the student were on campus, and also allows the export of his institutional aid, or full credit for a tuition scholarship offered by a third-party provider, the out-of-pocket costs can prove prohibitive and make the cost of such a program out of reach. The costs of a passport, a visa, and inoculations add up to a significant sum that is not necessary for study at home. And on top of these incidentals, international airfare must be paid.

The *finances* associated with study away also have serious implications. After all, what college or university today, and especially in the competitive environment for new students, can afford not to offer study abroad programs to indicate they are internationalizing? No matter what financial model a campus uses for operating its study abroad program (and the models are numerous and diverse), significant costs are involved when a student makes a choice to study overseas. It is not all about tuition, but also lost income from housing and dining services. Whereas programs run by the student's own college or university may involve only a partial loss of tuition, students in third-party-provided programs always cause the loss of tuition. This loss of revenue may be still greater if the institution additionally allows a student to carry her institutional aid with her to such programs. Institutions that charge home school tuition (and sometimes room and board) may keep some revenue in-house, but this rarely offsets the total cost to a university when sending a student abroad.

A domestic off-campus program is certainly not cost free. For example, when a faculty member directs such a program and does not teach on campus for a term or a semester, this programmatic cost may be the same as for a study abroad program. However, campus-run programs that are based more locally should be less costly than those offered overseas, although this may not be as true for those based in certain metropolitan centers. In this case, established consortia programs may prove a better option than a campus running its own. However, an unintended financial impact of a domestic off-campus program is that it brings real financial resources into the local community where the program is based and with whose members it is actively engaged. Another consequence, whether intended or not, may be an increase in interest among the youth of these communities in higher education, and potentially the campus from where a program originates.

Participation is another facet of access in which domestic programming may offer a positive advantage. Its impact can range from increasing the participation of students of color to attracting students from disciplines underrepresented in off-campus study, such as STEM majors. The issues that inhibit greater participation by certain groups, which also include athletes and males, revolve around obstacles—obstacles that may be real, imagined, personal, or institutional. Although the study abroad field has been working diligently to change the limited range of student demographic characteristics and to accommodate a broader range of students, the majority of study abroad students are female—65.3% in the latest Open Doors (2014) survey of 2012/2013 participants—and the vast majority are White students (76.3% male and female). Although Open Doors does not include this statistic in its annual survey, the cost of participating in a study abroad program likely means that students are often upper-middle class.

Just as colleges and universities struggle with increasing the diversity of the student body, so too does study abroad, and cost is but one variable that impacts participation. For many students, especially those who are first-generation attendees without a college-going tradition in their family, just going to college is an important achievement. For other students, depending on where home is, traveling to the college's location may already require a significant cultural adaptation and adjustment. When these students are also faced with academic requirements for some intended majors, which can require setting up a course plan from the first semester, the idea of studying somewhere in Africa, Asia, Europe, or Latin America is the furthest thing from their mind. Foremost is succeeding in class, costs, and the sacrifices their family is making for them to be there. They must also adjust to campus cultural life, which may not include the traditions they practice at home where English may not even be the main language of communication. College for such students is primarily about graduating and getting a well-paying job. For nontraditional students with jobs, families, or both, the thought of studying abroad may not even enter their heads, much less be seen as a realistic possibility.

The homogeneity of gender; race/ethnicity; and, one suspects, age (Open Doors does not survey this factor) that characterizes study abroad participants also carries over into fields of study. Students in the social sciences and humanities, along with business, dominate: 22.1%, 10.4%, and 20.4%, respectively. Certain majors with specific course requirements and course sequencing also set up barriers to study abroad. This is reflected in the percentage of students in those degree fields: STEM (physical and life sciences, 8.8%; health professions, 6.4%; engineering, 4.1%; and math, 1.9%), and education, 4.0% (Open Doors, 2014). One way to expand participation is to increase domestic study away opportunities that are more appropriate for students in these underrepresented disciplines.

Another aspect of participation that is rarely discussed but should not be ignored: What if the number of students studying abroad has actually peaked? Is it possible there is a more or less finite number of students who can or will study abroad? The total number of students who study abroad each year continues to rise but only by small annual increments: according to Open Doors (2014), 1.2% for 2010–2011, 3.4% for 2011–2012, and 2.1%

for 2012–2013. There have even been suggestions that despite the increases, the percentage of college students studying overseas has remained relatively constant given the increase in numbers of students attending university. Then there are the conversations about the U.S. Department of State (n.d.) initiatives—100,000 Strong China and 100,000 Strong in the Americas—as to whether there are even remotely enough educational placements in China and the Americas to accommodate these numbers. This is not to take these admirable goals lightly, and it is fine to go halfway across the world to be immersed in a culture thoroughly different from one's own, but when you have neighbors who are also part of cultures that are different from one's own, why would it not also be useful to create opportunities for students to be immersed in these communities? Why would one assume what needs to be known about domestic cultural diversity, any more than cultures found overseas, can be learned from books and social media? Further, if there were greater openness as to how languages might be taught—for example, the respected but not widely used self-instructional language programs (National Association of Self-Instructional Language Programs, n.d.)—a study away program could also include language study.[12] With the increase in the numbers of immigrants and refugees from ever more diverse locations, the number of distinct language communities has also grown significantly (Blatt, 2014).

Allies and Partners: Building a Stronger Campus Constituency

While many faculty members are avid supporters of study abroad, and perhaps this is increasingly so as the professorial ranks are being filled by a younger generation of faculty who themselves studied overseas as undergraduates or graduate students, study abroad professionals often lament that they do not find more support for their efforts on campus. Yet in addition to those faculty members who teach subject matter with a strong or even exclusively international focus, there are perhaps as many if not more on every campus whose expertise is the United States. Might some of these colleagues be open to and even support having an off-campus option or two that is more appropriate for majors in their disciplines whose focus is the United States? Just as those faculty who support study abroad programs as a way to enrich their students' knowledge, would faculty whose teaching and research focus on the United States not be supportive of programs that do the same for their students— programs that engage students in the curriculum in ways that cannot easily be duplicated in a classroom setting, are supportive of different learning styles, and provide an extended range of opportunities for hands-on learning? Some may even be interested in offering their own off-campus program.

Where study abroad does not involve these faculty members, study away can and should include them. Not only is this logical, it is in the self-interest of those colleagues who teach international content courses to be included. In fact, I would go so far as to suggest that those interested in internationalization ignore the domestic at their own peril. For example, when budget cuts come, and we know they do, international programming is seen and regularly identified as expensive; it can become an easy target. This is especially true at institutions with tuition-driven budgets. Instead of viewing domestic and community-engagement programs as a threat to study abroad, they need to be seen as partners.

Further, campus partners should also include all those campus constituencies that increasingly have initiatives focused on diversity, multiculturalism, community-based learning, and internship in their unit. The addition of domestic programs to off-campus opportunities for students makes it possible to better align the work of these professionals with that of those whose initiatives are presently understood to be explicitly international or global. Working together with a shared vision and a common understanding of the multidimensional nature of study away can allow different academic and administrative units to construct meaningful outcomes and build stronger partnerships across what are too often seen as institutional boundaries.

Health and Safety or World Order Disorder

Another factor that is inevitably front and center in conversations about off-campus programming is health and safety. Indeed, given its growing prominence, the field of education abroad has itself spun off organizations that are focused exclusively on risk and liability issues. The realities of a chaotic and increasingly multipolar—some would argue asymmetrical—world make concerns for students' physical safety a top priority. On any morning of the week, a scan of OSAC's (Overseas Security Advisory Council) Crime and Safety Report (n.d.), a valuable tool that a study abroad office is prudent to follow, demonstrates this. In fact, it can easily lead one to wonder if there is any safe place for students to study overseas. Woe unto the international education administrator who cannot respond to a call or an e-mail from the college's or university's president as to how many students are in New Zealand and are they all accounted for when CNN or NPR first reports an earthquake in Christchurch. Or when the office of the risk manager calls to find out if the students in Shanghai are all safe since a shooting at the railway station in Urumqi just occurred, unaware the two locations are nearly 2,500 miles apart. This is, in part, why professional positions exist: to stay on top of all the world's happenings (and occasionally to teach geography). Add the television media to this disservice, flitting from one world crisis to another with their so-called "in-depth" coverage, and is it any surprise that parents have concerns about sending their undergraduate overseas? In this light the United

States looks a lot less threatening. As pressure continues to build for more students to have an off-campus study experience, there seems little doubt that study abroad will continue to wrestle with issues of safety in various locations around the world. In this environment, why would one ignore the rich range of possibilities offered by study away programs in the United States?

To ignore the potential advantages that can accrue from expanding study away opportunities seems shortsighted from an educational perspective, even if one does not take into account the significant issues of cost (from sending tuition dollars off campus and keeping residence hall rooms filled to the impact on financial aid), the risk and liability issues that keep administrators and parents and guardians awake at night, and the numbers games played with signed partnership agreements and Open Doors totals.

Moving Forward

In 2012 Elliot Gerson wrote an article in *The Atlantic* that has been heartily embraced by study abroad professionals. In "To Make America Great Again, We Need to Leave the Country," he argued that all Americans, but especially young Americans, must travel outside the United States to learn about other countries and people to make the United States a stronger country. "Value will come not just from the greater global consciousness, but from the direct experience that many nations simply do many things far better than we do." He goes on to suggest that when students compare and benchmark the way Americans provide health care, public transportation, energy policy, and rational political discourse against other nations, they will return home "no less patriotic than when they left" but "with an openness about the world that many of their parents lack." I would certainly not argue against this possible outcome, but would suggest that the various chapters in this volume demonstrate that one can also traverse borders—state borders, cultural borders, ethnic borders, linguistic borders, religious borders—all right here, right in the United States. Further, doing so may provide a stronger background that will make benchmarking more meaningful and more patriotic in the sense that Kwame Anthony Appiah writes about when he speaks of cosmopolitanism: "The cosmopolitan patriot can entertain the possibility of a world in which *everyone* [emphasis added] is a rooted cosmopolitan, attached to a home of one's own, with its own cultural peculiarities, but taking pleasure from the presence of other, different places that are home to other, different people" (1997, p. 618). In sum, I prefer the image of Appiah's cosmopolitan patriot to that of Gerson's vision of American greatness. The celebration of difference, rather than seeking a form of global homogeneity, is more in line with what I understand global competence to be about.

Notes

1. On many campuses today, *globalization* and *internationalization* are being used inter-changeably. There is a distinction. For the purposes of this chapter I follow Knight (2003), who defines *internationalization* as "the process of integrating an international, intercul-tural, or global dimension into the purpose, functions, or delivery of postsecondary educa-tion" (p. 2) while ensuring that an international dimension is central, and not marginal. This is distinct from *globalization*, which belongs more to the domain of economics and politics: "the process of increasing connectedness and interdependence of relationships across the world, in which cultural, moral, political, and economic activities in one part of the world have significant effects in other parts of the world" (Dower, 2013). A useful introduction to the key debates about globalization can be found at the Global Policy Forum, "Defining Globalization," www.globalpolicy.org/globalization/defining-globali-zation.html

2. As the Harvard Pluralism Project makes clear, "pluralism is not the sheer fact of diversity alone, but is active engagement with that diversity. One can be an observer of diversity. One can 'celebrate diversity,' as the cliché goes. One can be critical of it or threatened by it. But real pluralism requires participation and engagement" (Ech, 2013).

3. See, for example, the Lincoln Commission's report (Commission, 2005) and U.S. Department of State's (n.d.) 100,000 Strong Educational Exchange Initiatives, www.state.gov/100k/

4. Today, community-based learning and service-learning are being used somewhat inter-changeably. Increasingly *community based-learning* is seen as a broader term and service-learning fits under it. The preference for community based-learning is, on one hand, to steer away from the various connotations attached to "service" and, on the other hand, to recognize who is providing the instruction and who is learning.

5. An image of this painting can be found at www.metmuseum.org/toah/works-of-art/59.204.2

6. The U.S. White majority will be gone by 2043. In 2012, the population younger than 5 years old stood at 49.9% minority; the projection is that in 5 years minorities will make up more than half of children under the age of 18. Today, about 40% of Whites 25–29 years old graduate from college, compared with 15% of Latinos and 23% of Blacks. Retrieved from http://usnews.nbcnews.com/_news/2013/06/13/18934111-census-white-majority-in-us-gone-by-2043?lite

7. Somalia is one of only a few countries in the world with an ethnically homogeneous popu-lation—consider the commonality found there today.

8. This concept of Native Americans belonging to two nations is perhaps made clearer in Canada, where the reference is not to "tribes" but "First Nations."

9. Others express this transformation as *intercultural competence*, or *multicultural competence*. While useful terms, the heavy emphasis this places on communication and behavior as the principal competency, for me at least, places too little emphasis on the acquisition of awareness and knowledge that are foundational to changing patterns of communica-tion and behavior. In reality, it is awareness and knowledge that are fundamental to why students, parents, and campuses think about and support off-campus study/study away, rather than making students more interculturally competent.

10. See www.susqu.edu/academics/52062.asp and chapter 13 in this volume.

11. As part of an ACE Internationalization Workshop, Pacific Lutheran University articulated a global education continuum that outlined four stages of development: introductory, exploratory, participatory, and integrative, more or less corresponding to the four years of

an undergraduate degree program to suggest such a sequence (Kelleher, 2005). The reality is that I am not aware of any good evidence or research that suggests what, if any, sequence of experiences is better than another for increasing global competence.

12. The list of 84 different languages taught by NASILP institutions as of June 2014 can be found at www.nasilp.net/index.php/languages

References

Appiah, K. A. (1997). Cosmopolitan patriots. *Critical Inquiry, 23*(3), 617–639.

Association of American Colleges & Universities. (2014). 2014 Global learning in college: Cross-cutting capacities for 21st century college students. Retrieved from https://www.aacu.org/meetings/global/14/index.cfm

Blatt, B. (2014, May 13). Tagalog in California, Cherokee in Arkansas. *Slate.* Retrieved from http://www.slate.com/articles/arts/culturebox/2014/05/language _map_what_s_the_most_popular_language_in_your_state.html

Braskamp, L. A., & Engberg, M. E. (2011, Summer/Fall). How colleges can influence the development of a global perspective. *Liberal Education, 34*–39.

Chen, G. M., & Starosta, W. J. (1996). Intercultural communication competence: A synthesis. *Communication Yearbook, 19,* 353–384.

Chickering, A., & Braskamp, L. A. (2009). Developing a global perspective for personal and social responsibility. *Peer Review, 11*(4), 27–30.

Commission on the Abraham Lincoln Study Abroad Fellowship Program. (2005). *Global competence & national needs: One million Americans studying abroad.* Retrieved from http://www.aplu.org/library/global-competence-and-national-needs-one-million-americans-studying-abroad/file

Cornwall, G. H., & Stoddard, E. W. (1999). *Globalizing knowledge: Connecting international and intercultural studies.* Washington, DC: Association of American Colleges & Universities.

Dower, N. (2013, February 1). Globalization. *The international encyclopedia of ethics.* Wiley Online Library. Retrieved from http://onlinelibrary.wiley.com/ doi/10.1002/9781444367072.wbiee761/abstract

Ech, D. L. (2013). From diversity to pluralism. Retrieved from http://www .pluralism.org/encounter/challenges

Engberg, M. (2013). The influence of study away experiences on global perspective-taking. *Journal of College Student Development, 54*(5), 466–480.

Gerson, E. (2012, July 10). To make America great again, we need to leave the country. *Atlantic.* Retrieved from http://www.theatlantic.com/national/archive/2012/07/ to-make-america-great-again-we-need-to-leave-the-country/259653/

Hais, M., & Winograd, M. (2012, May 7). A new generation debuts: Plurals. *Huffington Post.* Retrieved from http://www.huffingtonpost.com/michael-hais-and-morley-winograd/plurals-generation_b_1492384.html

Hoffa, W. W. (2007). *A history of U.S. study abroad: Beginning to 1965.* Carlisle, PA: The Forum on Education Abroad.

Hovland, K. (2014, Spring). What can global learners do? *Diversity and Democracy, 17*(2), 8–11.

Jones, R. P. (2014, August 21). Self-segregation: Why it's so hard for whites to understand Ferguson. *Atlantic*. Retrieved from http://www.theatlantic.com/politics/archive/2014/08/self-segregation-why-its-hard-for-whites-to-understand-ferguson/378928/

Kegan, R. (1994). *In over our heads: The mental demands of modern life*. Cambridge, MA: Harvard University Press.

Kelleher, A. (2005). Global education continuum. *Diversity Digest, 8*(3). Retrieved from www.diversityweb.org/digest/vol8no3/kelleher.cfm

Knight, J. (2003, Fall). Updating the definition of internationalization. *International Higher Education* (pp. 2–3). Center for International Higher Education, Boston College.

Kuh, G. D. (2008). *High-impact educational practices: What they are, who has access to them, and why they matter*. Washington, DC: Association of American Colleges & Universities.

National Association of Self-Instructional Language Programs. (n.d.) Retrieved from http://www.nasilp.net

Olson, C. L., Evans, R., & Shoenberg, R. F. (2007). *At home in the world: Bridging the gap between internationalization and multicultural education*. Washington, DC: American Council on Education.

Open Doors. (2014). Open Doors data. Retrieved from http://www.iie.org/research-and-publications/open-doors/data

Overseas Security Advisory Council (OSAC). (n.d.). *Crime and safety report*. Retrieved from https://www.osac.gov/pages/contentreports.aspx?cid=2

Public Religion Research Institute (2013). *American values survey: In search of libertarians in America*. Retrieved from http://publicreligion.org/research/2013/10/2013-american-values-survey/#.VR8Xoim3BWg.

Sinor, J. (2013, Summer). Say anything: The stories we tell ourselves. *The American Scholar*. Retrieved from http://theamericanscholar.org/say-anything/#.U9_V_Fa3DKc

Slimbach, R. (2012). *The fate of civilization and the future of education abroad: From doorstep to planet*. Carlisle, PA: The Forum on Education Abroad.

Sobania, N., & Braskamp, L. A. (2009). Study abroad or study away: It's not merely semantics. *Peer Review, 11*(4), 17–20.

Theroux, P. (1967/1997). Tarzan is an expatriate. *Transition, 75/76*, 46–58.

Turner, V. (1969). *The ritual process: Structure and anti-structure*. Chicago, IL: Aldine.

U.S. Department of State. (n.d.). 100,000 strong educational exchange initiatives. Retrieved from http://www.state.gov/100k/

Warner, M. (2013, June 7). Review of Rebecca Solnit's book of collected essays titled *The Faraway Nearby*. *Guardian*.

Woodard, C. (2012). *American nations: A history of the eleven rival regional cultures of North America*. New York, NY: Penguin.

2

MATCHING PROGRAM AND STUDENT CHARACTERISTICS WITH LEARNING OUTCOMES

A Framework for Study Away Curriculum Development

Mark Salisbury

O ne of the biggest challenges to demonstrably improving an educational program lies in converting findings derived from some sort of global assessment of learning into concrete and specific programmatic or pedagogical changes that matter in the moment. For many advocates of off-campus study (no matter if it is on the other side of the world or the other side of the town), the growing body of evidence highlighting the variability in educational effectiveness across off-campus study experiences has inspired numerous suggestions for programmatic and pedagogical alterations and additions. Yet, too often practical and theoretical frameworks that would help program directors and designers determine exactly *which* alteration or addition is best suited for improving *which* program are far less prevalent. This chapter proposes a framework for identifying an appropriate range of attainable learning outcomes that integrates a scaffolded conception of student learning with the unique learning environment of an off-campus program and the nature of the student participant (both as individuals and as a group). This framework can be applied to both existing programs that are now being asked to articulate specific learning outcomes and demonstrate student attainment of those outcomes, as well as new programs that are being created to meet specific learning outcomes across the expanding range of off-campus program designs.

A Thing or Two About Learning Outcomes

During the period when off-campus study programs evolved into the more formalized entity we now know, the learning outcomes of a college or university education consisted of a breadth of introductory knowledge across numerous disciplines (general education) and a depth of knowledge within a particular discipline (major). In each case, this knowledge focused primarily on content information—facts, theories, and processes. Within this context, off-campus study (i.e., study abroad) seemed a logical way to improve foreign language, cultural, and historical knowledge. But in the last several decades, higher education has increasingly adopted a new notion of learning outcomes that extends beyond content knowledge, focusing instead on the complex skills and dispositions necessary to excel across many fields of study, professions, or personal circumstances. Although the structure of a college education has remained largely unchanged in terms of its focus on content areas, higher education institutions now assert that the overarching goal of an undergraduate education is for students to develop complex skills, dispositions, and abilities such as critical thinking, intercultural competence, quantitative literacy, or innovative thinking/problem solving, with the content knowledge serving as a means to a greater end. Consequently, institutions are increasingly asking individual curricular and cocurricular programs to identify specific learning goals—over and above the content knowledge accrued through a particular experience—that map onto the institution-wide learning outcomes (or "up to" if one conceives of mapping outcomes like an organizational chart for learning).

In this context, study away faculty and program administrators need to identify learning outcomes for their programs that are reasonably attainable and can be demonstrably linked to the broader institutional learning outcomes. In order to accomplish this task—and in order to make sense of the framework presented in this chapter—study away faculty and program administrators need to understand two important characteristics of learning outcomes. First, although often conveyed as singular constructs, institutional learning outcomes are in reality broad combinations of knowledge, epistemologies, skills, and attitudes that are demonstrated fully when they are applied together in a specific context for a specific purpose. For example, students can demonstrate critical thinking in its fullest form only when they bring previously acquired relevant knowledge to bear on a specific context; analyze and interpret the intersection of this prior knowledge and new information to see implications, make inferences, and identify information they do not yet know and that would further shape those implications and inferences; and, finally, synthesize all of these strands to construct a new way of understanding the context in question. Each of these pieces of the larger critical thinking puzzle—remembering prior knowledge, applying prior knowledge to analyze new information, evaluating the implications, making inferences, and synthesizing to construct a new idea—require continual effort over years of learning to develop. With this in mind, because discrete educational experiences such as study away are generally designed to last for a semester, a trimester, or other periods of time in concert with an institution's academic calendar, it isn't realistic to think that one such experience would contribute demonstrable gains in student learning toward a given institutional learning outcome in its fullest form. Instead, study away programs are likely better suited to contribute specific elements of a given outcome, elements that are more realistically learned within the time provided for that program.

Second, the individual skills necessary to exhibit any broadly construed outcome (such as critical thinking) are not somehow roughly equivalent or interchangeable. They differ widely in cognitive complexity, requisite prior knowledge, and depth of experience. The individual skills required of any broad institutional learning outcome integrate successfully when students learn these skills in a purposeful, intentionally ordered way that treats these elements as building blocks, introducing them to students through an ordered process that starts with foundational, more simply understood knowledge and constructs before moving on to more complex, nuanced skills and dispositions. For example, intercultural competence is a complicated learning outcome that takes years to develop. When we work with students to develop this construct we break it down into a series of more concrete elements that are best learned in a particular order. We start with developing a basic awareness of difference, which needs to be in place before we can start talking about the cultural and geopolitical implications of historically embedded difference. Only after helping students understand the pervasiveness of these implications can we start to develop in them a genuine sensitivity that then empowers them to incorporate this new knowledge into their interactions across difference—no matter the context, location, or purpose of that interaction. This disposition is a critical precursor to successfully employing intercultural competence in real-world situations regardless of geographic location or national borders.

Even in this simplistic description of the building blocks necessary to develop intercultural competence, there is a clear pattern of increasing complexity, from simple awareness that differences exist to a nuanced sensitivity of the implications of contextually unique difference during a specific interpersonal interaction. This pattern of increasing complexity holds true for the building blocks of all institutional learning outcomes (e.g., critical thinking, socially responsible leadership). In each case, institutional outcomes encompass a list of specific knowledge, skills, and dispositions that can be organized on a spectrum from simple to complex.

While the exact nature of this increasing complexity has been the subject of much research and explication (see Anderson, Krathwohl, & Bloom, 2001; Fink, 2003), one way to summarize this pattern is to examine the extent to which these building blocks range from mere comprehension of information, facts, and theories to the increasingly sophisticated ability or skill to combine disparate knowledge, filter it through an analytic perspective unique to the situation at hand, and ultimately put the "right" information to use. As such, the simplest learning outcome will be one that can be demonstrated without any context through a quiz or a test. By comparison, a more complex learning outcome will require an increasingly nuanced context in order for one to demonstrate competence, such as an in-depth analytic paper, a portfolio, or a multistage project. Another way to think about a continuum of simple to complex is to consider the intellectual sophistication required to demonstrate a particular outcome. Similar to Bloom's Taxonomy, comprehension requires the least amount of intellectual sophistication. Conversely, creating (sometimes called synthesizing) requires extensive intellectual sophistication. In addition to knowing applicable information, one must know how to select the most useful or compelling information and combine it effectively to address a particular challenge in a new and convincing way.

No matter the learning outcome, the organization of its constituent skills and dispositions (building blocks) from "simple" to "complex" presents two key implications for student learning. First, although it might seem obvious to some, it is important to recognize that the constituent elements of each of these broad learning outcomes can and should be introduced in the order of their complexity. Second, no matter the unique set of constituent skills and dispositions required to develop students' abilities on a particular broad outcome, effective teaching of each constituent element requires learning conditions conducive to the intended learning outcome. Thus, as the discrete learning outcome becomes more complex, the learning conditions also become more complex. For example, while some basic content knowledge might be effectively delivered simply through a lecture or a text-book, developing more complex skills or dispositions, particularly those best demonstrated in context, needs a more complex learning environment that puts students into situations in which they must apply the concepts and skills they are learning toward a particular purpose.

Matching Learning Outcomes to Program Design

This framework isn't the first to propose a way of conceptualizing study away programs in a manner that clarifies the potential for educational effectiveness (see Kelleher, 2005). And by no means does this framework claim some sort of superiority over prior efforts to create taxonomies of study away program design. Instead, the goal in this chapter is to match the constituent elements (building blocks) of broader institutional learning outcomes with (a) key characteristics of study away program design, and (b) important variants in the nature of student enrollment in such programs that will allow faculty and program administrators to identify realistic and attainable learning outcomes for their programs that map onto the broader institutional learning outcomes.

Just as the building blocks of any institutional learning outcome can be organized from simple to complex, so too can differences within four key characteristics of off-campus study programs be organized along a spectrum of learning conditions that would be conducive to more simple or more complex learning. These characteristics include the length of the learning experience, the cultural gap between the student participants and the location of the study away program, the depth of immersion into the local community and culture, and the pedagogical approach of the instructors. Length of learning experience includes both the length of the actual time away from campus and the degree to which the program is integrated into pre- or post-program learning experiences. Cultural gap includes the many dimensions of difference that can influence the interaction between students and the host locale such as race, ethnicity, socioeconomic status, religious beliefs, social values, history, power, environment, or geopolitics. While depth of immersion includes many of the oft-discussed variations in residency classifications in the study abroad literature (e.g., homestays versus island programs), depth of immersion in the current framework is intended to extend beyond mere residency to encompass the entirety of the student's experience, including in-class sessions, out-of-class assigned work, organized social activities, and purely informal excursions and gatherings. Finally, pedagogical approach may be the most familiar construct that parallels the spectrum of simplicity to complexity among learning outcomes. The teaching and learning literature has long explored the relationships between various pedagogical approaches and student learning, and the evidence overwhelmingly indicates that passive learning contexts in which students merely listen to lectures and (hopefully) take notes do not produce the same kind of learning as active learning contexts (e.g., problem-based learning, team-based learning, flipped classroom learning), especially when that active learning includes an iterative and reflective component that feeds back into further active learning.

The following sections describe in some detail each of the aspects of program design and student characteristics that influence the range of learning outcomes that might be realistic for a given program. At the conclusion of these descriptions, the chapter will apply this framework to identify realistic learning outcomes for several different study away experiences as well as use the framework to identify ways in which alterations to the sample programs might redefine the type of potentially attainable learning outcomes.

Length of Learning Experience

While there has been plenty of controversy among study away advocates about program length, the reality is that, *depending on the intended learning outcomes*, short-term programs can be sufficiently effective. But it is more than fair to say that the opportunity for more complex learning inherently exists in longer term programs such as a semester or a full academic year. The actual length of the time away from campus by no means ensures educational effectiveness, but it may create a larger window of opportunity.

At least as important (albeit a regular casualty of the Faustian bargain to prioritize participation rates over demonstrable learning), the degree to which a study away program is designed to overlap with predeparture learning experiences and an organized postreturn educational experience turns out to matter a great deal in expanding the potential complexity of the learning conditions. Basic learning theory describes two critical phases for deep and permanent learning: a period of disequilibrium in which the student is placed in a context that is outside his or her comfort zone, and a period of meaning-making in which the student is given the opportunity, having returned to a more familiar environment, to make sense of his or her disequilibrium experience. One key feature of a successful meaning-making experience is that the learner benefits from some support, guidance, and even the dynamics of a group where others are also engaged in a similar processing experience.

Cultural Gap

The extent of a cultural gap between a group of study away students and a particular program's host community is another characteristic of an off-campus study program that influences the potential opportunity for varying complexity in learning conditions. The term *cultural gap* refers to any way in which substantive or systemic differences between individuals or groups might hinder interaction or collaboration toward a common goal. For the purposes of this framework, it is important to recognize that cultural gap is not set in stone or defined by lines on a map. Cultural gap is much more complex and nuanced. It can theoretically exist in multiple dimensions simultaneously, even if all of those dimensions aren't explored or exposed. Cultural gap does not require extensive travel; instead it is predominantly shaped by the relative cultural "location" of both participants in the interaction. For example, within the confines of a typical American college campus there often exist cultural gaps between gay and straight students, wealthy students and low-income students, or students from rural and suburban settings. There are numerous domestic study away programs where students experience extensive cultural gaps, such as students from rural Iowa spending a term in South Central Los Angeles or students from the wealthy western suburbs of Chicago spending weeks in rural Appalachia (and vice versa). In the context of more traditional overseas study programs, it isn't difficult to imagine substantive differences in cultural gap between two programs of American students in Paris if one program spends its time examining great works of art at the Louvre while the other spends all of its time studying experiences of North African immigrants.

In this framework, cultural gap is valuable because its existence creates the possibility for more complex learning conditions. The extent to which cultural gaps exist expands or limits the potential for students to develop, in a real-world setting, sensitivity to difference and the ability to engage in perspective-taking (the act of viewing and recognizing the complexities of a given situation through cultural lenses different from their own). Without the presence of identifiable cultural gaps, such educational efforts tend to become largely hypothetical and therefore less likely to take root. Yet cultural gap is really only half of the equation for making substantive learning emerge from such complex learning conditions.

Depth of Immersion

Depth of immersion represents the "other half" of the equation that works in concert with cultural gap. In this framework, depth of immersion includes both the degree to which student participants interact with the host community and the nature of that interaction. On one end of the spectrum, in a manner similar to the stereotypical grand tour among overseas study programs, students are often situated as distanced observers who never really interact interpersonally with the local culture. On the other end of the spectrum, students might live, work, and study within the local community, communicating in the local language and embedding themselves entirely as invested participants, even members, of that community.

In many ways, this characteristic of program design works in tandem with the existence of cultural gaps between the students in the program and the local community. Yet, as many island and tour programs demonstrate, the existence of multiple gaps does not necessarily ensure that these gaps are explored in any great depth. It is not the intention of this framework to suggest that programs that delve deeply into exploring extensive cultural gaps are somehow better than those that do not; however, it is important to recognize that the decision to minimize the depth of immersion (either by locating a study away program where there are few cultural gaps or by limiting—or failing to encourage—immersive experiences) also minimizes the potential for students to engage in more complex learning conditions, thereby limiting the potential for developing more complex learning outcomes.

Pedagogical Approach

Finally, the pedagogical approach implemented by faculty or program directors plays a key role in shaping the potential for complex learning conditions conducive to attaining more complex learning outcomes. This characteristic of a study away program is certainly not new to experts of experiential education, including service-learning, volunteering, internships, or undergraduate research. Yet there continue to be many traditional overseas study programs that follow the grand tour model or conduct classes on location in a manner that differs little from lecture courses held on campus. While the purpose of this framework isn't to condemn the lecture format, research on teaching and learning leaves little doubt regarding the differences in learning conditions or outcomes between passive and active learning environments (see Bransford, Brown, & Cocking, 1999). Simply put, active learning pedagogies are far more effective in teaching complex learning outcomes than passive learning pedagogies.

Furthermore, reflective components add additional depth to active learning endeavors that provide a critical dimension of affective development to student development. Although learning in colleges and universities has traditionally been framed as a primarily cognitive domain, we now know that virtually all learning benefits from attention to the affective domain. Properly designed reflective activities can engage this domain directly and partner with active learning approaches to create ideal learning conditions for integrative, complex learning outcomes. Thus, in this framework the spectrum of *pedagogical approaches* is defined as entirely passive in its most simple form and both active and reflective at its most complex.

Considering Student Characteristics

The reason we use the phrase "teaching and learning" to fully describe the work of educators is because the ultimate effectiveness of the endeavor occurs at the point of interaction between the teacher and the learner. In the same way, laying out a framework for identifying plausible off-campus study learning outcomes would be incomplete if we only focused on program design. In addition to the key features of program design, we must take into account the nature of our student participants, both individually and as a group.

Maturity and Knowledge

Although it is by no means a given that age equates with maturity or that prior coursework equates with prior knowledge, it is generally safe to say that students who are more mature and who have accumulated substantive prior knowledge are likely to engage study away differently than students who are less mature or who are coming into the experience without any prior relevant knowledge. Though this assertion isn't likely to strike anyone as groundbreaking, it is important to recognize that the types of students enrolling in a given program will influence the degree to which faculty can expect to successfully push them to engage in more complex learning. There are times when programs are designed with a specific type of student in mind but the curricular policies and student patterns of course enrollments at an individual institution tend to work against enrolling the types of students for whom the program is designed. Fairly or unfairly, faculty and program directors who refuse to adapt to these conditions do so at the expense of the potential for effective student learning.

Variation Across Participants

Of the two student characteristics that influence the learning conditions of any particular experience, the extent of variation across participants is certainly the more difficult to address. Sometimes certain programs are set up specifically for students late in their major and the group is generally tightly clustered in terms of its prior knowledge, maturity, and postgraduate aspirations. In other cases, especially for the sort of "come one, come all" program, it is not unusual to find a wider range of participants' prior knowledge, maturity, and postgraduate aspirations. As anyone who has taught open-enrollment courses such as general education or freshman composition, this can make it exponentially harder to teach. Focus on those students who need the most help and the more advanced students are more likely to get left on their own. Focus on the middle students and those on both ends can get lost in the shuffle. The same is true in many off-campus study programs, especially at institutions where there is a concerted push for increased participation rates. This variable isn't so much a cognitive development issue as it is a pragmatic function of the time available for teaching, grading, preparation, and so on. Groups of students that vary widely in knowledge, maturity, and purpose are more often better suited for less complex learning outcomes. Conversely, more tightly clustered groups (even if that group of students comes to the program less prepared overall) tend to be more likely to make progress on more complex learning outcomes. Of course, this is certainly the case with programs that enroll a tight cluster of late-major students.

Matching Outcomes With Program Design and Student Characteristics

Laying this framework out visually provides a potentially useful way of putting these ideas together (Figure 2.1). In addition, it can be particularly helpful as a sort of work sheet for study away directors and faculty. After determining in a general sense the institutional learning outcome to which a given study away program might contribute, the constituent elements of each broad institutional learning outcome can be listed in an order of increasing

Figure 2.1 Matching achievable learning outcomes with program design, student preparation, and program enrollment

Complexity of Intended Learning Outcome	Program Design					Student Preparation	Program Enrollment
	Length of Learning Experience	Cultural Gap	Depth of Immersion	Pedagogical Approach	Maturity and Knowledge	Variation Across Participants	
Simple (e.g., remembering facts)	Short and unrelated to any pre- or post-program experience	Largely similar across most dimensions	Distanced observer	Entirely passive	Young and naive	Widely dispersed	
Complex (e.g., synthesizing to create a new solution)	Long and integrated with pre- and postprogram experiences	Clearly different across multiple dimensions	Embedded participant	Active and reflective	Older and informed	Tightly clustered	

Note. The gray arrows represent a progression from simple to more complex learning conditions that parallel a progression from simple to more complex learning outcomes.

complexity along the spectrum of plausible learning outcomes. Then faculty or program directors can plot the specific characteristics of their individual study away program across the four aspects of the program design and the two aspects of the student participants. The result of this exercise provides a sense of the range of realistically attainable learning outcomes, particularly in terms of whether the program in question lends itself to more simple or more complex learning outcomes that line up within the range of plot points across the six descriptive categories.

To demonstrate how this framework might work in context, it seems appropriate to apply this approach to two different examples of study away programs in order to show how it might be helpful in either identifying realistic learning outcomes for a program as it is presently designed or identifying ways to alter a program in order to align its design more closely with newly determined intended learning outcomes. Hopefully, something about each example will ring familiar and provide some useful and concrete insights.

Example 1: A Semester Studying Nineteenth-Century German Literature

Let's start by imagining a long-standing faculty-led overseas study program that travels to numerous locations in Germany over the course of a 15-week semester to study nineteenth-century German language, literature, and culture. The program generally draws sophomores and juniors, only some of whom are German majors or minors (the rest are taking the course for some sort of general education credit), who travel and stay together throughout the term. The faculty teach the courses in a seminar format with extensive discussion of readings and locations, employing numerous local guest lecturers. The institution has recently asked the faculty directors to articulate learning outcomes for the program that map onto the institution's learning outcomes.

Applying the framework described in this chapter helps to isolate a realistic range of learning outcomes given the current design of the program and the current type of students who participate. Let's postulate that the faculty directors have selected the institution's outcomes related to critical thinking and intercultural competence, the constituent elements of which have already been discussed earlier in this chapter. The full semester program length allows the opportunity for more complex learning conditions, although additional predeparture and postreturn programming would increase that potential. The cultural gap available to be explored within the current design of the program is relatively small, though not insignificant. Maybe as a function of the content knowledge historically embedded in the program's design, the depth of immersion is relatively shallow in that the students interact

Figure 2.2 Identifying realistic learning outcomes for a nineteenth-century German language, literature, and culture semester study away

Complexity of Outcomes	Program Design				Student Preparation	Program Enrollment
Critical Thinking & Intercultural Competence	Length of Learning Experience	Cultural Gap	Depth of Immersion	Pedagogical Approach	Maturity and Knowledge	Variation Across Participants
Comprehension & awareness of difference						
Analysis			X			X
Application & sensitivity to difference		X		X	X	
Synthesis evaluation creating & relativistic appreciation of difference	X					

Note. The outcomes highlighted in gray indicate the learning outcomes that are likely realistic and attainable if all else remains the same.

across the few available dimensions of difference primarily as passive observers rather than participants. The pedagogical approach includes both lecture and substantial discussion, with students encouraged to analyze, critique, and extend the ideas expressed by the authors, artists, and thinkers. As noted previously, the students who enroll in the program are typically sophomores and juniors; however, the group's prior knowledge and motivation to engage and learn from the experience is highly diffuse.

Each of the elements of the program design and student characteristics is plotted in Figure 2.2. As you can see, the constituent elements of critical thinking and intercultural competence are listed from simple to more complex. Based on the plotted points across each of the program design and student characteristics, the range of realistic learning outcomes for both critical thinking and intercultural competence (again, assuming that students experience the program in its current form), highlighted by the gray shading, do not extend to the most complex elements of critical thinking or intercultural competence. Instead, although the length of the program presents some opportunity to develop students toward more complex learning, the rest of the design elements constrain this possibility. Furthermore, although the students might be moving toward a level of maturity that allows for more complex learning conditions, the diffuse nature of the participants will likely make it difficult to incorporate pedagogies and assignments that require extensive prior learning or intrinsic motivation among all students. In the end, the faculty directors ought to consider selecting critical thinking related learning outcomes that range from comprehension and understanding to analysis and some level of application. Likewise, the realistically attainable learning outcomes related to intercultural competence would be best suited to focus on awareness of difference and some sensitivity to the implications of difference but not extend to relativistic appreciation of difference in an interactive context.

This framework also provides some guidance in identifying alterations that might increase the complexity of plausible learning outcomes. First, let's examine the notions of cultural gap and depth of immersion together. It is true that taking students to Germany to study nineteenth-century language, literature, and culture excludes some of the more obvious dimensions of cultural gap (e.g., as opposed to taking students to the Global South to study the implications of poverty in the developing world), but this does not mean that there aren't other dimensions of cultural gap such as historical context and perception that could be more explicitly explored in the context of nineteenth-century Germany. However, in order to take advantage of these complex learning conditions, the program designers would need to alter the touring nature of the students' experience and put them in situations where they must engage in an extended interaction across this dimension of difference.

Second, let's consider the interrelated nature of the pedagogical approach and the variations in academic context across the student participants. The mix of students in terms of the academic purpose of their enrollment (taking the course as a part of their major versus taking the course to earn general education credits) surely constrains the degree to which faculty can apply more complex pedagogical approaches or expect a higher level of academic commitment from all of the students in the course. This in turn limits the complexity of learning outcomes that are realistically attainable. Although some might raise concerns over meeting participation thresholds, one alteration that could deepen the potential for complex learning would be to limit access to the program to majors and minors, which would limit the diffusion of the participants and allow faculty to assume a different level of motivation, interest, and effort across all participants.

Example 2: A Short-Term Study of Urban Planning in New Orleans

This framework can also be applied to identify plausible learning outcomes for shorter study away programs. This second example involves a domestic study program in New Orleans focused on urban planning. This program is restricted to junior and senior urban planning and political science majors. It is conducted over a *J-term*, a four-week term offered by many schools as a month-long, one-course-at-a-time term to contrast with their fall and spring semesters. The students in this program live with host families, conduct group projects in conjunction with the needs of local nonprofit agencies, and participate in some small-scale service-learning experiences. The in-class meetings with faculty are conducted in a seminar format based on lengthy discussions of readings, experiences, and observations and the development of the group projects. The course also utilizes numerous local experts as guest lecturers and discussion facilitators. Like the prior example, the program director has been recently asked by the provost to articulate learning outcomes for this program that map onto the institution's learning outcomes. For the purposes of this exercise, let's assume that the program director has decided to link the program's learning outcomes with the institution's overall goals regarding civic responsibility and collaborative leadership skills.

Plotting the current state of the program design and student characteristics again enables the program directors to identify realistic learning outcomes. First, it is critical to articulate the constituent knowledge, skills, and dispositions that combine to produce a sense of civic responsibility and interpersonal leadership skills. For the purposes of this exercise, the spectrum of constituent simple to complex learning outcomes that contribute to civic responsibility are derived from the AAC&U 2011 publication *A Crucible Moment: College Learning and Democracy's Future*, whereas the requisite aspects of collaborative leadership are loosely borrowed from the Social Change Model of Leadership Development (HERI, 1996) and John Dugan's work on the development of socially responsible leadership (2006). At the least cognitively complex level, the constituent learning outcomes are composed of gaining knowledge and understanding about notions of democracy, citizenship, and leadership, as well as theories of organizations and how leadership within them works depending upon how they are organized. At the most complex level, the constituent learning outcomes that contribute to civic responsibility and collaborative leadership involve working within a community to collaboratively design and implement a solution to a real-world issue or problem.

As you can see in Figure 2.3, the length of the learning experience is relatively short and doesn't necessarily lend itself to more complex learning conditions. The nature of the cultural gap is not expansive, but it is moderately accessible particularly in the areas of socioeconomic status, local culture, and the impact of relatively recent natural disaster. However, the

Figure 2.3 Identifying realistic learning outcomes for an urban planning J-term study away

Complexity of Outcomes	Program Design				Student Preparation	Program Enrollment
Civic Responsibility & Collaborative Leadership	Length of Learning Experience	Cultural Gap	Depth of Immersion	Pedagogical Approach	Maturity and Knowledge	Variation Across Participants
Understanding democracy/citizenship & organizational theories	X					
Applying self-knowledge, collaborative skills within diverse interactions		X				
				X	X	
Engaging with a community collaboratively to solve a real-world issue			X			X

Note. The outcomes highlighted in gray indicate the learning outcomes that are likely realistic and attainable if all else remains the same.

extent to which this program plumbs the available depths of immersion substantially expands the existence of complex learning conditions. In addition, the pedagogical approach employed by the faculty directors further extends this possibility for complex learning. The students enrolled in this program are older and often more mature and the group of students is tightly clustered in similar majors with relatively similar postgraduate aspirations.

Taken together, the nature of the program design and the nature of the student participants allow the program to realistically aspire to more complex learning outcomes. Moreover, the alignment of the depth of immersion and pedagogical program, supported by the nature of the student participants, sets in motion a scenario in which the previously articulated learning goals of the learning experiences in the course align almost completely with the learning outcomes that contribute to the institution's goals of civic responsibility and collaborative leadership. Finally, if the program wanted to explore ways in which it might further solidify its ability to develop complex learning in all of its students, program directors might explore ways in which they could explicitly link the J-term experience with a post–study away experience, in the form of a class or a cocurricular program, that would facilitate the students' process of making meaning of their one-month experience in New Orleans.

Conclusion

The framework proposed in this chapter allows study away faculty and program directors to match the design of an existing program and the characteristics of the student participants, as individuals and as a group, with a range of realistic and attainable learning outcomes that can be mapped to their institution's learning outcomes. Obviously, this process could also work in the other direction, whereby faculty or study away program directors could design a new program to specifically meet a range of constituent learning outcomes. This might be particularly valuable for an institution that recognizes a need to build new programs so that all students have the opportunity to develop the knowledge, skills, and dispositions necessary to meet institutional learning outcomes.

It is important to note, however, that this framework is not a panacea. As anyone who has put his or her heart and soul into teaching knows from experience, educating is a complicated endeavor. There are so many ways that we can stumble into brilliance or career into catastrophe. Educating is never about certainty; it is a perpetual effort to increase the likelihood that our students learn and embrace what they have learned after they leave us. Using this framework to improve the likelihood of meaningful success can be one important step in ensuring that they find just the right balance of challenge and support in a learning experience that can impact them for a lifetime.

References

AAC&U (Association of American Colleges and Universities), National Task Force on Civic Learning and Democratic Engagement. (2011). *A crucible moment: College learning and democracy's future.* Washington, DC: Author.

Anderson, L. W., & Krathwohl, D. R. (Eds.). (2001). *A taxonomy for learning, teaching, and assessing: A revision of Bloom's taxonomy of educational objectives.* White Plains, NY: Longman.

Bransford, J. D., Brown, A. L., & Cocking, R. R. (Eds.). (1999). *How people learn: Brain, mind, experience, and school.* Washington, DC: National Academies Press.

Dugan, J. P. (2006). Involvement and leadership: A descriptive analysis of socially responsible leadership. *Journal of College Student Development, 47,* 335–343.

Fink, L. D. (2003). *Creating significant learning experiences: An integrated approach to designing college courses.* San Francisco, CA: Jossey-Bass.

HERI (Higher Education Research Institute). (1996). *A social change model of leadership development: Guidebook* (version III). College Park, MD: National Clearinghouse for Leadership Programs.

Kelleher, A. (2005). Global education continuum. *Diversity Digest, 8*(3). Retrieved from www.diversityweb.org/digest/vol8no3/kelleher.cfm

3

WHERE EXPERIENCE MEETS TRANSFORMATION

Pedagogy and Study Away

Amanda E. Feller

"It is a year later and I am using this class to process my last study away [in central Europe]." A student shared this with me one morning over breakfast in our hotel. We were in Northern Ireland studying the Troubles and the peace process, but we could have just as easily been in Chicago, Los Angeles, Appalachia, or the American Southwest. I told the student that it was natural for one set of learning experiences to connect with others, especially when subject matter aligned. Then I asked what she was processing. "We went to four sites of violence in five days and never talked about it." I was puzzled. However, giving the benefit of the doubt to the student and her teacher, I asked questions about assignments, class discussion, the progression of a day, the instructor's facilitation style, and the student's overall participation. I arrived at a conclusion as we finished our porridge and tea. Based on this student's answers to my pedagogical questions, the instructor had facilitated a rich content-based curriculum, but seemingly neglected the complexities of the learning process. The first part is not unusual as faculty members teach subjects in which they have expertise. However, the intricacy of the learning process is an aspect of our teaching that we faculty do not spend enough time considering.

Why do we want students to study away? What do we imagine they gain away from campus that they do not gain on campus? What is our role as educators in leading programs, teaching courses, and designing curricula? More importantly, what is our responsibility as teachers in the study away context? What do we assume about learning and about our students as learners? Pragmatically speaking, what can we do as teachers to align study away outcomes with actual student learning?

This chapter focuses on pedagogy in the study away context. As my conversation over porridge revealed, we must recognize what can occur for students. We must recognize our responsibilities as educators to shape, manage, and facilitate the process of learning. We need to understand that exposure and content conversations are not enough. We cannot assume that because a person is studying away *as a student* learning is automatic. Nor can we assume that what works in the campus classroom works in the study away environment. We need to know with certainty that student change and meaningful perspective shifts are due to how we teach and not simply happenstance. We need to be knowledgeable, specific, and deliberate in our study away teaching, whether we are taking students into the field periodically, leading intensive short-term courses, or teaching as part of a long-term semester program.

In terms of learning, study away is special and unique, and not just with reference to cultural experience. As educators we must be equipped to engage students on all levels. Being in a new environment means to engage that environment with all the senses (which is less common for campus-bound students). We must help students make meaning from sensory engagement. We know that just being away from the familiar generates a range of responses: excitement, fear, self-doubt, insensitive or defensive remarks, fatigue or even depression, hyper or overly animated communication, and so on. However, do we understand that these responses are about more than just bad manners, naiveté, or homesickness—that they can be indicators of potential deep learning? Our tendency is to address these behaviors as general "teachable moments" about health, safety, or maturity. However, failing to address these behaviors pedagogically can have negative consequences for the student, personally and academically.

This uniqueness necessarily calls into being two pedagogical levels: specific content knowledge and deeper recursive learning. Whether a student is studying away from campus domestically or overseas, there is content knowledge for the student to learn that we recognize in our programmatic learning goals. That said, there is a reason we are away from campus. I can teach a campus-based course on conflict in Northern Ireland or on the U.S.-Mexico borderlands and meet the same basic knowledge goals as are met when I teach off campus. So, why take the time and expense to go "there"? The answer is twofold: I assume that being "there" (a) provides a quality of learning *about the content* that cannot be achieved on campus and (b) provides deeper learning *about more than the content.* However, these assumptions can be realized only if my pedagogical knowledge and practices are up to the task. Poor or misguided study away teaching is like having an inexperienced mechanic work on your car—there is a chance it might be fixed, but there is a greater chance it will not. The outcome can be expensive, counterproductive, and can shade your view of the automotive industry.

Whether a student is enrolled in a short-term course or a semester program, immersed in a domestic culture or far away in another land, studying a seemingly familiar culture or one dramatically different, we must equip that student for the learning experience. To do this we must learn more about pedagogy and how it works in this specialized environment. As teachers, we must know (a) how to engage students to meet the objectives of study away, (b) how to foster learning in that context, and (c) how to recognize and work with deeper learning behaviors. We must also know the difference between what learning we hope to see happen and the learning that does happen. Not knowing the difference can have severe consequences. This was obvious to me and to my student; "It is hard for me to be present and to process our time in Northern Ireland because my time at those sites of violence last year is so present." I not only heard the student express this sentiment, but also witnessed how she tried to manage this consequence—how it impaired her past study away experience as well as her present one.

To investigate the pedagogical nature of study away, this chapter reviews (a) student learning and study away, (b) experiential learning, and (c) transformative learning. Along the way, details are provided to better equip us as study away teachers, program leaders, and curriculum developers. A central theme of the case studies in this book is that the arrival of the student to the study away environment with a stated subject as the focus is just the beginning of learning.

Getting There: Expectation to Positive Outcomes

Attention to the pedagogical complexity of study away is both significant and consequential. As teachers, failure to attend to our pedagogical practices negatively impacts students. These effects can be minor and short term to more drastic and lasting, including unmanaged cultural shock (Furnham, 2010); unmanaged reverse cultural shock (Davis et al., 2008); cultural backlash (Christofi & Thompson, 2007); developmental regression (Pederson, 2010); unwarranted risk-taking (Hartjes, Baumann, & Henriques 2009; Popescu, 2007); entrenchment of hegemonic, imperialist, or colonialist attitudes (The Editors of the Committee for Academic Freedom in Africa, 2002;

Habu, 2000); attitudes of economic instrumentalism and personal cultural capital (Dowd, 2004; The Editors, 2002); and legal or criminal challenges (Deardorff, de Wit, & Heyl, 2012). Therefore, we must understand the promise and pitfalls of study away as determined by the sophistication of the teaching and facilitation.

Roholt and Fisher's *Expect the Unexpected* (2013) opens by raising the question, What makes international programs a viable learning method? Their question leads to important pedagogical considerations. Across the threshold is a needed discussion of perhaps familiar educational terms such as *role fulfillment, propositional learning, sensory capacities, learning styles,* and *student self-awareness.* This foundational discussion makes possible the subsequent framing of study away in terms of experiential and transformative education, two essential ways of approaching and maximizing study away.

When deliberating upon what is assumed to be familiar, I draw on a persuasive speech a student delivered in my public speaking course. She opened by asking, "Do you adequately wash your hands after going to the toilet?" Heads nodded emphatically. However, once she explained the standards for "adequate," nearly all realized they were doing a poor job and likely spreading germs. Robust conversation followed the speech about water temperature, soap quality, hand sanitizer, methods of hand drying, and the like. The following week I asked how many had changed hand-washing habits. All said that they had. This analogy reminds us that we imagine and feel that we are "adequate" (or better) in our study away teaching practices, when we really need to take time to check the assumptions, definitions, and standards. It is then that we improve and meet our intended outcomes for ourselves and for our students.

There are three foundational assumptions upon which study away pedagogical standards are built. The first has been alluded to, and that is our expertise with subject knowledge. As study away practitioners, we are quick to separate ourselves from "the Grand Tour," and the language of trips, tourism, and vacations. The fundamental difference is the emphasis on exploration and knowledge rather than on luxury and ensconced movement. As facilitators we must know the subject of our courses and have local knowledge. Students (and their parents/guardians) count on us for this. This first assumption is an acknowledgment that subject expertise matters. We possess information and interpretations of that information that the students do not, even if they have been "there" before.

The second assumption of effective study away teaching is somewhat ephemeral, that teaching "goes beyond." John Dewey's voice has echoed throughout the decades, reminding us that education involves far more than the transmission of information and propositional analysis (Dewey, 1938).

Those of us involved in study away education are typically thoughtful in this regard. We accept that "there is no guarantee that study abroad experiences in and of themselves will broaden and challenge students' worldviews" (Roholt & Fisher, 2013, p. 48). Therefore, we must understand our role in teaching study away goes beyond (a) "information transmitter" (leading students in lecture–discussion around cultural encounters), and (b) "propositional pundit" (urging students to wrestle with theory, concepts, and critical epistemological questions). Knowledge acquisition and debate of the proposition are only part of what we engage.

The third assumption flows from the second—"going beyond" what? This question is rooted in the fundamental belief that life away from campus is inherently a better offering. Upon first considering the question, "Why go there?" we think about the tactile, sensory experience of standing inside the Roman Colosseum, navigating a Moroccan kasbah, people watching in Greenwich Village's Washington Square Park, or sitting in a Navajo hogan. We say offhandedly, "You can't get that from a book." Yet, what is the referent? For some, "that" refers to full sensory input—sight, smells, sounds. For some, it is spiritual and emotional, even cosmological—connecting self to the length of human history. For some it is the circumstance of the direct tactile (touch) and for others it is the kinesthetic (moving within the environment). For some it is the imprinting and grafting of memories, and for others the immediate moment is most essential and rich, regardless of lasting memories.

This consideration points to the educational concept of learning styles: "Our concentration on the substantive elements of . . . courses means that *how* we teach often receives secondary, even minimal attention in favor of *what* we teach" (Carson, 2009, p. 95). Carson's point is well taken—we perceive that teaching the *what* in its immediate context is a valuable learning tool, such as reading Cicero at the Roman Forum or walking in Atlanta listening to a civil rights marcher recount his experience with Martin Luther King Jr. However, there is more to the *how* than matching *what* with *place*.

Learning style is a complex calculus of a person's strongest modality of making sense of new information including processing and retention (Krätzig & Arbuthnott, 2006). Learning modality deals with how well each person's brain processes sensory input. A basic example is the person who fixes a car based on reading the manual versus the person who learns by handling the car parts while receiving instruction. Research on teaching methods, learning styles, and achievement outcomes is a well-studied arena. Learning style research as part of meeting educational outcomes stems from the original question as to whether or not the once standard "chalk and talk" teaching method was effective. (The method was discovered to be effective only for those whose ability to process and remember information is based on high visual and high auditory capacities [Dunn & Dunn, 2005].) As research has continued throughout the decades, the concept of learning style is now understood to be multifaceted. For example, tactile learners and kinesthetic learners are not the same as they once were thought to be. For us as study away instructors, decades of learning styles research urges us to be informed about learning modalities and understand their importance to the formula of how-where-what we teach.

There is a secondary informative point here. When we say, "You can't get that from a book," what we mean is *I can't* get that from a book. *I know that I* can use the combination of my senses, thoughts, thinking ability, and emotional awareness to learn in the unfamiliar environment. *I know that I* can perceive, observe, parse, absorb, notice, take in, remove my native cultural lens, be comfortable with discomfort, and so on. This ability and capacity is not automatic; it is developed. Therefore, as teachers working with students in the study away environment, we must recognize how a student likely sees the unfamiliar environment—an overwhelming panorama of new sights, smells, touch, movement, and energies where no one part is distinguishable as exquisite or instructive. In addition, we then expect students to graft these stimuli onto assigned readings and respond to discussion questions. We next expect this unscientific grafting to successfully yield thoughtful inquiry, critical observation, and self-discovery. In reality, this sudden assault of the senses can cause a range of responses that are problematic to the learning environment: shutdown, fatigue, the defense mechanism of boredom, or seemingly arbitrary questions and observations. Therefore, we must teach students how to see, observe, process, and think while we teach them about the integration of what and place.

The last point on the matter of learning styles is that we must be knowledgeable about them, *and be instructive about them*. Students generally do not accurately evaluate learning styles:

> Students are poor at assessing their learning style before they have been exposed to the concept, and so they cannot be making "informed" choices in how to learn. This implies that a better introduction to learning styles and their implications for student learning could be provided to the students earlier in their higher degree studies. (Horton, Wiederman, & Saint, 2012, p. 114)

Assisting students in discovering their own learning styles is a responsibility we share across our institutions. However, those of us involved in study away are especially obligated in this matter. Many institutions are equipped with academic support centers, offering various inventories for students such as the Visual–Auditory–Kinesthetic (VAK) test or Kolb's Learning Styles Inventory (LSI), and can offer instruction for faculty. Similarly, education departments can be a resource, offering materials and consultations. Such inventories are an easy tool to find and administer. Even a single inventory and discussion can provide information to teachers and students alike.

In summary, these three foundational assumptions of effective study away teaching and learning must be examined in our own study away practices and programs. First, are we strong in subject matter, including local knowledge? Do we erroneously assume that place plus subject equals the learning outcomes we expect? Second, are we aware of how stimuli, modality, and processing capacities can interact or clash? Third, how well do we as individuals and as institutions help students learn about learning? Is our attention to *how we teach* as focused as our attention on *what* and *where*?

An interrogation of these assumptions sets the stage for understanding experiential pedagogy and transformative pedagogy. These two pedagogies are distinctive from one another. They are often assumed as both motives and outcomes of study away. As with hand washing, we imagine we know these pedagogical practices, yet there are details we do not know, have forgotten, or set aside.

The Cultural Excursion: Experiential Learning

The previous sections outlined how "experience" does not equate with "experiential learning," and that educators involved with study away often assume experiential learning is inherent by matching *what* with *place*. This section delves into the nature of *how*—how to teach process, engagement, thinking, attention, and absorption. The *how* is the catalyst that allows what and place to react together. Just as in chemistry, our pedagogical expertise as catalyst means that the reaction time is faster, requires less energy, and guarantees a particular reaction.

The movement away from pure cognitive pedagogy ("chalk and talk" and rote memorization) and pure behavioral pedagogy (objective and demonstrative) was driven by both John Dewey and Kurt Lewin (Kolb & Boyatzis, 2000). In *Experience and Education*, Dewey constructs a pedagogy deeply rooted in experience. In this he critiques typical pedagogical approaches, noting that "any experience is mis-educative that has the effect of arresting or distorting the growth of further experience . . . to engender callousness . . . lack of sensitivity . . . then the possibilities of having a richer experience in the future are restricted" (1938, p. 26). In contrast, he established criteria for experience to be educative, including the following:

- Education serves democratic, humanistic, and progressive societal goals.

- Teaching is action based and perpetual, *growing* versus *growth*.
- All pupils possess subjective experience-based understandings of the world.
- Teachers must possess objective subject-matter knowledge.
- Subject matter must be subordinate to experience-based understandings.
- Subject matter must not be separated from cultural and local contexts.
- Teachers must instruct in methods of perceiving significance and context.
- Teachers must instruct in methods of reflection.
- Subject matter and perception must be brought together through reflection.

While each is important, the key criterion is subordination. If something is subordinate, then it is secondary in importance or priority; it is even sequential and therefore dependent upon what comes first or is superordinate. For instance, remember those first lessons in learning to drive a motor vehicle? The laws, while vital, were completely removed from your mind while you tried to manage the gas pedal, braking, steering, and signaling as well as your instructor's commands. All you could process were emotions (excitement, frustration, thoughts of freedom) and the basic information of trying to coordinate seemingly disparate features of a vehicle and moving it through space. Today, years later, we drive without really thinking about the process, and all is coordinated, including our understanding of the laws; our only emotional responses come as a reaction to traffic jams, reckless drivers, and the like. In this case, when learning to drive (a new experience that intersects place, knowledge, and instruction), our reaction is superordinate and the knowledge is subordinate. There cannot be another relationship between the two. Therefore, the driving instructor must teach from the experience of the student, not from the experience of a seasoned driver. Knowledge is taught, shared, and built upon over time as the student's reaction evolves from perhaps panic to relative calm.

In the case of study away, information, theory, instrumentation, facts, and the other features of propositional education must be in reference, and therefore subordinate, to the student's experience of the world, which is superordinate. However, *subordination* does not mean *deferential*. Subjective, personal conclusions about the world are often erroneous and subject to challenge. As educators we are all too familiar with the range of arbitrary, misguided "commonsense theories" students bring to the classroom. Yet, in keeping with the concept of super- and subordination, these "theories" are born out of the habitual and natural way of making sense of experience.

Students are learning to drive, so how they operate a vehicle and understand the laws of the road is limited while their emotional and attitudinal experience is expansive. In the study away context, how a student understands the intersection of place and subject—immigration on the U. S.-Mexico border, for example—is a rough ride at best. Our approach as teachers must include managing the student view of and reactions to the world and (re)shaping knowledge. We can no more take students to the border and demand that they absorb subject-matter knowledge and graft one onto the other than a driving instructor can expect a student to successfully operate a motor vehicle and know all the driving laws in a single course. Dewey rightly argued that as teachers we must be aware that human beings formulate understandings of the world through life experience.

In Dewey's eyes, the central difference between experience and experiential learning is the difference between habit and growing. Teachers are the ones who break habits, deconstruct commonsense theories, and (re)shape knowledge. In study away, we must bring Dewey's criteria into our facilitation of student learning. We must recognize that students are overwhelmed by the immersion (some more than others, depending on learning styles and modalities). Therefore, we must attend to reactions to stimuli, which are superordinate to the objective material. We are the driving instructor who must still instruct through the panicked reaction. For example, when taking students to Los Angeles to learn from residents and community organizations about urban life, the majority of students, who have little to no experience with urban neighborhoods, will have visceral and disturbed responses. During an initial visit to a struggling neighborhood, urban blight is inescapable: street corners where certain gang-related deaths occurred are pointed out; the minimart is noted as the only grocery store in three square miles; a vibrant, yet underresourced community center is noted; and stories of the neighborhood are told. The litter, graffiti, and boarded-up homes appear unsettling and even frightening. The stories of violence, poverty, and even community outreach are upsetting. After a day out students return to the classroom space for a facilitated conversation about what they are feeling and what they are assuming. The next day is scheduled as "free day" where the students explore as they wish. Some opt for community sites, some for sightseeing; some even stay in to write, call home, and reenergize. Throughout, the instructor is there to tease out emotions; help make sense of them; adjust any emerging erroneous conclusions; and provide reminders for when, where, and how to process, including how to connect experience of the place to the prescribed knowledge.

This example demonstrates two points about teaching and learning in study away. First, the stimulation from the experience is intense, and students typically only have the capacity to sit with their reactions to it. In other words, initial awareness is typically at the level of personal emotion and reaction, and even identifying emotions or connecting reactions to the experience can be limited. Second, it is our responsibility as teachers to facilitate meaningful conversation about those reactions and how to begin to make sense of them. Instruction usually begins with "It was a long day and we won't stay in the classroom long; what are you thinking and feeling?" That simple question naturally gives way to content-based observations, thoughts, questions, and ponderings. The conversation connects feelings with content, giving the teacher the opportunity to gently check on where the feelings are taking thoughts about content. For instance, because the visit is designed to show the challenges that the community faces, it is common for the students to feel the situation is hopeless and community-building efforts are regressive. Although the thought is inaccurate, the intensity of the day can easily lead to such thoughts, exemplifying the potential for experience to be miseducative.

As teachers, our role is to engage students in thoughtful, guided reflection of feelings. We can tease out thoughts while they are still in formation. The larger group conversation is a collaborative exploration of feelings, attitudes, thoughts, assumptions, and more. Importantly, we do this as a group for three reasons. First, by facilitating a conversation about feelings, the students get the message that feelings matter and are instructive. As the teacher, I even share my feelings, typically saying, "I always have an emotional reaction to this type of day/visit. It varies and today it was . . ." Second, unspoken feelings are unarticulated and therefore less well understood. A group conversation becomes a way to say, "I feel a knot in my stomach, but I don't know why," and someone responds, "I have a knot too!" which opens the space to talk about what that means. Third, group conversation allows students to know that they are not alone in their feelings—why they have reactions, what those reactions mean or don't mean. It is easy for anyone, especially a student, to assume that one's feelings are unique and therefore isolating.

The conversation is a reminder that learning is holistic, challenging, and personal. I typically end such sessions with "This was an intense day. Please take time to take care of yourselves and each other; take time to reflect and write; maybe go back to your notes from earlier class sessions. . . . Enjoy your day tomorrow." Later I wander the halls and meeting rooms. I find students chatting in small groups or just sitting together as they write, share a meal, call home, or watch a fluff movie. I might be asked a question or have a student share with me thoughts and feelings. These are quiet, yet steady moments that are important to the overall learning dynamic.

In addition to exemplifying Dewey's concept of subordination, this group element of study away underscores the reality that learning is a gestalt process where initial lessons are founded in life experience. As illustrated previously, students take in an entire tableau at once and are unable to parse it into meaningful elements. When trying to make meaning, we do so in reference to our life experience as well as in reference to those around us. Where Dewey emphasized subordination and reflection, Lewin emphasized the dynamics of group interaction as an influence on making sense of experience and on personal as well as societal change (Lewin, Heider, & Heider, 1936). We create meaning, assumptions, and working theories from life experience, and do so in reference to the group. One natural interpretive lens of life experience is our perception of the normative attitudes and behaviors of those around us (Lewin & Grabbe, 1945). When faced with new or unfamiliar circumstances, we use others as reference points on a compass to gain our bearings.

Lewin's work has two implications for study away. First, we must recognize that each student interprets the often overwhelming stimuli of the study away environment through the lens of self placed in the new societal environment. In other words, an internal conversation unfolds: "Who am I here in this strange land? How do I operate? How do I navigate?" Perceptions of self and place are recursive, pointing back upon one another. This underscores Dewey's notion of subordination of subject matter. Therefore, as with group reflection in Los Angeles, facilitated conversation must occur as to how the self is operating in relationship to the social environment and how each is shaping the other.

The second implication can best be understood through Lewin's analogy of a carpenter wanting to become a watchmaker:

> [This] is not merely a matter of teaching the carpenter a set of new watchmaking skills. Before he can become a watchmaker, the carpenter, in addition to the learning of a set of new skills, will have to acquire a new system of habits, standards, and values—the standards and values which characterize the thinking and behavior of watchmakers. At least, this is what he will have to do before he can function successfully as a watchmaker. (Lewin & Grabbe, 1945, p. 55)

The "standards and values" and even the "thinking and behavior" of a watchmaker are constituted by those in the industry and culture. When we assume that being away from campus will change students' sense of self and of the world, then we are assuming the entailments of the analogy—that students will perceive, view, and understand the culture of the watchmaker. Students then naturally see the local people as the watchmakers and the at-large culture as the industry. However, because the students think, value, speak, and behave like carpenters, the watchmaking group might as well be invisible as an interpretive source. It is a paradox that can be handled only if we recognize our central roles as the facilitators, translators, and guides.

We cannot simply expose students to a cultural experience; rather we must direct that exposure. For instance, encouraging students to strike up a conversation with the local people at a neighborhood café or farmer's market is not enough. Students need instruction on what to look for, what to avoid, what questions to ask, how to read nonverbal communication, and how to listen. Dewey's and Lewin's work reminds us once again that *how we teach* study away is absolutely essential. In reference to experiential learning, thus far *how* involves subordination of subject, superordination of student reaction, facilitation of group reflection about reaction, gentle checking of knowledge construction during reflection, and creating means for interaction.

One final important part of the *how* of experiential learning and study away is rooted in the works of David Kolb and John Heron. These contemporary scholar–practitioners have developed the pedagogy by adding practices of connecting the elements of self, stimuli, reaction, group dynamics, and subject. Kolb's addition that best serves study away teaching is his method for mapping learning styles onto the cycle of exploration. Similarly, Heron's method of cooperative inquiry provides a detailed guide for our teaching, in helping students navigate the complexity of study away. There are, of course, critiques of both scholars as well as complexities to their works. This, however, does not alter the basics discussed here as to how to become more proficient in experiential pedagogy.

Kolb and Kolb summarize the aspects of experiential learning explored thus far:

1. Learning is best conceived as a process, not in terms of outcomes.
2. All learning is *re*learning. Learning is best facilitated by a process that draws out students' beliefs . . . about a topic so that they can be examined, tested, and integrated with new, more refined ideas.
3. Learning requires the resolution of conflicts between dialectically opposed modes of adaptation to the world.
4. Learning is a holistic process of adaptation to the world. Not just the result of cognition, learning involves the integrated functioning of the total person—thinking, feeling, perceiving, and behaving.
5. Learning results from synergetic transactions between the person and the environment.
6. Learning is the process of creating knowledge. (2005, p. 194)

The Learning Styles Inventory (LSI) developed by Kolb is useful in helping students understand what senses they privilege and rely upon most. What is more important is how learning styles are overlaid on the cycle of exploration (see Figure 3.1). We each approach a problem or new situation differently. Some of us prefer to start by defining and understanding the situation. Some prefer to jump in, using trial and error. When teaching group communication I use the LSI to help students understand how the members of an assigned group will tend to approach the project, and therefore know where in the cycle each member is strong. This minimizes conflict by maximizing awareness. In study away, the LSI helps students understand why they react or engage the way that they do. It is also useful for me so I know why I see what I see and how to guide each student.

This is crucial. The previous pages have emphasized the self and reaction, yet not in rejection of subject. By layering together learning styles and the exploration cycle, we can see the relationship of experience, feelings, and meaning-making. We can also see how to manage that relationship in a coherent way. In the instance of the Los Angeles site visit, the days prior and days following include direct instruction of community-building theory and concepts. This instruction provides a means to interpret the encounter. In fact, the course can be imagined as an upward spiral, where conversations

Figure 3.1 Kolb's learning styles and cycle of exploration

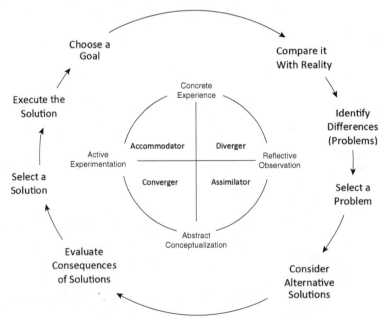

and assignments continuously manage the relationship of self, experience, and content.

In terms of study away and pedagogical prowess, Kolb's integration of learning styles with the exploration cycle is similar to Heron's method of cooperative inquiry. Like the other pedagogies mentioned, Heron views knowledge creation as holistic, inseparable from the self, dependent on self as central, involving multiple learning modalities (practical, propositional, presentational, experiential), and requiring a rigorous system for processing (Heron, 1996). His method involves four stages, which are repeated depending on the nature of the inquiry. While these stages are comprehensive, the following is a brief description applied to the study away context:

> *Stage 1. Focusing, Framing, Planning, Determining.* We aid students in focusing on key subject-matter questions and personal aims. Together we cocreate the framing or parameters of the study. We aid students in planning how to approach experience—how to engage with purpose, how to operate in the new environment, how to manage the self, how to manage stimuli, how long to be engaged. We guide students in determining the methods of recording—note-taking, blogging, critical writing, research writing.
>
> *Stage 2. Action.* Students move with purpose in the cultural environment. Actions and reactions are documented.
>
> *Stage 3. Experiential Immersion.* This stage is an extension of stage 2. Students check predispositions and preconceptualizations with what is occurring in the action phase. This is the core of study away inquiry because place, subject matter, and self are interacting meaningfully through our expert teaching. This is where knowledge is born, grows, and evolves.
>
> *Stage 4. Grouping, Reflection, and Adaptation.* This stage brings the students and faculty together to reflect on how data gathered in stages 2 and 3 fit with the focus and framing laid out in stage 1. What information and tentative meaning has been produced that addresses the key questions and personal aims? Based on this inquiry, approaches to action and recording are adapted. The cycle is then repeated.

Whether students are in short-term or long-term programs, the learning plan changes depending on what is happening with students. For instance, consider a course in which students are to engage as interviewers, documenting local attitudes, perceptions, and stories. Yet student silence and lack of prescribed interaction persists. A stage 4 conversation explores the students' silence and understanding of the environment, clarifies the purpose of the interviews, and adapts the data-gathering approach. This small example points to just how involved, nuanced, systematic, and detail oriented study away teaching is.

When pursued with expertise and care, experiential pedagogy results in the expansion of self-awareness, the embodiment of theory, and an enlarged view of others. This section has illustrated the complexity of experiential pedagogy because it is inexorably intertwined with successful study away courses and programs. However, we must be mindful that experiential learning produces nothing more; it is dangerous to assume otherwise. This means that study away—whether a week, three months, or a year—does not inherently transform a student.

In study away we see the potential of transformed views of self and the world. Indeed, we have witnessed profound growth. We have read, heard, and seen student self-reports of life-changing courses and programs. Yet in these moments we must ask, How did it come about? Again that word *how*. Until we thoroughly understand that experiential learning is not transformational learning, our study away teaching is limited. Signs of excitement, change, and "afterglow" are not signs of transformational learning. We can mistake "aha! moments" for deeper insights. We imagine excited reports home indicate paradigm shifts. We miscalculate that growth of knowledge wrapped around a plethora of feelings adds up to increased humility and compassion. When we assume experiential and transformational learning are the same, we miss essential clues indicating how well a student is making sense of self, place, and subject, as well as how likely he or she is to regress.

You Can't Go Home Again: Transformative Learning

Transformative pedagogy is a distinctive way of understanding learning and approaching teaching. Jack Mezirow, the founding father of transformative learning, began in the same way as Dewey—observing what was happening in the learning environment and setting forth a new theory of education. The originating observation for Mezirow came when teaching a group of women who had returned to school. While moving through the curriculum—the readings and assignments—Mezirow observed that these women were "disturbed" in the sense that the material was going beyond the intended instructional outcomes, and unexpected behaviors were being presented (Mezirow, 1990). He redirected the classroom conversation to focus on the behaviors and what they might indicate. Discussion revealed that the subject material was confronting existing worldviews held by the students, down to core assumptions of self, identity, placement in the world, and more. From this, Mezirow postulated transformative learning. Although the pedagogy has evolved, core aspects remain consistent. Two are most pertinent to teaching students in the study away context: (a) how to understand student behavior and (b) how to guide transformation. Significantly, where we can create experiential learning, we cannot create transformative learning. As teachers, we can create a setting and use our facilitation prowess to watch for students on the transformative learning path. The possibility for transformative learning depends on (a) how well students engage self and material and (b) how well we as teachers manage transformative learning once it is set in motion.

Transformative learning is based on the same principles as experiential learning, such as superordination of self, critical reflection, holism, systematic process, and so on. What sets transformative learning apart from experiential learning—the key distinction—is found in the concept and nature of disorientation. We are familiar with feelings of vertigo—nausea, dizziness, free-falling, a lost sense of direction. When a person absorbs new information so deeply that core assumptions are challenged, disorientation occurs. This is far more than cognitive dissonance, as it involves the full self and orientation to the world. The deeply felt dilemma of competing worldviews challenges the self on many levels at once: (a) old knowledge ("I was wrong about this?!"), (b) the people and institutions that did the teaching ("Everyone who's ever taught me was wrong?!"), and (c) the means of knowledge creation ("I wasted all those years studying this wrongness?!"). From this, a cascade effect occurs where everything about self, others, the world, and worldviews can be called into question (Feller, 2009). The challenges and feelings are too numerous and chaotic to catalogue. The disorientation can be unrecognizable, especially by the disoriented student.

In the study away context, we may not recognize behavior as an indication of disorientation, as something that can lead to transformation. Instead, we might interpret aberrant behavior as culture shock, a lack of cultural sensitivity, a personality trait, a momentary discomfort, or a sense of being overwhelmed. If we develop a sharpened pedagogical sensibility and use Heron's approach, we can better interpret the behavior that we see. What's more is that we cannot rely on student self-report here. We cannot ask: "Is there new information here that is disturbing your sense of self?" Rather, we have to watch, ask questions, and if we develop a sense of something deeper occurring for the student, then we need to employ a different process of teaching and learning.

The transformative learning process can look similar to Heron's cooperative inquiry, moving systematically through stages that bring together key questions, actions, thinking, and reflection. The critical difference is that the questions are now based upon the disorientation. There are four phases: awareness of a disorienting dilemma, evaluation of the dilemma, exploration, and recalibration. In the first and second phases, our role is to help students explore what they are feeling, to pull items in question out of the chaos, and to get at the deeper implications of the "wrongness." When transformational disorientation strikes and the cascade effect begins, one task of the facilitator is to help students sort out what aspects of self are still intact and which are open to evolution. As discussed, we hope that study away creates fundamental shifts in how one sees the world, increases empathy, and increases appreciation for difference. To fully realize this hope, we have to be the guide that brings the student out of the disorientation and helps recalibrate the compass.

The first two phases are the most dangerous and therefore the most important for us as teachers. The danger is to ignore the disorientation. As already noted, poor teaching in study away can have minor to major consequences. An ignored disorienting dilemma means we leave the student to make meaning of place and subject through an unsteady self. An outcome can be cultural backlash and an entrenched view of native cultural supremacy:

> The discourse of adventure on the one hand reproduces relations of power between students' host society (constructed as isolated and behind the times, with an insufficient education system) and home society (constructed as omnipresent and up to date, with sound education system), and on the other hand interpellates and governs the study-abroad student as a particular type of subject: a "student adventurer." (Doerr, 2012, p. 257)

We know some students return home from study away with attitudes that all aspects of the home country are best and that anyone from the outside is inferior or unworthy. The fault in such cases does not lie with the student; the fault lies with the nature of the study away teaching in that case.

If we successfully guide a student through awareness and evaluation of a disorienting dilemma, then we largely avoid the greatest dangers and negative outcomes. Also, the process gets a little easier. The third phase of deeper exploration happens when the student surveys what new meanings of self and the world are emerging and what that all means (Mezirow, Taylor, & Associates, 2009). We can guide this process too. We can help pose questions and posit implications. We can create more purposeful spaces and durations for reflection. We can design more specific types of reflection.

How many study away programs encourage students to keep a journal or blog documenting what happened, how they reacted, what they thought, and how it all points to learning? And how many times do we hear students say, "I'm terrible at keeping a journal" (meaning they don't have the discipline)? Therefore, a task we have is to teach students how to develop and maintain the discipline of thoughtful, critical reflection. Further, we cannot assume that even our most active students in social media or our strongest writers know how to write thoughtfully about moments of self-reflexivity. Whatever the format or manner of critical reflection and writing, we must instruct—this too is part of our study away pedagogical practice.

Making it through the exploration phase leads to the fourth and final phase of recalibration: internalized new knowledge of self and of the world. This means that perspectives and frames are changed. The change is progressive and humanistic. In this phase, the main task of the teacher is to affirm and build confidence. We appreciate the intense energy, trepidation, and excitement accompanying newfound ways of being, seeing, and acting. This leads us to an important matter of preparation—preparing students for operating as the new self in the old world. While their compass is recalibrated, those familiar to them have the old compass. In study away, we often improperly identify this as reverse culture shock.

Reverse culture shock is typically defined as the reentry encounter with home, dominated by the following themes: (a) the home culture is no longer idealized or romanticized, (b) newly adopted cultural practices are preferred but difficult to incorporate, and (c) family and friends are not really interested enough in study away stories and experiences, thus leaving the student isolated. In materials from organizations like SIT, students and parents are given advice that frames the circumstance as a situation that will work itself out with time, patience, and listening (Cavallero, 2009). While such advice is useful, it is only appropriate to matters of reverse culture shock, which is not the same as phase four of transformative learning—the new self in an old world.

Our task in this final phase is to prepare students for being a new person regardless of place. We prepare them for encounters with friends and family members who may not see, much less understand, the new person before them. We prepare students for helping friends and family members see, embrace, and support this new person. We prepare students for the eventuality that some dear to them will be unable or unwilling to support the changed self and worldviews. We prepare students to make difficult choices about relationships—that once close friends find this new person and his or her beliefs too strange to continue a relationship.

When facilitated well, a disorienting dilemma can prompt a journey, leading a student through a truly life-changing process. In this way study away can produce the hoped for, assumed, and even documented outcomes. Simultaneously, we can avoid the most negative of outcomes; however, this depends on our ability as teachers and facilitators to recognize a disorienting dilemma for what it is and our ability to guide students through a specific process. In the end, our tasks as facilitators of transformative learning are unique and can bear witness to seemingly magical results:

The magic of travel is that you leave your home secure in your own knowledge and identity, but as you travel the world in all its richness intervenes. You meet people you could not invent; you see scenes you could not imagine. Your own world, which was so large as to consume your whole life, becomes smaller and smaller until it is only one tiny dot in space and time. You return a different person. (Nerburn, 2005, p. 48)

The Journey Guide: Training and Preparation

Aspirations for students who pursue study away are numerous. We hope they learn something about the place and the subject; we hope they interrogate self and identity; we hope they develop cultural sensitivity, understanding, and empathy; we hope they return a different person. These hopes are realized when we adequately train and prepare ourselves in pedagogical practices relevant to the nature of study away. By reviewing the nature of learning in study away, experiential learning, and transformative learning, the definition of *adequate* is clear. My students who thought they adequately washed their hands after using the toilet realized that falsehood once presented with specific standards of health and hand washing. It is a simple, almost silly, analogy. And that is the point. As educators who have years of classroom and even study away teaching experience, we imagine we know how to teach and how to facilitate learning. Yet both anecdotal and assessment data reveal that study away aspirations are realized in fits and starts. As demonstrated by the student who visited many sites of violence during a study away course, the faculty member seemed to assume that place (*where*) plus subject (*what*) was sufficient and that it was up to the student to make meaning, and the right meaning. If this formula is correct, then there is no distinction between travel and study away, no reason for faculty members, curricula, or programs. Students could read subject-matter materials and travel with the same outcomes.

The fact is *how we teach* is the catalyst in the formula. How we guide students in the journey of self, subject matter, and place makes all the difference, makes the learning richer, more efficient, and more likely. While we cannot guarantee all positive outcomes all the time for every student, pedagogical prowess increases the odds. As teachers we must become proficient in understanding learning styles and modalities; experiential learning principles, phases, and practices; and transformative learning indicators and processes. Beyond increasing our individual proficiency, we must become institutionally and programmatically proficient. While organizations and institutions dedicated to study away are experts in program design, logistics, health and safety, and providing practical guides for teachers and students, there remains a limitation in recognizing the pedagogical complexities of study away. This is an area of institutional development for consideration.

> The fundamental issue is not of new versus old education nor of progressive against traditional education but a question of what anything whatever must be to be worthy of the name *education*. . . . What we want and need is education pure and simple, and we shall make surer and faster progress when we devote ourselves to finding out just what education is and what conditions have to be satisfied in order that education may be a reality and not a name or slogan. (Dewey, 1938, p. 90)

References

Carson, D. (2009). Is style everything? Teaching that achieves its objectives. *Cinema Journal, 48*(3), 95–101.

Cavallero, L. (2009). *A readjustment manual for parents: A handbook for parents of students returning home from studying abroad.* Brattleboro, VT: SIT Abroad.

Christofi, V., & Thompson, C. L. (2007). You cannot go home again: A phenomenological investigation of returning to the sojourn country after studying abroad. *Journal of Counseling & Development, 85*(1), 53–63.

Davis, D., Chapman, D., Bohlin, B., Jaworski, B., Walley, C., Barton, D., & Ebner, N. (2008, November). *Reverse culture shock: A comparison of United States and Japanese students' experiences returning from a study abroad sojourn.* Paper presented at the annual meeting of the NCA 94th annual convention, San Diego, CA.

Deardorff, D., de Wit, H., & Heyl, J. (2012). *The Sage handbook of international education.* Thousand Oaks, CA: Sage.

Dewey, J. (1938). *Experience and education.* New York, NY: Kappa Delta Pi/Collier Books.

Doerr, N. (2012). Study abroad as "adventure": Globalist construction of host–home hierarchy and governed adventurer subjects. *Critical Discourse Studies, 9*(3), 257–268.

Dowd, J. J. (2004, August). *Consuming travel: American students abroad.* Paper presented at the annual meeting of the American Sociological Association, San Francisco, CA.

Dunn, R., & Dunn, K. (2005). Thirty-five years of research on perceptual strengths: Essential strategies to promote learning. *Clearing House, 78*(6), 1–6.

The Editors of the Committee for Academic Freedom in Africa (2002). Globalization & academic ethics. *Review of African Political Economy, 29*(92), 362–364.

Feller, A. E. (2009). Balance on the water. In E. McKenna & S. Pratt (Eds.), *Jimmy Buffett and philosophy* (pp. 57–78). Chicago, IL: Open Court.

Furnham, A. (2010). Culture shock: Literature review, personal statement and relevance for the South Pacific. *Journal of Pacific Rim Psychology, 4*(2), 87–94.

Habu, T. (2000). The irony of globalization: The experience of Japanese women in British higher education. *Higher Education, 39*(1), 43–66.

Hartjes, L. B., Baumann, L. C., & Henriques, J. B. (2009). Travel health risk perceptions and prevention behaviors of US study abroad students. *Journal of Travel Medicine, 16*(5), 338–343.

Heron, J. (1996). *Co-operative inquiry: Research into the human condition*. London: Sage.

Horton, D. M., Wiederman, S. D., & Saint, D. A. (2012). Assessment outcome is weakly correlated with lecture attendance: Influence of learning style and use of alternative materials. *Advances in Physiology Education, 36*(2), 108–115.

Kolb, A., & Kolb, D. A. (2005). Learning styles and learning spaces: Enhancing experiential learning in higher education. *Academy of Management Learning & Education, 4*(2), 193–212.

Kolb, D., & Boyatzis, R. (2000). Experiential learning theory: Previous research and new directions. In R. Sternberg & L. Zhang (Eds.), *Perspectives on cognitive, learning, and thinking styles* (pp. 193–210). Mahwah, NJ: Lawrence Erlbaum.

Krätzig, G. P., & Arbuthnott, K. D. (2006). Perceptual learning style and learning proficiency: A test of the hypothesis. *Journal of Educational Psychology, 98*(1), 238–246.

Lewin, K., & Grabbe, P. (1945). Conduct, knowledge, and the acceptance of new values. *Journal of Social Issues, 1*(3), 53–64.

Lewin, K., Heider, F. T., & Heider, G. M. (1936). *Principles of topological psychology*. New York, NY: McGraw-Hill.

Mezirow, J. (1990). *Fostering critical reflection in adulthood*. San Francisco, CA: Jossey-Bass.

Mezirow, J., Taylor, E., & Associates. (2009). *Transformative learning in practice: Insights from community, workplace, and higher education*. San Francisco, CA: Jossey-Bass.

Nerburn, K. (2005). *Simple truth: Clear and gentle guidance on the big issues in life*. Novato, CA: New World Library.

Pedersen, P. J. (2010). Assessing intercultural effectiveness outcomes in a year-long study abroad program. *International Journal of Intercultural Relations, 1*(34), 70–80.

Popescu, R. (2007). Get me out of this place. *Newsweek, 150*(18), 14.

Roholt, R., & Fisher, C. (2013). Expect the unexpected: International short-term study course pedagogies and practices. *Journal of Social Work Education, 49*(1), 48–65.

4

EVALUATIVE APPROACHES TO DOMESTIC OFF-CAMPUS PROGRAMS

Mark E. Engberg and Lisa M. Davidson

I n order to evaluate whether domestic off-campus programs are achieving their intended outcomes, administrators of such programs must ensure that their intentionality in program design is met with an equal emphasis in program evaluation. Incorporating evaluation into the larger program ethos provides quality assurances that domestic programming initiatives are meeting the larger needs of the local communities being served, that program delivery is steeped in best practices and aligned with the prevailing tenets of program theory, and that intended outcomes are being met and contributing to the larger institutional mission. Further, by establishing an assessment team inclusive of stakeholders who are entrenched in the day-to-day operations of campus programs as well as those who share assessment expertise and administrative oversight, campuses can optimize the utility of such efforts and ensure that assessment plans are connected to meaningful program improvement.

Inquiries into evaluative approaches for domestic off-campus opportunities have largely focused on student learning relative to participation in service-learning, alternative break programs, and community-based education efforts. As such, we discuss findings from and draw parallels between these particular educational opportunities and other domestic off-campus programs (e.g., domestic study away and exchange programs). Like these other domestic off-campus programs, the learning environments embedded within service-learning, alternative break programs, and community-based education are situated externally to students' home college campuses, and these opportunities share related learning outcomes. For example, the National Student Exchange connects its exchange programs to institutional missions around globalization, cultural diversity, and off-campus learning initiatives (National Student Exchange, 2014), whereas Break Away, the U.S. national alternative break nonprofit organization, cites the development of lifelong active citizenship, a complex view of social issues, and a different perspective of one's place in society as central to its developmental model and the transformative learning embedded within quality alternative break programs (Break Away, 2014). Considered together, the components, stakeholders, and outcomes of domestic service-learning, alternative break programs, and community-based education are in many ways analogous to those in other domestic study away and exchange programs. As such, we examine and synthesize various approaches used within the research and evaluative literature and best practices related to these experiential learning opportunities.

We begin the chapter with a brief discussion of the importance of both aligning program evaluation with program design and creating a comprehensive, continuous, and formative plan of assessment to maintain the highest standard of program readiness and intent. Then, we present an overview of basic approaches to program evaluation, with an eye toward both approach (i.e., needs, process, and outcomes) and the evaluative criteria that guide effective assessment plans (i.e., utility, feasibility, accuracy, and propriety). The next section examines methodological considerations in evaluating domestic off-campus programs, with a critical eye toward summarizing the various approaches used in the research and evaluative literature. In the final section, we present a set of recommendations to guide institutions as they move forward in developing an assessment plan for their domestic off-campus programming initiatives. Particular attention is placed on the importance of planning, inclusivity, continuity, utility, and demonstrating an ethic of care.

Overview of the Evaluative Process

As the regulatory environment surrounding college campuses has intensified, there has been a concomitant focus on measuring student learning outcomes to meet external and internal mandates to demonstrate the "value added" of different curricular and cocurricular offerings. While such an environment leans toward more summative forms of assessment—in which evaluative findings are used to make determinations around program continuation and resource allocation—the focus of this chapter is on more formative approaches to campus assessment. Formative approaches are steeped in the language of program improvement, empowering those who work most closely with a particular program to discover and uncover over time how resources and activities translate into student learning and development. Domestic off-campus programs, however, involve both campus and community partners, and the reciprocal nature of these relationships demands an equal emphasis on how such programs impact both students and the communities they serve.

In addition to advocating for more formative approaches to assessment, we emphasize that effective evaluation is both well planned and continuous in nature. Too often, campuses approach evaluation from a reactive rather than proactive stance, and while the former may be necessary when specific issues surface (e.g., campus climate) or national attention is brought to particular issues (e.g., campus violence), program evaluation is most effective when it is carefully planned with short-, intermediate-, and long-term goals in mind. As such, we adopt Suskie's (2009) emphasis on assessment as a continual process—one in which assessment results are continually used to refine programmatic goals, which in turn influences both the nature of programmatic offerings and the learning that develops from such experiences. In this regard, evaluation is seen less as a static form of learning in which the same approach is implemented year after year and more as a responsive form of learning that inspires adaption, innovation, and experimentation.

Preliminary Stages of the Evaluative Process

Philosophical and Epistemological Perspectives

Program evaluation is steeped in questions related to how one approaches the construction of knowledge, whether there is one "truth" or multiple realities that govern how one understands program effectiveness, and who has access to such information in the decision-making process. Each of these questions is rooted in philosophical traditions, including logical positivism, postpositivism, and constructivist paradigms, and aligns with different objective- and participant-oriented approaches to evaluation (Fitzpatrick, Sanders, & Worthen, 2011). At the beginning of the evaluative process, it is essential to contemplate the value of these different traditions and approaches, as each possesses certain benefits and challenges, which, in many cases, may drive methodological choices. The choice of an approach, however, is not necessarily singular in nature; rather, there is value for any new entrant into the evaluative world to review these traditions and approaches and develop a more customized approach that recognizes the program's philosophical orientation coupled with the contextual and institutional demands of the campus environment. In our own practice, we lean more toward participant-oriented approaches that recognize and place value on the beliefs and understandings of multiple stakeholders, as this constructivist stance seems most responsive to the needs of different campus and community partners and can often increase the overall utility and validity of the evaluative work (see Stake, 2004, for more detailed information on responsive forms of evaluation).

Developing and Prioritizing Guiding Questions

Although there is often a desire to plunge headfirst into the evaluative process, it is essential to first gather the necessary information and intelligence to optimize the value and utility of a program evaluation. Cronbach's (1982) earlier work identified two essential stages in developing an evaluative focus: a divergent stage in which data are more informally collected from stakeholders, professional associations, prior research and evaluative studies, and other available documentation to formulate a laundry list of available foci; and a convergent stage in which initial lists are filtered and culled for common or critical themes identified by both stakeholders and informational resources. The process itself can range in length depending on the scope of the program, number of stakeholders, complexity of ideas presented, and the larger political landscape that situates the program. One of the benefits of using a longer term and more continuous framework is this can often help in charting a more systematic way of approaching different questions while appeasing the often competing demands of different stakeholders.

Mapping Questions Into Evaluative Categories

In our experience, the list of evaluative questions that accrue from the divergent and convergent questioning processes can often be sorted into categories that help guide the direction of the evaluation process. While myriad typologies exist, we employ a tripartite classification system in which questions are sorted according to their emphasis on needs, processes, or outcomes (Fitzpatrick et al., 2011; Wholey, Hatry, & Newcomer, 2010). Needs-oriented questions often arise in the early stages of program development and we must consider whether a particular issue or problem exists that warrants a new program or intervention. A needs assessment can also address questions about the suitability of current program models in meeting the needs of all students along with understanding the accessibility of and interest in different programmatic offerings. As campuses develop strategic plans that include domestic off-campus opportunities, they may consider questions like the following about which students are involved in such opportunities: How did the students learn about domestic off-campus opportunities? What are students' motivations for engaging in different opportunities? What challenges or barriers do students who were unable to engage in such opportunities face?

Process-based questions focus on the underlying activities and delivery mechanisms that constitute a particular program, examining the effectiveness of different programmatic components, the learning environment, instructor characteristics and teaching contributions, and students' overall level of satisfaction with different aspects of the program. Administrators and practitioners overseeing particular programs might consider questions about the value and worth participants placed on different programmatic components; their overall satisfaction with different components; their perceptions of the quality of instructional delivery and supervisory support; and which aspects of the off-campus experience were perceived as most meaningful, challenging, or confusing.

Finally, outcome-based questions focus on the impact of the program on different stakeholders and community partners, ranging from immediate to long-term effects. Outcome-oriented questions seek to understand growth across outcomes that are congruent with the goals and objectives of the program, relative differences in outcomes among program participants or across national norms representing peer or aspirant institutions, and the larger impact of the program on the communities being served. Given the breadth of domestic off-campus opportunities and individuals involved, careful attention is needed in selecting outcomes that resonate with both the goals of the program and the various types of activities and services students and other stakeholders are exposed to throughout the duration of the program. Off-campus programs emphasize a range of different learning outcomes for student participants focused, for instance, on globalization and cultural diversity (National Student Exchange, 2014) or active citizenship and transformative learning (Break Away, 2014). Further, Gelmon, Holland, Driscoll, Spring, and Kerrigan (2001) developed a comprehensive assessment matrix to measure the impact of service-learning initiatives on students, faculty, and community partners, highlighting the reciprocal and multidimensional benefits of such programs.

In our own work, we often employ a process–outcome-based approach, which allows for a more comprehensive understanding of how different programmatic components influence program outcomes. In doing so, we are able to not only demonstrate relative differences among participants, but also examine how different programmatic components mediate students' growth and development. This is particularly valuable in identifying those processes that are malleable and most conducive to change, and developing formative strategies that target specific programmatic areas. Regardless of the approach one takes, systematically organizing the information and emergent questions that derive from the data-gathering stage of the evaluation process is an essential task in developing a comprehensive evaluation plan.

Program Theory and Logic Models

In the process of collecting data and information about the program, the evaluator gains important insight into not only questions surrounding the nature of the program, but also differing perspectives on how and why the program is expected to create change. According to Weiss (1997), it is essential to uncover the underlying assumptions that connect programmatic components to their intended outcomes—what is often referred to as the theoretical "black box"—as such knowledge unmasks the underlying program theory and provides a basis upon which to test the efficacy of different theoretical premises. Many domestic study away programs, for instance, rely on Kolb's (1984) experiential learning model and the incorporation of reflective and meaning-making strategies to enhance student learning and development (Jones & Abes, 2004). However, too often these theoretical ideas are assumed to be understood without explicit attention to how such premises relate to specific strategies and interventions and translate into different programmatic outcomes. Further, in making the assumptions that underlie program theory more explicit, evaluators can better understand the conditions that matter most in optimizing their programs and anticipate ways to evaluate the extent to which such conditions were met. In a service-learning program, for instance, evaluators may determine that certain conditions for intergroup contact must be met first for reciprocal learning to occur or that students working in underserved communities must first recognize and reflect upon their own privileges to enlarge their understanding and propensity to engage in social justice work.

In the process of describing a program theory and as an added means of organizing the data collected in the preliminary stages of the evaluative process, we often rely on different heuristic devices to help communicate findings to different stakeholders and build a shared understanding of how the program is expected to work. One of the more useful tools in this regard is the logic model, which represents a schematic of how program resources are used to develop different activities, which in turn influences outcomes ranging from short to long term in scope (Kellogg Foundation, 2004). The level of detail used to develop a logic model will vary based on the emphasis placed on program theory, implementation, or outcomes, and most models make explicit both the underlying assumptions and external conditions necessary to ensure an effective program delivery. By taking the time to make explicit these connections and underlying conditions, evaluators will increase the overall utility of their designs and anticipate methodological considerations related to both program antecedents and externally derived factors.

Evaluative Standards

Before discussing important methodological considerations, it is important to highlight the four pillars upon which most evaluations are built: utility—the extent to which the results will be used to make formative changes; feasibility—whether the design can be carried out given the resources of the program; accuracy—the validity, reliability, and truthfulness of the findings; and propriety—the ethical nature of the evaluation (Fitzpatrick et al., 2011). In our experience, there are inherent trade-offs with many of these pillars, and it is essential to carefully consider the weight placed on each of these standards. An evaluative design, for instance, that places the most weight on demonstrating causality in relation to the intervention may not be feasible given the resources of the program or the naturalistic setting in which most domestic off-campus programs occur. Additionally, while collecting mixed-methods data may be feasible, it must be weighed against the time needed to analyze and sift through the collected data (feasibility concern) and the likelihood that such data will inform future programmatic improvements (utility concern). Further, while commercially developed instruments may carry more accuracy in terms of validity and reliability testing, this must be examined in relation to more locally developed instruments, which offer a more contextualized understanding of a program and often carry greater utility in making program refinements. We adhere to McCormick and McClenney's (2012) emphasis on the "consequential validity" of assessment efforts—"that is, to produce data that are meaningful and actionable" (p. 330).

Methodological Considerations

There are multiple ways to evaluate domestic off-campus experiences, including standardized scales, observations, interviews, focus groups, archival data, and other qualitative data (Bringle, Phillips, & Hudson, 2004). As discussed previously in this chapter, the type of inquiry is contingent upon answers to philosophical and practical questions around the nature of truth, the role of the evaluator, who and what is studied, and the outcomes under investigation (Borland, 2001). In comparing the various attributes of qualitative and quantitative evaluative designs, both yield valuable insights and when used conjointly can lead to a more holistic view in informing institutional research, assessment, and decision making (Borland, 2001; Bringle et al., 2004; Gelmon et al., 2001). We organize this section by examining qualitative, quantitative, and mixed-methods approaches, with a particular focus on the assessment of student learning as it relates to off-campus service participation. Although the extant research on evaluative approaches to domestic off-campus programs largely examines service-learning, alternative break program, and community-based education outcomes, the parallel learning environments and outcomes between these and other domestic off-campus programs allow our discussion around methodological considerations to extend more broadly to domestic off-campus programs, regardless of any concurrent service component.

Qualitative Research Designs

Qualitative inquiry is primarily an inductive process that focuses on how participants make meaning of their experiences, relying on the evaluator as the primary instrument to collect and analyze emergent data (Merriam, 2009). Examining domestic off-campus opportunities through a qualitative lens incorporates relatively smaller samples (i.e., from a single program or course) and aims to provide rich descriptions of particular components of the experience. Sampling is typically more purposeful in this regard, utilizing criterion-based methods to maximize or minimize subject variation and gain a more nuanced understanding of participant experiences. In examining the application of qualitative methods to various domestic off-campus opportunities, we review several approaches that emphasize the use of reflection, content analysis, rubrics, and interviews.

Reflection

Opportunities for meaningful and consistent reflection are essential in reaching the learning outcomes embedded within many domestic off-campus programs, including developing a deeper understanding and application of the subject, more complex critical thinking and problem-solving abilities, openness to new ideas, and multiple interpretations of service observations (Eyler & Giles, 1999). Yet, if not practiced with intentionality, reflective activities can appear disorganized, unattached to course material, ineffective in challenging students' preexisting knowledge and beliefs, and less conducive in measuring student outcomes (Ash & Clayton, 2004; Eyler, 2000). To counter these limitations, Ash and Clayton (2004) propose a model of reflection that "pushes students beyond superficial interpretations of complex issues and facilitates academic mastery, personal growth, civic engagement and critical thinking" (p. 140). This method allows students and faculty to appropriately use reflection to evaluate learning by focusing on four essential tasks in which students explicate what they learned, how they learned, the significance of the learning, and how they will use the learning in the future.

Content Analysis

Content analysis allows investigators to analyze themes and patterns related to student learning through an inductive process (Merriam, 2009). Litke (2002), for example, utilized content analysis to determine whether differences existed when themes from students' final papers were compared across academically lower and higher performing students. Sixty students' papers were coded using the following six themes based on Eyler, Giles, and Schmiede's (1996) previous work: personal development, sense of belonging and connection with others, commitment to active citizenship, enhanced academic understanding of subject matter, ability to apply knowledge and skills elsewhere, and ability to reframe complex social issues. Mpofu and Imalingat (2006) also used content analysis—based on documents relevant to existing assessment practices and interviews with students and key individuals from academic departments—to develop a set of assessment guidelines for the different community-based education programs on their campus. Following the analyses, relevant experts in community-based education facilitated a workshop to identify essential items for inclusion in the proposed assessment tool (i.e., knowledge, transferable skills, professionalism, and attitudes), and the instrument was subsequently piloted with two departments in various community settings.

Rubrics

A variety of rubrics exists that practitioners and faculty can use to evaluate student learning outcomes associated with domestic off-campus programs. For example, in its Valid Assessment of Learning in Undergraduate Education (VALUE) initiative, the Association of American Colleges and Universities provides rubrics that assist in evaluating 16 different undergraduate learning outcomes related to intellectual and practical skills, personal and social responsibility, and integrative and applied learning (Rhodes, 2010). Other rubrics used to measure learning outcomes related to domestic off-campus programming include the Cognitive Level and Quality Writing Assessment Instrument to evaluate student essays (Flateby & Metzger, 1999, 2001), the Problem-Solving Analysis Protocol and accompanying rubric to assess students' critical thinking in analyzing social problems (Steinke & Fitch, 2003), and the Campus Compact (n.d.) rubric to assess students' reflection papers. A number of rubrics and matrices also exist to evaluate faculty and community partners, including an assessment matrix to measure the role and impact of faculty in service-learning courses (Gelmon et al., 2001) and a rubric to gauge the strength of the community partnership potential in both domestic and international alternative break programs (Piacitelli, Barwick, Doerr, Porter, & Sumka, 2013).

Interviews

Individual or group interviews are useful in obtaining valuable qualitative insights when observations of others' behaviors, feelings, or interpretations are not possible, or when an investigation involves studying a past event that cannot be replicated (Merriam, 2009). Eyler and Giles (1999) illustrate the value of focus group interviews in the early stages of research and evaluation efforts to identify and clarify the type of learning that occurs through service experiences and to inform their subsequent survey efforts. In particular, Eyler and Giles (1999) developed the Problem-Solving Interview Protocol to investigate how service experiences change students' analyses of an initial problem they identified in the pre-service interview using four scoring categories: locus of problem and solution, causal complexity, solution complexity, and knowledge application. The Perry Network (n.d.) also developed a semistructured customizable interview protocol (specific to particular learning opportunities and different types of intellectual development), based on Perry's (1970) scheme of intellectual and ethical development, to retrospectively investigate students' development over the course of their college career and understand how this relates to prospectively thinking about their life after college.

Quantitative Research Designs

While qualitative inquiry provides a deeper understanding of how students make meaning of their domestic off-campus programs, such an approach often leads to findings that are too narrow to generalize and more broadly apply to the impact of different service experiences (Bringle & Hatcher, 2000; Waters & Anderson-Lain, 2014). In reiterating the value of generalizability in service-learning research, Waters and Anderson-Lain (2014) argue for the use of quantitative survey instruments that are "intended for numerous classes, programs, and institutions" (p. 90). Quantitative approaches to domestic off-campus programs primarily utilize cross-sectional and longitudinal designs either to make relative comparisons or to understand how students change over time. Comparison group designs have also been reported in the literature to examine differences in particular outcomes across those who participate in courses with and without service-learning components (Bernacki & Jaeger, 2008; Moely, McFarland, Miron, Mercer, & Ilustre, 2002; Vogelgesang & Astin, 2000). While sampling can range from proportional to purposive techniques, most designs are limited in their use of randomized samples given the naturalistic setting in which most domestic off-campus opportunities occur.

While qualitative approaches rely more heavily on inductive techniques, quantitative approaches are more deductive in nature, placing a higher premium on a priori assumptions about learning and the types of measures used to demonstrate student learning and development. Eyler and Giles (1999) argue that a "central element of service-learning is to link personal and interpersonal development with academic and cognitive development" (p. 9), underscoring the ways in which experiential education connects different aspects of students' learning and development and these outcomes. Similarly, Conway, Amel, and Gerwien (2009) conducted a meta-analysis of 103 quantitative studies and uncovered a taxonomy of learning categories that highlighted academic, personal, social, and civic outcomes. Given the premium placed on outcome selection in quantitative approaches to domestic off-campus programs, particularly service-learning experiences, we review several studies that have investigated learning across these four outcome categories.

Academic Outcomes

Academic outcomes associated with service-learning experiences include "cognitive and academic changes involving knowledge, ability to apply knowledge, cognitive processes, and motivation to learn" (Conway et al., 2009, p. 234). To measure service-learning's relationship to different academic outcomes (i.e., college grade point averages and students' self-reported growth in both writing and critical thinking skills), Vogelgesang and Astin (2000) conducted a longitudinal study using Cooperative Institutional Research Program (CIRP) data that compared over 22,000 students across three student groups (community service, course-based service-learning, and nonservice participants). Other researchers have utilized the Cognitive Learning Scale (Steinke & Fitch, 2003; Steinke, Fitch, Johnson, & Waldstein, 2002) and the Global Perspective Inventory (Braskamp, Braskamp, & Engberg, 2013; Engberg, 2013; Engberg & Fox, 2011) to examine changes in students' cognitive development based on their participation in service-learning experiences.

Personal Outcomes

Personal outcomes associated with service-learning experiences largely concern students' "thoughts and feelings about themselves or their motives or values, and their well-being," as well as the importance of students' self-esteem, self-efficacy, and career development relative to their service-learning experiences (Conway et al., 2009, p. 234). To illustrate this, Bernacki and Jaeger (2008) examined the relationship between students' service-learning and outcomes related to moral development, use of an ethic of care and justice, and positive changes within themselves. Engberg and Fox (2011) also uncovered positive relationships between service participation and students' intrapersonal identity (e.g., understanding of personal values and sense of self).

Social Outcomes

Social outcomes examine "participants' relationships to others including skill in interacting with others (e.g., leadership skills) and thoughts and beliefs about others (e.g., attitudes toward the population one is serving)" (Conway et al., 2009, p. 234). Moely et al. (2002) investigated the relationship between service-learning participation and students' self-evaluations on six scales: civic action, interpersonal and problem-solving skills, political awareness, leadership skills, social justice attitudes, and diversity attitudes. Beyond examining possible relationships between particular variables, Moely et al. (2002) also examined the degree to which students' course and service evaluations predicted scores on the six scales noted previously. Engberg and Fox (2011) also found a positive relationship between service participation and students' intrapersonal affect (e.g., tolerance and acceptance of difference) and social interaction (e.g., proclivities to interact across difference).

Civic Outcomes

Conway et al. (2009) utilize Westheimer and Kahne's (2004) categories to describe civic-oriented outcomes related to service-learning, including personally responsible, participatory, and justice-oriented citizenship. Within each of these categories, outcomes could potentially involve actual behaviors, beliefs, and commitment or intentions to engage in behaviors resultant from service-learning experiences. Mayhew and Engberg (2011) also investigated whether first-year success courses with a service-learning component influenced the development of students' civic responsibility. The results of a longitudinal sample of 173 students in 10 different first-year success courses showed that infusing first-year success courses with a service-learning component contributed to students' development of charitable responsibility, though there was no significant posttest difference related to students' development of social justice responsibility. Engberg and Fox (2011), however, demonstrated a strong association between students' service participation and their scores on a measure of social responsibility.

Mixed-Methods Research Designs

As previously discussed in this chapter, it is beneficial to consider mixed-methods approaches under particular circumstances, using multiple data collection and analytical approaches. According to Creswell (2014), mixed-methods designs are typically used in one of three ways: a convergent parallel design in which quantitative and qualitative data are collected separately and then compared to one another to confirm or disconfirm key findings, an explanatory sequential approach in which quantitative results are used to purposefully select individuals and frame questions for purposes of a qualitative follow-up, or an exploratory sequential approach in which qualitative interviews are first used to develop and refine a quantitative instrument that can then be used to make broader generalizations. Here we review two examples of mixed-methods designs used to examine the benefits of service-learning experiences.

Rockquemore and Schaffer (2000) used a mixed-methods design to investigate how students learn from their experiences in the community. The authors used a sample of 120 students enrolled in several different service-learning courses, employing a 26-item pre- and post-service-learning survey and a cross-course subsample of students' reflection journals. The journal questions encouraged students to generate three types of data: (a) a descriptive account of the events that transpired during the students' service-learning experiences, (b) an account of their emotional reactions to the events they encountered within their service-learning sites, and (c) a description of their integration of the course content and service experiences. The pre- and post-service-learning survey uncovered positive changes in students' attitudes toward social justice, equality of opportunity, and civic responsibility over the duration of the semester, whereas the students' journal entries identified three stages of development related to shock, normalization, and engagement.

Eyler and Giles (1999) also utilized a mixed-methods approach in the two national research projects detailed in their text. The authors employed initial pilot focus groups and interviews and subsequent surveys that included more than 1,500 students from 20 different schools to examine the impact of service-learning on students. Of particular importance in this study was the focus on service-learning program characteristics (i.e., placement quality, application, written reflection, discussion reflection, diversity, and community voice) as predictors of service-learning outcomes (i.e., stereotyping/tolerance, personal development, interpersonal development, closeness to faculty, citizenship, learning, understanding, application, problem solving, critical thinking, and perspective transformation), effectively shifting the focus of inquiry from student outcomes to program characteristics.

Recommendations

Throughout this chapter, we have emphasized the importance of careful planning in the assessment process and the various trade-offs involved in maximizing the utility, feasibility, and accuracy of assessment efforts. In the sections that follow, we summarize and extend the recent recommendations by Braskamp and Engberg (2014) in judging the effectiveness of assessing student learning, with a particular emphasis on planning, inclusiveness, usefulness, communication, and demonstrating an ethic of care.

Establishing a Plan for Action

Evaluation works best when it begins with a comprehensive planning process that includes a range of stakeholders, especially those who are entrenched in the day-to-day operations of the program such as assessment experts, administrators with budgetary oversight, and other local partners (campus experts and/or community members). The complex nature of domestic off-campus programs necessitates a consideration of the needs and priorities of multiple constituents, and as such, the process is often highly politicized and requires a high degree of interpersonal and facilitation skills. Developing a comprehensive plan prior to engaging in data collection allows for stakeholders to develop a consensus around evaluative priorities while charting out a temporal course that recognizes the long-term and continuous nature of the most effective plans. Similarly, the planning stage addresses the feasibility of the evaluative plan at the onset, and ensures that the necessary resources needed to execute the plan (including data collection, data analysis, and dissemination) are accounted for and allocated in a responsible and intentional manner.

Creating an Inclusive Environment

In our experience, top-down evaluative mandates are rarely conducive to maximizing the utility of evaluation efforts. Rather, we believe there is great benefit in beginning the process with an inclusive mind-set that purposefully and strategically brings together different stakeholders who are both directly and indirectly connected to the program. In doing so, the evaluative planning process recognizes the critical perspectives and positionality of stakeholders who represent different social, cultural, and racial/ethnic backgrounds, and seeks to build a culture of openness and trust to guide decision making in all phases of the process. It is also critical to identify those individuals who can serve as "tipping point connectors" (Wholey et al., 2010, p. 330) through their commitment, connection, and leadership skills—in other words, individuals who can champion the evaluation plan throughout the entirety of the process.

Collecting Credible and Useful Evidence

With the proliferation of different assessment tools to measure student learning, it is essential to choose a data collection plan that is both congruent with the goals of the program and aligned with the larger mission of the departmental and institutional setting. We recommend using multiple methods in approaching evaluative questions, and this is particularly true for domestic off-campus programs that are uniquely situated in local communities that may not easily align with more standardized measures of student learning. Locally developed survey instruments may be more suited for many domestic off-campus programs, although this requires a particular savviness in questionnaire development and a willingness to incorporate pilot testing to ensure the face validity and interpretational consistency across items. Qualitative approaches, especially focus groups, can be particularly valuable when they are used to elicit patterns of student learning and contextual elements that contributed to such learning prior to developing more localized survey instruments. The use of multiple methods, however, requires a high degree of sequential intentionality that concomitantly can be used to triangulate emergent findings and account for rival or discrepant findings. Finally, while there is often a temptation to assess all aspects of a program at the onset, we advocate for an approach that favors depth over breadth, as this often yields the highest rate of utility and avoids an overly complex and cumbersome process.

Communicating Results Through Storytelling

Dissemination of results is one of the most important aspects of the evaluative process, yet all too often information remains in the hands of a few or is delivered en masse with little direction on how to incorporate such information into program improvement. Evaluation findings are communicated best through storytelling—stories that are clearly stated, focused, and understood by the various stakeholder groups involved in the process. Communication in this regard is key, and it is essential to consider which dissemination strategies will be most effective given the various constituents involved in the process (e.g., written report, webinar, in-service training, formal or informal meetings). Prior to dissemination, it is critically important to gain the varied perspectives of stakeholders on the meaning they derive from the evaluative findings, as stakeholders will invariably approach their understanding based on their different positions within the campus and community coupled with their own unique lived histories and varied social identities. Finally, it is important as well to recognize that the story itself may not be complete, and that questions or concerns that arise from campus deliberations will invariably lead to the next chapter in the ongoing evaluation story.

Approaching Evaluation Through a Continuous Lens

At the completion of any evaluation cycle, it is critical to take a step back to examine the effectiveness of the endeavor, particularly in light of the standards of feasibility, utility, accuracy, and propriety (Fitzpatrick et al., 2011). In doing so, it is important to recognize the various limitations inherent in any approach and to discover how ongoing evaluative efforts might miti-gate these threats in the future. It is also essential to make deliberate deter-minations of which program areas need improvement, and to fold such improvements into future evaluation plans. In our experience, programmatic improvements often take several years to manifest identifiable results, and it is important to adapt evaluation plans to take into account the findings from each consecutive cycle. The process of evaluation often uncovers more ques-tions than immediate answers, and thus, it is essential to recognize the imper-manence of many findings, especially given the changing environments that comprise many domestic off-campus programs.

Incorporating an Ethic of Care

Throughout the evaluation process, it is essential for evaluators to dem-onstrate an ethic of care and concern for the dignity and self-worth of all stakeholders, particularly those who are most directly impacted by domestic off-campus programs. In considering domestic alternative break programs, for instance, there are potential risks in isolated and dispersed institutional efforts that may stem from a lack of necessary knowledge and experience on the part of students and institutions to deliver adequate service work (Piacitelli et al., 2013). Evaluators must strive to demonstrate a high level of integrity throughout the entirety of the process, ensuring transparency in relation to procedures, findings, and recommendations coupled with a com-mitment to minimizing potential risks to program recipients while maintain-ing respect for all who are impacted and involved in the process.

References

Ash, S. L., & Clayton, P. H. (2004). The articulated learning: An approach to guided reflection and assessment. *Innovative Higher Education, 29*(2), 137–154.

Bernacki, M. L., & Jaeger, E. (2008, Spring). Exploring the impact of service-learning on moral development and moral orientation. *Michigan Journal of Com-munity Service Learning, 14*(2), 5–15.

Borland, K. W., Jr. (2001). Qualitative and quantitative research: A complementary balance. *New Directions for Institutional Research, 2001*(112), 5–13.

Braskamp, L. A., Braskamp, D. C., & Engberg, M. E. (2013). *Global perspective inventory (GPI): Its purposes, construction, potential uses, and psychometric properties.* Retrieved from GPI website at https://gpi.central.edu/supportDocs/manual.pdf

Braskamp, L. A., & Engberg, M. E. (2014). *Guidelines for judging the effectiveness of assessing student learning.* Chicago, IL: Loyola University Chicago.

Break Away. (2014). Retrieved from http://www.alternativebreaks2014.org/philosophy/

Bringle, R. G., & Hatcher, J. A. (2000, Fall). Meaningful measurement of theory-based service-learning outcomes: Making the case with quantitative research. *Michigan Journal of Community Service Learning*, 68–75.

Bringle, R. G., Phillips, M. A., & Hudson, M. (2004). *The measure of service-learning: Research scales to assess student experiences*. Washington, DC: American Psychological Association.

Campus Compact. (n.d.). Rubric to assess service-learning reflection papers. Retrieved from http://www.compact.org/resources/rubric-to-assess-service-learning-reflection-papers/992/

Conway, J. M., Amel, E. L., & Gerwien, D. P. (2009). Teaching and learning in the social context: A meta-analysis of service learning's effects on academic, personal, social, and citizenship outcomes. *Teaching of Psychology, 36*(4), 233–245.

Creswell, J. W. (2014). *Research design: Qualitative, quantitative, and mixed method approaches* (4th ed.). Thousand Oaks, CA: Sage.

Cronbach, L. J. (1982). *Designing evaluations of educational and social programs*. San Francisco, CA: Jossey-Bass.

Engberg, M. E. (2013). The influence of study away experiences on global perspective-taking. *Journal of College Student Development, 54*(5), 466–480.

Engberg, M. E., & Fox, K. (2011). Service participation and the development of a global perspective. *Journal of Student Affairs Research and Practice, 48*(1), 85–105.

Eyler, J. (2000, Fall). What do we most need to know about the impact of service-learning on student learning? *Michigan Journal of Community Service Learning*, (1), 11–17.

Eyler, J., & Giles, D. E., Jr. (1999). *Where's the learning in service-learning?* San Francisco, CA: Jossey-Bass.

Eyler, J., Giles, D. E., Jr., & Schmiede, A. (1996). *A practitioner's guide to reflection in service-learning: Student voices and reflections*. Nashville, TN: Vanderbilt University.

Fitzpatrick, J., Sanders, J., & Worthen, B. (2011). *Program evaluation: Alternative approaches and practical guidelines* (4th ed.). New York, NY: Longman.

Flateby, T. L., & Metzger, E. (1999). Writing assessment instrument for higher order thinking skills. *Assessment Update, 11*(2), 6–7.

Flateby, T. L., & Metzger, E. (2001). Instructional implications of the cognitive level and quality of writing assessment. *Assessment Update, 13*(1), 4–5.

Gelmon, S. B., Holland, B. A., Driscoll, A., Spring, A., & Kerrigan, S. (2001). *Assessing service-learning and civic engagement: Principles and techniques*. Providence, RI: Campus Compact, Brown University.

Jones, S. R., & Abes, E. S. (2004). Enduring influences of service-learning on college students' identity development. *Journal of College Student Development, 45,*(2), 149–166.

Kellogg Foundation. (2004). *Logic model development guide: Using logic models to bring together planning, evaluation, and action*. Battle Creek, MI: W. K. Kellogg Foundation.

Kolb, D. A. (1984). *Experiential learning: Experience as the source of learning and development*. Englewood Cliffs, NJ: Prentice Hall.

Litke, R. A. (2002). Do all students "get it?": Comparing students' reflections to course performance. *Michigan Journal of Community Service Learning, 8*(2), 27–34.

Mayhew, M. J., & Engberg, M. E. (2011). Promoting the development of civic responsibility: Infusing service-learning practices in first-year "success" courses. *Journal of College Student Development, 52*(1), 20–38.

McCormick, A. C., & McClenney, K. (2012). Will these trees ever bear fruit? A response to the special issue on student engagement. *The Review of Higher Education, 35*(2), 307–333.

Merriam, S. B. (2009). *Qualitative research: A guide to design and implementation.* San Francisco, CA: Jossey-Bass.

Moely, B. E., McFarland, M., Miron, D., Mercer, S., & Ilustre, V. (2002, Fall). Changes in college students' attitudes and intentions for civic involvement as a function of service-learning experiences. *Michigan Journal of Community Service Learning, 9*(1), 18–26.

Mpofu, R., & Imalingat, A. (2006). The development of an instrument for assessing community-based education of undergraduate students of community and health sciences at the University of the Western Cape. *Education for Health, 19*(2), 166–178.

National Student Exchange. (2014). Overview. Retrieved from http://www.nse.org/aboutNSE.asp

Perry Network. (n.d.). Interview format. Retrieved from http://perrynetwork.org/

Perry, W. G. (1970). *Forms of intellectual and ethical development in the college years.* New York, NY: Holt, Rinehart, & Winston.

Piacitelli, J., Barwick, M., Doerr, E., Porter, M., & Sumka, S. (2013). Alternative break programs: From isolated enthusiasm to best practices. *Journal of Higher Education Outreach and Engagement, 17*(2), 87–109.

Rhodes, T. (2010). *Assessing outcomes and improving achievement: Tips and tools for using rubrics.* Washington, DC: Association of American Colleges and Universities.

Rockquemore, K. A., & Schaffer, R. H. (2000, Fall). Toward a theory of engagement: A cognitive mapping of service-learning experiences. *Michigan Journal of Community Service Learning, 7*(1),14–24.

Stake, R. E. (2004). *Standard-based and responsive evaluation.* Thousand Oaks, CA: Sage.

Steinke, P., & Fitch, P. (2003). Using written protocols to measure service-learning outcomes. In S. H. Biller & J. Eyler (Eds.), *Advances in service-learning research: Research exploring context, participation, and impacts* (Vol. 3, pp. 171–194). Greenwich, CT: Information Age Publishing.

Steinke, P., Fitch, P., Johnson, C., & Waldstein, F. (2002). An interdisciplinary study of service-learning predictors and outcomes among college students. In A. Furco & S. H. Billig (Eds.), *Advances in service-learning research: Service-learning research through a multidisciplinary lens* (Vol. 2, pp. 73–102). Greenwich, CT: Information Age Publishing.

Suskie, L. (2009). *Assessing student learning: A common sense guide* (2nd ed.). San Francisco, CA: Jossey-Bass.

Vogelgesang, L. J., & Astin, A. W. (2000, Fall). Comparing the effects of community service and service learning. *Michigan Journal of Community Service Learning, 7*(1) 25–34.

Waters, S., & Anderson-Lain, K. (2014). Assessing the student, faculty, and community partner in academic service-learning: A categorization of surveys posted online at Campus Compact member institutions. *Journal of Higher Education Outreach and Engagement, 18*(1), 89–122.

Weiss, C. H. (1997). *Evaluation* (2nd ed.). Upper Saddle River, NJ: Prentice Hall.

Westheimer, J., & Kahne, J. (2004). What kind of citizen? The politics of educating for democracy. *American Educational Research Journal, 42*(2), 237–269.

Wholey, J. S., Hatry, H. P., & Newcomer, K. E. (Eds.). (2010). *Handbook of practical program evaluation* (3rd ed.). San Francisco, CA: Jossey-Bass.

5

NO COMMON GROUND

The Spectrum of Policies Related to Domestic Off-Campus Programs

Michael Edmondson

This chapter examines the vast difference of opinions, policies, and support that colleges and universities have toward domestic off-campus programs administered by other institutions or consortia. While surveys, best practices, and reports detail the state of affairs related to study abroad or international education, no such resources exist for domestic programs. Even though some domestic programs have been around since the 1960s, educating tens of thousands of undergraduates across the United States from Arizona, California, and Oregon to Massachusetts, Pennsylvania, and Washington, DC, no review of institutional support toward domestic programming exists. To fill this tremendous gap in the literature, interviews were conducted with presidents, faculty, off-campus administrators, and other stakeholders during the four-month period from September 2013 to December 2013.[1] Also included in this chapter are findings from a review of the policies that institutions have toward study abroad in general and domestic off-campus programs specifically. Secondary literature was also utilized. This assessment examines a variety of issues including the different campus constituents that are directly or indirectly involved with domestic off-campus programs, the value and function that presidents place upon them, the amount of financial aid provided for participating students, the extent to which schools accept academic credit from managing institutions of programs, and the various strategies higher education institutions use to communicate the availability of domestic programs to students.

The evidence overwhelmingly demonstrates that a great disparity exists as to how institutions treat off-campus programs administered in the United States. For some institutions, domestic programs receive the same level of administrative and fiscal support as their study abroad/international counterparts. Faculty and staff at these institutions publicly support open access to all international and domestic off-campus programs. For others, however, domestic study away programs managed by another institution or consortia receive nominal administrative or fiscal support. On these campuses, programs located outside of the United States take precedence over ones that operate domestically. Between these two polar opposites fall a range of methods used by institutions to support, manage, and market domestic study away programs. Understanding the causes for this spectrum of support that colleges and universities have for domestic programming is essential reading for anyone interested in understanding how higher education institutions can update their strategic plans, curricula, and enrollment tactics in order to expand the number of deep, meaningful learning opportunities for students in today's dynamic and ever-changing global environment. To exclude domestic off-campus programs from a global education perspective runs counter to today's hyperconnected and interdependent marketplace that unites people from around the world to engage in commerce, communication, and collaboration at levels previously unimaginable. As Thomas Friedman of the *New York Times* noted, today's connectivity and creativity have "created a global education, commercial, communication and innovation platform on which more people can start stuff, collaborate on stuff, learn stuff, make stuff (and destroy stuff) with more other people than ever before" (Friedman, 2013).

Introduction

During the 2012–2013 academic year approximately 819,000 foreign students traveled to study in the United States. Conversely, 283,000 U.S. undergraduates studied abroad—a 3% increase from the previous year ("Foreign Student," 2013). The majority of U.S. students, however, tend to do much shorter stints than foreign students coming into the United States. Of U.S. students participating in a study abroad program, 38% participated during the summer, 13% studied abroad for eight weeks or less, and fewer than 4% spent the entire academic year abroad (McMurtie, 2012). Faculty-led programs continue to drive participation in study abroad programs as institutions look for new and creative ways to engage students and possibly save money or create a new revenue stream. Unfortunately, since there is currently no system that accurately calculates the number of students participating in programs around the globe, including the United States, the total number of students having an off-campus experience remains unknown. Although officials suggest that the United States needs to increase the number of students studying abroad ("Open Doors 2013"), the reality is that many colleges and universities create a "series of obstacles that prevent enthusiastic students from seeking the opportunities they desire" (Williamson, 2010).

"The barriers to increased student participation in off-campus programs are real. In addition to the high costs, academic demands, and lack of encouragement by faculty and staff, institutions may restrict financial aid, withhold course equivalencies, and/or deny valuable academic credit" (Williamson, 2010). A 2008 report observed that colleges and universities may "talk the talk but don't walk the walk as they construct many of the barriers that hamper students" (American Council on Education, 2008). Examining the lack of common ground among institutions regarding domestic programming sheds some much-needed light on the institutional policies that "hamper students." The first barrier to understand is getting an institution to even recognize the existence and value of domestic off-campus programs.

Recognition

The first element of disparity exists in the recognition of domestic programs as a viable option for students. Interviews with campus officials and a review of policies at 65 colleges and universities related to spending a semester off-campus found that only 68% of institutions recognize off-campus programs in the United States as a possible opportunity for students. Thus, 32%, or nearly one third, of colleges and universities fail to recognize these programs. The opinions of presidents toward domestic off-campus programs as a viable option for students span the entire spectrum of support. On the one hand, there are presidents who believe that these programs are a key component of their institution's experiential education curricula. One president noted that the inclusion of domestic off-campus programs should be in the institution's strategic plan. Doing so ensures that the students have as many choices for off-campus participation as possible.

On the other hand some presidents believe that domestic programs lack the cultural immersion or language requirement mandated by their institution. One president noted that "since I can drive to Philadelphia, why would I send my students there? I can't drive to Thailand so that's a better experience for our students." Such a myopic view is often supported by the faculty, staff, and other administrators who believe that students need to study outside of the United States to "increase their chances of success in the ever-globalizing world that we live in—a world where bilingual is the international norm, and where multiculturalism is becoming the standard of the United States" (Buff, 2013). Doing so negates the contribution that domestic off-campus programs have had, and continue to have, on a student's learning experience around difference and multiculturalism. As one student who participated in a domestic program observed,

> A perk about going to college is the ability to study off campus for a semester. This could mean studying while tasting flavorful tapas in Spain or studying in the gardens of Versailles. I could have chosen either of those for my semester off campus. Instead, I chose a program that would take me to places much further than across the Atlantic Ocean. I chose to be a part of a program in the United States that would help me discover new ways to grow as a creative and critical thinker. As a result I discovered a stronger sense of "self" that had been missing and felt like an independent adult for the first time. (Marina R., College of Wooster, Philadelphia Center program participant, 2013)

The level of support for study abroad is so high on some campuses that they provide 100% of a student's institutional financial aid if they participate in a program in a foreign country. With the level of support lopsided and in favor of foreign destinations on some campuses, if a student chooses to spend a semester in a domestic program, the school provides no institutional aid whatsoever. The proclamation of one president—"What cultural diversity could possibly exist in Philadelphia?"—serves as an example of this policy. Actually, Philadelphia is an amazingly diverse city. The extent of that diversity varies widely across Philadelphia's 46 neighborhoods. In the years since 2000, compared to earlier years, Philadelphia has seen increases in the percentage of immigrants coming from Latin America and Africa while the percentage from Asia, which is the largest group, has been relatively constant. Of all the foreign-born individuals living in Philadelphia, 45% have come since 2000 (PEW Charitable Trusts, 2013).

The lack of common ground at the presidential level is based on several factors, but the interviews suggest one may be the newness involved in sending students off campus. Opportunities to integrate, synthesize, and apply knowledge around global understanding, while a familiar feature at many institutions, are a relatively new arrival among the goals of undergraduate education. Its meaning is still imperfectly understood, with no consensus that adequately defines the body of skills, attitudes, and knowledge needed to help students understand and negotiate a more interdependent world. As former Harvard President Derek Bok wrote, "Educators have identified a set of educational experiences that would appear to be relevant and useful. How to put them together in the most effective, mutually reinforcing way remains obscure" (2006, p. 52). Presidents are also concerned about the finances involved with sending students off campus. Once again there is little common ground across institutions.

Finances

Every president interviewed noted that financing off-campus programs was a major concern. For most students, financial aid is the biggest factor when deciding upon the affordability of participation. Several presidents noted that endowments or special funding campaigns help defray the financial obligations of sending students off campus. "Government grants and loans can usually travel with a student, but colleges are less generous with the aid from their own coffers" (Pappano, 2007). Only 65% of colleges and universities provide 100% of institutional aid for a student participating in a domestic off-campus program. This leaves one third, or 35% of institutions, that provide some or none of a student's institutional aid. These findings complement an older survey conducted by The Forum on Education Abroad that uncovered 74% of colleges let students apply need-based institutional aid to programs they run themselves (Pappano, 2007). One president expressed grave concern that in the future "only the richest schools with large endowments will be able to afford to send students off-campus."

"The financial challenges of operating a study-abroad program differ from one college to another. Some private institutions have found ways to generate a surplus even after direct and indirect costs have been met. Tuition at public institutions, however, is often too low to cover study-abroad costs and despite a university wide fee to support students going off-campus, they lose money on almost every student" (Williamson, 2010). In addition to the tuition costs, over 60% of institutions surveyed charge fees that range from as little as $80 to as much as $2,500 to attend an off-campus program. Institutions justify their fees to help cover administrative, technological, and overhead costs associated with managing off-campus programs. Some institutions allow the fee to be rolled up into a student's financial aid package as it is recalculated based on the costs of a program. Each institution differs, however, in the way it finances students who have decided to participate in a domestic off-campus program. Institutions find funding for students enrolled through a number of avenues such as endowment campaigns, grants, scholarships, or line items in the operational budget. In an era where one third of all institutions find themselves on an unsustainable fiscal path where expenses outpace revenue, limiting the export of financial aid, coupled with the increase in an application fee, is a strategic imperative for institutions that allow students to participate in an off-campus program (Blumenstyk, 2012).

"Colleges would be mistaken to blame study abroad's sluggish growth entirely on economic conditions," according to Allan E. Goodman, president of the Institute of International Education. "Rather, institutions need to make the option more accessible to more types of students, including science majors and athletes, and also to offer these experiences earlier than in the junior year" (McMurtie, 2012). In referring to the increased number of students participating in short-term study abroad programs, Goodman concluded that "we have the wrong paradigm" and that the requirements in one's major prohibit more students from participating in off-campus programs (McMurtie, 2012). In this he refers to the third element in which there is little common ground when it comes to domestic off-campus programs—administrative policies.

Administrative Policies

Higher education institutions also differ on the various administrative policies they use toward study abroad programs in general and domestic off-campus programs specifically. Administrative barriers are another layer of concern that the student must navigate in addition to security concerns, high costs, academic demands that accommodate neither study abroad nor other international-learning experiences, and lack of encouragement by faculty and advisers (Williamson, 2010).

As with study abroad programs, institutions differ widely on the way they accept academic credit and the transfer of grades from domestic off-campus programs administered by a third party. Unfortunately, the complexity of policies regarding credit acceptance often presents additional barriers for students interested in attending an off-campus program. When it comes to the transfer of academic grades from an off-campus program to the home institution, very few colleges and universities allow such transfers. Students who lack clear information about the transfer of credit fear their qualifications may not be adequately recognized when pursuing an off-campus program and are, therefore, less likely to participate in one (Myers, 2012).

This inconsistency regarding the transfer of academic credit is especially true for those off-campus programs that include an internship as part of the experience. A survey of more than 700 colleges by the National Association of Colleges and Employers found that only 30% of colleges and universities permitted their students to obtain academic credit from internships (Perlin, 2011). While institutional support around issuing credit for internships is inconsistent, there is a general consensus from students about the learning that takes place during their experience. As one student wrote:

Before coming to Philadelphia I was very interested in human resources and did not have any interest in sales. After my internship my attitude has completely changed. I still like human resources, but I have also found a passion for sales and event planning. Discovering my attraction to sales was not something that I thought I would learn here in Philadelphia, but I am glad I did! My internship also showed me the importance of organizational culture. The reason why I enjoyed going to work every day was because of the family atmosphere. Everyone I worked with was extremely nice and I formed strong relationships with my coworkers. (Jessica M., Hanover College, Philadelphia Center program participant, 2013)

Institutions also vary greatly in the administrative policies toward defining and communicating the value of off-campus programs. According to a survey of more than 10,800 British and American students, just 24% of students said they had enough information to make a decision about studying abroad (Fischer, 2013). In my review of policies at 14 liberal arts institutions, 50% allowed a representative for an approved off-campus program to visit classrooms for a brief presentation. Willingness of faculty to give up class time for anything other than the subject matter they are teaching is always a challenge. For example, only 20% allow a program representative to contact faculty members directly to schedule a brief class visit or meeting to discuss the program's educational opportunity for students. The issue is exclusively with faculty. Faculty members from several campuses complained that they received only one e-mail from a representative reminding them of the deadline for students interested in spending a semester off campus. On these campuses faculty rely on the staff members in the Off-Campus Programs Office, where study abroad programs dominate, to educate students about the available options.

The application process is another administrative policy area where there is little common ground. Students routinely report that the application process was confusing. "When a student decides to study abroad, the process they have to go through is actually somewhat long and complex" (Redden, 2012). None of the presidents I spoke with acknowledged this as an issue. The process is so complex that one survey discovered that the greatest predictor of students' participation in study abroad was the seriousness of their intention and ability to complete the application process. Compounding the application process for those interested in participating in a domestic off-campus program is the location of the responsible office. On some campuses domestic off-campus programs go through the study abroad/international education office while others go through the career development office. For other institutions the career center helps students understand the value of a domestic opportunity, especially if the program includes an internship.

Other examples of different administrative units overseeing U.S.-based programs include the offices of off-campus programs, study abroad, or experiential education.

Part of the complexity stems from the lack of collaboration between campus constituents. All too often the offices processing the applications for students are detached from academic departments. As Bok observed, "The units that need to work together are often unequal in status, a disparity that can further inhibit cooperation in subtle ways" (pp. 251). The needed integration requires the cooperation of several separate units of the university: the relevant academic departments, the off-campus office, the financial aid office, and—if it is a credit-bearing experience—the registrar. "Effective collaboration among these units is the exception rather than the rule" (Bok, 2006, p. 52).

The lack of common ground regarding these administrative policies is synonymous with the divergence of action steps institutions are taking in order to innovate and adapt to today's dynamic and ever-changing global marketplace. While many institutions resist any significant change, others are experimenting with more integrative and interdisciplinary curricular designs, developing thematic and problem-based courses and programs, connecting curricular and cocurricular goals and activities, and engaging with communities and employers to apply academic study to the workplace and service to the community. Much more work is needed, however, if higher education institutions are to prepare students "for their future, and not our past" (Pink, 2009). Substantial progress mandates an entirely new way of thinking. "We need to accept the possibility that every off-campus program (across an international border or not) can achieve powerful learning outcomes if it is designed around specific learning goals and linked to on-campus learning experiences that occur before departure and upon return. Then we need to situate these programs fully within the larger education endeavor so that they can reach their potential as a powerful spark that lights a lifelong flame" (Salisbury, 2012). Doing so requires the support of the faculty. This, however, maybe difficult. In their survey of provosts, George Kuh and Stanley Ikenberry concluded that "gaining faculty involvement and support remains a major challenge" (as cited in Tagg, 2012, p. 6) for an institution to implement significant change.

Conclusion

Off-campus programs, whether they are study abroad or domestic in nature, provide amazing opportunities for learning. Students participating in these programs learn how to translate theory into practice, deepen their understanding of cultural diversity, and explore various vocational or professional possibilities. Such opportunities often fundamentally change a student and can ignite a passion for learning long after the program has ended. By allowing their students to participate in a domestic off-campus program, higher education institutions can fundamentally restructure their approach to offering innovative elements that complement their curriculum through an integrative and applied learning experience. "This emphasis on integrative and applied learning is helping to build capabilities that we need as a society facing some of the most difficult challenges that we have faced in recent history—fundamentally issues about survival. These critical times will define the future that we will create together and our students' capacity to integrate will be the key to our success" (AAC&U, 2013). Study abroad programs in general, and domestic off-campus programs specifically, can play a vital role as institutions look to identify valuable approaches to integrated learning. Creating a common ground among higher education institutions regarding domestic off-campus programs, whether a college's own or administered by a third party, is a step in the right direction.

Note

1. These interviews coincided with my professional education plan as a member of the 2013–2014 Council for Independent Colleges' Senior Leadership Academy.

References

AAC&U (Association of American Colleges and Universities). (2013, Fall). *Peer Review, 15*(4). Retrieved from http://www.aacu.org/publications-research/periodicals/president-0

American Council on Education. (2008). *Mapping internationalization on U.S. campuses: 2008 Edition.* Washington, DC: Author.

Blumenstyk, G. (2012, July 23). One-third of colleges are on financially "unsustainable" path. *The Chronicle of Higher Education.* Retrieved from http://chronicle.com/article/One-Third-of-Colleges-Are-on/133095/

Bok, D. (2006). *Our underachieving colleges: A candid look at how much students learn and why they should be learning more.* Princeton, NJ: Princeton University Press.

Buff, K. (2013, October 17). The cost of not studying abroad is real. *New York Times.* Retrieved from http://www.nytimes.com/roomfordebate/2013/10/17/should-more-americans-study-abroad/the-cost-of-not-studying-abroad-is-real

Fischer, K. (2013, April 30). Dearth of information keeps many students from studying abroad, survey finds. *The Chronicle of Higher Education.* Retrieved from http://chronicle.com/article/Dearth-of-Information-Keeps/137707/

Foreign students in US and Americans studying abroad reach all-time high. (2013, November 11). *Guardian*. Retrieved from http://www.theguardian.com/education/2013/nov/11/us-study-abroad-research-china-uk

Friedman, T. (2013, April 30). It's a 401(k) world. *New York Times*. Retrieved from http://www.nytimes.com/2013/05/01/opinion/friedman-its-a-401k-world.html

McMurtie, B. (2012, November 12). Growth in study abroad approaches standstill. *The Chronicle of Higher Education*. Retrieved from http://chronicle.com/article/Study-Abroad-at-a-Standstill/135716/

Myers, J. (2012, January–March). *Solving the problem of transferring study-abroad credits*. University Park, PA: Penn State College of Education.

Open Doors 2013: International students in the United States and study abroad by American students are at all-time high. (2013). New York, NY: Institute of International Education.

Pappano, L. (2007, November 4). Why study abroad costs so much: What to do about it. *New York Times*. Retrieved from http://www.nytimes.com/2007/11/04/education/edlife/studyabroad-1.html?pagewanted=all

Perlin, R. (2011, April 2). Unpaid interns, complicit colleges. *New York Times*. Retrieved from http://www.nytimes.com/2011/04/03/opinion/03perlin.html?pagewanted=all

PEW Charitable Trusts. (2013). *Philadelphia 2013: The state of the city*. Philadelphia, PA: Author.

Pink, D. (2009, January 26). Preparing kids for THEIR future. Retrieved from https://meartsed.wordpress.com/2009/02/20/daniel-pink/

Redden, E. (2012, July 10). Study abroad, graduate on time. *Inside Higher Education*. Retrieved from https://www.insidehighered.com/news/2012/07/10/new-studies-link-study-abroad-time-graduation

Salisbury, M. (2012, July 30). We're muddying the message on study abroad. *The Chronicle of Higher Education*. Retrieved from http://chronicle.com/article/Were-Muddying-the-Message-on/133211/

Tagg, J. (2012). Why does the faculty resist change? *Change: The Magazine of Higher Learning, 44*(1), 6–15.

Williamson, W. (2010, July 25). 7 signs of successful study-abroad programs. *The Chronicle of Higher Education*. Retrieved from http://chronicle.com/article/7-Signs-of-Successful/123657/

PART TWO

SEMESTER-LONG FACULTY-LED PROGRAMS

6

GLOBAL ISSUES MANIFESTED IN A LOCAL SETTING

The Arizona Borderlands

Patty Lamson and Riley Merline

The border between the United States and Mexico spans approximately 2,000 miles from Texas to California and is "the world's longest contiguous international divide between a superpower and a developing nation" (Romero & LAR, 2008, p. 42). This border has a long history of contested space, cultural shifts, and political and economic forces that inform the disparate and complex realities of both countries and the border region. The signing of the Treaty of Guadalupe Hidalgo in 1848 ended the Mexican–American War and resulted in the addition of 525,000 square miles of land to the United States. With the Gadsden Purchase, a treaty signed in 1853 between the United States and Mexico, the United States acquired another 29,640 square miles of territory that established the border of New Mexico and Arizona. The eastern border follows the Rio Bravo/Rio Grande River but the western borderline cuts through harsh, remote territory including rugged mountain ranges, the historic lands of the Tohono O'odham, and the binational Sonoran Desert.

At different times a marker of military sovereignty, a site of transborder trade, a home to binational communities, a customs and immigration checkpoint, a divide between political and legal regimes, and even at times a battlefield. What began as a line on a map became a space of evolving and multiple meanings and forms. (St. John, 2012, p. 3)

Today, the U.S.-Mexico border is a complex cultural, linguistic, political, and economic region where people cross the border to work, shop, and socialize. It is an area sometimes referred to as a "denationalized" zone because it extends miles into each country and serves as a cultural buffer area (Griffith, 1993). Norma Cantú (1993) writes of the "pain and joy of the borderlands" where "contradictions abound, cultures clash and meld, and life is lived on the edge." Today, the region is a tangled web of transnational migration, and border scholar Joseph Nevins (2008) suggests that the boundary is one "between life and death" (p. 169) referring to the access to resources that one has according to his or her country of citizenship.

The twenty-first century is witnessing a dramatic rise in the development and implementation of border enforcement and immigration policies in combination with increased flows of goods and capital. The U.S.-Mexico border is a primary staging ground in which these policies are enacted:

Today there is a pervasive sense of urgency to control the increased flows of people, information, currency and goods that cross borders, despite the difficulty this task entails. This issue has reached a paradoxical state: on one side, there has developed an obsessive necessity to control border flows, while on the other, despite increased security, we are witnessing the highest flows of people and goods across international borders in history. The traditional functions of international borders are being tested by globalization—a phenomenon whose momentum has the potential to severely alter the future state of the world. (Romero & LAR, 2008, p. 15)

The Arizona–Sonora border region has, in particular, become a center of heated debates about immigration and border enforcement policies as the migratory flow from the south has been forced into the dangerous Arizona desert. Millions of crossers have passed through the Tucson sector, and southern Arizona experiences one of the highest numbers of migrant crossings and fatalities along the U.S.-Mexico border (Binational Migration Institute, 2013, p. 11). The magnitude of migration over the past 15 years has contributed to increasing social tension, making the location one of extraordinary significance in national debates on global economic policy, human rights, and national identity.

Lawmakers' responses to the tensions in the Arizona borderlands have thrust the state into the national spotlight. In 2010 and 2011, Arizona passed a series of highly profiled and controversial laws that target unauthorized immigrants. Additionally, Arizona has come under scrutiny for its practice of expedited removal proceedings and the widespread use of controversial for-profit private detention facilities. These practices have been carried out in multiple locations across the country since their implementation. Copycat laws have been passed in Alabama, Georgia, South Carolina, Indiana, and Utah, and "fast-track" justice has been implemented in numerous geographic and political contexts across the country.

In contrast to these harsh policies, Arizona has also long been a place of pro-immigrant organizing. Cesar Chavez was born in Arizona and supported the struggles of farmworkers to achieve better working conditions. In the 1980s, the Sanctuary Movement began at Tucson's Southside Presbyterian Church and quickly spread across the country as churches, individuals, and communities offered hospitality and support to Central Americans fleeing the wars in their countries. Later, in response to the many migrants who died crossing the desert, humanitarian groups such as No More Deaths became internationally known for their lifesaving work. Meanwhile, community groups in Arizona such as Puente [Bridge] Movement, Fortin de las Flores [Women's Fort of Flowers], Corazon de [Heart of] Tucson, and numerous others have organized networks to protect immigrants and immigrant communities. Yet, while the sociopolitical tensions in the region are palpable, the borderlands are also home to cross-border cultures bound by history, family, friendship, and solidarity.

The contrasting realities are shaped by the interplay of policy decisions made on local, national, and international levels and thus present a rich location for students to engage global issues through the examination of how they are manifested in a local setting.

Tucson and the Arizona–Sonora Borderlands as "Place"

The Earlham College Border Studies program began in 1997 with support from the Great Lakes Colleges Association (GLCA) in the El Paso/Ciudad Juarez border region. After 10 years, the program moved to Tucson, where it developed a sharp focus on border and immigration policies. The program now offers a fall and spring semester for undergraduate students from colleges and universities across the country. Their academic majors vary widely across the disciplines, including political science, sociology/anthropology, environmental studies, religion, biology, peace and global studies, Latin American studies, American studies, and more. The on-site directors and faculty organize, teach, and lead all aspects of the program in coordination with Earlham College, and faculty from several colleges that send students to the program form an advisory committee to contribute to ongoing program development.

The educational program is centered on the examination of critical social, economic, and political questions surrounding immigration to the United States and the development of international borders in the twenty-first century. The complexities of migration inform the content and structure of the program, and, as such, the courses and lived experiences enrich one another in an integrated curriculum. The nexus of study, experience, and reflection is foundational to the pedagogy of the program. This framework encourages students to draw informed conclusions about the world around them and to act in thoughtful ways while continually recognizing the impacts these actions have for individuals and communities.

Throughout the semester, students live with families where they experience border realities on a daily basis. The families become important teachers, and students learn how immigration policies directly impact the multiple generations that comprise a household. The home is a learning environment where the student "can personally experience the dynamics of an immigrant family, their history, the close relationships that stretch across the border, and the bi-national culture of the family" (personal communication, Rosalva Fuentes, BSP host mother, December 5, 2013).

Three core courses—Roots and Routes of Migration, Critical Issues in the Borderlands, and Toward Social Change—form the academic heart of the program. Each is designed to inform and complement the experiential aspects of the program by offering historical, contextual, and theoretical study of the issues and region. Discussions include analysis of the readings and reflections on the lived experiences of the students. This combination creates an intense experience that gives students a comprehensive understanding of and personal connection to the people, places, and issues in the region.

The program design falls clearly within the field of *experiential education*, which is defined here by the Association for Experiential Education:

> Experiential education is a philosophy that informs many methodologies in which educators purposefully engage with learners in direct experience and focused reflection in order to increase knowledge, develop skills, clarify values, and develop people's capacity to contribute to their communities. (n.d.)

The Border Studies program is grounded, more specifically, in the type of experiential education that Jay Roberts calls "Experience and the Political" to "signal the ways in which experience . . . is embedded within the dynamics of power and social justice" (2012, p. 69). The approach of the program is situated in critical pedagogy, based upon Paulo Freire's key works *Education, the*

Practice of Freedom (1967/1976) and *Pedagogy of the Oppressed* (1968/1970). Critical pedagogy leads to "conscientization," resulting from cycles of focused study, informed action, and critical reflection, which then lead to transformation (Freire, 1968/1970). Amy Hunter defines *transformative learning* as

> a process that precipitates a deep and structural shift of perspective in students through new experience. When learners are challenged to reflect critically on disorienting dilemmas in light of personal biases, when they are encouraged to test and validate their thinking in discourse with others, and when they are given the opportunity to integrate their learning into the fabric of their lives through action, the possibility of transformation exists. (2008, p. 100)

Transformation, though, is not the end process but rather a starting point for social action that leads to social change (Hunter, 2008). Glen Kuecker (2013) takes this a step further, suggesting that "predicament thinking" in the messiness of world situations is key for the future:

> Contending with the messy world of predicaments—where difficult trade-offs fraught with disturbing moral and ethical challenges displace problems with clear solutions—will define the life-long learning of our students as well as the ways they will create new knowledge in the twenty-first century. Predicament thinking will be at a premium, and liberal education is well suited for this teaching task.

Program Seminar on Migration: The Global Is Local

The Roots and Routes of Migration course challenges students to use a historical and global perspective in relation to immigration from Central America and Mexico to the United States. Readings concentrate on migration history, the global economy, and free trade, and students examine the significance of an increasingly militarized U.S. border with Mexico and the choices and everyday realities for individuals and communities affected by migration.

Embedded in the Roots and Routes course are travel seminars ranging in length from 3 to 20 days that explore the causes and effects of migration. Students interact with communities in Guatemala, southern Mexico, and along the Mexico-U.S. border that are directly impacted by migration. Students have experienced manifestations of the international boundary from the Pacific Ocean to the west and Big Bend National Park to the east. In Guatemala and Mexico, they have engaged with communities that experience high rates of emigration to the United States, causing disruption or transformation in all levels of society. Students have learned about the hazards of crossing the southern border of Mexico and the trains that carry migrants north, have spent nights with migrants in shelters, and have had discussions with indigenous groups and organizations who are developing alternative practices to function in the twenty-first century.

Through these intentional interactions, students acquire a depth of insight and diversity of perspectives on the debates that surround immigration and border policies. As one student commented, the course syllabus "came alive" in an excursion to Nogales, Sonora. This interplay allows students to apply theory to experience and experience to theory, thereby enriching the learning experiences in each setting. Students gain a deeper connection to and understanding of what borders and migration mean for sending communities, receiving communities, and families caught in both. The following statement by student Keiler B. describes how his interactions deepened his learning experience:

> I was able to see first-hand what we had been discussing in our classes in a way that never would have been possible. For me the most powerful part was seeing the communities that migrants had left behind, and understanding not only the forces at work that precipitated their migration, but also the effect their absence has on those left behind. Speaking with migrants in a shelter in Tapachula [Chiapas, the southern Mexican state that borders Guatemala] really hit me hard, because their hopefulness for their journey sometimes stood in stark contrast with the heartbreaking stories describing the route up to the U.S. border I had heard earlier in the semester in a shelter in Altar [Sonora, the northern Mexican state that borders Arizona]. (Whitman College, program participant, 2013)

As Keiler illustrates, this course gives students a holistic and personal encounter with migration as a global and local phenomenon. Students develop an understanding of globalization and its relationship to international migration, but they also take with them the numerous personal experiences they have had.

Critical Issues in the Borderlands: Community as Classroom

In the Critical Issues in the Borderlands course, individuals in the Tucson region act as the students' primary teachers, thereby eliminating the separation between the traditional classroom and the community. Notions of where, how, and with whom education occurs are broadened by expanding the concept of teachers to include community members who offer multiple perspectives. With the community as text, students reflect critically on these interactions and personal experiences through readings, discussion, and weekly writing assignments.

This course is particularly powerful for students because literature, analysis, and theory become real through visceral encounters with and reactions to a diversity of places, circumstances, and people. For instance, students read about the migrant journey north, the dangers of crossing in the desert, the growing border enforcement apparatus, and the connections immigrant detention centers have to the for-profit prison industrial complex. Simultaneously, students visit with migrants in a shelter in northern Mexico, tour the Border Patrol facility and walk along the towering border wall, hike migrant trails and leave lifesaving water in the desert, witness detained migrants in court as they are processed and sentenced to deportation or incarceration, and tour Immigration and Customs Enforcement (ICE) detention centers in the prison town of Florence, Arizona. Occasionally students meet a migrant in a shelter in Mexico and then see that person shackled before a judge in federal court in Tucson. Students thus incorporate powerful experiences into their developing understanding of migration and enforcement policies.

The Field Study

The field study provides an essential learning space for students to participate on an individual basis in an organization or agency that works with immigrant groups. Students devote approximately 12 hours a week at their site to learn from seasoned practitioners and activists. Organizations like No More Deaths and Coalición de Derechos Humanos [Human Rights Coalition] strive to end border suffering and to bring dignity to immigrant communities. At these sites, students contribute to abuse documentation and participate in the desert aid camps. Fortín de las Flores promotes the rights of women and offers leadership training and community building. It also aids women with practical needs through its secondhand clothing store that provides appropriate clothes for job interviews. Students participating here have assisted in various aspects of supporting these women. In the Ecological Program at Manzo Elementary School in Barrio Hollywood, students learn from teachers and youth in project-based learning programs. The school has developed a garden, a greenhouse, and an animal habitat that youth care for as part of their school activities. Moses Thompson, the school counselor at Manzo Elementary and the supervisor of the Border Studies program's students who are placed there, framed the relationship in the following way:

The partnership between the Border Studies program and Manzo Elementary School is a perfect example of place-based learning. Border Studies students gain valuable work experience while immersed in the rich culture and heritage of Barrio Hollywood and help fill the programmatic gaps of an underfunded public school. (personal communication, February 6, 2014)

Throughout the semester the field studies instructor and the student have ongoing conversations through meetings and the exchange of detailed field notes, allowing the instructor to push students in their understanding and analysis of border issues. Kaitlin M. wrote about her "new normal" in a blog entry while participating at No More Deaths:

My new normal does not include days off. My new weekends are spent doing desert aid training. It is sharing a meal with Javier who spent the last 24 days traveling from his home in Guatemala riding on top of a train. . . . My new normal is feeling so many emotions at once that I don't even know what I'm feeling anymore. It is desperately longing and needing to talk to a familiar loved one but when I get on the phone you're speechless. I can't relate my experiences, there's just this disconnect because we no longer live in the same world. Well in actuality, the scariest thing is, is that we both still live in the same world, I'm just looking at it from a different angle. It's like those illusions in which you can see two pictures in the same drawing, and although we're looking at the same picture we are seeing two different things. (personal communication, Earlham College, program participant, February 14, 2011)

Kaitlin's statement illustrates a transformative shift in her perspective and demonstrates that students do not necessarily need to travel far to have their knowledge system destabilized. Indeed, the domestic location might be more destabilizing because the shift happens within the home context. The combination of intense ongoing personal encounters, focused analysis of readings, and critical reflection encourages this difficult, but powerful, transformational learning process.

Toward Social Change

The Toward Social Change course challenges students to develop an understanding of what it means to work for social and environmental justice. Students address systems of inequality and work toward defining issues such as solidarity, justice, and liberation. In this course, students must draw from all of the intellectual and personal experiences they have encountered in the program, and "are encouraged to explore the different aspects of power and privilege that adhere to them by virtue of living in the United States"

(Swanger, 2002, p. 4). Questions they address include: What is the significance of committed, thoughtful engagement, and what might this look like in our lives? How can we maintain hope alongside hardship and injustice? How does resistance emerge? How do the things we witness and experience in the borderlands also occur in the places we come from? What roles do we each play in this?

At the end of the semester, students complete an autoethnography that incorporates both theoretical learning and personal growth. They are asked to contemplate a variety of ways to address the problems, messiness, and predicaments they have observed and encountered and, through this, to articulate their own worldviews and their own positions. Reflection in this context is treated as a substantive critical reasoning skill. Inevitably, students reflect on questions of race, class, language, power, privilege, age, gender, and self as they relate to the experiences they have lived throughout the semester. The question of what it means to be human after the dehumanizing experiences they have seen is often at the heart of their discussion. They struggle to negotiate privilege, how to make sense of it, and how to incorporate thoughtfully that privilege into their own lives. Here we can see the "deep and structural shift of perspective in students through new experience" that Hunter (2008, p. 100) describes in transformative learning. Alex C. wrote that it is important for him to

> consider my own position and my own privilege as I continue to understand the Borderlands and how I am implicated in and even perpetuate their current state. Further, the problem encountered here is not one that pertains solely to this experience; I expect to encounter it throughout the rest of my life. However, with this problematic in mind, I continue to seek insight into how to better conduct relationships committed to listening, accountability and human flourishing. (Earlham College, program participant, 2014)

Jenny R. wrote about her work at Owl and Panther, an organization that promotes art therapy with refugee youth, commenting on how her experiences might translate into action:

> Those moments when I was mostly listening as I watched the kids color furiously or paint meticulously . . . aren't going to change the world in any big, spectacular way. . . . But I'm thinking now that the idea of putting art supplies and pencils in the hands of refugee children and parents is something radical. The radical world I want to create includes more avenues for beauty and joy in the lives of all people. Owl and Panther has ultimately taught me that radical change does not always mean Big Change—it means

being willing to dive into the grey area, sit with discomfort, and to work to make the world a little more beautiful. (Kenyon College, program participant, 2013)

Similarly, Rena B. wrote of the role of building community as a central tenet of justice work, something she observed through her time with UNIDOS (United Non-Discriminatory Individuals Demanding Our Studies), a student-run group that advocates for ethnic student courses in Tucson high schools:

An integral part of my stay in Tucson has been the openness and warmth with which I've been welcomed by UNIDOS and other people in the activist community. . . . Before this program, the idea of graduating terrified me. Now I feel more excited, more hopeful about the world beyond college, the ability of people and communities to live intentionally, take care of themselves and each other and strive together for a better life for everyone. (Oberlin College, program participant, 2013)

Conclusion: Education for the Twenty-First Century

Tucson and the greater borderlands are an exceptional setting for the cross-cultural and transformative learning expected from off-campus study programs. The Border Studies program places students in situations where they face and grapple with complicated twenty-first-century predicaments in the "messy" context of the U.S.-Mexico borderlands. Oberlin College professor of history Steven Volk describes how this affects students upon return to campus:

What happens on the Border Studies program is that students are able to integrate a number of approaches, from sustainability and environmental studies to law, immigration, history, health care, and many more, around a specific geography and a specific set of burning issues. . . . They come back not just energized and motivated, but better able to take command over their own education. (personal communication, February 3, 2014)

Reece Jones contextualizes the nature of the dilemmas posed by contemporary border walls by noting that an era marked by globalization, interconnectedness, and expectations of "an increasingly borderless world" has ironically been an era of record-setting levels of border militarization and wall construction between so-called first- and third-world nations (2012,

p. 1). The ethical questions regarding the construction of walls intensify when we consider the extreme levels of global inequality contributing to mass migration. The states that build walls argue that they are necessary for the security of those within, while others describe this predicament as the "age of global apartheid," a clear condemnation of border restrictions (Nevins, 2008). Such a predicament compels students to ask: What is the future of national boundaries and how will that affect the people and environments of the borderlands and beyond? What is the future of human mobility in the globalized free markets of the twenty-first century? How am I implicated in these questions and what role can I play in addressing them?

Through their participation with the Border Studies program, students tackle such questions and apply what they learn through the realities of migration and borders to a wide range of social, economic, environmental, and political dilemmas that they will encounter throughout their lives. The program prepares participants to actively work and to shape the world around them in ways that reflect their values and principles.

References

Association for Experiential Education. (n.d.). What is experiential education? Retrieved from http://www.aee.org/what-is-ee

Binational Migration Institute. (2013). *A continued humanitarian crisis at the border: Undocumented border crosser deaths recorded by the Pima County Office of the Medical Examiner, 1990–2012.* Tucson: University of Arizona. Retrieved from http://bmi.arizona.edu/sites/default/files/border_deaths_final_web.pdf

Cantú, N. (1993). Living on the border: A wound that will not heal. Borderlands Festival Program Booklet. Smithsonian Institution. Retrieved from http://smithsonianeducation.org/migrations/bord/live.html

Freire, P. (1970). *Pedagogy of the oppressed* (M. B. Ramos, Trans.). London: Penguin. (Original work publisher 1968)

Freire, P. (1976). *Education, the practice of freedom* (M. B. Ramos, Trans.). London: Writers and Readers Publishing Cooperative. (Original work publisher 1967)

Griffith, J. (1993). The Arizona–Sonora border: Line, region, magnet, and filter. Borderlands Festival Program Booklet. Smithsonian Institution. Retrieved from http://smithsonianeducation.org/migrations/bord/azsb.html

Hunter, A. (2008). Transformative learning in international education. In V. Savicki (Ed.), *Developing intercultural competence and transformation: Theory, research, and application in international education* (pp. 92–107). Sterling, VA: Stylus.

Jones, R. (2012). *Border walls: Security and the war on terror in the United States, India, and Israel.* London: Zed Books.

Kuecker, G. (2013). Teaching philosophy statement. Retrieved from http://www.depauw.edu/academics/departments-programs/history/faculty--staff/detail/1112592582468/

Morris, K. (2011, February 14). My new normal [Blog entry]. Retrieved from http://spring2011borderstudies.blogspot.com/2011/02/my-new-normal-revolves-around-bus.html

Nevins, J. (2008). *Dying to live: A story of U.S. immigration in an age of global apartheid.* San Francisco, CA: Open Media/City Lights Books.

Roberts, J. (2012). *Beyond learning by doing: Theoretical currents in experiential education.* New York, NY: Routledge.

Romero, F., & Laboratory of Architecture (LAR). (2008). *Hyperborder: The contemporary U.S.–Mexico border and its future.* New York, NY: Princeton Architectural Press.

St. John, R. (2012). *Line in the sand: A history of the western U.S.–Mexico border.* Princeton, NJ: Princeton University Press.

Swanger, J. (2002). Letter from the editor: The critical pedagogy of ethnography in the Border Studies program. *International Journal of Qualitative Studies in Education, 15*(1), 1–10.

7

SEEING THINGS WHOLE

Immersion in the West

Phil Brick

I n his 1862 essay "Walking," Henry David Thoreau wrote that, for him, the future lies wesward. Like Thoreau, Americans have long visualized the West as an open frontier with seemingly limitless possibilities. With its majestic mountains, its wide-open spaces, and its vast expanses of forests and grasslands, the West is what we imagine this country once was, and perhaps paradoxically, what it could be. By the end of the nineteenth century, most of the West was either privatized or became public land (nearly one third the land mass of the country), managed by federal agencies such as the Forest Service and the Bureau of Land Management. Many Westerners bristle at the regulations such management brings, and Western public lands have long been the focus of cultural conflict between traditional extractive values (exemplified by industries such as logging, mining, ranching) and environmental values, which emphasize conservation, wilderness preservation, biodiversity, and watershed protection. In recent years, growing evidence of climate change has forced a reckoning of sorts. As the region becomes hotter and drier, how can the beauty and richness of the region be preserved while still maintaining the rural lifestyles cherished by many Westerners? In essence, this is just a variant of the same question every region of the country must now ask itself: What does it mean to live well in this place in an era of unprecedented change?

The West's open spaces still beckon us to believe that both human and natural communities are more resilient than we might think. The West is thus an excellent learning laboratory for a field program in environmental studies where human values, a wealth of natural resources, and rapid changes intersect. After taking students out into the field for a weekend here and there, I decided that the region, conceptualized as a whole, deserved a full semester's treatment.

Program Overview

Whitman College's Semester in the West (SITW) is an interdisciplinary, environmental studies field program focused on landscapes of the interior American West, a remarkably diverse learning laboratory.[1] Our curriculum sits at the intersection of natural resource policy, ecology, and environmental writing, mirroring the structure of the environmental studies program on our home campus, which includes requirements in all three areas of liberal learning: the social sciences, the natural sciences, and the humanities. If anything sets environmental studies aside as an academic field of inquiry, it is the importance attached to seeing connections between things, such as the nexus between nature and culture, the global and the local, and the coevolution of humans and natural systems (Soulé & Press, 1998). Our goal for SITW is to develop both practical and intuitive understandings of these connections, to "see landscapes whole," and to develop narratives through which we can share these understandings with a public increasingly disconnected from the landscapes that sustain them.

SITW is a deeply immersive, experiential learning program, covering a wide geographic area that includes the vast forests of the Pacific Northwest, the mountains and canyons of the Colorado Plateau, and the deserts of the Southwest. Nature writer Ellen Meloy, who played a key role in the creation of the program before her sudden death in 2004, encouraged students to develop what she called "a deep map of place." Participants travel nearly 8,000 miles to visit with over 80 Westerners from many professions and walks of life. These guest speakers, which may include forest activists, Navajo elders, writers, poets, ecologists, county commissioners, ranchers, loggers, miners, journalists, hydrologists, archeologists, and so on, become the primary "texts" for the work in the field, and students are expected to learn how to read and (politely) interrogate them as they would any scholarly text. Although we meet a diverse set of guests in the field, it is striking how nearly everyone struggles with the same question: What does it mean to live well in a place that includes so much open and common space, wild country, and contested human and ecological history? Originally conceptualized to focus on the rural/urban cultural divide over regional environmental issues such as forest, water, mineral, and grassland management, in recent years the program has shifted nearly completely to focus on how climate change is altering natural and human dynamics in the region, unsettling expectations, and forcing us to reconceptualize our relatively stable assumptions about natural systems and our many senses of place.

The American West in Global Context

The West has always been subject to global processes such as immigration, colonial imperialism, and the commodification of its natural resources, which have shaped the region in profound ways. Climate change promises to bring changes of similar or even greater magnitude. The American West is the perfect place to begin looking for these changes because the West is warming significantly faster than national and global averages. Whereas average global temperatures rose 1.1°F over the past century, the interior American West was 1.4°F warmer, and climate models predict a further increase of 3.6°F to 12.6°F by the end of this century ("National Climate Assessment," 2014; NRDC, 2008). Already, the West is experiencing a taste of what is to come: declining mountain snowpack, dwindling water reserves, record heat waves and drought, dust storms, insect infestations, wildfires, and gradual loss of critical wildlife habitats. Even the most optimistic climate models suggest that global temperatures will continue to warm substantially before stabilizing late in this century. The West will likely feel the effects of such warming much more acutely than other regions, with potentially transformative changes in the region's vast expanses of forests, grasslands, deserts, and high alpine meadows. Perhaps the biggest challenge will be the expected diminishment of available water for farms and cities, while the human population in many parts of the region is expected to grow.

On SITW, students have the opportunity to meet with conservationists, ecologists, land managers, local citizens, and community leaders in the West who have been inspired by the prospect of climate change to rethink priorities for the region's vast wealth of natural resources, much of which remains in public hands. Even though the West has more than its share of climate skeptics, the climate change debate is reinvigorating long stalemated conversations about best management practices for the nation's public forests, prairies, mountains, and rivers, opening new pathways to conceptualize public resources in more sustainable and democratic ways. At the same time, the prospect of climate change can also be used to justify large-scale state and federal projects that may fix short-term problems but do little or nothing to alter existing patterns of resource exploitation and ecosystem decline. Thus, one goal of SITW is to highlight the choices that climate change will place in front of everyone who cares about Western landscapes, sustainable communities, energy security, and biodiversity. Two paths diverge from here. One path bulldozes a familiar but expensive route through the landscape, building still more dams, pipelines, power lines, and subsidizing unsustainable exploitation of the region's public forests, grasslands, and waterways. This will surely summon traditional opponents in industry and conservation groups to their familiar battle stations. But a second path is possible, where expectations of climate change become the catalyst for a more ecologically sensible reconceptualization of the region's natural resources. Traditionally, the nation's public lands have been simply a storehouse for needed commodities: lumber, water, forage, oil and gas, minerals, and recreational opportunities. Climate change encourages the rethinking of this orientation. A hotter and drier West will need healthier forests and grasslands for clean, reliable sources of water, carbon sequestration, and biodiversity. Public lands will be more valuable for these "ecosystem services" than the simple dollar value of commodities extracted from them. And if done properly, rural Westerners will continue to be able to make a sustainable living by producing traditional commodities *and* managing ecosystem services.

An Interdisciplinary Learning Community in the Field

One of the unique features of SITW is that students and faculty spend a full 90 days in the field, camping each night in remote areas while keeping to a rigorous academic and travel schedule. Days off are rare, and adventures begin each day at first light and go well into the evening. Students work in rotating teams to produce healthful meals in the field kitchen, and everyone is responsible for a wide range of camp chores. We travel with a solar-powered computer laboratory (a converted horse trailer), which has a satellite link to the Internet, essential for research and keeping in touch with the wider world. Students travel in rented Suburbans and the trailer is towed by a pickup truck owned by the college, which also carries water and sanitation systems. Full-time program staff include the program director and two field assistants, who help organize camp life and maintain our Web connections to the outside world.

Learning to cooperate with fellow students in close quarters and in sometimes stressful conditions (extreme weather, cold, darkness) is an important part of the student experience, and integral to the goal of creating a tight-knit learning community. Students are admitted to the program in a highly selective admission process, and the goal is to assemble a team with diverse talents and skills so that students can help one another with the wide variety of daily tasks, which range from manipulating data in geographic information systems (GIS) to crafting poetry and reading it aloud in front of the whole group.

Students formally enroll in four courses, each four credits: Environment and Politics in the American West, Ecology of the American West, Environmental Writing and the American West, and Western Epiphanies, the last being an independent project at the end of the semester. Once in the field, however, the boundaries between these courses largely fade away, and even seem to merge into one. For example, a key learning segment is at the intersection of beaver ecology, hydrology, global environmental history, natural resource politics, and aesthetics. This segment is currently led by Mary O'Brien, an ecologist with the Grand Canyon Trust, and Suzanne Fouty, a hydrologist for the U.S. Forest Service. Both O'Brien and Fouty are engaged in projects to restore beaver to our national forests. They argue that if beaver could be restored to even a fraction of their presettlement numbers and range, enough water could be stored and cooled behind their dams to offset expected water shortages due to climate change. Instead of paying the Army Corps of Engineers billions of taxpayer dollars to build and maintain dams, they argue, beavers could do a better job for free, *and* they create useful wetland habitat for scores of other species at the same time.

In field labs designed by Drs. O'Brien and Fouty, students learn how to run stream transects and enter these data into a GIS interpretive map. The goal is to assess habitat suitability and create baseline data for areas that don't yet have beaver, and to document changes in streamside vegetation for areas that do. This work is exhausting and time-consuming, but it is more than an academic exercise. The data they collect are essential for political efforts to convince the Forest Service that beaver can be an effective restoration tool. At the same time, students learn that these efforts face substantial opposition, which is grounded in the complex and often difficult relationship humans have had with a species that is perhaps most like us in terms of its ability to reshape its environment to its liking. As part of their instruction, O'Brien and Fouty model how scientific knowledge can be used responsibly and strategically in political struggles. Furthermore, they help students understand the global historical context of beaver in North America. Once the de facto currency of global trade and imperial designs on the continent, beaver were trapped nearly to extinction by the end of the nineteenth century. Removing this keystone species caused watersheds to unravel. Streams that were historically perennial became ephemeral, and over time these degraded streams have come to be accepted as normal. To add a layer of complexity, most students find beaver streams, which are dense with brushy willow and cottonwood, less attractive aesthetically than more open, degraded streams.

At the end of the segment, students recognize that understanding human history is essential to understanding natural systems, even those that may appear pristine. And sometimes, what is ecologically most rich and diverse may not necessarily be the most aesthetically pleasing or amenable to human use, which complicates efforts to restore ecological function to Western public lands.

Service-Learning

Another important facet of SITW is service-learning, which stems directly from the program's experiential, community-based learning. In exchange for the time that some of the guests, who are also instructor–educators, spend with us, we design projects that allow students to work side by side with our hosts to accomplish much-needed work. Each semester typically includes a half dozen such projects. Two examples from the 2012 program involved service work in cross-cultural settings, where we have ensured that our hosts welcome the program's presence and that students are aware of power relationships implicit in such arrangements.

One project, a favorite among students, was helping to install a solar power system for a family living in a remote hogan on the Navajo reservation. It was particularly meaningful because the two previous days had been spent touring Navajo coal mines on Black Mesa, which feed the Navajo Generating station in Page, Arizona, one of the largest coal-fired power plants in the United States. Power generated at the station is exported to Phoenix, Los Angeles, and Las Vegas along high-tension lines strung high across the Navajo reservation, where many people still live without power and running water. It was particularly important to our Navajo hosts that we understood the irony and injustice of the situation. At the same time, students learned that many Navajo *want* to live in remote locations where grid electrical service is impractical. Thus, a solar power system for this situation was a good solution, and the students really loved the chance to help install it.

A second project involved work with a binational conservation effort down on the Colorado River Delta region in Sonora, Mexico. Once one of the richest river deltas in the hemisphere, much of the Colorado River Delta is today dry and barren. The once mighty Colorado River no longer reaches the sea because its waters are almost entirely drained for human uses by the time it reaches the Mexico border near Yuma, Arizona. Undaunted, environmental and community groups on both sides of the border have collaborated to develop small-scale wetland restoration projects using recycled water from the city of Mexicali's wastewater treatment plant and from brackish irrigation runoff. Students helped plant cottonwood and willows in newly restored areas, which was both a rewarding task for students and a useful one for our Sonoran Institute and Pronatura Noroeste partners. With so many hands on task, many days of work can be accomplished in just a few hours.

In both cases, the informal, cross-cultural conversations that happen during the workday are perhaps the most valuable and memorable. These are the kinds of "global" experiences that can't be scripted or explicitly organized. However, on SITW, they seem to happen organically by our working closely with partner organizations that already know us and have a good sense of the kinds of projects that will be of mutual benefit. And we are ready for anything: we travel with tools and work gloves for everyone.

Western Epiphanies: Finding a Narrative Voice

A recurring struggle on SITW is the tension between dominant cultural conceptions and narratives of the West as "pristine," and the reality that most landscapes in the region have clearly been shaped by the human hand, even if the presence of that hand is not immediately visible. Ecologist and program instructor O'Brien says,

> The West is beautiful until you look closely, and then you can readily see how two centuries of abuse of these lands have left them ecologically impoverished. . . . Forests that look perfectly fine to the untrained eye are on the verge of collapse, and we have lost most of our native grasslands to livestock production. . . . These ecosystems used to be rich, verdant, and full of life, now [with climate change] they will likely become burned-out woodlots and deserts. (personal communication, July 2013)

This paradox hits our students hard throughout the semester, and a sense of loss, perhaps of the innocence of their naive conceptions of nature, is our constant companion. Conservationist Aldo Leopold once noted, "One of the penalties of an ecological education is that one lives alone in a world of wounds. Much of the damage inflicted on land is quite invisible to the layman" (1993, p. 165). One of the challenges of this program is to develop ways to tell stories about the West that convey complex and sometimes bitter realities without losing sight of the fact that for many Americans, the West remains the place where we keep our nature pure and undisturbed, "the native home of hope," as Wallace Stegner (1969, p. 37) once wrote.

The humanities are uniquely suited to this task, and throughout the semester, several writers and media experts help students develop the narrative, visual, and auditory skills to make sense of what they are experiencing, and to be able to share it effectively with others. In addition to gathering ecological field data, we make excursions to "stock our metaphor banks," practice landscape and character descriptions, and put them together in short, insightful essays (we call them "epiphanies") that we read and workshop together in a chair circle under the night sky. For students, this is one of the more intimidating and challenging parts of the semester—to lay their thoughts and work bare for peer review and criticism. Part of what makes the program so successful is the culture of support and encouragement the program fosters. By the end of the semester, when the students must present one of their epiphanies before a large audience, they can read their pieces with poise and confidence. The epiphanies are accompanied by a slide show tailored to each piece, drawn from photographs students have taken throughout the semester, with guidance from staff about lighting, framing, and composition.

Final Project: National Public Lands Radio

In the early years of the program, we struggled to come up with a final project that would tie the many diverse strands of student experiences in the program together. Starting in 2008, we began experimenting with audio podcasts, which has turned out to be an excellent final exercise that students find both challenging and rewarding. While in the field, students are responsible for audio recording each speaker they meet, plus recording ambient sounds in the places we visit. We come in from the field two weeks before the program's end to debrief and work on final projects. We do this at a "wilderness campus" that we are fortunate to have in the mountains just 16 miles from the Whitman campus. While there, each student is responsible for producing an eight-minute, NPR-style story, chronicling some aspect of an issue with which we engaged in the field. We hire journalism and media experts to teach the students how to develop a coherent and compelling narrative, and then how to use software to blend narration, subject voices, music, and ambient sounds to transport the listener to the place and subject of the story. Although quite time-consuming, these podcasts create an opportunity for students to go back and listen again to speakers they encountered in the field, this time with more context and with the goal of distilling issues down to their bare essentials, in order to artfully integrate those messages into a coherent narrative that is accessible to a wide audience. These final podcasts, which we call "National Public Lands Radio," are then placed on our website and linked to target audiences such as readers of *High Country News* and blogs that focus on environmental and social issues in the West.[2]

Aftermath

Like so many students returning to the traditional classroom after study abroad, the "Westies" (as they call themselves) often find it difficult to adjust to life back on campus. Westies perhaps face a few unique challenges. Some students report difficulty navigating the built environment after so much time living outside, while others simply miss the deep camaraderie forged in the field. One advantage of an off-campus program run by one's own institution is that students can continue friendships and learning communities established in the field, and many Westies do so by living together and hosting regular social events for the remainder of their time at the college. After graduation, many Westies maintain enduring friendships and they frequently network with each other for jobs and other opportunities. In the fall of 2012, we hosted a 10-year reunion of all Westies at a remote location in southern Utah, six hours from any major airport. It was the best-attended reunion in the history of Whitman College, with over 70% of our program alums making the trip from all parts of the country.

At the reunion, we set up a "video booth" where alums could record brief testimonials about how the program influenced them. Here is a sampling of the responses:

> Being challenged with these issues that you can't close your textbook on at the end of the day but you wake back up to and thus they transform you, whether you wake up on the Navajo Nation and look around and imagine your life if you were raised there, or watching the Central Arizona Project canal recede in the distance and really get a sense for what moving water 300 miles uphill means. Any of those things that you experience with all five senses instead of in a purely cerebral way necessarily changes who you are. And so everything became intensely personal and it still is, and I guess I wish that on other people, not as a curse but as an inspiration, as a driver to serve something that is all of ours, these are our public lands and I think heartbreak is an important part of it. The line for me from SITW to who I am and what I do today is clear and bright. (Camilla Thorndike, program participant, 2008, politics major, conflict resolution specialist)

> I heard about SITW and thought it would be a great way to explore what I consider to be my place and to learn about the West, where I came from. I remember trying to find study abroad programs that spoke to me and nothing really did, but SITW just felt like it was perfect. SITW really celebrates life, and changes in life, and the history of this place, I was just captivated by that the entire time. I think that as a biology major I felt a lot of connection to the natural world and the thing that was most challenging was the politics and the social side, and that really changed me. It changed my way of viewing problems and finding solutions, and just connecting on a totally different level other than the scientific method. It wasn't just qualitative data either, a lot of it was just the experience of sitting in a

place or hearing a conversation, meeting a farmer or a crazy environmental radical and trying to process all that, was really challenging for me, but the only way I think now is very critically about the world, and I learned that through this program. (Debbie Nelson, program participant, 2004, biology major, organic farmer)

I am really blessed to be working at a newspaper that values journalism as a public service. That's also what SITW teaches you. It is a semester of public service, both learning from all the people who donate all of their time to you and also the time you spend building people's fences and collecting firewood for them, and knowing what their life is like and how you are helping them. In journalism, the best stories are the ones that are controversial, and the ones that look at what all sides are saying in a convincing way, and not just putting a face behind one story, but also putting a face behind the opposing story as well. That is a very similar thing to SITW. (Katrina Barlow, program participant, 2008, environmental humanities major, journalist, *Seattle Times*)

At the base of it I guess I learned to listen better to people who are different than me, and to hear them and to take it to heart and think about what they said. It is hard to have empathy with a point of view unless you are presented with someone's person, their reasoning, their circumstances, their surroundings, and their context, which are all part of why they see things the way they do. This is how SITW really helped me see things in a much larger context and that is crucial to the work I now do. The program is designed in such a way that it is much like reporting. Instead of focusing on books, which may be a part of the picture for context, you go and talk to people who are involved in all sides of the issues and you are forced to find a way to draw meaning out of all their conflicting ideas and come to some kind of conclusion, of not telling people what's right, but by synthesizing their information into some whole that people can use. That's great training for journalism. (Sarah Gilman, program participant, 2002, art and biology double major, associate editor, *High Country News*)

As a senior at Whitman College I was at a point where I was oversimplifying environmental issues, everything was cut-and-dried and I knew that there was a right and a wrong answer. When I started SITW I started realizing the complexity and nuance to these issues, and being someone who is interested in environmental ethics and really thinking about the right and wrong, I realized that nothing is cut and dried, and that was my first epiphany, these are really complex issues and the human side is the most important part of environmental issues. (Jay Heath, program participant, 2006, environmental humanities major, education technology specialist)

Notes

1. For more information, visit the program website www.semesterinthewest.org
2. Visit www.hcn.org

References

Leopold, A. (1993). *Round river.* New York, NY: Oxford University Press.
National climate assessment. (2004). Retrieved from http://nca2014.globalchange.gov/
NRDC (Natural Resources Defense Council). (2008). Hotter and drier: The West's changed climate. Retrieved from www.nrdc.org/globalwarming/west/contents.asp
Soulé, M. E., & Press, D. (1998, May). What is environmental studies? *BioScience, 48*(5), 397–405.
Stegner, W. (1969). *The sound of mountain water.* New York, NY: Penguin Books.
Thoreau, H. D. (1862). "Walking." Retrieved from http://thoreau.eserver.org/walking.html

8

SOJOURNS IN THE LOWCOUNTRY

Gateway to Africa in the Americas

Jacquelyn Benton

In 2006 the U.S. Congress designated an area stretching from Wilmington, North Carolina, through the states of South Carolina and Georgia, and on down to Jacksonville, Florida, as the Gullah/Geechee Heritage Corridor. The act was initially proposed by South Carolina Congressman James E. Clyburn. Its passage was an effort to acknowledge and help preserve a unique culture in the American landscape, a culture described as African as much as it is American. Gullah/Geechee people, a distinct segment of the African American community, have traditionally resided in the Sea Islands off the southern coast of the United States. Their distinction lies in the fact that they have been able to preserve much of their African heritage in their everyday lives even after centuries. How was this possible? It has much to do with their history, which speaks to a specialized slave trade, the isolation of the Sea Islands, and a tropical environment inhospitable to their slave owners.[1]

The Sea Islands lie in what is known as the Lowcountry, so called because the area falls below sea level. During the slavery era, planters in this area were interested in creating rice plantations, but they had no knowledge of rice cultivation; therefore, they specifically sought Africans with that expertise. Highly desirable were Africans from an area formerly known as "The Rice Coast," which extended down the west coast of Africa from the Senegambia region to the country of Liberia, where rice had been cultivated for thousands of years. Sierra Leone is one of the countries falling within that area, and in South Carolina at the Charleston City Market, one can still see images of old slave bills that advertised Africans from Sierra Leone specifically. Shipped from the slave-trading fort on Bunce Island (formerly Bance Island) in the Sierra Leone River, these Africans were the ancestors of Gullah/Geechee people. In fact, historical data on the relationship between Englishman Richard Oswald, one of the fort's owners, and Henry Laurens, his American agent in South Carolina, have helped historians to uncover the Gullah/Geechee–Sierra Leone connection. This includes the terms *Gullah* and *Geechee*, now thought to be derivatives of the *Gola* and *Kisi* ethnic groups found in Sierra Leone.[2]

Instead of being taken to mainland areas, these Africans were kept on the Sea Islands, which at that time had no bridges connecting them to the mainland. Contact was only possible by means of a small boat, which Gullah/Geechee people call a "bateau." In fact, the song "Michael, Row the Boat Ashore" is thought to be a Gullah/Geechee creation reflecting this reality. However, the lack of bridges is what created their isolation, allowing them to maintain their African culture. This was strengthened by the fact that their numbers were continually being replenished with more Africans from the rice-growing areas, so deeply was their expertise needed. In fact, it is no exaggeration to say that the entire Southern economy in this area was absolutely dependent upon slave labor.

However, growing rice successfully requires a tropical environment, and with a tropical environment comes the spread of tropical diseases. This is where one of the ironies of history occurs because as the planter slave owners grew richer from their successful rice plantations, they also grew sicker. Brought from a tropical environment, the Africans had some immunity from diseases like malaria and yellow fever, but their slave owners did not, the diseases often proving fatal. As a result, slave owners soon realized that they could not stay on their plantations year round and instead left Black overseers in their absence. Therefore, for extended periods of time, there was an all-Black—and initially all-African—environment, the lack of a White presence further supporting the ability to keep the African cultural elements strong.[3]

With an interest in studying linkages between African and African American culture, I was drawn to the history still prevalent in the Sea Islands. As a faculty member in the Department of Africana Studies at Metropolitan State University of Denver, I began to introduce Gullah/Geechee history and culture into my classes. This introduction included Penn School on St. Helena Island, which opened its doors in 1862 as one of the first schools for newly freed slaves during the Reconstruction era.[4] Following my visit there in the summer of 2004 and a return visit in the following November to experience Heritage Days, a showcase of Gullah/Geechee culture, I wrote a course proposal to take students there. The result was "The Gullah Experience," an upper-level 15-week semester course, first offered in fall 2005. The first 11 weeks of the course provided students with a background in Gullah/Geechee history and culture through text readings, articles, and documentaries. This was followed by a five-day study visit to South Carolina. Today this three-credit course is offered every other year (fall 2007, 2009, 2011, and most recently 2013), and the study visit has now expanded in both time and location with community members from Colorado and beyond becoming active participants in the course.

All the study visits have taken place in November so that we could attend Penn Center Heritage Days, held annually on the second weekend. On-site are Gullah/Geechee artisans sewing cast nets used for fishing, shrimping, and crabbing, as well as weaving sweetgrass baskets made from long grasses and palmetto, which grow along the riverbanks. Food vendors are also in abundance, selling staple Gullah/Geechee dishes, like red rice, shrimp and grits, and Lowcountry boil. All these activities make the culture come alive. However, it is Reverend Joseph Bryant on St. Helena Island who brings the history alive when he takes us to one of the last remaining Praise Houses[5] on the island. It was at Brick Baptist Church on St. Helena Island that the Emancipation Proclamation was first read on January 1, 1863, and Reverend Bryant tells us that the tradition has continued at this Praise House on New Year's Eve at Watch Night services. "This is very important in the Gullah/Geechee community to hear the Emancipation Proclamation read, saying we were no longer slaves. When it's read, you can hear a pin drop" (personal communication, November 13, 2009). As Reverend Bryant takes us through a Watch Night service, he mentions that the only remodeling to the building has been on the roof and that we're sitting on benches once sat upon by slaves.

Reverend Bryant has been critical to the study visits in another way, since he speaks the Gullah language, a language past linguists had seen as solely English based. That perception changed with the publication of *Africanisms in the Gullah Dialect* (1949/2002), written by African American linguist Lorenzo Dow Turner.[6] Unlike his predecessors, Turner had begun his research in the Sea Islands with the premise that there had to be an African influence on the language of Gullah speakers, leading him to study a few languages spoken in West Africa. As a result, his research revealed Gullah as a hybrid language, whose vocabulary was largely English based but whose fundamental structure was based on African languages. The country of Sierra Leone again came to the fore, the language of Krio spoken there sharing startling similarities with Gullah.

Our immersion in the Sea Islands allows Gullah/Geechee culture to become actualized on the study visits, largely through the rich oral tradition permeating the lives of Sea Island residents. I certainly experienced this with my initial visits to South Carolina but soon discovered that I was missing a lot by limiting my focus solely to that state. In 2007, spurred on by the creation of the Gullah/Geechee Heritage Corridor, I expanded the study visit to include sites in Georgia, lengthening our stay from five to seven days. This expansion brought further authenticity to the experience, since we witnessed the continuity of African culture on Sea Islanders in both states. This is also when I felt that college students and community members began to recognize that for Gullah/Geechee people history is not something in the distant past, but rather an ever-present reality in their lives. In Georgia, we experience this vividly when we see a performance of the "Shout."

First noted by outside observers during the Civil War years, the "Shout" consists of practitioners forming a circle, which they move around counterclockwise using a distinctive shuffling step, the purpose of which is to invoke spiritual forces.[7] A religious practice brought from Africa by enslaved people, the "Shout" had always been described to us by Reverend Bryant when we were in St. Helena, but we did not get to actually see it performed until 2009 when we met the McIntosh County Shouters. The practice was thought to have died out until in 1980 it was discovered that it was still being practiced in McIntosh County at a church in Eulonia, Georgia. Led by Lawrence McKiver, the McIntosh County Shouters performed the practice for the first time publicly that year at a Georgia Sea Island Festival and have since been in demand for performances throughout the South and on the East Coast. The performance we see is invigorating with call-and-response singing and intricate clapping, as practitioners move counterclockwise in circular fashion. It is also accompanied by the rhythmic pounding of a stick on the floor, which keeps the beat, and during slavery was a broom handle. The "Shout" is thought to be the oldest known performance practice of African retention surviving in North America, and though the original McIntosh County Shouters are now deceased, their children, grandchildren, and great-grandchildren are keeping the practice going (Rosenbaum, 1988).

When we visit the peninsula of Harris Neck, Georgia, we meet Mary Moran, where another rich experience awaits. As shown in the documentary *The Language You Cry In* (Serrano & Toepke, 1998),[8] Moran still remembers a song she learned from her mother, Amelia Dawley, though she could not understand the words because they were in an African language. Scholars now know that the language was Mende, spoken in Sierra Leone. The students see the documentary before we leave Denver so as to recognize the significance of Mary Moran's centuries-old song. Yet hearing Moran, now in her nineties, sing the song for us takes the understanding to another level: "Actually hearing Mary Moran sing that song is what made me cry" (Melanie M., program participant, 2013).

Moran is significant to our study visit for another reason. During World War II she was part of a group of Geechee landowners who forfeited their lands at the request of the U.S. government so that an airstrip could be built. Though the airstrip was built, it was not used and the land was never returned to the owners after the war as promised. Students have seen a 1983 segment of *Sixty Minutes*, in which Mike Wallace covered this issue, and read a more recent *New York Times* article entitled "Black Landowners Fight to Reclaim Georgia Home" (Dewan, 2010); however, in Harris Neck they hear firsthand accounts from former residents, who witnessed their homes being bulldozed and burned. They have never stopped fighting to get their land back, and their children and grandchildren have now taken up the struggle. We also see the abandoned airstrip, as well as the lands once theirs, which are now part of the Harris Neck Wildlife Preserve.

Land issues are a major reason why much of Gullah/Geechee culture is being lost, and after reading Cornelia Walker Bailey's memoir *God, Dr. Buzzard, and the Bolito Man* (2000), my students are familiar with the land struggles on Sapelo Island; however, during our visit on Sapelo, we meet the author and hear her personal reminiscences of growing up in the Sea Islands. Until the 1950s, five Geechee communities were found on the island; however, between 1950 and 1964 all closed except Hog Hammock, with residents being forced to relocate to this last remaining community, while the rest of the island was sold to the state of Georgia.[9] Similarly, development has taken over other islands, Hilton Head being the most recognizable example. Generally thought of as an island paradise, like Sapelo, it once held only Gullah/Geechee residents. Reverend Bryant had made me aware of Sea Island residents' struggle to hold on to their land on my initial visit with him. In fact, he had put a responsibility on me, saying, "Now that you know we're struggling, what are you going to do to help?" (personal communication, November 14, 2005). I credit him as being the catalyst for the Gullah Experience course and resulting study visits because his question prompted their creation.

The study visits serve to help student and community participants understand the urgency of keeping this culture alive. Continuing interest in the Sea Islands has resulted in land being lost to investors who build fabulous homes and resorts at the expense of the history and heritage of Gullah/Geechee people, a heritage the residents are very deliberate about trying to preserve and protect. When our sojourners hear their stories, they begin to understand why this culture is worth fighting for and often want to help in the ongoing preservation efforts. They also start thinking about history differently, all of which I see reflected in the journals they keep while on the visits, which is a requirement of the course:

> [I] [m]et Cornelia Walker Bailey. She corrected me, saying she is a Geechee, that you switch the term depending if you're in GA (Geechee) or SC (Gullah). She exuded the calm indignation of their situation. I asked what we could do to help. (Yvonne B., program participant, 2009)

> Slavery has been a topic in many classes that I've taken over the years, but somehow it seems more real now. Seeing actual shackles that were used to bind actual people to a life of masters and hard labor, it . . . I guess you could say that it illuminated some uncharted passage in my mind. (Laura K., program participant, 2005)

> The experience of seeing the Penn School and walking paths that the characters in our reading walked made a great impression on me. It is one thing to read about moss hanging in giant [live oak] trees in the night, and then walking amongst them in the cool evening alone. Now the books and articles have come alive for me. (Chokyi K., program participant, 2013)

> The fact that the [First African Baptist] church [in Savannah] was a stop on the Underground Railroad was remarkable. . . . It's one thing to read history but to go to the historical sites is another. (Alycia M., program participant, 2011)

> Final thoughts: It is impossible to grasp all of Gullah/Geechee culture in a single visit. That's what gets Mrs. Bailey worked up when people imply such. . . . I must return . . . I want to know more. I want to do something to help. I can start by incorporating more of the culture into my daily professional practice by including Gullah music in my repertoire and sharing with my students, or anyone who'll listen. (Yvonne B., program participant, 2009)

These reflections come from students; however, community members are similarly impacted. One recent participant said the visit reminded her of things her father had tried to pass on to her: "I just couldn't appreciate what he was saying then. After we got back, I apologized to my father" (Lela S., program participant, 2013).

Ultimately, I have to credit and acknowledge the community members for the success of the program, since their participation has never waned. The Gullah Experience course was first offered off campus, with class sessions being held at Park Hill United Methodist Church. This was in keeping with the university's desire to provide opportunities for interaction between campus and community. As word of the course began to spread throughout the Park Hill neighborhood of Denver, community members started asking if they could sit in on class sessions. The result was that the 2005 study visit comprised college students fulfilling course credits and community members accompanying us out of their own interest. In fact, that first year more community members than students participated, which has continued today. This feature has proven significant, since the larger number of participants has reduced overall individual costs; however, community involvement has also resulted in bringing greater exposure to Gullah/Geechee culture, both on campus and in the larger community.

In 2007, a Gullah Studies Institute event called "The Water Brought Us"[10] was held on campus over a weekend. This outstanding event brought eight Gullah speakers, artisans, and scholars from South Carolina, Georgia, and Virginia. Concurrent to the lectures and presentations, a sweetgrass basket workshop was ongoing, as were showings of Gullah/Geechee documentaries and feature films. In 2012, an exhibit called "The Water Brought Us: Passport to Africa in America" was held in an art space called RedLine, located in a historic Black community in Denver. Taking place over three weekends in September, the exhibit brought some of the same presenters who came for the institute, but in addition brought the McIntosh County Shouters, as well as Gullah visual artist Jonathan Green.[11] Both these events were community-initiated gatherings, and both were a direct result of the Gullah/Geechee study visits.

Being able to sit on the Praise House benches, to see a performance of the "Shout," and to hear Mary Moran's song have been impactful experiences, often transformative ones, for both students and community participants. Being able to witness African retentions in this country firsthand is a truly unique aspect of the program. In fact, I have found that for people coming from Colorado, just the experience of being in the South can be a revelation, since there they are confronted with the reality of the slave experience, as opposed to just written accounts. For example, in Charleston, South Carolina, the Slave Mart Museum is located on the site where slaves used to be auctioned; it also houses exhibits that document the city's role in the domestic slave trade. In Savannah, Georgia, the slave holding pens called "barracoons" still remain, though they now are used to hold parked cars. Just being able to see tangible historical evidence has enhanced the educational experience of students and community participants alike.

As a result, several community sojourners have participated in the study visit multiple times and former college students have returned to have the experience again as community members. This was particularly evident in the 2013 program, the most recent and largest program. For one of the community members, it was her fourth time participating and for three former students a return visit. The study visits have also evolved from South Carolina alone to Georgia and now on to Amelia Island and Jacksonville in Florida, thus covering three states in the Gullah/Geechee Heritage Corridor. The 2013 program was different too in that it included participants from outside Colorado—from New York, Missouri, and California—who heard about the program when Denver community members shared their experiences and reflections with them. This drove home in a significant way the important role community involvement has played in the program's success, involvement that also prompted a filmmaker to document the study visit component of the program.[12]

In recent years, the course has been offered as a hybrid, with meetings on campus once a week and course materials available online. As a result, members of the community have been able to audit the class with access to course materials and to meet with the students on campus. The result has been a bond that extends beyond the study visit to afterward when community members consistently come to campus to support the students presenting their final course projects.

Student enrollment in this upper-level Gullah Experience course has been stimulated by my inclusion of a unit on Gullah/Geechee history and culture in my lower-level Introduction to Africana Studies course. The unit includes a virtual visit of the Sea Islands, and because I teach four to five sections of this course each fall and spring semester, this addition has significantly increased student awareness of this culture and its traditions. Recent acknowledgment of the Lowcountry in popular culture also has an impact. Here I'm thinking of the inclusion of a Gullah float in President Obama's second inaugural parade and the fact that Candice Glover, a Lowcountry native of Beaufort, South Carolina, was declared the 2013 *American Idol* winner. Then too there has been the attention given the film *Twelve Years a Slave*. When we went to the Kingsley Plantation in Florida in 2013, a prominent quote by Solomon Northrup was part of the slave quarters' display, and the fact that he was the enslaved man on whom the acclaimed film is based was not lost on our group.

Following Reverend Bryant's example, I have also placed a responsibility on each student enrolled in the Gullah Experience course. From day one, students know that they will be required to complete a final project that will in some way help to preserve Gullah/Geechee culture. The projects have ranged from research papers and school curricula to interview journals with people met on the study visits. One student created a mini film and another created a Gullah quilt, both reflecting aspects of what they experienced. For some, the impact has gone far beyond the course: one student from 2005 was inspired to relocate from Denver to St. Helena Island in South

Carolina, where she still resides. Another earned a master's degree and is now completing a doctoral degree, both with a Gullah focus. However, whether to students or community participants, the course and study visits have made clear a reality long thought false: enslaved African peoples brought far more with them to the New World than just their labor. Evidence of this abides in Gullah/Geechee culture in the Sea Islands, and witnessing it firsthand has been an invaluable benefit of this domestic study away program.

Notes

1. As a graduate student at the University of Wisconsin, I found the Gullah/Geechee story a hidden piece of American history that still remains largely unknown.
2. Early scholars thought Gullah might be a derivative of Angola and that Geechee might be a reference to the Ogeechee River found in Georgia; however, with more recent scholarship revealing connections with Sierra Leone, it is now felt that *Gola* and *Kisi* may be more plausible origins for the terms.
3. For further reading on Gullah/Geechee history and culture, the following are highly recommended: *The Legacy of Ibo Landing: Gullah Roots of African American Culture* (Goodwine, 1998); *African American Life in the Georgia Lowcountry: The Atlantic World and the Gullah Geechee* (Morgan, 2009); *The Gullah: Rice, Slavery, & the Sierra Leone–American Connection* (Opala, 2000); *Rehearsal for Reconstruction: The Port Royal Experiment* (Rose, 1964); *Shout Because You're Free: The African American Ring Shout Tradition in Coastal Georgia* (Rosenbaum, 1998).
4. In the 1960s, Penn Center (formerly Penn School) was well known by Dr. Martin Luther King Jr., since it was one of the few places he and his followers could meet together in a still-segregated South.
5. Praise Houses were Gullah/Geechee places of worship. Barred from White churches initially, they would gather here for prayer meetings usually held three times a week.
6. Turner is now considered the "Father of Gullah Studies." A book, so subtitled, was written on his life by Margaret Wade-Lewis and published in 2007. A traveling exhibit out of the Smithsonian called "Word, Shout, Song: Lorenzo Dow Turner Connecting Communities Through Language" also features his work. Participants on the 2013 study visit got to see this exhibit when it was featured at the Ritz Theatre and Museum in Jacksonville, Florida.
7. For African peoples, giving praise to God often requires more than a sermon, prayers, scriptures, and so on, since actualization of the "Spirit" or spiritual energies is sought during the worship. For Gullah/Geechee people, the "Shout" seemed to accomplish this, and descriptions I have read of the traditional practice are comparable to Candomble ceremonies I have seen in Brazil, Candomble being an Afro-Atlantic religion first practiced by enslaved Africans there.
8. In the documentary, American anthropologist Joe Opala and ethnomusicologist Cynthia Schmidt take Turner's recording first to Sierra Leone to see if anyone there still remembers the song, and they find a woman named Baindu Jabati who can still sing it. Back in the United States, they discover that Mary Moran can as well, and the two women end up meeting in Sierra Leone, an ancient song uniting the histories of these two women.

9. The last private owner of the island was a man named Richard Reynolds, who began selling the land to Georgia's Department of Natural Resources, which made way for the University of Georgia Marine Institute.

10. The title alludes to a well-known event in Gullah/Geechee history, which occurred on May 15, 1803, when a slave ship arrived on St. Simons Island. While the ship was being unloaded, the Igbos, members of an ethnic group in Nigeria, walked back into the water, chanting in their own language, "The water brought us, the water will take us away." Some versions say that they held themselves under water, committing a mass suicide, others that they walked on water back to Africa.

11. Jonathan Green is probably the most recognizable Gullah artist because he has attained international recognition for his paintings. His subject matter is Gullah culture, and participants on the 2007 study visit had the opportunity to meet him when we were at the Penn Center. We saw him again at the Penn Center in 2013.

12. Filmmaker Erica McCarthy from Athens, Georgia, was amazed to learn of the interest the Denver community had taken in Gullah/Geechee culture. As a result, she came to Denver to interview students taking the Gullah Experience course before the study visit, and then filmed the entire visit until we boarded the flight in Savannah to return to Denver. Her film is now in production.

References

Bailey, C. (2000). *God, Dr. Buzzard, and the Bolito man: A saltwater Geechee talks about life on Sapelo Island, Georgia.* New York, NY: Anchor.

Dewan, S. (2010, July 10). Black landowners fight to reclaim Georgia home. *New York Times,* pp. 1–4.

Goodwine, M. (Ed.). (1998). *The legacy of Ibo landing: Gullah roots of African American culture.* Atlanta, GA: Clarity Press.

Morgan, P. (Ed.). (2009). *African American life in the Georgia Lowcountry: The Atlantic world and the Gullah Geechee.* Athens: University of Georgia press.

Opala, J. (2000). *The Gullah: Rice, slavery, & the Sierra Leone–American connection.* Freetown, Sierra Leone: The United States Information Service.

Rose, W. (1964). *Rehearsal for reconstruction: The Port Royal experiment.* New York, NY: Oxford University Press.

Rosenbaum, A. (1988). *Shout because you're free: The African American ring shout tradition in coastal Georgia.* Athens: University of Georgia Press.

Serrano, A. (Producer), Serrano, A., & Toepke, A. (Directors). (1998) *The language you cry in* [Motion picture]. Sierra Leone, Spain: Inko Producciones

Turner, L. (2002). *Africanisms in the Gullah dialect.* Columbia: University of South Carolina Press. (Original work published 1949).

Wade-Lewis, M. (2007). *Lorenzo Dow Turner: Father of Gullah studies.* Columbia: University of South Carolina Press.

Wallace, M. (1983, February 20). Harris Neck Land Trust. *Sixty Minutes.* New York, NY: CBS.

9

PEDAGOGY INTO PRACTICE

Teaching Environmental Design Through the Native American Sustainable Housing Initiative

Rob Pyatt, Jennifer L. Benning, Nick Tilsen, Charles Jason Tinant, and Leonard Lone Hill

Theory and practice are not only interwoven with one's culture but with the responsibility of shaping the environment, of breaking up social complacency, and challenging the power of the status quo.

—Samuel Mockbee (1998)

Home to the Oglala Sioux Tribe, the Pine Ridge Indian Reservation covers more than 2.8 million acres in southwestern South Dakota, making it the second-largest reservation in the United States. Nationally acknowledged as one of the poorest regions in America, it has few natural resources and almost no industry (Curtis, Henson, & Taylor, 2008). The unemployment rate on Pine Ridge has been reported to be 89% (U.S. Department of the Interior, 2005). Socioeconomic indicators, such as education and health care, and basic resources like electricity, water, and sewer, have all been referred to as inadequate and substandard (U.S. Commission on Civil Rights, 2003). More than 60% of the residents on Pine Ridge live below the poverty line, with a per capita income of $6,000 (U.S. Census

Bureau, 2010). These conditions all contribute to lower life expectancies, extraordinarily high suicide rates, and disproportionate rates of alcohol and drug addictions (U.S. Commission on Civil Rights, 2003).

Affordable housing is a critical need for the Oglala Lakota Nation. According to the Tribal Housing Case Study: Pine Ridge, SD in the Environmental Protection Agency's OAR Tribal Asthma and Housing Update, more than 4,000 new homes are needed to combat homelessness; 59% of the current reservation homes are substandard; 26% of the housing units on Pine Ridge are mobile homes; 33% lack basic water, sewage systems, and electricity; many homes lack adequate insulation and central heating; and at least 60% may have an infestation of mold (Griffin, 2010). Due to the physical shortage of housing and the high Lakota cultural value placed on caring for extended family, overcrowding is common (NAIHC, 2001).

Pine Ridge is also known for its harsh climatic conditions, with summer temperatures that can soar to 120°F and winter temperatures that are known to plummet to −30°F. The negative effects of climate change, including high winds, frequent storms, and an increasing number of tornadoes, pose an extreme risk to families living in substandard homes. In a region characterized by systematic poverty, the high costs of heating and cooling substandard and inadequately insulated houses can cause significant economic stress to families with already low incomes, highlighting the critical need for new homes that are safe, affordable, and energy efficient, as well as adapted to the effects of climate change. However, new home ownership is often out of reach for families on Pine Ridge because "Native Americans also have less access to home ownership resources, due to limited access to credit, land ownership restrictions, geographic isolation, and harsh environmental conditions that make construction difficult and expensive" (U.S. Commission on Civil Rights, 2003, p. x).

In light of these severe conditions, many Oglala Lakota tribal members are seeking new approaches to solving the systematic challenges impacting their communities, as well as actively facilitating the advancement of the Oglala Lakota Nation.

Education as a Catalyst for Change

Recognizing that tribal colleges and universities (TCUs) are a critical resource in Native American communities, with the potential to be a source of lasting technological innovation, the Native American Sustainable Housing Initiative (NASHI) was created by Rob Pyatt in 2010 to address the lack of applied service-learning programs among mainstream universities and TCUs that focused on sustainable, affordable, and culturally appropriate housing design and construction. Pyatt developed the partnerships and community support on Pine Ridge through a series of meetings with Gerald One Feather,[1] a former tribal president, current housing advocate, and member of the Oglala Lakota College Board of Trustees. One Feather facilitated additional meetings with the college administration and faculty from OLC's construction technologies program and math and science department, who had been developing a pre-engineering program with the South Dakota School of Mines & Technology (SDSMT).

These collaborative meetings were held when the Oglala Lakota Nation was undergoing significant change. Beginning in 2010, Thunder Valley Community Development Corporation (CDC) and BNIM Architects coordinated a regional-planning process for the Oglala Lakota Nation on Pine Ridge through the inaugural grant of the Department of Housing and Urban Development's (HUD's) Sustainable Communities Regional Planning Program. This regional plan, called Oyate Omniciye (Oglala Lakota Plan), takes a comprehensive integrated approach to creating a sustainable future for the Pine Ridge community and has been adopted by the Oglala Sioux Tribe as the official regional plan for sustainable development. Similarly, OLC's president Thomas Shortbull had initiated a new program, Oyate Kici Kaya (Building for the People), focused on the college's role in addressing the housing shortage on Pine Ridge as a desperately needed community service.

NASHI participated in this unprecedented planning process in 2011, as an Oyate Omniciye consortium member, directly aligning the development of the NASHI program activities in support of the community's goals for education, sustainable housing, and model community development.

With community support and an advisory board in place, the NASHI service-learning program was launched in spring 2012 as part of the new curriculum in CU-Boulder's program in environmental design (ENVD),[2] and in fall 2012, CU-Boulder, OLC, SDSMT, and Thunder Valley CDC were awarded a Sustainable Construction in Indian Country Initiative[3] grant from HUD's Office of Policy Development and Research (PD&R) to support the sustainable housing research and service-learning partnership on Pine Ridge. This unique public/private partnership has three main shared goals:

1. To address an overwhelming shortage of healthy homes on Pine Ridge, and across Indian land
2. To educate architecture, engineering, and construction students at mainstream universities and tribal colleges in environmental design projects that build their awareness of the societal and cultural aspects related to their respective fields

3. To empower Native American participation in architecture and the science, technology, engineering, and mathematics (STEM) fields

Addressing the Need for Holistic Professional Skills Through Service-Learning

In an increasingly globally connected world, the challenges faced by future designers, whether architects or engineers, are also increasingly complex in nature and are often outside of the boundaries of traditional practice (Fisher, 2006). Holistic design approaches of real-world relevance that stress technical, ecological, economic, social, cultural, aesthetic, and ethical concerns are needed to meet these challenges. Organizations such as the American Institute of Architects (AIA) and the National Academy of Engineering (NAE) have called for educational curricula that not only incorporate technical skills, but also advance professional skills such as awareness of social and cultural implications of their designs; understanding and appreciation of diversity; and skills in project management, collaboration, and effective communication (AIA, 2014; NAE, 2004; Nicol & Pilling, 2000). Accreditation criteria for architecture and engineering degree programs require addressing these types of skills as awareness of these needs has grown. The National Architectural Accrediting Board (NAAB) states that students must understand "the diverse needs, values, behavior norms, physical abilities, and social and spatial patterns that characterize different cultures and individuals" (NAAB, 2014, p. 17). Similarly, for engineering program accreditation, the Accreditation Board for Engineering and Technology (ABET) states that engineers must have "the broad education necessary to understand the impact of engineering solutions in a global, economic, environmental, and societal context" (ABET, 2013, p. 2). However, it is often difficult for faculty to address these needs in conventional classroom or studio courses.

As exemplified by NAAB's and ABET's attention to professionalism and sustainability, both the architecture and engineering professions are increasingly shifting toward holistic, sustainable design and development. Stakeholder participation and attention to culture and social issues are recognized as critical components of sustainable development and management of natural resources (Fischer & Shipman, 2013; Greene, 1987; Guest et al., 2009). Furthermore, it is recognized that diversity in perspectives can help to foster innovation (Cohen & Levinthal, 1990; Greene, 1987).

Agencies such as the National Science Foundation (NSF) have created initiatives that focus on increasing diversity in STEM fields. It has been demonstrated that service-learning projects focused on sustainability have the capacity to increase diversity in STEM by engaging women and underrepresented groups in projects that emphasize these groups' learning goals and values (Oehlberg, Shelby, & Agogino, 2010; Zimmerman & Vanegas, 2007). NASHI seeks to advance the goals of the architecture and engineering professions by increasing the awareness of cultural and social values in mainstream students, while also increasing diversity of practitioners in these professions.

NASHI Pedagogy

Project-based service-learning has been acclaimed by numerous programs as a pedagogical method that is capable of challenging students to develop the skills needed for consideration of social and cultural contexts of their designs. All studies focused on service-learning in design education have concluded that pedagogies that actively engage students in project-based service-learning have shown improvements toward the profession's goals for more holistic problem solvers (Coyle, Jamison, & Sommer, 1997; Hugg & Wurdinger, 2007; Shuman, Besterfield-Sacre, & McGourty, 2013; Tsang, 2007). The NASHI program was developed to address the need for the critical professional skills called for by AIA and NAE, creating opportunities in which students are engaged and challenged to acquire these professional skills.

What is particularly unique about NASHI's approach to design pedagogy is its inclusion of all stakeholders in a participatory design process that supports cross-cultural learning; students are able to learn, while working in a multicultural and multidisciplinary team environment, how culture can and should be acknowledged and incorporated into the design process in order to achieve truly sustainable results. This pedagogical approach encourages the understanding of architecture as both a social art and political act (Dutton, 1991) centering learning at the intersection between academic knowledge, application in the design professions, and the sociocultural context of the Pine Ridge community. There is a clear emphasis placed on learning by doing, encouraging students to explore and reflect on their experiences.

> I am grateful that I was able to be part of the NASHI Praxis Program because I have learned and experienced the power of architecture as a catalyst for change. NASHI helped me understand and apply an integrated approach to design that is often overlooked in traditional architectural education. Through considering social factors and people as a core element in the development of a project along with sustainable materials and methods of construction, I was able to experience architecture and design as an instrument in addressing contemporary real-life challenges. (Fernando A., CU ENVD Student, 2012)

The Native American Sustainable Housing Initiative is a program that connects the fundamentals learned in school to actual life experiences. This program alone has taught me more than I have learned in any previous class. NASHI connects by bringing awareness to the different responsibilities of architecture. Through NASHI, not only did I have the opportunity to learn about the Lakota culture, I was immersed in it! The NASHI Praxis Program is different from other programs in that both parties involved are so passionate about what they are doing. It not only benefits the Lakota people, but the students, interns, and everyone involved. Being a part of this program has been one of the most rewarding experiences I have had, and has been life changing for me. I am so grateful to have worked with such an incredible group of people. (Gina Y., CU ENVD Student, 2012)

Community-Engaged Scholarship

The NASHI program was developed with the intention of having broader benefits to local and professional communities through engaged teaching and scholarship. A critical need was identified on Pine Ridge for safe, affordable, and culturally appropriate housing, and the NASHI program was designed to give faculty, students, and volunteers the opportunity to address this critical need by leveraging university research, education, and outreach activities in support of the community, thereby contributing to the public good. A key objective of the NASHI program is to develop a comprehensive case study to help inform the future housing choices for the Thunder Valley Regenerative Community Development as well as the Oglala Sioux (Lakota) Housing Authority, and to establish an applied research laboratory at Thunder Valley to educate CU, OLC, and SDSMT students in the design and construction of sustainable, affordable, culturally inclusive, and regionally appropriate housing for Pine Ridge.

> Lakota tribal members on Pine Ridge not only face an overall severe lack of housing, but a majority of the homes in existence are substandard, plagued by black mold, are energy inefficient resulting in high heating/cooling costs in our harsh temperature extremes, and are not designed to withstand the high number of occupants living under the same roof, as it is common for extended families to share living space. We are actively working to develop solutions to this problem and believe the NASHI program, with its focus on implementing sustainable and culturally relevant construction methods in our communities, collecting data on the efficiency of the methods employed, and strengthening the skills and knowledge of our youth to continue these efforts in the future, complements and leverages our work and will provide a lasting contribution to our efforts. (Nick Tilsen, Oglala

Lakota Tribal Member, Executive Director of the Thunder Valley Community Development Corp., 2011)

NASHI is showing that it is possible to make a significant difference on tribal lands, and in people's lives, through sustainable design. In meeting basic needs one building at a time NASHI is creating homes that are not only affordable, but also beautiful and inspiring. It's a paradigm for education in service to community; an exercise in understanding, problem solving, and reaching out. Students learn through hands on engagement with nature, place, craft, and restraint. All this while confronting the nearly overwhelming challenges faced every day by the Oglala Lakota at Pine Ridge. What NASHI, its volunteer supporters, and the Oglala Lakota themselves are teaching us . . . is that there is a better more sustainable way to live and build simply, something we seem to have forgotten along the way, and an inspirational lesson for us all to remember. (Robert Harris, FAIA, LEED Fellow, Partner, Lake/Flato Architects, April 9, 2013)

Universities also benefit from programs like NASHI because they create new opportunities for teaching, research, and scholarship, as well as increase campus diversity. The University of Colorado Boulder created the Flagship 2030 Strategic Plan, working from the bold vision of "becoming a leading model of the 'new flagship university of the 21st century' by redefining learning and discovery in a global context and setting new standards in education, research and scholarship, and creative work that will benefit Colorado and the world" (University of Colorado Boulder, 2007, p. 2). The Flagship 2030 core and flagship initiatives include "transforming how we teach, discover, and share knowledge," and "promoting diverse backgrounds, perspectives, and intellectual endeavors" as well as the creation of "a coordinated, targeted, and expanded outreach program" (p. 43) that calls for incorporating "experimental learning programs more broadly into every student's education" (p. 5) and "transcending traditional academic boundaries" (p. 6). The NASHI academic service-learning program seeks to advance the goals outlined in Flagship 2030 by enhancing cultural understanding, supporting underserved populations, and fostering diversity:

The Native American Sustainable Housing Initiative is a program designed to spread confidence and understanding across cultures. NASHI harnesses the power of people and of place to inform design, based on the foundation of improving quality of life. As individuals, we rarely have the opportunity to bridge the gaps between cultures that NASHI so easily overcomes. By finding common goals between people from vastly different communities with complementary skill sets, this group of dedicated, forward looking individuals have sculpted a new way of facing the challenges in each of our worlds. By focusing on the sustainability of our futures, a value we hold in common, we have the capabilities to inform what our futures look like. (Aaron T., CU ENVD Student, 2012)

NASHI powerfully demonstrates the benefits of making knowledge useful and how it becomes consequential. This outreach effort has had a direct and tangible impact on both the Pine Ridge community and the university's academic mission. If NASHI had simply and remotely advised the Pine Ridge community on their housing problems, we could say, "That's nice and that's it." But through this reciprocal, deep and sustained partnership, our faculty and students have obtained valuable insights about environmental design that have shaped their teaching and learning. And now, we can say, "That's outreach informing the university's core mission." (Anne K. Heinz, PhD, Associate Vice Chancellor, Summer Session, Outreach and Engagement, University of Colorado Boulder, 2014)

Empowering a New Generation of Native American Designers

Because NASHI has partnered with OLC and SDSMT, there is also a component of the collaboration that is focused on increasing Native American participation in STEM fields. There is a critical need for increasing the numbers of Native Americans with degrees in architecture, engineering, and related STEM fields. A 2007 study indicated that only 5.7% of the American Indian population on Pine Ridge had obtained a bachelor's degree (U.S. Department of the Interior, 2005). Because NASHI is a collaboration between two mainstream universities and a tribal college, it is uniquely positioned to address this need by empowering Native American students through a learning process that is embedded in the social and environmental context of Pine Ridge. It is specifically this type of collaborative, community-based methodology that has achieved a high degree of success in addressing Native American community issues and interests (Kovach, 2010; Smith, 1999).

How Each Institution Is Incorporating Project-Based Service-Learning Through NASHI

Each year, Rob Pyatt, the NASHI director, coordinates the activities between the faculty from CU-Boulder, OLC, and SDSMT to integrate courses that create real-world opportunities in which the students and faculty can collaborate to address the need for sustainable, affordable, culturally inclusive, and regionally appropriate housing. The process is designed to be iterative, allowing research, education, and outreach to be integrated through five phases of activity:

1. Discovery
2. Synthesis
3. Application
4. Evaluation
5. Sharing

University of Colorado Boulder

For students enrolled in the environmental design degree program at the University of Colorado Boulder, NASHI is part of their sixth-semester curriculum and combines courses in Native American and indigenous studies, architectural design, and sustainability in the spring semester, with a six-credit sustainable construction and cultural immersion course on Pine Ridge during the summer session; ENVD students work with the Oglala Lakota College construction technology students to build sustainable housing.

> During the summer, the hands-on construction experience played an invaluable role in my architectural education. Having the opportunity to work side-by-side with Lakota students, leaders, and community members while gaining an understanding of the construction process proved the highlight of the summer for me. The struggles and challenges we faced along the way, while tough, turned out to be the most interesting and inspiring moments; navigating the complex social, political, and cultural underpinnings of the reservation while trying to successfully initiate a sustainable housing program was an irreplaceable experience. (Katie S., CU ENVD Student, 2012)

Spring Semester

Cultural Studies Course (3 Credits)
Native American & Indigenous Studies: Explores a series of issues including regulations of populations, land and resource holdings, water rights, education, religious freedom, military obligations, the sociopolitical role of men and women, self-governance, housing, and legal standing as these pertain to American Indian life.

Architectural Design (Community Outreach) Studio (6 Credits)
The NASHI Community Outreach Studio offers students a unique opportunity for a project-based approach to architectural education. Students

gain valuable experience working in a multicultural environment with tribal members and community groups. Students are responsible for site analysis, project design, structures, building systems, production of working drawings, material donations, fund-raising, and ultimately construction of a culturally appropriate sustainable and affordable house on the Pine Ridge Indian Reservation. The NASHI Community Outreach Studio emphasizes collaboration, communication, community interaction, and an integrated and holistic approach to design.

Technical Studies Course (3 Credits)
Advanced Materials Workshop: The focus of this course is an exploration of the materials, methods, and craft of construction, including alternative materials and methods, as well as an exploration of the nature of materials as a conceptual framework for the understanding of tectonics in architecture and material culture. Students will expand their knowledge of material properties and assemblies through research, detail drawing, and a series of hands-on construction workshops.

Summer Semester

Architectural Build (Pine Ridge Indian Reservation) (6 Credits)
Sustainable Construction in Indian Country: Construction of a culturally appropriate, sustainable, and affordable house on the Pine Ridge Indian Reservation. Lakota cultural immersion. The NASHI Build Studio emphasizes collaboration, communication, community interaction, and an interdisciplinary approach to construction.

Fall Semester

Student Internship (3 Credits)
Service and research projects include postoccupancy analysis, data monitoring, community outreach, and program support.

Through this curriculum, the NASHI academic service-learning program provides a distinctive "real-world," project-based approach to architectural design education by integrating design theory and practice, sociology, and Native American/Indigenous studies courses with an ongoing design/build community engagement. The program allows students to develop the critical skills needed to address the social and environmental challenges facing numerous local and global communities (Nicol & Pilling, 2000).

This specific combination of collaboration, research, interdisciplinary coursework, and field experience ensures a deeper contextual basis for the housing designs and allows for the opportunity to work on relevant contemporary and innovative solutions to problems affecting the Oglala Lakota community in both the immersive summer design/build studio and ongoing research projects.

Oglala Lakota College

Students enrolled in the construction technology and the pre-engineering programs at OLC have opportunities to work with CU-Boulder and SDSMT students and faculty through all five phases of development. Students participate in the design process, construction, and collection and analysis of data. The NASHI program seeks to engage Native American students in the STEM fields of architecture and engineering with a long-term goal of increasing Native Americans with STEM degrees on Pine Ridge.

OLC construction technology students worked together with CU-Boulder environmental design students during construction of the first of the NASHI research homes, a straw bale house; this collaborative construction effort will continue for the construction of the remaining NASHI homes. Additionally, students and faculty in this program visit CU-Boulder during the spring planning phase of the NASHI project. This allows the development of professional skills for all students, and also directly provides job training for the OLC students in innovative, sustainable construction technologies.

Most recently in the summer of 2014, OLC construction technology students and engineering students from OLC and SDSMT attended a weeklong summer class on renewable energy. In this weeklong training, led by Solar Energy International and organized by CU-Boulder, approximately 19 students and faculty from all institutions learned about the design and installation of grid-tied photovoltaic (PV) energy systems. The team worked together to install 18 solar panels (5 kW) on the roof of the net-zero energy research and demonstration home being built at Thunder Valley.

Additionally, student research projects in support of the NASHI program have included indoor air-quality monitoring, soils and concrete testing, wind resource analysis, and a weather station tower design, and students from both universities also attended the second-phase design charrette, thus gaining experience in a community-based participatory design process. The students involved in these experiences have directly benefited from their service-learning project investigations, and all students have stated that they are more motivated in the pursuit of their architecture, engineering, and construction degrees.

South Dakota School of Mines and Technology

NASHI has been implemented into a junior-level course focused on sustainability and is required for all students in the civil and environmental engineering program. Through the process of reverse engineering, students learn to interpret construction documents and apply calculations to evaluate building energy demands. Student learning is extended to incorporate ideas of stakeholder needs and social and cultural impacts of their designs through community design charrettes, focus groups, and class discussions allowing them to develop their understanding of the professional skills increasingly demanded in the engineering professions. Impact and awareness of these social and cultural needs is effectively communicated through the outreach video produced by NASHI (http://vimeo.com/74495999).

Thunder Valley Community Development Corporation

In 1998 the ancient rite of traditional Lakota Sun Dance was reintroduced in the Thunder Valley community. This celebration of sacrifice, life, and rebirth laid the foundation for change, offering culture, tradition, and a renewed sense of responsibility toward family and community. As this circle of change grew larger with each passing season, more and more individuals and families became involved in creating the energy and passion needed to set a powerful path forward.

The Thunder Valley Community Development Corporation was created in 2007 using this same energy of resiliency and community values. It was nurtured from conversations voiced by youth to elders who realized we honor the best of our past by utilizing new tools, new ideas, and new strategies as we create the opportunities of the future.[4]

Making an Impact on Higher Education

NASHI has had an impact on higher education as it prepares students for the modern demands of practice in architecture, engineering, and related professions as demonstrated by awards from professional societies and university-affiliated associations.[5]

> I truly believe that Project Based Service Learning is the best way to teach architecture and engineering design. I learned more from working as a research and teaching assistant for the NASHI academic service-learning program than in any other class. The NASHI program empowered me as much as the Lakota students and communities, demonstrating through

a real community based project the social, economic, and environmental responsibility of architecture. It was a life changing experience for me. (Janna F., CU ENVD Student, 2011)

I have gained so much experience and knowledge during my time participating in the NASHI Praxis Program. I have been involved with the initiative for over a year now, and in that time I have had the opportunity to learn firsthand about culture, designing for place, community engagement, and construction technologies. NASHI has truly changed my perspective about the capabilities and responsibilities of architecture; and through this experience I have developed skills that I can take with me and apply to any future project. (Keegan R., CU ENVD Student, 2012)

NASHI is an invigorating combination of service-learning academic courses, which provide strong course content and the application of such to community engagement addressing severe Native American housing needs. NASHI has been exemplary in providing all the important ingredients for a program which both provides students with a superior learning experience and helps meet housing needs for the Oglala Lakota Nation and other tribal communities throughout the west. This program is the most outstanding example of design, collaboration, and build during the history of our institute. The high quality and successful planning, development and implementation done in collaboration between CU-Boulder, Oglala Lakota College and the Oglala Lakota Nation is nothing short of amazing—a rare feat considering all the partners, the distances involved and many other factors which had to be addressed. Not only has NASHI been exemplary, but it has also served as a rich and robust scholarship of engagement model for other similar efforts both at our university and other schools, particularly as an interdisciplinary effort. (Peter Simons, Director, Institute for Ethical and Civic Engagement, University of Colorado Boulder)

Notes

1. Gerald One Feather (Oglala Lakota) attended the University of Colorado Boulder in the 1960s, as a graduate student in sociology. In 1970, at age 32, he was elected the president of the Oglala Sioux Tribe, where he worked with many of the CU-Boulder faculty (including Howard Higman, Len Pinto, and Bob Hunter) to establish the Oglala Lakota College on the Pine Ridge Indian Reservation in South Dakota. In later years CU faculty Jim Downton, Paul Wehr, and Liane Pedersen-Gallegos also worked closely with him on various projects. Gerald One Feather supported the establishment of the NASHI program, naming it "Tiwahe Tipi Oaye"—which means "Lakota homes for families forever." Gerald received an honorary doctorate degree from the University of Colorado Boulder during the 2013 spring commencement ceremony.

2. The vision of the ENVD degree program in Boulder is to provide innovative interdisciplinary education to prepare students for practice and advanced study in the design-based

fields of architecture, landscape architecture, and planning, with the knowledge that those professions are in the midst of significant change. ENVD faculty have created curricula to address the new challenges facing design professionals—greater sustainability of buildings and cities, global needs for housing, responsible resource management, and adaptation to the impacts of climate change. Our students are enrolled in studios, lectures, and seminars taught by 30 faculty with outstanding academic and professional expertise in adaptive buildings, urban design, and landscapes that support society's domestic, civic, cultural, and industrial/commercial activities. Students are learning to apply state-of-the-art educational technology including computing tools, digital image databases, fabrication equipment, and media for display and presentation of designs. Their curriculum also draws from Boulder campus scholarship in the sciences, social sciences, and technology fields in order to enable ENVD graduates to develop new standards and materials for "green" buildings; anticipate the environmental, social, and economic impacts of development; and design for energy and water efficiency in buildings and communities.

3. The Sustainable Construction in Indian Country initiative is a congressionally mandated effort of the U.S. HUD Office of Policy Development and Research (PD&R), in partnership with the HUD Office of Native American Programs (ONAP). The initiative seeks to promote and support sustainable construction practices in Native communities, helping tribes to provide their members with healthier, more comfortable, and more resource-efficient homes.

4. Thunder Valley CDC is an Oglala-led, Native American 501(c)3 nonprofit organization based out of the Thunder Valley community of the Porcupine District on the Pine Ridge Indian Reservation. TVCDC's mission is "empowering Lakota youth and families to improve the health, culture, and environment of our communities, through the healing and strengthening of cultural identity" (www.thundervalley.org).

5. Both NASHI and Pyatt have received awards and recognition for this work. NASHI received the 2014 ACSA/AIA Housing Design Education Award, which is granted jointly by the Association of Collegiate Schools of Architecture (ACSA) and the AIA to recognize the importance of good education in housing design to produce architects ready for practice in a wide range of areas and able to be capable leaders and contributors to their communities; Pyatt received the 2014 Scholarship in Action Award from the Campus Compact of the Mountain West (CCMW). This award recognizes a faculty member at a CCMW member institution whose employment of service-learning pedagogy concretely impacts students' comprehension of course material, enhances students' awareness and understanding of current social issues, and addresses a pressing, community-identified need or challenge.

References

Accreditation Board for Engineering and Technology (ABET). (2013). *Accreditation policy and procedure manual (APPM) 2013–2014.* Baltimore, MD: Author

The American Institute of Architects (AIA). (2014). Citizen Architect. Retrieved from http://www.aia.org/advocacy/getinvolved/AIAB051121

Cohen, W. M., & Levinthal, D. A. (1990). Absorptive capacity: A new perspective on learning and innovation. *Administrative Science Quarterly, 35*(1), 128–152.

Coyle, E. J., Jamison, L. H., & Sommer, L. S. (1997). EPICS: A model for integrating service-learning into the engineering curriculum. *Michigan Journal of Community Service Learning, 4*, 81–89.

Curtis, A. E., Henson, E. C., & Taylor, J. B. (2008). *The state of native nations: Condition under U.S. policies of self-determination* (Harvard Project on Indian Economic Development). New York, NY: Oxford University Press.

Dutton, T. (Ed.). (1991). *Voices in architectural education: Cultural politics and pedagogy* (Critical Studies in Education and Culture). New York, NY: Bergin and Harvey.

Fischer, G., & Shipman, F. (2013). Collaborative design rationale and social creativity in cultures of participation. *Creativity and Rationale, 20*, 423–447.

Fisher, T. R. (2006). *In the scheme of things: Alternative thinking on the practice of architecture*. Minneapolis, MN: University of Minnesota Press.

Greene, J. C. (1987). Stakeholder participation in evaluation design: Is it worth the effort? *Evaluation and Program Planning, 10*(4), 379–394.

Griffin, C. (2010). OAR tribal asthma and housing update: And tribal IAQ-learning, sharing, and networking (presentation from the U.S. EPA Indoor Environments Division). Retrieved from http://www.epa.gov/region6/6dra/oejta/tribalaffairs/pdfs/bie_2010/asthma_griffin.pdf

Guest, J. S., Skerlos, S. J., Barnard, J. L., Beck, B., Daigger, G. T., Hilger, H. . . . Love, N. G. (2009). A new planning and design paradigm to achieve sustainable resource recovery from wastewater. *Environmental Science and Technology, 43*(16), 6126–6130.

Hugg, R., & Wurdinger, S. (2007). A practical and progressive pedagogy for project based service learning. *International Journal of Teaching and Learning in Higher Education, 19*(2), 191–204.

Kovach, M. E. (2010). *Indigenous methodologies: Characteristics, conversations, and contexts*. Toronto, Ontario: University of Toronto Press.

Mockbee, S. (1998). The rural studio. In Wigglesworth, S. & Till, J. (Eds.), *The Everyday and Architecture (Architectural Design)* (pp. 7–9). Academy Press.

NAAB (National Architectural Accrediting Board). (2014). *2014 conditions for accreditation*. Washington, DC: Author

NAE (National Academy of Engineering). (2004). *The engineer of 2020: Visions of engineering in the new century*. Washington, DC: The National Academies Press.

NAIHC (National American Indian Housing Council). (2001). *Too few rooms: Residential crowding in Native American communities and Alaska native villages*. Washington, DC: Author.

Nicol, D., & Pilling, S. (2000). *Changing architectural education: Towards a new professionalism*. New York, NY: Spon Press.

Oehlberg, L., Shelby, R., & Agogino, A. (2010). Sustainable product design: Designing for diversity in engineering education. *International Journal of Engineering Education, 26*(2), 489–498.

Shuman, L. J., Besterfield-Sacre, M., McGourty, J. (2013). The ABET "Professional Skills" — Can they be taught? Can they be assessed? *Journal of Engineering Education, 94*(1), 41–55.

Smith, L. (1999). *Decolonizing methodologies: Research and indigenous peoples.* London, UK: Zed Books.

Tsang, E. (Ed.). (2007). *Projects that matter: Concepts and models for service-learning in engineering.* Sterling, VA: Stylus.

University of Colorado Boulder. (2007, October). Flagship 2030 Strategic Plan. www.colorado.edu/flagship2030/

U.S. Census Bureau. (2010). Census 2010. Retrieved from http://www.sdtribalrelations.com/

U.S. Commission on Civil Rights. (2003). *A quiet crisis: Federal funding and unmet need in Indian country.* Retrieved from http://www.usccr.gov/pubs/na0703/na0731.pdf

U.S. Department of the Interior, Bureau of Indian Affairs, Office of Tribal Services. (2005). *2005 American Indian population and labor force report.* Retrieved from www.bia.gov/cs/groups/public/documents/text/idc-001719.pdf

Zimmerman, J. B., & Vanegas, J. (2007). Using sustainability education to enable the increase of diversity in science, engineering and technology-related disciplines. *International Journal of Engineering Education, 23*(2), 242–253.

IO

STUDY USA

Preparing Students to Enter the Most Diverse Workforce in the World

Connie Ledoux Book, J. McMerty, and William Webb

As it is on most college campuses, administration and faculty often follow in the footsteps of our students; and so was the case when Elon University decided to establish its first domestic program, Elon in Los Angeles. In 2007, after several students stopped by the central office in the School of Communications to have a transfer of credit form approved so that they could enroll in an alternate school's summer program in Los Angeles, the decision was made to further investigate the program and report student benefits.

Over the next several months, Elon faculty and staff visited our students in Los Angeles to understand the assets of the program they had enrolled in and, most importantly, asked our students the reasons that compelled them to spend a summer studying and interning in Los Angeles. We also visited several other academic programs present in Los Angeles, such as Ithaca, Emerson College, and the University of Texas at Austin. Additionally, we conducted post–Los Angeles focus groups with the students when they returned to campus to further understand how they were connecting the dots between that summer experience and the curriculum we offered at Elon.

Our fact-finding clearly demonstrated that the Los Angeles experience was providing our students an opportunity to expand their understanding of professional life in Los Angeles within their respective disciplines, primarily television and film. The benefit we also observed was that the U.S.-based experience allowed students to develop a sense of their discipline in a context we could not create on our main campus and in our classrooms—the diverse city of Los Angeles. Unexpectedly, this urban experience was allowing students to unmask Los Angeles and its rich cultural opportunities. Students reported significant interactions around difference, such as with new immigrants to the United States and celebrations of art and culture from diverse origins. Intuitively, we understood these encounters because they mirrored those we worked to develop in our study abroad program.[1] Global citizenship is a mission of the university, and under the university's current strategic plan, one of the first priorities is to ensure our students have 100% access to a global experience.

When we studied those who chose not to study abroad, roughly a quarter of the student body, the most common reasons included that study abroad opportunities were too expensive or did not clearly connect to their career and academic goals. This was particularly true for males and our minority students, and both groups were more likely to be represented among the students seeking permission to transfer credit from the Los Angeles program.

Domestic study seemed a clear alternative to the study abroad experience and, if designed correctly, could help reach some of the same intercultural learning goals we sought through our study abroad program. The question that loomed over the university was whether or not we should invest in developing our own program versus relying on the provisions of other universities with open enrollment programs already based in Los Angeles.

We analyzed the data and learned that with more than a dozen students enrolling, Elon now had enough of a critical potential revenue to hire our own staff and launch an Elon-supported experience in Los Angeles. The value of building our own program versus enrolling in a competing school's program rested on what we believed was the ability to create a learning outcome bridge, one that connected the Los Angeles experience to Elon's general education and communications curriculum with a hard, black line. We also believed that we could provide this high-impact teaching environment at a more affordable cost to our students.

This chapter details the decision to launch the Elon in Los Angeles summer program, the curricular design we used, faculty development opportunities, our attempts to integrate goals in diversity and multiculturalism, and the lessons we have learned, from marketing to legal issues. We will also detail the decisions to add New York City, to open the Study USA office, to expand from summer programs to offer traditional semester programs, and how we are moving forward.

Launching the Elon in Los Angeles Program

In the book *Transforming a College: The Story of a Little-Known College's Strategic Rise to National Distinction,* George Keller (2004) wrote about the nimbleness of Elon as a university that worked to innovate and create a high-impact environment for students. In keeping with that pace, in November 2007 the university decided to move forward with developing our own domestic program to begin six months later in Los Angeles.

A pilot program of 20 students, the wide majority majoring in communications, arrived in Los Angeles in the summer of 2008. Students enrolled in an introductory digital media course that focused on creating messages using entry-level production equipment. Before leaving campus, students worked with career advisers to identify and apply for discipline-connected internships. Each student enrolled in one traditional face-to-face class, which was taught on Monday by an Elon faculty member, and the remainder of the week was dedicated to internships, practicums, and group projects.

Without a classroom facility, the university relied on the common facilities provided by the housing complex to stage class meetings. Without a robust public transportation system in Los Angeles, faculty and students also relied on car rental agencies to navigate travel throughout the city.

During recruiting for the pilot program, the clear driver for student enrollment was professional development opportunities. Students (and their parents) were most interested in where they would intern and how they would secure the internship. From a program-implementation perspective, the internship would in fact be the least challenging piece of the puzzle to establishing a domestic program. Most professional communities in the United States understand the value of internships and were ready partners.

The more challenging pieces of leveraging the domestic experience for learning would be related to creating a meaningful curriculum, integrating learning gains from the domestic experience with the student's campus experience, and moving the mission of global citizenship into the learning outcomes of the program. As we enter into our eighth year of programmatic development, these challenges are the critical ones for the future of domestic study at Elon University and higher education more generally.

Part of the larger question is, When does the "learning" happen for a student in a domestic study away program? John Dewey would argue it happens when they reflect on it (1997). Elon University has significant investment in experiential education and the process of reflecting as a means to leverage student learning and integration of knowledge. The writing exercises in our pilot program, from internship reflections to a weekly blog assignment, demonstrated that students were immersed in experiences that drove creativity and integration of knowledge. But these reflections also demonstrated significant gains in student development and confidence. For example, one student wrote that first summer, "People work differently here. They start the work day later and end later. The environment is more relaxed, but more creative. Perhaps creativity needs this type of environment to flourish. I'm not used to it" (Johnson, T., program participant, 2008). Another student would later write, "I'm practicing my Spanish every day. It amazes me how many cities are in this city. Nothing at all like home in Georgia" (Enurah, N., program participant, 2010).

These articulated gains in student learning, evidenced in reflections and in their subsequent coursework when returning to campus, prompted us to establish another summer program in New York City. With strong undergraduate programs in theater, arts administration, strategic communications, and business, the learning opportunities in New York City were a natural fit with student interests. Additionally, the confidence in running these summer programs led to further development of winter term programs based on place and opportunity for learning, such as in New Orleans to document emergency broadcasting during Hurricane Katrina; Aspen, Colorado, to engage in independent film development at Sundance; and Pikeville, Kentucky, to consider social services in an Appalachia area. Faculty became adept at using the backdrop of domestic experiences to drive context, to drive learning. Other programs exist in civil rights, international policy, and immigration issues.

After four years of running successful summer and winter programs, the faculty began to consider whether the programs should be expanded to a traditional semester, much like our study abroad programs. Doing so would allow students additional time in the selected city and allow deeper engagement in internship and coursework that drew on the assets of the location. In 2012 the university ran a pilot of a semester program in Los Angeles specifically designed for communications majors. One faculty and one staff member led 20 students in the expanded experience, which included four courses, an internship, and a robust calendar of student enrichment. At this time, the university is supplementing the courses our faculty teach by using adjunct faculty with deep entertainment-based education and experience. Additional courses offered in the semester program include media law, marketing entertainment, and art history (drawing on cultural opportunities in Los Angeles). Enrollment has been steady in the Los Angeles semester program, and in 2014 the School of Communications adopted a degree requirement that students seeking a bachelor of fine arts in communications complete a semester or summer in Los Angeles, in effect ensuring a vibrant enrollment for the semester program going forward. In 2014 a parallel pilot semester program in New York City was offered and is being closely monitored for success. If these programs continue to be sought after by students, we hope to offer year-round opportunities in domestic study away.

Two additional important themes in domestic study evolved as faculty and administration worked to develop programs. The process found significant gains not only in student learning, but also in faculty learning. Elon University is located in a rural area of North Carolina. While the drive to a more urban setting is just 20 minutes away, the opportunities presented in Los Angeles and New York City could not be replicated in the Piedmont region of North Carolina.

The faculty providing instruction in our domestic programs were also engaged in their own professional development, leveraging the opportunity to engage in scholarly and professional work made available through the location. For example, a dance faculty member collaborated with a studio in Los Angeles to develop deeper pedagogical skill sets in dancing for the camera. A historian leveraged the New York Public Library archives to assist with a project on the history of one of the world's great advertising companies, Ogilvy. A human service studies faculty member conducted field interviews in Appalachia as part of a qualitative study in persistence in social services.

Additionally, the domestic experience was allowing us the opportunity to interact in new and meaningful ways with our alumni. One of the significant assets of any university is its alumni network. Being on-site in key professional markets like Los Angeles and New York City allowed the university to engage with our alumni and develop them as mentors to currently enrolled students, as well as to provide support to young alumni just arriving to these competitive cities for employment.

Domestic program directors collaborated with our alumni office to host welcoming events, networking opportunities, mentoring programs, and informational interviews with current students. The domestic programs have also allowed for teaching moments to continue with alumni. Faculty and administrators engaged on-site in the domestic programs continue to provide learning opportunities for alumni by inviting them to workshops, panels, and even one-on-one mentoring. They also are able to celebrate the achievements of young alumni by supporting their own professional milestones such as theatrical openings, film screenings, new employment, and launching a start-up. This deepening of alumni relations is especially critical for our university, with more than 70% of its alumni under the age of 40 and with an increasingly national footprint.

The challenges faced during the transition from student to employed graduate during these interactions with young alumni were so apparent, particularly because of the state of the national economy from 2008 through

2013, that the university launched an effort to help bridge the student to effective employment using our domestic programs as the support mechanism. Domestic program staff in career services, already supporting internships on-site, worked to stage recent graduates for employment by offering networking opportunities, interactions with professional organizations, transitional housing, and general support through the job hunt. Called "Bridges," the program sends a message to our graduates that we are here for them on campus and off campus as they transition to professional life.[2]

Evidence of Intercultural Gains

As the gains in domestic learning became increasingly evident, the university sought to establish an office on campus to support the existing programs and to develop a robust schedule of new programming. A new position was approved to direct our Study USA efforts and a decision made to move the operational components of the program to our center for global education. This new Study USA office maintains the support mechanisms for enrollment and program management, but also provides the critical role of enterprising the area for the university. The curricular elements of Study USA, course offerings and internship supervision, continue to be managed by the offering departments and faculty.

Building upon the anecdotal observations by students that demonstrated intercultural gains, a required and guided reflection on diversity in the workplace was added to the syllabus. This reflection asks students to consider the diversity they encountered in their internship from a broad perspective (e.g., race, ethnicity, social class, religion, geography, age) and how these differences impacted the work environment. They are also asked to consider their own personal encounters around these differences. Lastly, because students in Los Angeles and New York are often engaged in content-producing sectors such as film, advertising, and other creative works, students are asked how the diversity in the workplace impacts the output of the work the organization produces.

These reflections offer clear evidence of the urban impact on global-engaged learning we sought in our students' development. For example, one student working at an agency in Los Angeles wrote,

> I recognized my own privilege as a White person attending a private liberal arts university watching my African American boss who attended a public university and shared that he grew up without having much. He works with rich, White people who went to Harvard or Stanford every day. He works harder than anyone I've ever met. I think he wants to prove he can

overcome those odds and make a difference. It's working. (Hamilton, L., program participant, 2014)

Another student working at a record label wrote,

I have been exposed to much more diversity than I encounter at home in Massachusetts. Back at home, I had fallen victim to the popular notion that Caucasians commonly fill the shoes of upper management in big corporations. Now having an experience on West Coast under my belt, I have seen how people of all different beliefs and appearances can thrive in these roles as well. An example of this is how one of the top dogs at my internship is an Asian man with tattoos from head to toe. His hair is shaved on one side of his head, and the other side of hair falls down to his ankles. He is one of the most fascinating people I have ever met and I can see how his demeanor is a difference-maker in the office. The relationships between these wildly different characters in the office are undeniably genuine. (Lowery, M., program participant, 2014)

Beyond these reflections, the university has recently engaged the Global Perspective Inventory (GPI) in a pre- and posttest assessment with students in our Los Angeles and New York City programs. As we build our data set we will learn more, but our initial sample (N = 55) demonstrated some promising gains from the design of our domestic programs. The GPI assesses three dimensions: cognitive, intrapersonal, and interpersonal. While Elon University students participating in summer programs showed at least some gains in each area, the most significant gains were in intrapersonal affect as tested by the GPI. This includes sensitivity to other cultures, acceptance of other cultures, openness to other cultures, and learning from other cultures. Even though a relatively small sample, 50% of participants responding (N = 55), these findings demonstrate the promise and potential of our Study USA program and generally of domestic programs in higher education. In March 2014 we also engaged students taking the National Survey of Student Engagement with the supplemental series of questions focused on study abroad and intercultural gains. From this data set, the university is working to further understand how study abroad learning outcomes and Study USA learning outcomes parallel and differ from each other.

Academic service-learning is another area with robust participation on campus that has demonstrated gains in student development. In recent years we have worked to incorporate this feature into our domestic programs as a way to increase intercultural awareness and to become more fully connected to the city where they are "citizens" for the summer. Service-learning staff from the main campus visited the programs and considered how the summer programs might be able to create these moments. Additionally, site visits to universities in Los Angeles and some of the established community partners working effectively with these universities provided opportunities for Elon students.

Reflections from students during the pilot found that the academic service-learning was providing a new perspective to their experience in the city and about being an active citizen in this community, even though temporary.

> My major takeaway from volunteering at the LA Food Bank was just realizing how many people are impoverished in Los Angeles and who can't afford to simply feed themselves. It's so easy to get caught up in the glamour and sophistication of LA, but there are so many people who are so removed from this and don't even have access to the most basic human needs. (Fox, C., program participant, 2014)

Another wrote,

> This isn't the side of Los Angeles that shows up on the silver screen, but it's the part of L.A. with real people out of work and in need of food. Working at the Food Bank made me feel like I added something to what could be my new home in a couple of years. It also made me more conscious of the food that I use and sometimes discard, and how people are in dire need of that food not less than 5 miles away. (Jacobs, W., program participant, 2014)

Ideally we will be able to create permanent support for service-learning opportunities that run parallel to the students' curricular and professional experiences in Study USA. The early evidence is clear that important learning is staged in these moments.

Goals Going Forward

The university is continuing to invest in the promise of domestic experiences to move students forward in the mission of global citizenship. Our institutional priorities have clearly stated goals to support the development of new opportunities and to create robust experiences that are available to students during the traditional academic year. We believe American higher education is seeing an increase in the disruption of a four-year traditional campus experience. More and more, particularly for universities like Elon that are in rural settings, students, faculty, and staff will desire the capacity to move in and out of the four-year learning cycle engaged in high-impact experiences such as our Study USA program.

This work doesn't come without challenges. The creation of curriculum that allows a student to persist with a four-year graduation rate will be essential. Faculty support for these domestic learning opportunities will be based on the perceived learning gains as students return to their classrooms. Additionally, from a retention of faculty and staff perspective, Study USA offers critical opportunities for members of campus. Creating access and funding for these experiences will be essential to the widespread support and development of engaging Study USA programs.

Elon University is deeply committed to the development of young people as global citizens in the morning of their learning. Our programs across the United States and around the world are evidence of the steadfastness we have to engagement in this arena of student development. Study USA is of high value in the current environment of accountability in higher education for employment upon graduation, four-year graduation, and the promise of a return on the investment in a college degree. The cost of student participation comes at a much lower rate than an international experience. Additionally, it brings significant student development in intercultural skill sets as they prepare to enter the most diverse workforce in the world—the United States. For these reasons, Elon University is committed to continuing to enhance Study USA and promote it as a critical asset for higher education going forward.

Demystifying Los Angeles

When Elon University first conducted student interest meetings about the possibility of an internship-based program in Los Angeles, we asked a lot of questions. First, we asked about the students' current perceptions of LA. The answers were typically clichés or references to popular television shows. For example, in 2008, HBO's *Entourage,* a television show about friends sticking together as they navigate the complicated Hollywood entertainment industry, was a big hit. Second, we asked about the students' career aspirations and how they intended to achieve their goals. Many answered this with big goals and big gaps in a real pathway to their own defined success.

Los Angeles was much like another country to students, existing in fiction and dreams, but not an actual place to make a living, a home, and a lifestyle. The university set out to demystify many aspects of Hollywood as a part of the students' educational and experiential learning. In the 1980s and 1990s we learned about California through the lenses of *Beverly Hills, 90210*; *Three's Company*; and *Baywatch*. Surfing and sun songs by the Beach Boys shed light on the California coast. Bringing students to the streets of Venice and beaches in Malibu, as well as to see the poverty next to gentrified warehouse lofts downtown, brings the city of Los Angeles from simply lines in songs to a more comprehensive and meaningful understanding for the students.

The Elon in Los Angeles experience is anchored by internships that provide the student a gateway to the possibilities of a future professional life. The career path becomes more tangible as students interview supervisors for their academic internship class. The demystifying begins for making a living in Los Angeles as they work 32 hours a week interning while taking a rigorous course load.

Interacting with Elon alumni who have sat in their seats and have entry-level jobs in companies with big and small names opens up this possibility for their own ambitions and a strategic path to realizing those goals.

We have a quote we use in the Elon in LA program borrowed from Oliver Wendell Holmes Jr.: "Man's mind, once stretched by a new idea, never regains its original dimensions" (www.quotery.com/quotes/mans-mind-once-stretched-by-a-new-idea-never-regains/). Students have demystified the idea of working and living in Los Angeles, with approximately 50% of those students who have attended our program returning to make LA their home. Our Los Angeles alumni have grown 200% since we opened our program in 2008.

The Streets of New York City

Developing a deep and meaningful connection to a place can be a transformative opportunity for a student. The ability to immerse oneself in a location extends the classroom experience in ways that are not replicable. As part of the Elon in New York City summer study program, students enroll in a course titled The Streets of New York City, designed to encourage their citizenship in the city. The course utilizes the nuts and bolts of ethnographic research to engage students in an exploration of the rich historical, cultural, political, and economic roots of New York City. This is driven by an assignment over the course of the nine-week experience that requires students to choose an area, a street, or a neighborhood in one of the five boroughs of New York City and study it using introductory ethnographic research techniques.

The Elon in NYC experience begins in North Carolina and ends in North Carolina. Students select the area to research in the city while still on campus, developing initial impressions through media and library materials prior to traveling to the city. Once in NYC they begin the project in earnest with an on-site training session at the New York Public Library archives, immersing themselves fully in their chosen location. The selected area is examined through its history, changing demographics, race and ethnicity, as well as its local economy. Students then spend time observing the people who live and work there, in addition to learning the geography, streets, and often unique architecture, and finally move on to ask questions, such as, Who lives here? What types of businesses prosper here? What is the intercultural and intracultural climate? What is the history of the area and how has it changed? The final deliverable of the project is a case study narrative detailing what they have learned and a presentation to their classmates of the unique assets of the area. Among the areas students select for study are Times Square, Hell's Kitchen, West Greenwich Village, Bryant Park, and Harlem.

A goal of any domestic or international study program is to develop a deep and meaningful connection to a location, and to gain a sense of place beyond that of a tourist simply visiting for the summer. The Streets of New York City class is tailored to this idea. Students leave New York City feeling connected to the location they selected to study. They develop a bond with the area and have a sense of ownership toward it. These are two fundamental assets of citizenship—belonging and allegiance. Students also gain confidence in their ability to conduct field interviews, make observations, and utilize original documents via the library archives. They are not tourists, and they are not casual passersby; they are more like citizens of NYC, becoming part of the areas they have chosen to study.

Notes

1. More than 70% of Elon University students study abroad at some point during their time at the university. Elon University ranks first among master's-level universities in the Open Doors survey (Institute of International Education, 2014) on study-abroad participation.
2. As the economy has rebounded, interest in the program is less robust among our most successful students, but continues to provide important support for students who may not have had their eyes on the outcome of employment upon graduation.

References

Dewey, J. (1997). *Experience and education.* New York, NY: Free Press.

Institute of International Education. (2014). *Institutions by total number of study abroad students, 2012/13.* Open Doors Report on International Educational Exchange. Retrieved from http://www.iie.org/opendoors

Keller, G. (2004). *Transforming a college: The story of a little-known college's strategic rise to national distinction.* Baltimore, MD: Johns Hopkins University Press.

PART THREE

FACULTY-LED SHORT-TERM PROGRAMS

11

FROM IMMERSION WITH FARMERS AND AUTOWORKERS TO REFUGEES AND IMMIGRANTS

40 Years of Transformational Learning

Jeff Thaler

Yet, for the person who is indifferent, his or her neighbor are of no consequence. And, therefore, their lives are meaningless. Their hidden or even visible anguish is of no interest. Indifference reduces the Other to an abstraction.

—Elie Wiesel (1999)

It's a universal law—intolerance is the first sign of an inadequate education. An ill-educated person behaves with arrogant impatience, whereas truly profound education breeds humility.

—A. Solzhenitsyn (1971)

The state of Maine has long been renowned for its rocky coastline, lobsters, and L.L. Bean, and in recent years Portland, Maine's largest city, has become nationally known as a food, music, art, and

166

tourism destination. The state of Maine is not known for its diverse population, however. Over 95% of the state's 1.3 million residents are White. But
behind the art galleries and gastropubs, Portland is more diverse than many
know. For over three decades, the city has been one of the United States'
refugee resettlement centers. Portland's 66,000 residents include immigrants
from over 80 countries speaking more than 60 different languages—people
trying to adjust to a new culture, create a new home, find a new occupa-
tion. The Williams College Resettling Refugees in Maine program occurs
annually during Williams's January Winter Study period. Since 2007 it has
immersed over 40 students in international experiences without going overseas. Students live with immigrant and refugee families in the Portland area
while working as teacher's aides in public schools or as medical apprentices
in community health clinics.

However, the Maine program has a much longer history, inspired by
a transformative yearlong experiential program, directed by political science Professor Robert Gaudino, called Williams-at-Home (WAH).[1] I was
one of the 17 students in the original 1971–1972 program and it changed
my life. That unique program immersed students in the homes and workplaces of Deep South small businesspeople, Appalachian rural poor, Iowa
family farmers, and Detroit autoworkers, and extended over five months.
Professor Gaudino created that program in part because he felt that the
students were not sufficiently challenged by classroom learning and did
not know their own country well. I felt the same was still true many years
later.

Even though today both Williams and America are more diverse than
in the early 1970s, ironically we know less about our neighbors, coworkers,
and communities and are more prone to the easy path of indifference about
what they think or what happens to them. In a twenty-first-century America
where the average person spends almost eight hours per day in front of a
television, computer, or smartphone screen, we know even less about people
who are different from us. It is more important than ever that we push outside of our comfort zone to actively and considerately question, listen to, and
learn from people we do not know and normally would not encounter, and
to confront uncomfortable ideas and situations.

So, while the Williams student body and American populace have
changed greatly in 40 years, the core educational techniques and transformational value of domestic experiential education have not. The model pioneered
by Professor Gaudino and continued today in Maine since 2007—academic
rigor combined with immersion into diverse and uncomfortable cultural
experiences, and ongoing reflection upon those experiences—works. In this
chapter I explain how and why, and ways it can be replicated elsewhere.

Can diverse student bodies and semester-abroad programs alone achieve the Gaudino–Maine results? They cannot. With fewer than 2% of higher education students studying abroad, and over half of those going to Europe, most American students do not immerse themselves in a foreign culture during their higher education. Furthermore, hardly any immerse themselves in the growing number and diversity of "Third World" cultures found "at home" in the United States that would make them directly and personally confront important questions such as, What makes up the American identity and "dream"? Who defines it? How do race, ethnicity, national identity, religion, and/or socioeconomic class impact people and public institutions on a daily basis?

The premise common to both overseas and domestic cross-cultural immersion is uncomfortable learning. While often a subtext in international programs, it is a core tenet of the Williams programs, which are premised on taking students into places they would not normally choose to go, uncomfortable places—geographically, intellectually, emotionally—in order to not only have an uncomfortable immersion experience, but also use it to move through reflection to understanding and empathy. Students must take responsibility for their own learning: to ask questions and, more importantly, learn how to carefully listen to what people think and feel, to find deeper meanings and then apply them to their own lives. Ultimately, the purpose of the Williams programs, both the original and the current iteration, is for students to become more sure of who they are and then more tolerant, confident, empathetic, humble, knowledgeable—and more motivated to learn both in the classroom and from others over a lifetime.

This chapter explores how the Maine program is structured pedagogically and logistically, and demonstrates how it and the original WAH program have contributed to the transformational learning of Williams students and their host families—and can do so elsewhere (Thaler, 2011).

Underlying Pedagogical Goals and Tactics

Williams-at-Home: The Original Semester Program

One WAH goal was for students to look closely at public authority and institutions involving education, health care, and law enforcement, as well as the role and impact of race, class, gender, and age in America. Another was to "see the world in its ambiguities, contrasts, dislocations, paradoxes, confusions, ideals, hypocrisies . . . to prepare students to be both perceptive about and sensitive to meanings in life" (Gaudino, 1971).[2] Gaudino's recurring themes were that silence is suspect, discussion demanded engagement with others, and take every person's opinion seriously. Then, after the experiential segment, students must return to the classroom more motivated to learn, testing and questioning their own grounds of opinion.

In the spring of 1971, after selecting rising sophomores and juniors, Gaudino distributed a 40-book summer reading list covering a variety of topics on American culture and institutions, and required us to write an essay about the meaning of public authority as reflected in our own lives, and how (not what) each of us had learned about public authority up to that point. During the fall semester we took Gaudino's course, Public Authority in America, and participated in field experience with a local public institution (I worked with the police). With invited community members working in the particular public institution, we watched and discussed documentary films by Fred Wiseman such as *High School, Hospital, and Police.*

Then on New Year's Day 1972, we hit the road. In an era before computers and cell phones, logistics were challenging—especially for Gaudino, who drove 10,000 miles to check in on each of us during each placement, and to conduct group discussions. The first placement was six weeks living and working with small business owners in Georgia and Mississippi, paying $5 per day for room and board. Each student kept a journal, picked a particular institution (school, hospital, police) with which to interact, and wrote a reflective paper after each homestay. Gaudino pushed us to be more than houseguests, to question people about their lives, but it was hard. He chastised me for not questioning my host family and employer (the one Black funeral home in town) about what it was like being Black in Waycross, Georgia, how they had been treated, and how racism in the South compared with that in the North.

Conditions during the second placement, a month in Appalachia, were very challenging and led to malaise on my part. Gaudino turned it into a lesson, suggesting my "freedom had shrunk"—from poverty, racism, hunger, rural isolation, and from multiple types and levels of discrimination. The third placement, five weeks on a small Iowa farm, was more comfortable for us but had its own new experiences—like learning how to castrate pigs. During the last placement of six weeks in Detroit, each student lived with an autoworker family and worked a 40-hour week as an autoworker. I worked in a stamping plant, running a huge machine stamping nuts onto a piece of metal over 600 times every hour. On the weekends we met with Chrysler and union executives, while also writing our journals and papers. The program was very time, energy, and emotion intensive.

During the ensuing summer, we wrote a comprehensive paper about our present opinions of public authority and how those had changed; we were also to judge the educational aims and methods of the program, and how it had affected us. This approach was critical to Gaudino's goal of having each of us learn not only about America but also our own education, and to return with a more purposeful, focused vision of ourselves and our opportunities during our time left in college. Indeed, the program inspired me to take the few education courses offered at Williams, and to write my senior thesis on my four years of liberal arts education and learning.[3]

Resettling Refugees and Immigrants in Maine: The Current Winter Program

In the early 2000s, with my own transformational experience continuing to resonate in my life, it dawned on me that students do not have to go abroad to have a powerful international learning experience. Only four hours' drive from Williams, Portland, where I live and teach, has served as a refugee resettlement center for over 30 years. With only 66,000 residents, Portland is home to roughly 13,000 resettled refugees, asylees, and other immigrants. Despite this multicultural influx, Maine is one of the Whitest states, and thus the increasingly diversifying Portland area has proven to be a very accessible site for the twenty-first-century version of a study abroad program within a Williams-at-Home construct.

Preparing students to act in a globally interdependent world; to be more competent in relating to and working with persons different from oneself culturally, socioeconomically, and/or religiously; and to develop increased confidence, tolerance, and humility, all goals stated in some way or another by study abroad programs, can also be achieved through a domestic study away program.

The goals of the Maine program are both similar to and different from those of the original WAH program. With a focus on host family and work placement among people from all over the world trying to adapt to American society, there is more reflection on what it means to be an "American." Front and center is how one deals with generational and other differences while trying to perpetuate one's "old home" country culture and values, and at the same time trying to learn different "new home" values. Each student thus becomes part of a "foreign" culture within the dominant "domestic" culture. There is two-way learning with host families as they too learn about the student's life, culture, and language skills. The Maine program is not a field study anthropological course—it is structured for students to both see and feel forces of resettlement, adaptation, literacy, race, class, and ethnicity in real time but also in context; to bridge the traditional gap of school time with real life, then merge the two during and after the program. As one student said after her return to Williams, "The goal is to meld the personal with the intellectual; to not only observe and take note of others' opinions, but also be aware of your own reactions and prejudices" (Rosenfeld, 2013).

From late September to November, I conduct on-campus information sessions, then find and visit family and work placements to match, as much as possible, student preferences with my own sense of which placements would be the best fit. The range of program participants, mostly sophomores and female, has been vast—Nepal, Tanzania, and the Bronx; first- and later-generation immigrants, African American and Caucasian, and a wide range of majors. In turn students have lived in Portland with host families from Asia, the Middle East, Central and South America, and Central and Eastern Europe, while working with people from all over the world. Each family is paid a per diem amount of money to cover room and board expenses for the student they host.

In preparation for this intensive January course, students receive a list of books on refugee and immigrant resettlement issues written from an individual's perspective. This is followed by materials I compile on refugee, immigrant, cultural, educational, and public health issues, as well as articles and a TEDx talk on experiential education programs like WAH and the Maine project.[4] Texting, e-mailing, and phoning before, during, and after the program make staying in contact with the students vastly easier than collect calls and driving the thousands of miles Professor Gaudino did in the original program.

Upon arrival in Maine around New Year's Day, students submit a five-plus-page reflective essay on how forces such as race, ethnicity, national identity, religion, and socioeconomic class have impacted their lives. Throughout the program they keep a journal and at the end of the month submit it and a closing essay on what has changed or been learned since the opening essay; I then provide detailed comments and questions to encourage further reflection. As Lindsey V. wrote in her 2014 journal, "We are keeping our minds sharp and exercised in a similar manner as someone sitting in a classroom would. Yet we are out of the classroom, still using our intelligence and thoughtfulness and stretching our analytical muscles, learning and soaking up new knowledge that you can't glean from a textbook no matter how many hours you spend highlighting."

Students stay their first night in Maine at my house to meet, discuss what is about to happen, and watch a film called *Rain in a Dry Land* that follows two Somali families from an African refugee camp, onto their flights to America, and then for 18 months as they resettle in Atlanta, Georgia and Springfield, Massachusetts (Makepeace, 2006). During the program I remind students of some of the movie's scenes to compare and contrast with their Portland experiences. The next day I show them where they will be living and working, hold a group lunch, and bring them to their homes.

Two meetings are held weekly during the four-week program, with a two- to three-hour session each Saturday. During these self-assessment sessions, students not only discuss their home and work experiences, but also share any ongoing changes in attitudes, including those toward their previous modes of learning. At the same time students are alerted to ongoing local events that may be of interest involving immigrant issues and arrange sessions where they meet public officials, reporters, or Williams alumni so that they must reflect on and then articulate for others what they have been experiencing and learning. The last Saturday is a "host family potluck," with each family bringing a dish from their home country to share. Work hosts are invited, and thus all the elements of the program are brought together for the program's conclusion.

Without having been familiar with the theory, my goals for and design of the Maine program have mirrored those of "transformative learning," which, while having many definitions, includes individuals changing their frames of reference by critically reflecting on their assumptions, beliefs, and experiences, thereby "experiencing a deep, structural shift in the basic premises of thought, feelings, and actions" (O'Sullivan, Morrell, & O' Connor, 2002, p. xvi). The question is, Have the Maine program participants experienced transformative learning?

Transformative Outcomes

The best way to answer that question is to hear from the students and hosts themselves—first about the host–student dynamic, then about three different sets of learning outcomes.

Host Families

> It is quite easy to say that my host family taught me more than I taught them. There is vulnerability in such an opening up, letting a stranger so far into your life. There was something quite humbling about their willingness to trust and to share despite the limitations of my ability to understand. As they let me further into their lives, I found myself letting them into mine. (Charlotte S., program participant, 2008; Cambodian host family)

> My children learn from the Williams students what it takes to go to college, and how to work to succeed. It has given them friends and guides for life, as well as confidence. (Fatuma H., Somali host mother, 2009–2014)

> With the Nkulu [Congolese] family, Jason Rapaport enjoyed far-ranging conversations about religion, culture, and politics. They exchanged

traditional prayers and shared meals. They introduced him to tilapia and cassava. Rapaport showed them how to make spaghetti and tuna salad sandwiches. . . . "It is really wonderful to have Jason in our home," Alain Nkulu said. "He is an intelligent young man and it is a privilege to have someone from his tribe in our home." (*Press Herald*, 2010)[5]

When I asked Regina why she opened her home to an unknown college student, her answer was twofold. First, she believed that with me living there and understanding how Sudanese people and refugees live, I could become something of an advocate, helping to bridge this community to the wider community, and speak out against the negative stereotypes that people may hold of the Sudanese and refugees, such as how refugees take advantage of the social welfare system or cause crime. Secondly, she believed that young people should have the opportunity to explore and understand the diversity within America, and try to help other people, as she says, "This is not my country. This is our country." (Diane K., program participant, 2014; Sudanese host family)

It is particularly telling that the program is one of the only ways available that gets students out of their comfort zones, and that is life-changing through human connections that are forged through the experiences. I think the essential point of the Gaudino program is in these connections— in the empathy it creates, and the bonds and love that emerge. (Erica L., program participant, 2013, writing 18 months later after graduation; Ethiopian host family)

Increased Awareness of Cultural and Religious Differences and Similarities

It was having a much greater appreciation for the interaction among different cultures and how that plays out. To give a more concrete example, working in the ESL classrooms at the high school, I've had to explain simple parts of grammar that really have no explanation, it's just the way English works. What I'm realizing is that there are certain parts of American society that are very hard to explain as well, just the way things in America tend to work. So actually having to reflect on the aspects of society while being exposed to aspects of other sorts of cultures has been very interesting and has definitely left me maybe not with a lot of answers, but with a lot more questions. (Charlotte S., program participant 2008; Cambodian host family)

This was more powerful than study abroad homestays I have done where you feel more of a visitor in a family whose way of life is different as opposed to being with new Americans where the line is more blurred, a culture within a culture. It is harder to apply abroad experience back here, compared to this program exposure to so many cultures in your own back-yard. (Elly T., program participant, 2009; Somali host family)

I was able to gain incredible insight to [the] beauty of Islam and their devo-tion to it—something I have studied in courses but completely different in this learning setting. I found a new truth in wearing the hijab, going to mosque, having first-hand conversations, and developing the willingness and determination to break down stereotypes. When, one day, I responded to the girls' invitation to wear a hijab myself, for the first time in my life I was looked at as the "other." (Lauren N., program participant, 2013; Somali host family)

I was experiencing three layers of culture. Nepal is in every possible way different from the United States—different in its size, its geography, and the looks of its people, the culture, the beliefs, the religion, the economy, the politics, and the lifestyle. And now, I was living with this Somali Mus-lim refugee family, very different from both Nepali and American families. But rather than creating confusions within me with the fusion of these three cultures, they actually developed to be like one of Silly's milkshakes, a bit unusual in its composition, which however, tastes good when it's ready.[6]

The final milkshake from the amalgamation of three cultures and three belief systems for me was one main idea, that my host mum often echoed, and the one that I believe has been expressed by wise people over the years in various forms—that setting our physical, mental, emotional, social, and cultural differences apart, we at the end are all human beings, and we all have the same basic needs and desires. With this thought in mind, there's no room for harsh judgments, criticism of others or feeling of superior-ity over others. (Pushpanjali G. [from Nepal], program participant, 2013; Somali host family)

Increased Awareness of Self, Identity, and Complexity

I did not come back to Williams with a clearer perspective on refugee resettlement, urban poverty, or racial discrimination. I can only say that I came back with a fuller sense of how complicated social and political issues were: there isn't a theory or a structure that can solve them, let alone represent them in full. In the seminar room, considering the opinions of other students or the perspective of the text suddenly wasn't enough. There were more viewpoints and voices that needed to be heard. I realized that academic arguments couldn't be confined to the classroom but instead needed to spread outside its walls; indeed, this is where they found their life. Learning to listen to other people—across broken accents, fractured histories, and different cultures—became a task with no end. (Charlotte S., program participant, 2008; Cambodian host family)

It seems that one of the overarching goals of this Winter Study has been to provoke self-reflection, to complicate our perceptions of our own identities—in fact, to complicate and challenge our perceptions of how all identities are formed and mediated. I would much rather say that Portland has complicated my life. That is, I think, part of the beauty of this program—afterwards, what you take away from it is completely dependent on self-motivation and self-initiative. (Jenny T., program participant, 2011; Burundian host family)

Several Asian American students, living with refugee hosts, questioned their own identity of what it means to be American; one referenced "Jook-sing," the Cantonese description of a Chinese person living in a Western culture, thus not part of either culture.[7] Yet another concluded, "I thought my hyphenated identity made me less American, but I'm starting to realize that I'm just part of the diversity of the U.S." (Diane K., program participant, 2014; Sudanese host family).

Increased Ability to Ask Questions and Listen Well to Stories

The lessons that I learned in Portland five years ago continue to guide me. Listening to other people's stories has become a way of learning. Each person has his or her own story, each place its own history. (Charlotte S., participant, 2008; Cambodian host family)

Mamo [host father] opened my eyes to some struggles seemingly universal to refugees—questions of returning home, questions of belonging and nationality, questions of assimilation and hard work and not getting what you expected and how to raise a family caught between two cultures.

But I was also pushed to examine questions that I had not necessarily anticipated—questions about public and private schools, teaching and learning methods; questions about my own education and its purpose, about my goals for the future and the kind of life I want to live; questions about religion, race and class and nationality in general, but also about my own approach to these forces. Evenings spent with my host family and their community, days spent at Lincoln Middle School, weekend afternoons spent at the mosque, nights spent reading books about refugees and my classmates' personal essays, and mornings at thought-provoking meetings with Jeff [and] the other Williams students constantly bombarded me with new experiences and ideas to consider. Looking back, I can now see that the moments where I felt most uneasy were often the moments when I learned the most or felt most satisfied after, because they forced me to grow.

I am glad that Jeff [Thaler] put so much of an emphasis on uncomfortable learning and the idea that every person in the world has a story to share and something to teach you. Both conversations with the group and readings about Williams-at-Home helped create a constant awareness of what

I could miss out on if I did not push myself to start that conversation with Mamo or join my host family for Koran school at their mosque. I interpreted the course and readings to mean that in my month of "experiential learning," I needed to not only experience and expose myself to as much as possible, but [also] reflect on it and examine it. Looking back, I am surprised how much this experience pushed me to examine myself rather than just teaching me about refugees and Portland like I had expected. As much as I learned about others and tried to reflect on forces of race, class, and nationality, I also constantly thought about my own life, my strengths and flaws, and my goals for the future. I wasn't expecting how much the uncomfortable learning of experiential education would throw my own values and choices into light and force me to examine them. I'm very glad it did. (Jill G., program participant, 2012; Ethiopian host family)

Conclusion

In a world deluged with numbers, one student summarized well what we increasingly need to know about our neighbors: "Each person in a statistic has a face and family, and only by entering into individual lives can the world change for the better" (Natalie D., program participant 2010; Somali host family). As demonstrated in this chapter, "study at home" programming can have powerful impacts not only upon the host parents and siblings but also upon the students, even changing college and career paths, while also forcing them to wrestle with essential questions of American values, identity, and culture. Immigration is transforming our country; high-impact educational programs like Williams-at-Home and Resettling Refugees in Maine can be developed at other schools as well, in order to transform students' lives to better prepare them for the country and world in which they will work and live, and to be able to better lead others in overcoming indifference and intolerance.[8]

Notes

1. Gaudino explained: "Williams-at-Home, then, is not an innocent or haphazard title. It suggests a contrast. . . . Williams is the place for reflection, putting a distance between self and subject matter in order to objectify reality. Home is the place for direct experience, the expression of the whole self, the reduction of reality to locality. It is with this basic distinction that Williams-at-Home begins. . . . Its purpose is wider personal observation. The aim is to prepare students to be both perceptive about and sensitive to meanings in life, to encourage them to look closely at people and situations."

2. This mirrors George Kuh's "high-impact educational practices" that bring "one's values and beliefs into awareness; . . . develop the ability to take the measure of events and actions, and put them in perspective. As a result, students better understand themselves in relation to others and the larger world" (2008, p. 17).

3. Although Gaudino planned a second WAH program, a medical condition worsened and he died at 49, shortly after our graduation in 1974. The second WAH has still not happened. A group of alumni, working with the college, established the Gaudino Memorial Fund, http://gaudino.williams.edu, so that his educational philosophy and methods might continue to make an impact on the entire campus. I was one of those alumni and served on the fund's board for almost 20 years before deciding there was more work to be done in the field.

4. See, for example, http://bangordailynews.com/2014/01/30/news/portland/eye-opening-program-places-college-students-with-portland-immigrant-families/?ref=search; www.pressherald.com/news/learning-thats-life-changing_2011-01-18.html; www.pressherald.com/archive/a-real-world-education-in-portland_2010-01-14.html; www.pressherald.com/archive/refugee-families-offer-life-lessons_2009-01-21.html; and www.youtube.com/watch?v=2WzWxVA_3o4

5. www.pressherald.com/archive/a-real-world-education-in-portland_2010-01-14.html.

6. Silly's is an eclectic Portland restaurant whose milkshakes contain many diverse and unusual combinations, like peanut butter and bacon, or avocado and limeade. See www.sillys.com/menu/shakes/

7. *Jook-sing* references a container made of bamboo, which is hollow and compartmentalized; thus, water poured in one end does not flow out the other. The metaphor is that jook-sings are not part of either culture. Victoria Sung, http://victoriavickis.wordpress.com/2011/06/28/caught-between-worlds-in-defense-of-the-jook-sing/

8. For example, Colby College recently agreed to develop with the author a program in Portland, Maine, for January 2016 similar to that of the Williams program.

References

Gaudino, R. (1971). *Williams-at-Home Proposal: A study of private and public life in America.* Gaudino papers, Williams College Archives.

Kuh, G. (2008). *High-impact educational practices: What they are, who has access to them, and why they matter* [excerpt]. Washington, DC: AAC&U. Retrieved from http://www.aacu.org/leap/hip.cfm

Makepeace, A. (Producer), & Makepeace, A. (Director). (2006). *Rain in a dry lond* [Motion picture]. United States: PBS.

O'Sullivan, E., Morrell, A., & O'Connor, M. A. (Eds.). (2002). *Expanding the boundaries of transformative learning: Essays on theory and praxis.* New York, NY: Palgrave.

Rosenfeld, S. (2013). Living as learning: The future of experiential education at Williams. Retrieved from http://www.youtube.com/v/q4uzHTyPe3c?version=3&f=playlists&d=AZD1aDIYgwFzhXuSPev0I14O88HsQjpE1a8d1GxQnGDm&app=youtube_gdata

Solzhenitsyn, A. (1971). *August 1914.* New York, NY: Farrar, Straus and Giroux.

Thaler, J. (2011). Immersion in the unfamiliar: An education [TEDxDirigo talk]. Retrieved from http://www.youtube.com/watch?v=2WzWxVA_3o4

Wiesel, E. (1999, April 12). The perils of indifference. Retrieved from http://www.americanrhetoric.com/speeches/ewieselperilsofindifference.html

12

BEYOND WAIKĪKĪ

Discovering the *Aloha* Spirit in Hawai'i

Oumatie Marajh and Esther Onaga

T he commonly held stereotypes and depictions of Hawai'i as a travel destination are often associated with beautiful images of fun, sun, sand, and sea in combination with some aspect of traditional Hawaiian dancing or food. The decision to make Hawai'i a place of study was in some ways "an easy sell." However, what students learn by participating in this study program is much more than exotic scenery and beaches. Academically, Hawai'i is an ideal location for observing and experiencing ethnic and multicultural identities and conflicts. It is a place where traditional Hawaiian culture has played a large role in influencing the "local" people, people who today come from many other parts of the world to live in Hawai'i but are not Hawaiian. Students learn that *aloha* means more than "hi" and "good-bye." From the royal history of the islands and the use of *aina* (land), to how Hawai'i became part of the United States and the consequences of Western influence that came with this, students are given a unique opportunity to observe, learn, discuss, and reflect on the many challenges that face Native Hawaiians.

Michigan State University (MSU) has had a long and successful history with its study away and study abroad programs. Perhaps one of the most innovative has been the Hawai'i program, launched more than 25 years ago in partnership with colleagues from the University of Hawai'i (UH) in Hilo and Mānoa. In the early developmental years the program was housed in the main Study Abroad Office, which administers all MSU programs. As stories go, the rumor has it that at a study abroad fair on campus, some good-natured joking from our visiting Australian partners led them to question the reasons for Hawai'i being placed in a foreign country/study abroad category. The program was then relocated to its current academic home in the College of Social Science. This chapter will focus on telling the story of how and why a successful combination of program design, structure, leadership, and location continues to provide a high-quality immersion and academic experience for numerous students. A phenomenon that is no surprise to professionals in the field, when long-standing programs continue to grow successfully at an institution, it is often attributed to the passion, vision, and dedication of program leaders and their ability to forge partnerships with others that enable this sustainable model. The Hawai'i study program is a true example of such a model.

The partnership between the two universities was based on a common interest and goal to educate about ethnic and cultural differences. Through this partnership, MSU students were afforded the opportunity to learn with the UH students in the classroom and in their service-learning projects. Students were able to access high-quality community settings where the learning goals could be met. While the MSU instructor constructed and was ultimately responsible for the coursework, Native Hawaiian expertise became part of the educational team.[1] A two-island combination permitted the MSU students to begin their journey through a one-week immersion experience on Hawai'i Island (Hilo), the southernmost island in the island chain, followed by four weeks with UH students on Oahu. Thus, students who did not have the local Hawaiian experience (and many of MSU students did not) could be provided with an orientation to "place" before meeting with the UH students. Year to year, MSU faculty and staff would assess what combination of factors might best serve students' learning. As a result the program structure has had several modifications, depending on faculty leadership and availability of local community leaders. The original faculty member who led the program was from criminal justice, teaching in the integrative social science program. The current faculty member is an ecological/community psychologist with a human development and family focus. We anticipate that the faculty leadership and their respective disciplines will continue to be organic and evolving as the program continues to be offered through the College of Social Science.

The Setting

Two of Hawai'i's islands, Hawai'i Island and Oahu, are the settings in which the students engage with their academic and field experiences. Embedded in the program design is a deliberate structure created to provide meaningful encounters with others whose cultural lenses and perspectives are different from what our students would have typically experienced in their own lives. The two-island model emphasizes distinct and unique perspectives, one in a rural setting where Native Hawaiians are more likely to be active practitioners of their culture and another in an urban setting. In Oahu, although the Native practitioners are also identified for the projects aligned with the goals for the students' learning, the context is now in a big city (Honolulu). There are clearly defined differences within each portion of the study program. During the first week, program elements are designed to provide full-scale immersion activities for five days with Native practitioners and field observations of the less populated area of Hawai'i in contrast to Honolulu, the 44th-largest city in the United States. This interaction with community leaders provides the context for an in-depth understanding of important political and social issues that Native Hawaiians face today, including the history of the illegal takeover to become part of the United States and significant other historical benchmarks that have affected the Native Hawaiian people. During this week, students visit homes and families and are invited to visit sacred sites, which include instruction and role modeling about respectful behavior in such settings and full interpretations about the underlying principles and rationale for the rituals. In addition, they engage in several small service projects such as planting coconuts in a lava field or planting *taro*, a revered root vegetable for Native Hawaiians. In the Hawaiian genealogy, *taro* is the original life from which Hawaiians emerged. Through these service activities students learn firsthand about the current issues within the communities, such as diversion of natural rivers to provide water access to hotel development, and the destruction of the fishponds and burial sites. This first week's immersion experience is accompanied by cultural activities that include learning traditional dancing, preparing local food, and observing and participating in traditional customs and rituals that provide the setting for intense academic reflection and discussion of what it means to be "the other" while discovering some of the values associated with their own identities and backgrounds. Students come away from this first week with a solid introduction to and appreciation of the significance and meaning of Hawaiian culture.

By contrast, on Oahu the teaching/learning model is quite different. The course is a joint endeavor with UH and MSU, and cotaught by two professors, in an innovative attempt to support interactions between local and Michigan State students in both the classroom and the service-learning placements. The goal is that each group can contribute and learn from the other. Through interactions with their peers, MSU students are able to continue to extend their exposure to Hawai'i. The service projects include mixed teams (UH and MSU) that travel and work together. Also included are two days of group activities embedded in a community setting (e.g., community planting projects with native species) that provide interesting contrasts to their experiences in Hilo. Living in close proximity to Waikīkī Beach, students are often exposed to both the experience and impact of a high-volume tourist destination with all the services and amenities while working on small service projects in the community.

The Students

For many people Hawai'i represents a dream vacation destination, and undergraduate students are no exception. For many participants, who range from first-year students to seniors and represent different ethnicities, this is their first time visting Hawai'i. Therefore, campus information meetings are specifically designed to introduce students from any major with interests in other cultures and social science credits to details of the Hawai'i Study Away Program—a place-based immersion introduction to Hawai'i and its cultures. Subsequent predeparture sessions continue this introduction and take advantage of program alumni panels. In addition, the program offers some students an internship track component after the one-week Hilo experience, where they are full-time interns at specific sites in Honolulu, based on their academic discipline and professional interests.

The Pedagogy

Service-Learning

Similar to a course taught on campus, students are assigned readings and coursework. However, that is where the similarities end. In this study away program, the majority of learning occurs outside the classroom, where students are immersed in the community and have the opportunity to interact with people with different backgrounds from theirs. The study program is based primarily on the sociocultural learning theory, which assumes that students' social experiences, influence their perception and interpretation of the world (Vygotsky, 1978). Much of the structure of the learning is built upon the work of scholars who laid the foundational principles (Dewey, 1938) and scholars who have defined service-learning (Eyler, 2002) and use Kolb's (1984) learning model. The context in which the learning is embedded requires each student to provide meaningful service as identified by the members of the site. While our primary focus is on Native Hawaiians, students also come into contact with other South Pacific Islanders, local undergrads, and educators, who can represent a multiplicity of cultures. The intent behind this hybrid model of a joint classroom with both MSU and UH students is to provide a space where lively discussion and interpretation can occur based on the out-of-classroom experiences of both groups.

The service-learning opportunities include single-occasion service on Hawai'i, and a four-week span of service on Oahu. For example, single-occasion experiences have included pulling out invasive species on the campus of a Native Hawaiian Charter School. Students learn about the Native Hawaiian value of *malama* (caring for) the *aina* (land) by working with staff and students at the school. Working in the valley at a community garden is another example where students begin to observe customs and practices that illustrate how and why caring for the land is embedded in community practice. In addition, they participate in the Aloha Circle, a circle formed by all who are present, including community members, staff, and visitors, who later form teams to harvest, weed, cut trees, and work in the kitchen. The Aloha Circle, which begins the event, involves staff welcoming everyone to the garden, followed by all members in the circle introducing themselves, saying where they come from, and who they have brought with them to the circle. Much to the surprise of the MSU students, this can be a deceased relative or friend, thus providing a learning opportunity on the importance of ancestors for Native Hawaiians.

On Oahu, the service-learning continues for a total of 15–20 hours for the four weeks. Here the work revolves around two sites, a low-income housing community center to work with children during their summer activities, and a homeless shelter in the city. The community center serves South Pacific Islanders from Pohnpei, Chuuk, and American Samoa. The children share their musical talents and dancing skills, and in turn the students from the Midwest teach dances from the mainland. At the homeless shelter, staff introduce the teams of MSU and UH students to the families and children living in the shelter. Their task is to design recreation and play activities for the children when they return to the shelter. The people living at the shelter are required to leave the shelter in the morning and return around dinnertime each day. Each of these two sites offers students the experience of looking at a variety of cultures coming together and demonstrating the children's and families' resilience in spite of the unique challenges they face as part of their homeless condition. This service-learning is a potent mix of emotional, challenging, and rewarding moments.

Perspective Taking

Using the theory of perspective taking based on the early work of George Mead (n.d.), undergraduates learn not only about "the other" who is different from themselves, but also about their own identity through their service-learning engagements. Program participants bring their own cultural framework with them. They are encouraged to reflect and talk about this throughout the program, imagining not only how another feels but also how they would feel being in the different situations they are experiencing (Batson, Early, & Salvarani, 1997). Many come from Michigan but within this group there is also a good deal of racial, ethnic, and socioeconomic diversity. Thus, students leave with their own truths about cultural differences. White students from Michigan face being a minority group, or a *haole,* for the first time.

Asian American students find themselves surprised to be considered "local" and part of the large group of Asian Americans.

> Coming to Hawaii felt like coming home for the first time in my life. For me, the feeling goes well beyond just looking like a local and eating like a local. Instead, the locals' warmth, acceptance, and absence of most of the racial barriers of the mainland made me feel like less of an outsider, even within my hometown. (Brian S., program participant, 2005)

African Americans are often surprised to learn that Hawai'i had plantations. An important learning outcome of this program is the discovery that place and race do indeed matter. One of the most rewarding outcomes from a program leader's point of view is looking at the range of personal self-reflection and reactions that students are able to articulate once they leave the program.

> Given my level of excitement at this opportunity the first thing I thought of was do I call my elders auntie or uncle and . . . it occurred to me that I was following the traditions I had recently learned about family in Hilo. This was unexpected and surprising. I was grateful for learning what I did from Hilo because it kept me grounded in a way. I respect the land more, meaning I respect my elders, people, plants, and the scenery, also understanding why the people of the land love this island more than a visitor would. I was blessed to be able to experience that opportunity that most visitors would not, but now I would not consider myself as just a visitor. I work and live within the community. I am "hanai." (Charity H., program participant, 2009)

As the participants experience the generosity of the Native practitioners making food for them in an in-ground oven, or *imu,* teaching them music and dance, and talking about the importance of *ohana* (family) in Hawai'i, the "place" becomes so much more than a tourist destination. Students learn about how race plays into the lives of Native Hawaiians and how that has shaped their life experiences. Topics of discussion include meeting with people whose land was illegally taken, the desecration of the land through military practice, and the contemporary use of sacred land that disrespects values of Native practitioners. Students learn from the Native Hawaiians who organized protests against the allocation of sacred burial sites for the development of observatories and a freeway for the purpose of military transport, or the increased acreage of land for explosive testing for purposes related to homeland security. Together these meetings and guest lectures provide students with a perspective about Hawai'i that contrasts with that of the popular culture tourist depiction.

> My life was impacted because I was able to expand my reality. I met a different culture; the Hawaiians' history and their attempt to preserve their culture was something I could never imagine. I thought that Hawaiians were living in paradise 24/7 but it was shocking when I found out they were a minority. They want to keep their culture alive without being tainted by new trends. Now I am even more open-minded then [*sic*] I was before the program. College is about more than academics. It is also about one's growth in society, learning the realities of the world, and the like. I believe that no matter what major a student may be, the Hawaii Study Away program will give them an experience that will enhance personal growth and expand one's perception of culture in the USA. (Parissa B., program participant, 2012)

It is important to understand how critical perspective taking and learning are to the program. In the first week, students are instructed about how to enter a Native Hawaiian practitioner's site, in this case the charter school. The charter school was selected to highlight how an educational entity was structured to embrace Native Hawaiian values such as demonstration of respect to each other; the high value of caring for the *aina*, land; and the importance of Hawaiian language to preserve the survival of Hawaiian culture. Students stand at attention in two lines, males and females, and are chanted into the site by a Native staff person. The students can enter the school grounds only after the staff at the entrance chant to welcome them. This is followed by the *honi*, a greeting involving placing the host's forehead to the student's forehead, holding each other's shoulder, and inhaling the air from the other's breath. Preparing students to have an open mind about learning and sharing in rituals such as this is essential. Sharing food across different ethnicities and cultures is another important activity in which perspectives about food are shared. One of the highlights of this food exchange activity is our Midwestern students' realization that people have different perspectives about food! When the instruction was to bring snack food to class that represented comfort food, the Midwestern students brought apple pies. The American Samoan men, however, cooked large pots of food with coconut milk, commenting, "We don't snack."

Reflection

> The greatest thing I learned while in Hawaii would be the meaning of "ohana" or family. Not only did I make lifelong friends from MSU, I made everlasting relationships with the people I met in Hawaii. I will forever be thankful for this trip and the memories I have made. (Pitone J., program participant, 2013)

Reflection, a critical component of service-learning (Eyler, 2002; Eyler & Giles, 1999; Eyler, Giles, & Schmiede, 1996) is central to the program's learning process. Reflection can take different forms. Program participants keep daily journals with entries that address their understandings and interpretations of the experiences they have each day. Further, reflection takes place in small groups composed of people who work in the same service-learning sites. Each shares his or her perspective and summarizes what is commonly agreed upon and what may have been a unique perspective for an individual student. More recently, students share their reflections using technology to weave music, photographs, and poetry into their presentations.

When instructed to address what they learn from their experiences, not only about "the other," but also about themselves, this reflection serves as a means to assess students' critical thinking. In this way they are challenged to think about why the learning matters, much like the structured reflection of the DEAL model (Molee, Henry, Sessa, & McKinney-Prupis, 2010). The model is based on the practice of critical reflection through description and examination of an experience, and the ability to articulate the learning outcomes associated with the experience. Over the course of the program the reflections become more than an accounting of what happened or a venting of feelings. The students provide presentations that reflect that they have created their knowledge based on their experiences, woven in the information from their readings, and integrated their personal beliefs into their final analysis. Furthermore, the reflections touch upon ethical issues (Leming, 2001), illustrating where students stood in relationship to what transpired historically to Native Hawaiians. The stories students encounter in their field sites challenge what they learned in high school. Many had little to no information about the late nineteenth-century illegal takeover of the Hawaiian Kingdom and the continued desecration of the land for development and military and homeland security use. These become ever more difficult reflections as they learn about the actions of activists and those who believe in Hawaiian sovereignty.

Conclusion

The Hawai'i study program, through the structures enabling collaborations across universities and communities, provides students with a rich context for learning about cultural differences. The UH and MSU students learning together about Native Hawaiians, their history and current economic and social status today, and jointly experiencing service-learning provides for a unique learning opportunity. The diverse perspectives among the UH and MSU students creates a fertile context to address differences. For example, often the UH students offer their knowledge from their ethnic heritage of being Korean, Chinese, Hawaiian, Samoan, Filipino, and "mixed" or multiracial. The MSU students offered their perspectives from their generally Midwestern majority cultural lens and the African American experience. This type of learning structure enables students to counter the criticism of the failure of education that isolates learning from experiences. In keeping with the sociocultural learning theory approach (Vygotsky, 1978), the program provides students with the resources, such as contexts rich in adults interested in the education of students, transportation, preparation to enter cultural settings respectfully, and identification and engagement of meaningful service for their service-learning experiences. Thus, these resources and the program design are intended to maximize the students' strengths in learning about "the other."

Students leave Hawai'i with a new perspective about the people and the state. Although they enjoy the beauty of the place and the opportunities of going to the beach, they now know Hawaiians, through the people they meet, as people with names and stories. The group's perspective about what the experience means to them can be summarized around two themes: the caring people who extended themselves to students; and the exposure to diversity as expressed by ethnicities, socioeconomic groups, and people with privilege and those with less privilege. One can think of a mosaic of learning, each piece representing each student's unique truths about what the experience meant to him or her. Today with social media, students stay connected with each other, with Native Hawaiian practitioners who taught them, and with families they met. They each have found the meaning of *aloha*—not in Waikīkī, but in the people with whom they met, shared stories, and conducted their service-learning projects.

> The people and contacts I made I hope to remain in contact with years down the road. The culture of Hawai'i will always be with me. Our bus driver from Hilo, Auntie Maggie, told each one of us to spread the "ALOHA" spirit wherever we go and that is what I plan to do. Aloha means much more than a simple hello or goodbye. It is a way of life, a way to

spread love and respect, and the positive energy needed to bring harmony. I am extremely grateful for my experience in Hawaiʻi and hope to return! (Bradley P., program participant, 2013)

Note

1. We want to gratefully acknowledge and thank our colleagues in Hawaiʻi for the cooperation and friendship shown to our students and us that enables us to offer this study away program. Paul Neves is a cultural practitioner of the traditional ways of the *Kanaka Maoli*, Native Hawaiian people. He emphasizes *aloha* as a lifestyle within a *hula halau* (school) setting, *ohaha* (family), *alakaʻI* (leadership/discipline), and *lokahi* (unity) as the core of communal expression. He wishes to lay the foundation of *aloha* within the goal of making a difference in the world through the practice of Hawaiian culture and values. Palikapu Dedman is an opponent of geothermal industry and leader of the Pele Defense Fund, whose mission is to preserve and perpetuate Native Hawaiian traditional rights, customs, and practices and to protect the island environment for all of Hawaiʻi to enjoy now and in the future. Keikialoha Kekipi is the cofounder of the educational nonprofit Hoʻoulu Lahui formed in 1994, and Kua O Ka La Public Charter School. He also serves on the Hawaiʻi Burial Council.

References

Batson, C. D., Early, S., & Salvarani, G. (1997). Perspective taking: Imagining how another feels versus imagining how you would feel. *Personality and Social Psychology Bulletin, 23,* 751–758.

Dewey, J. (1938) *Experience and education.* New York, NY: Macmillan

Eyler, J. (2002). Reflection: Linking service and learning—linking students and communities. *Journal of Social Issues, 58,* 517–534.

Eyler, J., & Giles, D. E., Jr. (1999). *Where's the learning in service-learning?* San Francisco, CA: Jossey-Bass.

Eyler, J., Giles, D. E., Jr., & Schmiede, A. (1996). *A practitioner's guide to reflection in service-learning: Student voices and reflections.* San Diego, CA: Learn & Serve America National Service-Learning Clearinghouse.

Kolb, D. (1984). *Experiential learning: Experience as the source of learning and development.* Englewood Cliffs, NJ: Prentice Hall.

Leming, J. S. (2001). Integrating a structured ethical reflection curriculum into high school community services experiences: Impact on students' sociomoral development. *Adolescence, 36,* 33–45.

Mead, G. (n.d.). *Internet Encyclopedia of Philosophy.* Retrieved from www.iep.utm.edu/mead/

Molee, L. M., Henry, M. E., Sessa, V. I., & McKinney-Prupis, E. R. (2010). Assessing learning in service-learning courses through critical reflection. *Journal of Experiential Education, 33,* 239–257.

Vygotsky, L.S. (1978). *Mind and society: The development of higher psychological processes.* Cambridge, MA: Harvard University Press.

13

GO LONG OR GO SHORT, BUT GO

Study Away as Curricular Requirement

Scott Manning and Christina Dinges

The very existence of cross-cultural study away programs in the United States for American college students demonstrates how far we have come from the origins of modern study abroad. What was once a yearlong experience in Europe, shared mostly by an elite class of wealthy female college students, has evolved into outcome-based experiential learning, something many U.S. college students expect to complete as a part of their undergraduate curriculum. This evolution has coincided with the increasing focus on skills development and outcomes assessment in American higher education. We want to know that our graduates possess the skills they need to succeed in the workforce, and to live meaningful and productive lives. While it has long been accepted that traditional study abroad offers cultural enrichment, it has been less clear how it enhances career skills.

At Susquehanna University (SU), in a recent revision of the central curriculum, faculty began by asking these basic questions: What does every Susquehanna graduate need in order to be able to succeed in the workplace? How do we prepare them to obtain it? This led to the development of a set of university learning goals followed by a process to consider the best ways for students to achieve them. Finally, faculty developed individual areas of the central curriculum, each with their own specific, measurable learning goals that tied back to the university learning goals. One of the areas that developed from this conversation was a requirement that every student have a cross-cultural immersion experience off campus—study away—followed by a seminar on campus in which they reflect on their experience and integrate it into their academic and career objectives. It quickly became apparent that there was no reason to assume that such experiential learning could take place only outside U.S. borders as long as students experience immersion in a culture different from their own, in which they would be pushed outside their comfort zone, and with which they could compare and contrast their own cultural background and the assumptions that come with it. The cross-cultural learning goals that grew out of this process now serve as the foundation for every faculty-led program on campus, and the standard by which they are approved by the curriculum committee is the same whether they are traveling to New Orleans or Nepal:

Students complete a cross cultural experience that contains preparatory, experiential, and reflective components that enables them to:

1. demonstrate a complex understanding of culture including the ability to

    A. develop a critical working definition of *culture*
    B. articulate awareness of differences and similarities between their culture of origin and the one in which they are/were immersed
    C. define and recognize *ethnocentrism* and *ethnocentric assumptions*
    D. demonstrate critical awareness of their own cultural values and identity

2. recognize how their attitudes, behaviors, and choices affect the quality of their cross cultural experiences
3. reflect on their personal growth, social responsibility, and the value of active participation in human society (www.susqu.edu/academics/52062 .asp, 2007)

One of the most important factors in this program's success is that we placed the requirement's emphasis on the reflection that takes place *after* students return to campus. The cross-cultural experience essentially became a prerequisite for the requirement, allowing us to build a great deal of flexibility into how students acquire the experience. Some students go on a traditional semester-long study abroad program (GO Long) and attend an academic institution or program overseas; others participate in a short-term faculty-led program (GO Short); and some students complete a self-designed experience doing research, volunteer work, or an internship (GO Your Own Way).[1] The notion of study abroad/study away has evolved at Susquehanna as a result of this program. We have shifted away from a primary emphasis on completing academic work overseas to an emphasis on experiential learning that revolves around cross-cultural interactions. In all cases, the focus of the requirement is the critical reflection on the experience of being immersed in a culture different from one's own.

In order to provide a sufficient number of opportunities for a cross-cultural experience, we knew that we had to prioritize the development of faculty-led programs. About 30% of Susquehanna students were already studying abroad on semester programs. Further, students could already apply all institutional aid to traditional study abroad, so we knew that most students who wanted to pursue this option were probably already doing so. We assumed that most students *not* already choosing to study away would look for options reflected in current trends: shorter programs, more topically focused, more experiential in nature. We also considered other obstacles these students might face that could have prevented them from choosing traditional study away: obstacles such as financial constraints; cultural issues of students in underrepresented groups; academic constraints of completing course requirements; and cocurricular issues such as participation in athletics, student government, and other organizations. Finally, and importantly, we also recognized that some students in our traditional applicant pool might not consider themselves ready to commit to international travel, and we did not want to turn them away. All of this confirmed our belief that it was essential to include domestic study away options—especially short-term options—in the portfolio of programs available.

Now, with three years of data, we know that roughly 15% of our students choose to complete their cross-cultural experience in the United States, either on a faculty-led GO Short program or on a self-designed GO Your Own Way experience. Many of the factors mentioned above figure in their choices. A closer look at some of the details of two such domestic (U.S.) programs will illustrate more fully how they fulfill the SU cross-cultural learning goals in ways similar to an overseas program, and how they help address some of the concerns and choices of current students regarding this unique type of study program.

New Orleans

The GO New Orleans: Culture and Service program was adapted from a program that predated the Susquehanna cross-cultural requirement. Since 2005, three groups of students per year had been going to to New Orleans to work for a week to 10 days in neighborhoods devastated by Hurricane Katrina. When GO was formally adopted, these teams shared how much they had learned about the unique culture of the city while doing post-Katrina service work with locals. We recognized that we could lengthen the existing service program to two weeks (the minimum for GO Short programs) and include a greater focus on culture, enough to fulfill the cross-cultural learning goals.[2] Now, 10 years after Katrina, this is one of the most popular GO programs for several reasons: for example, service work is a strong value for many SU students, some students are concerned about leaving the United States and this seems like a less threatening choice, and it is the least expensive GO program offered. We have also learned that some students may choose it because they see this as an "easy" option, assuming that a program in the United States will be less challenging. Compared to other GO Short programs, we have seen that this program disproportionally attracts male students, athletes, highly cost-conscious students, and students who already work on other civic engagement projects on campus—an interesting mix.

While the service portion of the program helps students to gain leadership, critical thinking, communication, and team-building skills as well as disaster recovery experience, the coursework on campus before students travel sets the stage for so much of the experience to be internalized. Through the experiential and academic component, students deepen their understanding of positive citizenship, civic engagement, and social responsibility as they grapple with the complex societal forces at play both pre- and post-Katrina. The course encourages students to make human connections and allows them to step outside of themselves. The value of civic engagement or active participation in human society is emphasized on-site in New Orleans and in the coursework on campus. Service work is the main marketing tool for this program but, as noted, it evolved to include cultural activities and interactions in and around New Orleans.

As in all of our faculty-led GO Short programs, we find that the design of effective pre-departure coursework is essential to student success in the travel and reflection portions of the program. While most GO Short programs have the same program directors each time, GO New Orleans is offered twice per year, typically by different teams of program directors. Faculty from Environmental Science, History, and Psychology have served recently, along with staff from Cross-Cultural Programs, Public Safety, and the Health Center. A basic syllabus for the GO New Orleans predeparture class has been developed over the years, but each team of program directors may design their own activities and assignments to help students grasp the learning goals. The most recent team presented program learning goal 1A to students by showing them the traditional iceberg model of culture often used in study abroad preparation meetings. Students identify where certain aspects of culture will appear either above or below the visible surface. This leads to a lively discussion about how they will be able to get the most out of their experience in New Orleans. Students are asked to plan how they will move beyond awareness of surface cultural identifiers like food, gestures, literature, and music, in order to explore the deeper cultural values such as the concept of time, the concept of self, and notions of modesty, among others.

Since students may have a greater challenge recognizing cultural differences when on a program in the United States, preparation geared toward identifying them is all the more essential. One of the most popular and effective classroom activities is a game called "Where is this place?/Who are these people?" This exercise not only explores differences but also ethnocentric assumptions (learning goal 1C) they may have about people and places. Students are presented with a series of PowerPoint slides and four to five possible answers to identify each one. One photo shows an African woman dancing, wearing a white dress, and holding a snake. The students are asked where they think this woman is from: Haiti, Louisiana, Hawai'i, or Botswana; they typically vote overwhelmingly for Haiti. After learning the correct answer (Louisiana), a discussion about voodoo and its history in the United States, particularly in New Orleans, follows. Other photographs focus on social class, race, or location. Students learn that they have built-in stereotypes or misconceptions about certain ethnic groups, social classes, or locations in the United States and around the world. Other examples include a slide of a large mosque with choices of Saudi Arabia, Jordan, France, Michigan, and Turkey. It is, in fact, in Dearborn, Michigan. A third slide depicts a gay pride parade with choices of Miami, Istanbul, New York, and Amsterdam. Yes, it's Istanbul. The students are asked to keep an open mind about the location they will be visiting and recognize how their attitudes, behaviors, and choices affect the quality of their cross-cultural experiences (learning goal 2). Similar activities are completed with students who study abroad for a semester. Students in both groups, whether they go for a shorter or longer time, in the United States or overseas, always comment on how eye-opening the exercises are and how surprised they are at some of their answers.

A significant amount of the most recent predeparture class time was devoted to the history of the free people of color in the city, based on the specific interest of one of the program directors. Students were given background on this group's success under the Spanish regime. On-site, students examined related historical and cultural aspects of New Orleans. They visited historic African American neighborhoods such as Treme, and historically Black colleges and universities, meeting with students, staff, and faculty about African American history. Regardless of who directs the program, students journal and reflect on their experience while learning about the city by joining guided tours through a historic cemetery, by speaking with survivors of Hurricane Katrina, by trying Cajun and Creole foods, by visiting a former plantation that owned slaves, and by exploring New Orleans jazz at the famous Preservation Hall. Interspersed with these activities, students spend several days working with a local community organization building houses for those still in need post-Katrina. As part of this service project, students work alongside the new homeowner as well as meet with homeowners of houses built with the help of previous GO New Orleans teams.

When students return to campus in the semester after the program, they reflect on their experience and its impact. They reflect on their definition of *culture* and discuss the cultural aspects unique to New Orleans, influenced by Native Americans, African and Caribbean slaves, French, Spanish, and other groups. Students then use this background information, gained firsthand through their time in the city, to write a series of reflection papers on the cultural, socioeconomic, and governmental factors that contributed to the race/class dynamics exposed in the aftermath of Katrina. Finally, students give presentations on a topic that demonstrates what they have learned. At the end of the most recent course one student created a photo display and analysis of street fashion worn in New Orleans and how it is similar and/or different from what students typically wear on our campus. The discussion included speculation on social norms and cultural origins of some of these fashion choices as well as how they might be seen and interpreted differently by cultural "insiders" and "outsiders." A similar presentation focused on current musical tastes in New Orleans and similarities and differences from those on campus.

Hawai'i

The GO Hawai'i program was designed during a second wave of program development, with the benefit of lessons learned from assessment of the first set of programs. Unlike the New Orleans program, which blended the goals of an existing service program with the cross-cultural learning goals, the Hawai'i program was focused primarily on cross-cultural experience from its inception. As in the development of any new program, every activity and assignment had to answer the same questions: How does this relate to the SU cross-cultural learning goals? Which learning goal specifically? How will progress on that learning goal be measured? The program design benefited from the fact that one of the two program directors is Native Hawaiian, while the other is from the area of Pennsylvania where Susquehanna University is located. Throughout all of their planning and their site visit, they were able to imagine the shifting perspectives of SU students immersed in Hawaiian culture. Importantly, they were also able to benefit from the program director's connections on-site, which opened up access to numerous opportunities for cultural immersion.

Students begin the preparatory course in the semester before they travel with assignments that help them probe their own cultural background, as well as their initial knowledge of Hawai'i and its place in American culture more generally. These assignments are given again after the immersion experience when students are back on campus so that students themselves measure how much their understanding of both Hawaiian and their own (usually American) culture has changed. The program directors have noted that invariably students start with very little self-awareness about their own culture, and too little knowledge about their destination. This also becomes apparent to students themselves when completing their posttravel assessments on these issues. They have learned much more not only about Hawai'i, which is to be expected, but also about their own cultural backgrounds through the dissonance they felt when immersed in Hawaiian culture.

As on most GO programs, the keys to the success of GO Hawai'i lie in the amount of interaction that students have on-site with the community in which they are immersed, and in the degree to which the faculty program directors help them to process their experience while it is happening. The program is on-site in Hawai'i for only two weeks, so the pre-departure coursework is critical for preparing students with a baseline of knowledge and questions they will want to pursue; the activities on-site provide them with the opportunity to test their knowledge and develop it further. In one particular assignment, students (in pairs) seek out local people to talk with and learn from in a few different locations over the course of their travels. They ask questions and often answer many questions, too. As they approach the end of their travels, and after they return to campus, they take the material they have gathered as a resource for understanding Hawaiian culture and prepare a presentation to the group. Frequently, of course, students discover that the various people they encounter have very different perspectives on the same issues, calling into question their assumptions about the uniformity of another culture. They not only have to balance sometimes contradictory feedback, but also occasionally talk with people who are not willing to discuss their culture with outsiders. Their reaction to these experiences can also be a valuable addition to their understanding. The information collected during these interviews eventually becomes part of the final presentation that all GO Hawai'i students give at the end of their reflection course.

In some ways, the U.S.-based GO programs have some advantages in the study of culture that overseas programs do not have. A student going to the Philippines or Italy, for example, may be more keenly aware of being an outsider, which can lead to more objectification of the differences experienced on-site. In fact, a U.S.-based study away experience may at times be more impactful than one overseas simply because students do not expect to learn or experience a different culture within the United States. This tension between cultural similarities and differences in U.S. programs does mean that careful program design is even more critical than on an overseas program. Program directors must find ways both to expose students to cultural differences, and to help students understand and evaluate those differences critically, without ignoring the shared American cultural values.

For example, students on GO Hawai'i experience a cultural setting that is in some ways part of their own American culture, broadly speaking, but with a distinctive local culture that is not at all familiar. In Hawai'i this is often expressed directly in terms of cultural preservation and concerns about cultural assimilation, something many students have not previously considered. On one portion of the Hawai'i program, students work with local people on a traditional fishpond, one that has been at this site for centuries. They do not always understand the significance of this work at first—and sometimes they actually question its value. The pond is not actively used; the fish are not farmed—what is its purpose, they wonder? Its purpose, they discover, is simply to preserve the memory of a cultural practice that, though no longer necessary, remains an important cultural identifier to the local community. Many students later reference this particular activity as crucial to their understanding of cultural difference and its value.

Conclusion

U.S.-based programs have come to be an essential component of the portfolio of options available to students completing the Susquehanna cross-cultural requirement. At most institutions, study abroad/study away is an option; however, individual student circumstances can often present obstacles to study away, whether real or imagined, personal or institutional. While disappointing, there is no particular necessity for the student or the institution to find ways to overcome these obstacles. At Susquehanna this is not the case, and the shift to emphasis on cross-cultural experiential learning, which made it possible to include domestic study away options equal in outcomes to overseas options, has become one of the keys to helping make this possible.

Indeed, one hallmark of Susquehanna's program is its accessibility to every student—removing traditional barriers to study abroad related to ethnicity, gender, disability, academic level, major, or financial ability. Nationally, African American and Hispanic students tend to study abroad at lower rates than others, as do male students and STEM students. At Susquehanna, it is our responsibility to remove the obstacles that could have prevented many of our students from having an experience that every college student should have. We ensure that every student can *and does* GO.

All students with financial need are eligible for institutional aid however they choose to satisfy the cross-cultural experience. As stated previously, students on GO Long programs continue to pay home-school tuition and receive all aid. But Susquehanna also offers grant aid to students on GO Short programs. Based on expected family contribution level, students are awarded a percentage of the total cost of any GO Short program; those with significant need receive grants of 75% or more. In this way, cost can be lessened as the primary determining factor in student choice. At the same time, students with high need who wish to spend the least can pay only 25% of the fee for a domestic program, which is already offered at a lower cost compared to an overseas program.

Grade point average requirements and other academic issues pose obstacles for many students who might otherwise study abroad at other institutions or on third-party programs. As long as students are in good academic standing—with at least a 2.0 GPA—they may apply to a Susquehanna faculty-led GO program. Alternatively, GO Your Own Way allows students to have a cross-cultural experience that is not for credit and carries no such limiting requirements.[3] Students with other academic and personal issues, such as limited language ability or anxiety issues that cause them to fear being far from home, can find quality program options within the United States. Susquehanna believes that limiting study abroad to the students who are already the most engaged in their studies is the wrong approach. If we believe that study away is a transformative experience, shouldn't we focus our efforts on transforming those who need it most?

The presence of U.S-based study away options in the Susquehanna Global Opportunities requirement grew out of an effective process focused on student learning outcomes. But it has had practical advantages for the institution as well. It offers admissions recruiters a greater range of options to draw on when discussing this unique requirement with students. It also helps to bridge the artificial divide found at some institutions between U.S. diversity and internationalization efforts. In fact, the adoption of the GO requirement and the inclusion of the U.S.-based programs in the program portfolio, have coincided with a surge in student applicants from diverse backgrounds at Susquehanna, as well as a surge in international applicants. While we have no data available to provide concrete evidence of direct causality, we are obviously very pleased with this trend, and we do believe that the existence of this program has helped many prospective students and their parents to see that Susquehanna is a place where difference and an experientially based understanding of difference is central to the mission of the institution.

Notes

1. For more details on the Susquehanna Global Opportunities (GO) program see www.susqu .edu/academics/studyaway.asp
2. The post-Katrina recovery in New Orleans remains a work in progress. Media attention moved on long ago, but many years of sustained work are needed to help those who wish to rebuild and recover from the storm. While the Susquehanna program continues this work, it has expanded to include a focus on the culture of New Orleans, before and after Katrina.
3. Recent examples of GO Your Own Way: A student of European descent arranged a homestay with a first-generation Puerto Rican family in Allentown, Pennsylvania, while she completed an internship at a neighborhood theater. Another student volunteered at a Somali refugee camp in New England and had a homestay with a Somali immigrant family who had settled in the area several years ago. Two students recently volunteered on the Navajo nation, an experience arranged through a local service provider.

14

"IT'S SO GOOD TO SEE YOU
BACK IN TOWN"

Participating in Makah Culture

David R. Huelsbeck

The Makah are a Native American tribe. They occupy the area around Cape Flattery on the northwest corner of Washington State. About 1,500 Makah live on the reservation, which is a very small portion of their traditional territory. Makah language and culture is most closely related to the Nuu-chah-nulth to the north on Vancouver Island (Renker & Gunther, 1990).

At first glance Neah Bay looks like most coastal communities on the Olympic Peninsula. Looking closer you will notice traditional Makah art displayed on many buildings. The Makah have hunted whales for thousands of years and their attempts to revive this treaty right make the news often enough that students anticipate trying to understand this aspect of Makah culture (Bowechop, 2010; Brown, 2007), but many are surprised at the quantity of seafood, game, and gathered plants that are regularly consumed (Sepez, 2008). When you spend time in the community, you learn that traditional songs and dances are performed and passed on and that distinctive cultural values like the importance of family and respect for elders are very strongly held. "The Makah, both past and present, have demonstrated their ability to adapt, survive and flourish" (Peterson & the MCRC, 2002, p. 151).

The Course

Pacific Lutheran University (PLU) has a 4-1-4 calendar. The First Year Experience program includes an Inquiry Seminar. The seminar is supposed to introduce students to a discipline, help them practice the skills at the heart of general education, and, in January, introduce students to what it means to be part of an academic learning community. Completing a four-semester credit course in four weeks requires spending a great deal of time together, adding a study away component, and developing a sense of community.

The Makah Reservation is less than 200 miles from PLU's campus, and the Makah are experienced and skillful educators, communicating Makah culture to non-Makah (Bowechop & Erickson, 2005; Erickson, Ward, & Wachendorf, 2002). As I am an anthropological archaeologist who has worked with the tribe since graduate school, a short-term introduction to anthropology course that included spending time on the reservation seemed like a good idea.

Most introductions to cultural anthropology draw examples from cultures around the world; substituting all examples from Makah culture was fairly straightforward. Like all communities, there is no one Makah belief or perspective about anything; there is variation. To help students prepare to perceive variation, I intentionally recruit as diverse a group of students as possible, including first-, second-, third-, and fourth-year students from across campus. The more experienced students act as role models in a learning community, but how can we create the "safe space" in the classroom for first years? Another challenge, particularly important when studying a different culture, is learning to recognize authority. In the classroom, authority is obvious; it is at the front of the room. In another culture, it can be difficult for an outsider to recognize authority. A core principle of the course is that everyone has "voice" (the cumulative experiences that create the perspective from which they are speaking) and everyone has "authority" (the experience and knowledge that makes the speaker worth listening to). Students begin practicing identifying the voice and authority of their fellow classmates in the classroom on campus. This creates a safe space in the classroom for students to learn from each other and prepares them to learn from members of the Makah community. The classic example of how well this can work involves two first-year male students who had never taken an anthropology course and a senior female anthropology major. The male students were very quiet until we took up hunting and fishing treaty rights. They hunted and fished; the anthropology major did not.

The course involves about 20 hours of class meetings on campus to present a quick introduction to anthropology and to the academic literature on Makah culture. Whenever possible, connections to contemporary life in Neah Bay (the main community on the reservation) are highlighted. The staff of the Makah Cultural and Research Center (MCRC) in Neah Bay organizes the 12 days of activities on the reservation and then we meet on campus for the last two or three days of the term.

History of Development

With a small planning grant from PLU, four anthropology faculty traveled to Neah Bay to work with MCRC staff and provided the staff with a modest honorarium. We developed a course proposal much like the course outlined previously. The proposal included an applied anthropology research project that would focus on the Ozette collection and a cultural question in alternate years. The proposal was reviewed and approved by the MCRC board.

The on-campus portion of the first offering went well. When we arrived in Neah Bay, we learned that the person who was supposed to organize our program was not in town. Fortunately, a member of the MCRC board (a personal friend) called in favors around the community and scheduled activities. It was immediately obvious that doing any kind of research was out of the question (and would have been out of the question under the best of circumstances). We filled that block of time by helping MCRC staff move Ozette artifacts from the old storage facility into the new storage facility. We discovered service! There was a death in the village while we were there. The Makah cancel celebrations and "fun" activities out of respect for the grieving family. So the traditional dance practice session we were going to attend was canceled, but MCRC staff spent the evening explaining customs surrounding death to our class. At the end of the term, the student papers describing what they had learned were so good that I sent copies back to Neah Bay to share with the people who had worked with us.

The second time the course was offered, the Neah Bay schedule was organized by my friend, but we had the schedule ahead of time and brought along presents for those who interacted with us. In the third year the Neah Bay part of the program was organized by MCRC staff and we had honoraria for some of the people who worked with us. Service was still opportunistic, not planned. In the fourth year, we arrived at the model we've used ever since. The MCRC organizes the activities in Neah Bay and receives compensation for the time and effort. Community members who share their time and expertise are also compensated; we give each of them a certificate of thanks and a gift, and service is a regular part of the program. January of 2014 was the 18th time the course was offered in 20 years.

Collaboration, Authority, and Respect

The "content" goal of the course is to see traditional Makah culture in contemporary Makah life. I organize the on-campus portion of the course with input from the MCRC staff, and the MCRC staff organize the off-campus portion of the course with feedback from me on how well different activities have worked. Members of the tribe decide what about their culture to present or share with the students, and they decide who in their community will do the sharing.

Each year the specific activities we engage in vary, but most fall into three general categories. The first category is traditional practices that are still being practiced. The "bone game," sometimes called *slahal,* is a game that has been played since before Euro-American contact and is still enjoyed today. Makah stories still contain important lessons about proper behavior. Sometimes we are invited to "party"; a potlatch where people are fed, speeches are made, and presents are distributed. The Makah have a very active language program to support the revival of the Makah language. A variety of arts continue to be practiced. Baskets are woven and given as presents and are sold to support the artist. Carvers make masks for ceremonies and pieces for sale like model canoes. Painters illustrate drums and other cultural implements and sell limited edition prints. The cedar canoe is being reinvented: logs of the size and quality needed for a big dugout are rare, so strips of cedar are glued together to create a canoe with the features of the traditional design. Learning how to do some of these activities is fun. And of course, eating traditional foods is a real treat.

> Cultural importance can also be seen in local wood working, beading, weaving and other projects. Despite the fact that the methods themselves may have changed slightly or drastically through time, the significance of the object has not changed. Although drums may (or may not) be made differently than 300 years ago, they still serve as important components in ceremonies that include singing and dancing. . . . In fact, the act of cultural material production in itself helps to connect community members back to ancestral practices and creates a shared historical as well as contemporary experience for all community members that share in artists' endeavors. (Brittany P., program participant, 2014)

Another thing I noticed was how at every home we visited we were offered some sort of food or snack. It was very thoughtful of our hosts to provide

us with food even though there were so many of us and I was very apprecia-
tive. (Katy L. D., program participant, 2014)

Those activities are balanced by the second category, an exploration of
contemporary Makah life where traditional values remain central. Cultural
values are at the heart of the MCRC's collection management philosophy.
The operations of tribal government, the tribal court, and the regulation of
hunting and fishing all embody Makah values in very contemporary activities. The number of Makah who willingly serve in the U.S. armed services
and why they serve often surprises students.

The third general category is outdoors. Short and long hikes through
forest and tide pools include pointing out resources used for food and as raw
materials for making things. Trying to work as a team to propel a traditional-
style 40-foot-long cedar canoe introduces the important means of transportation (and makes it abundantly clear why they call it "pulling," not "paddling").

The schedule is put together with the goal of exposing the students to
different authorities in the community. There always is an activity where
students meet elders, usually lunch at the senior center. Some years a panel of
elders has answered student questions about the community.

> One extremely important value that I witnessed among the Makah was the
> importance and place of family in the culture. Family really is everything to
> the Makah and it was wonderful to see how tight-knit the families were in
> Neah Bay. . . . Where they come from and what family they belong to is a
> vital component of who the Makah are. . . . This was clearly demonstrated
> when the elder panel talked at length about their family histories and sto-
> ries about their ancestors when they were asked to say a little bit about
> themselves. (Christian W., program participant, 2012)

Whale hunting is a very important cultural practice, a treaty right of the
Makah, and a subject that frequently comes up in a variety of contexts. In
addition, we often meet with the president of the Makah Whaling Commission, a commissioner representing another family, and a member of the crew
from the successful hunt in 1999.

> Common perception is that Native American treaty rights are special
> rights. In actuality these treaties do not give rights, they take rights away.
> The Makah Treaty of 1855 is a living piece of law. It has been the means
> to secure fishing and whaling for the Makah. . . . The Makah can act as a
> sovereign government. . . . By participating in Tribal to state and federal
> political processes, representatives can improve and express their tribe's
> claims and relationship to the ocean. (Hannah H., program participant,
> 2010)

Students talk with a longtime hunter and fisherman, with a member of the tribe who has a degree in wildlife biology, a biologist working for the tribe who isn't a member of the tribe, and a commercial fisherman. We meet with successful artists who have an established reputation, artists who are just getting started, and high school students in a cultural arts class. The individuals have their own authority, which the students recognize and respect.

> It took me a while in Neah Bay to really appreciate how multi-faceted the experience we got was. At first, I wasn't sure why we were hearing so many people's stories about their lives. . . . I realized that everyone's stories were different, and everyone's views on the Makah were different. We were told to expect differing opinions, but I was expecting more outright statements to be contrary, almost like the research papers we read in class. I was surprised at the nuances that came through when talking to people. (Jacquelyn J., program participant, 2009)

Service, Trust, and Participation

Every textbook will tell you that participant observation is the primary field method of cultural anthropology. However, what can an undergraduate, new to anthropology and new to Makah culture, actually participate in? Service has been the key that opened that door for this class. (Also see chapter 15 in this volume.)

Service placements are a formally scheduled part of the 12 days we are in Neah Bay; weekday mornings of the complete week in the middle of our visit we do all kinds of service projects. Sometimes it is just helping with a backlog of filing in a tribal department. The archives always needs documents digitized. One year, students helped museum staff refresh displays. Three or four students volunteer at Head Start. The "Lend a Hand" placement helps members of the community with yard work or other chores. Recently we helped MCRC staff reorganize one of their storage facilities, moving hundreds of archive boxes of materials and reboxing dozens more. None of these service activities are very complicated—there isn't enough time in the four or five half days to train us. However, we accomplish things that need to be done, that might not get done, or that certainly would take much longer without our assistance.

These service activities accomplish two things: students have an opportunity to meet and interact with individuals in the community outside of the structured program, and we are recognizing the value of everything members of the community do for us during our stay. The program gives us a chance to interact closely with about 30 members of the community. The service placements double our contacts in the community. This effect is multiplied because the "word" gets around.

We frequently hear a member of the community say, "PLU doesn't just come to Neah Bay to take [to learn from us]; they come to give too." In this context "taking" isn't a bad thing; the Makah are very proud of their culture, they are eager to share who they are with outsiders, and they are very skilled at doing it. But it usually is a one-way transaction. Giving back to the community helps build a trust relationship.

Another important factor building the trust relationship is the length of time we've been doing the course. My relationship with the tribe goes back 40 years; the PLU student relationship with the tribe goes back 20 years. One of the first things we do when we arrive in the village is to go to the grocery store to stock the refrigerators of the cabins where we are staying. After about year 12 or so, it became common for people in the store to greet students who had never been within hundreds of miles of the community by saying, "It's so good to see you back in town." The community "knows" PLU students, and members of the community open up to the students in ways that wouldn't otherwise happen in such a short visit. One of the reasons that cultural anthropologists regularly invest a year or more in fieldwork is that it takes time to establish trust and the relationships necessary to be able to participate.

A significant cultural event in the Makah community is a funeral. A member of the community has passed, maybe a family member or a friend, but for almost everyone in this community, it was someone they knew. The community gathers to help the grieving family heal. There will be a funeral service and a dinner. After the dinner, acquaintances, friends, and community members will offer words of comfort to the family. Frequently invoking cultural values, they are part prayer, part sympathy, part celebration of life; they illustrate and demonstrate the community that is Makah. Then the family talks, about their loss, the rich life they shared, and how grateful they are to everyone in attendance.

The funeral service and dinner are regularly attended by more than 300 people. There is a cook who, with her family, is skilled at organizing the contributed cakes, pies, and other dishes and in preparing the main dishes of the meal. The family is responsible for organizing the event; setting up hundreds of chairs in the hall for the service, rearranging the chairs and setting up tables, setting the tables, serving the food, and cleaning up afterward. They've all done this before in one context or another, so it isn't as impossible as it would be for many of us elsewhere, but it is a burden in a time of grief. It is a place where it is easy to help and the help is greatly appreciated. It is a very special feeling for instructor and student to be allowed to participate in what for most of us who aren't Makah is a personal and private ritual. We participate in the role of junior family members and help the community help the grieving family.

> While we had consumed lots of information on Makah culture and history in and outside of class, some aspects of it just cannot be conveyed in an academic article. . . . Having real conversations and listening to stories helped me understand more of the day-to-day Makah culture, and what it is like to live in Neah Bay. (Angela S., program participant, 2013)

> We had discovered that in life what really matters is family and community, tradition and the pride that we have in what has been passed down to us, and the respect that we show to one another. These are lessons that I learned from the amazing people of Neah Bay and lessons that I hope to pass down to my children and grandchildren. (Anna M., program participant, 2014)

Each year is different. Sometimes we will set up and clean up, but not stay for the dinner. Sometimes we are invited to help out and participate in a happier event—like a birthday party. It depends on the events of that year and the host family in question. We never plan that we will be invited to participate, but we are always ready to help out.

Cementing the Connection

The course is designed to have an academic component on campus and an experiential component in Neah Bay. There is a test before we leave campus, but a test isn't an appropriate mechanism to assess experiential learning. Students keep a journal, which I read, but which otherwise is as private as they want it to be. Students also write a reflection paper. At the end of the first class, I asked students if I could send copies of the papers to the MCRC and they agreed. In subsequent years, students are told from the beginning that copies will be sent back to Neah Bay to be shared with the people who shared their knowledge of Makah culture. The original prompt for the reflection paper assignment was "What I learned about Makah culture in January." I suggested a target length of approximately five pages single-spaced. The assignment gives students a reason to process the experience. We meet as a class for the last couple of days of the J-term to discuss the experience, to discuss how to write about it, and often to discuss issues that can only be described as *reentry culture shock*.

> I think immersion in another culture, learning what they know from their perspective, is a great way to learn—it enabled me to think outside my

box and see the world from a different point of view. It also enabled me to reflect on that from the academic side as well. (Darlene R., program participant, 2014)

After a few years I finally realized that an important part of the experience was what students were learning about themselves. We often spent time discussing personal learning experiences in the debriefing sessions and students included this discussion in their reflection papers. I changed the prompt to "What I learned about Makah culture and myself in January" to acknowledge the value of this aspect of the experience. We all should be learning all the time, but college students, particularly college students experiencing a culture not their own, will learn things about who they are and who they want to be. (Isn't this the reason for study away?)

Not only did I learn a great deal about the past and present life of the Makah people, I learned about what it means to be me. Essentially, by learning about the lives of others, I better understood my own place in the world. (Ted C., program participant, 2009)

These often very personal accounts are shared with the community. Community members who interacted with us can see the impact that they had on 15 individuals. Sometimes a student will see something that a community member had never noticed, so the papers can be quite interesting. The papers always are honest and the community members know that they can trust the PLU students who "come back again" next January.

Conclusion

The Makah Culture Past and Present course is my most rewarding teaching experience. Students don't just read about learning about another culture—they experience learning about Makah culture. Students are confronted with treaties and treaty rights and must decide how to deal with those issues. By engaging Makah culture, students reflect on their personal and cultural identities. It is a very successful course on every level.

My experience in Neah Bay was one that I will never forget. I was challenged to reevaluate my own biases, to reexamine how I learn and why I think the way I do. I was given the opportunity to meet people who had something important to say, and I was lucky to be in an environment where I could hear it and think about it and discuss it not only with fellow students but with a professor who has been in my very place himself. There have been few classes that have affected me as much as this course. Being challenged on so many different levels is something we all need. First-year students are lucky to have had this class so early in their college careers. The insights they have gained here will help them more than they can know. I am so grateful to have had the opportunity to learn from the Makah people and I hope I can continue to learn from them as well as share with others what they so willingly shared with me. (Bridgette C., program participant, 2010)

Acknowledgments

Very special thanks to the people of the Makah Indian Tribe. Their openness and willingness to share who they are and what being Makah means to them creates a powerful educational experience. I want to thank the staff of the MCRC, particularly Janine Ledford and Theresa Parker, for organizing and overseeing the Neah Bay portion of this course. Without them, this course wouldn't happen. I would like to acknowledge the role played by the staff of the MCRC and my colleagues on campus in developing this course and in helping it evolve over the years. I want to thank the PLU students who have participated in the course; their openness to a different culture and their willingness to challenge their ethnocentrism makes the class a pleasure every year.

Note

1. I was part of the Ozette Village Archaeological Project. Ozette was one of five permanent Makah villages at the time of contact. A small portion of the village was covered by a mudslide about 300 years ago, creating anaerobic waterlogged conditions that preserved vegetal material. Archaeological excavations began in 1970 when a winter storm exposed baskets and boxes and other wooden artifacts. Excavations continued until 1981. Members of the tribe worked at the site and shared their cultural expertise assisting in analysis (Samuels, 1991, 1994; Whelchel, 2005). The tribe took advantage of the opportunity presented by the project to establish a cultural and research center that supports a wide range of tribal heritage programs (Bowechop & Erickson, 2005; Media Resource Associates, Inc., 1994). Altogether, the project was a very successful collaboration between the tribe and archaeologists.

References

Bowechop, J. (2010, Fall). Contemporary Makah whaling. *Columbia: The Magazine of Northwest History, 24*(3), 6–13.
Bowechop, J., & Erikson, P. P. (2005). Foraging indigenous methodologies on Cape Flattery: The Makah Museum as a center of collaborative research. *American Indian Quarterly, 29*(1/2), 263–273.

Brown, J. J. (2007). It's in our treaty: The right to whale. The Evergreen State College. Retrieved from www.evergreen.edu/tribal/cases

Erikson, P. P., Ward, H., & Wachendorf, K. (2002). *Voices of a thousand people: The Makah Cultural and Research Center.* Lincoln: University of Nebraska Press.

Peterson, M., & the MCRC (Makah Cultural and Research Center). (2002). Makah. In J. Wray (Ed.), *Native peoples of the Olympic Peninsula* (pp. 150–167). Norman: University of Oklahoma Press.

Renker, A., & Gunther, E. (1990). Makah. In W. Suttles & W. Sturtevant (Eds.), *Handbook of North American Indians: Vol. 7. Northwest Coast* (pp. 422–430). Washington, DC: Smithsonian Institution.

Samuels, S. R. (Ed.). (1991). *Ozette Archaeological Project Research Reports: Vol. 1. House structure and floor midden.* (Reports of Investigation No. 63). Pullman: Washington State University Department of Anthropology.

Samuels, S. R. (Ed.). (1994). *Ozette Archaeological Project Research Reports: Vol. 2. Fauna.* (Reports of Investigation No. 66). Pullman: Washington State University Department of Anthropology.

Sepez, J. (2008). If middens could talk: Historical ecology of continuity and change in Makah subsistence foraging patterns. *Ethnobiology, 28*(1), 110–133.

Thomas, K. (Producer), & Thomas, K. (Director). *Indian America: A gift from the past* [Video] United States: Media Resource Associates.

Whelchel, D. L. (Ed.). (2005). *Ozette Archaeological Project Research Reports: Vol. 3. Ethnobotany and wood technology.* (Reports of Investigation No. 68). Pullman: Washington State University Department of Anthropology.

15

PRACTICING LIFELONG LEARNING AND GLOBAL CITIZENSHIP ON THE PINE RIDGE INDIAN RESERVATION

Kathryn Burleson

Most colleges and universities strive to create "lifelong learners"—by which we mean we want graduates to maintain motivation and the tools to learn through life after graduation, yet what do we do to prepare students for learning in this way? Learning after graduation is marked by negotiation and cooperation with others and weighing different perspectives as they are presented. Learning in the classroom, where we intentionally eliminate distractions and isolate our material not only by discipline, but also in a way that fits together neatly within the time frame (50 or 80 minutes per session), is not by itself adequate preparation for lifelong learning. There is a place for this type of focused learning environment; it is a privilege to isolate material and engage with it in such a designated way. But if college students *only* experience learning this one way, then they are only prepared to learn one way.

I would like to formally acknowledge the significant contributions that my collaborators, students, and community partners played in the development of this chapter.

Learning in community, like other types of learning, is a skill; it will not magically appear after students have a diploma in hand. If we want students to apply knowledge in new settings, negotiate with others to define issues, derive new answers or paradigms, and persist toward goals when faced with multiple perspectives, we must guide them through these processes.

Following the logic that students need to be supported toward the outcomes we as the higher education institution desire, similar arguments can be made for "global citizenship." Many colleges and universities include global citizenship (or related concepts) in their mission statements (Green, 2012; Plater, 2011). Additionally, departments within a college or university may include it, as does my discipline in which the American Psychological Association identifies "ethical and social responsibility in a diverse world" as a top outcome for undergraduate education (APA, 2013). Meanings vary, but some key components include self-awareness as a cultural being, awareness of others as cultural beings, intercultural empathy, understanding multiple worldviews, responsible decision making, and meaningful participation in social and political life (see Green, 2012). Because global citizenship (like lifelong learning) is an informed action, fostering it requires going beyond talking about it. Delivering information and dialogue about global citizenship is important, but if we want students to think and act as global citizens, we need to offer opportunities for them to practice this way of being.

Intercultural Service-Learning

Carefully constructed intercultural service-learning is one pedagogy that can provide a platform for developing skills of lifelong learning and global citizenship (Kiely, 2004; Longo & Saltmarsh, 2011). At some level of analysis, all service-learning is inherently intercultural; however, the focus here is on service-learning that intentionally crosses explicit cultural boundaries in such a way that culture is made visible and can be a topic of serious and engaged discussion. Intercultural service-learning centers around a mutually beneficial collaboration in which faculty share the "teaching space" with trusted intercultural community partners (see Bringle & Hatcher, 2011; Steinman, 2011). The service component is unique because it serves as an entry point to work *with* diverse individuals, rather than learning *about* them, and the course objectives extend beyond the student-centered ones to include serving community-defined needs. As a result, students are not just pressed to learn for the sake of their own growth, but are also responsible for learning as an act of social responsibility. Ideally the collaboration represents a sustained relationship in which the desired outcomes or experiences for the community and learners are complementary, overlapping, or otherwise appropriately linked.

Case Study

In this chapter, I will describe the psychology course I taught (Cultural Psychology), that includes an intercultural service-learning component in which students travel from the mountains of North Carolina to the Pine Ridge Indian Reservation in South Dakota. It is my hope that this particular case is a useful depiction of one way in which students can be guided toward global citizenship within a context more similar to life postcollege.

Background: The Beginnings of the Relationship

The intercultural service-learning experience described here began with a Warren Wilson College student, who did not just share the idea with a faculty member but instead developed the relationship, sustained it, and led our first intercultural service-learning program to Pine Ridge. Justin Levy came to this leadership role in 2007 following an internship with the hunger-relief nonprofit Conscious Alliance (consciousalliance.org). While working with Conscious Alliance he met and began a relationship with Floyd and Natalie Hand (founding members of Conscious Alliance).

The Hands are leaders in the Lakota community and live on the Pine Ridge Indian Reservation in South Dakota. Floyd is a spiritual leader of the Lakota people and Natalie is a teacher, a community organizer, and the logistics coordinator for the Conscious Alliance food pantry located on their property. In working closely together, Levy and the Hands realized they share a goal of relieving hunger as well as educating others about Lakota culture:

> We are always interested in helping to educate the non-Indian world about the true history of this country and more about Lakota culture so that maybe there will be more respect. I want them to take away a better understanding of the real history of this country and how it was formed, how it displaced the indigenous population of this land. A lot of people were killed for this land, our ancestors. It's a very uncomfortable conversation to have—a lot of people don't want to have it—but it's an important conversation to have if we want to live together in this world. We don't have a plan B, a different planet to live on—we're just renting this space. We all have to come together to make solutions to the problems we have before it's too late. (N. Hand, personal communication, September 22, 2013)

This statement illustrates the Hands' underlying motivation to teach non-Indian students about the Lakota perspective. She acknowledges that the process of creating a more civically responsible world includes education that can be emotionally and intellectually distressing. But, ultimately, the education is a necessary process to bring people together and support reconciliation. With these common goals in mind, Levy and the Hands developed an alternative break program that invited college students onto the reservation to serve and learn with the Lakota community during fall break.

Intercultural Service-Learning in Cultural Psychology

After leading the program successfully, Levy graduated from Warren Wilson College in 2008. Seizing the opportunity to sustain and build the partnership, I reconfigured my course to embed the Pine Ridge service-learning program within it. The academic quality of the course is greatly enhanced by the experience because a founding principle of cultural psychology is that *people develop through participation in cultural practices* (Rogoff, 2003). With the experiences on Pine Ridge, students have direct opportunities to witness and live this principle.

Overview of the Model

While each course offering is different in important ways, the heart of the experience and structure has been the same. The overall structure of my course is a sandwich model (Jones & Steinberg, 2011); there are eight weeks of class prior to Pine Ridge, a weeklong intercultural service-learning experience during spring break, and eight weeks of class upon our return. Throughout the 17 weeks, there are clear learning goals, which include developing and practicing global citizenship and lifelong learning skills. To accomplish this, critical reflections to address and reinforce *what* and *how* the students are learning and serving are integrated throughout the course.

Preparation Embedded in the Course

Prior to our travel, we spend approximately two thirds of the class time on typical cultural psychology material. The material represents a variety of cultures, methodologies, perspectives, and conclusions. As students begin to understand the ever-changing nature of culture and the ways in which humans develop through participation in cultural practices, they are asked to uncover their own current and past cultural practices, and how those practices influence (and influenced) who they are. This personal understanding and the broader material provides a larger academic and personal context in which to ground our experiences on Pine Ridge, and it prepares students to understand themselves as cultural beings. We spend the other one third of our class time specifically and explicitly learning and preparing for our experience on Pine Ridge.

Authenticating Lakota Perspectives

Before we go, we learn about Pine Ridge from the widely available media coverage (most of which our hosts call "poverty porn"). We discuss the impacts of stereotypes and review grim statistics, such as the low life expectancy and high rates of suicide, diabetes, and addiction. Students understand that Pine Ridge is one of the most financially impoverished and food insecure places in the United States. Moving beyond problematizing the reservation, we strive to understand how issues on the reservation exist together and are perpetuated within a larger context of cultural oppression (current and historic). Importantly, the curriculum also validates Lakota viewpoints and elaborates on cultural strengths; we watch documentaries with Lakota voices and read Lakota authors (including *Learning Journey on the Red Road* [1998] by our host Floyd Hand).

Because service is a part of the course, an important additional way to authenticate a Lakota perspective is to approach service from our hosts' standpoint. This approach is aligned with a current best practice of service-learning: doing service *with* instead of *for* a community (see D'Arlach, Sánchez, & Feuer, 2009; Kahn, 2011; Plater, 2011; Steinman, 2011).[1] While students often expect service to be *doing* something *concrete* and *observable*, the primary need identified by our hosts is to improve relations through intercultural understanding. This is much harder to quantify and observe and is an unfamiliar idea to many students. As a result, the preparation for the service on Pine Ridge must include comprehensive discussions of how our concrete service[2] is secondary to our relational service:

> It is really important for us to help people to understand the racial tension that still exists very strong out here. The more outside people we have come here and get past the stereotypes, then maybe they will have more respect and go back to their homes and tell people about the positive things that happened to them here. There is a very rich culture here, a rich spirituality, and we want more people to know about it. (N. Hand, personal communication, September 22, 2013)

Similarly, Steinman (2011) reveals that his host community (the Makah Nation of Washington State) prioritized the service as "being there" and listening to tribal perspectives. (Also see chapter 14 in this volume.)

The contrast between what students expect will be "service" and what our host community wants is an essential lesson. Once after hearing the term *poverty porn* in class a student became alarmed and vehemently pleaded to her classmates that we cancel the trip, and mail all the money we raised for the program directly to Pine Ridge. This suggestion triggered a valuable opportunity to think critically about power, privilege, and service from various perspectives. It is true that families on the reservation could use the money that we spend on airfare. But that is not what our hosts asked for; it does not achieve progress toward breaking down stereotypes and learning to live together more respectfully. As one student participant explains:

> The major change and transformation that happens as a result of that learning is realizing that there is something bigger than yourself. It redefines how you look at service work. It is just as important to them [our hosts] that we sit and listen to their elders. Many of those people have been largely disregarded by America as a whole, they have been called racial slurs, they have been oppressed, so it's just as much a service to sit and truly listen, to be present with that person and learn about them respectfully and with an open mind. (Trey J., program participant, 2011; student leader, 2013)[3]

Listening is service (in this context) and to send the money would only prolong the distance between the two communities and do nothing to address misconceptions about the Lakota.

Learning as Service: Embodied[4] Cultural Practices

After eight weeks of preparation, we travel together to Pine Ridge. Once off campus, my stance shifts from delivering knowledge to observing and helping students navigate learning in community. Stemming from the lifelong learning objective, my primary role is to facilitate a respectful relationship between the students and our community partners by prompting the students to initiate meaningful interaction and adapt their learning and service to the new context.

Upon arriving on Pine Ridge, students immediately spend time with our hosts, the Hands. Natalie stresses that students need to strive to understand the historic and current underpinnings of the issues, continue to work toward solutions, and gain an appreciation of the community's strengths:

> Any time that we have a group here, I am adamant that they not just take pictures of dilapidated houses or poverty, they need to experience the strength of the tribe and all of the rich culture we have here. There are needs. We do have high unemployment and no infrastructure, and those things need to be addressed, but you need to see our strengths too, and you need to want to help in a meaningful way. You can't just fly in, "fix things" by your own cultural standards, and then fly out. (N. Hand, personal communication, September 22, 2013)

When my students demonstrate their respect and willingness to learn about the Lakota perspective, they are invited to engage in some Lakota cultural practices (the behaviors are explained and the students are coached through them). They participate in Lakota prayer, they listen to stories, they don't take notes, they don't make extended eye contact, they demonstrate respect for elders, they make a spirit plate for each meal,[5] they quiet down, they don't ask why, and they observe.

Students soon come to realize that the opportunity to participate in another person's cultural practices is an honor and uniquely reveals a new perspective:

> Initially it was very difficult for me to get out of even something so simple as a firm and direct handshake. I'm from Texas, and there it is very disrespectful not to give someone a firm handshake and meet their eyes, but in Lakota it is a very soft touch of the hand . . . , and looking them in the eyes [for extended time] would be rude. (Trey J., program participant, 2011; student leader, 2013)

Learning to view unconscious pleasantries and displays of respect as culturally relative is an intended consequence of the course. It is also moving to see how gaining a new perspective on old behaviors can resonate on a deep personal level:

> We were at an elder's house about to eat lunch and Natalie handed me the Spirit Plate for that meal. I was really honored and felt as if I was going to cry. There was a humbleness to it. It was not about me. It was about praying for the whole community and the food we brought forward and the people eating that meal. Speaking for the group with the Spirit Plate in my hands gave weight to my prayer that went beyond myself. It has made me more comfortable with my own prayers. (Julia L., program participant, 2013)

Students' experiential learning is strengthened through regular critical reflections (see Whitney & Clayton, 2011). After a few days, I can ask my students: How does it *feel* to pray in a Lakota manner? Our hosts tell us that you don't pray for yourself or what you want. You pray for others and express gratitude for what the creator has provided. How does doing that several times a day shape your decisions and mood throughout the day? What happens to your listening skills when you are immersed in a community that finds extended eye contact distracting and rude? When you aren't looking someone in the eye, do you hear the person more clearly? When you stop the small talk, are you more receptive to everything else going on? If your spirituality and language are daily reminders that the ground and the rocks that you walk on are composed of your ancestors' bodies, how does that inform the way you treat the earth? Do you feel different after participating in these practices for just five days? Answering these types of questions after embodying different cultural practices, and while surrounded by people in a landscape who have been engaged in them for centuries, prepares the students to articulate the meaning of the experience, and to see how the lessons are transferable to other situations.

> You just realize that every activity that you do is a part of your culture. The simplest act, like shaking hands, is cultural, not universal. I notice more when I return how people make statements all the time that they think are universal, but I tell them, "Well, that's in your culture. . . ." I think going to Pine Ridge takes you back to square one in figuring out what culture is. It makes you ask, what is it that I'm doing? (Trey J., program participant, 2011; student leader, 2013)

Even though these embodied cultural practices to some extent are surface level and temporary, it is sufficient to allow for a new perspective to be more fully developed than it would through just reading, observing, and listening to others speak. For some it is an intense experience that leads to questioning much of what was once assumed. Students report feeling a loss of words and feeling vulnerable[6] as they try to negotiate the new information and experience:

> When you go to Pine Ridge, you learn that all of your beliefs about the world are based on your own set of assumptions. In other words, the experience forces you to come to grips with the idea that perspective is a product of culture. Because of this, being on Pine Ridge is an incredible eye-opener, an agent for cultural-open-mindedness and transformation. (Barnaby O., program participant, 2013)

As these student quotes should make clear, allowing students to embody cultural practices brings to life the larger course tenet that *people develop through participation in cultural practices, which themselves are always changing* (Rogoff, 2003). Students are able to see how the new practices shape their own development, as well as acknowledge how cultural practices shape others' development, a key component of intercultural empathy.

Obviously not all community partners will want outsiders to engage in their cultural practices, and to be clear, we know that we are only visiting for a week and not capable of experiencing life as a person of Lakota heritage. We also know that there are people on the reservation who would not want us participating in their cultural practices. However, it is the opinion of our hosts (and I agree) that doing this is transformative; it breaks down stereotypes, creates healthier relations between cultures, and builds profound new understandings necessary for global citizenry.

Solidifying the Experience: The Last Eight Weeks

In the last eight weeks of the course, we continue the pattern of dividing our class time between broader cultural psychology literature and discussions and activities stemming from the Pine Ridge experience. Because learning on Pine Ridge unfolds in real time, often in unpredictable and consequential ways, we need the time back on campus to sift through *how* and *what* was learned. Students have the opportunity to actively listen to each other's perceptions, digest different points of view, and express the larger meaning of the lessons. The usefulness of the posttravel reflection cannot be overstated and is highlighted by an example.

During the experience on Pine Ridge in 2009, we were on our way to a significant scheduled activity when the students came upon a man bloodied with a head injury. He was not sober and in the moment the group had different, intensely held ideas of how to "take care of him." The man refused help, but some students weren't willing to leave him alone. Several students with medical backgrounds wanted to help him (from their perspective) to seek medical treatment. There was obvious disagreement within the group, but within a few minutes a Pine Ridge community member became involved and told us that we were not needed. At that point one of our leaders decided the group would leave (to make our scheduled activity). While it continued to disturb some students and created tension within the group, the week was so busy that we didn't have an opportunity to fully revisit the event in a facilitated fashion while on Pine Ridge. However, once back in the classroom we were able to unpack the emotions and opinions. We had a serious conversation about whether health needs are universal and whether the man was in a valid state to speak for himself. The discussion was full and thorough and transformed into an exchange on broader issues including the intersections of substance abuse and oppression, and the rumored relationship between admission to the hospital and admission to the Pine Ridge jail. If we had no opportunity to discuss this event in class, students may have not reconciled their viewpoints with one another or considered the cultural context of a head wound:

> This experience affected me deeply. At the time I was a young EMT and I learned that "fixing" the problem based on my needs and values may not always be in the best interest of the individual. This experience taught me to listen, taught me to treat with dignity no matter the individual's choices, and taught me not to assume I know better. This was tough to grasp at the time but has helped me immensely in learning to serve. (Conner S., program participant, 2007; student leader, 2009)

As the class renegotiates and reconsiders what we experienced, they prepare a public presentation to express what they learned from the intercultural service-learning experience. It is one way in which we attempt to fulfill our hosts' parting request to educate others on our experiences with the Lakota on Pine Ridge:

> One thing I remember most was sitting in Floyd and Natalie's living room on our last night. They told us that if we did anything at all, we needed to talk about our experiences there. We needed to help to tell the truth. Our voices had power and it was our responsibility to use them. (Tessa C., program participant, 2009)

Conclusion

We know the best way to develop any skill is to practice it. If colleges and universities want to foster *lifelong learning* and *global citizenship*, students can't just be sitting at desks in the sanctuary of the classroom implicitly being taught to *value* lifelong learning or to learn *about* (even explicitly) global citizenship. This is not to say that the classroom is obsolete; even for community-engaged courses the classroom is necessary to prepare students for community, to critically analyze assumptions about community-based experiences, and to articulate and unpack the learning that occurred. Together, the classroom and the community enhance critical thinking and better prepare students to be productive global citizens ready to discover and conceive solutions for a more just world.

To close, I share three quotes from participants that reflect main points of this chapter. Here they express how they were transformed by the intercultural service-learning experience on Pine Ridge:

> When you spend time in a place like Pine Ridge, learning is no longer a matter of memorizing facts or analyzing a theoretical argument. You are instead learning from your core. You are being changed. And you will carry those experiences on as part of you. What I learned has gone on to shape who I have become and what I have gone on to do. Along with learning in a new way, I have also learned about my privilege and the responsibility that comes along with my education. . . . This is not something I could have learned in a classroom. (Tessa C., program participant, 2009)

> I went to Pine Ridge in the spring of 2011, almost 3 years ago. Since that trip, I have stayed involved with the service-learning component by fundraising for the trip independently, volunteering with Conscious Alliance, and sharing my experiences as a Pine Ridge alum with students embarking on this trip. For me, the reflection process I learned and the

cultural encounters I had at Pine Ridge have been continual and have aided me in my work with a non-profit. I consider myself a life-long learner, and a big part of my efforts to grow as a global citizen can be attributed to the service-learning trip to Pine Ridge. (Gina G., program participant, 2011)

I am able to revisit the words of Natalie and Floyd Hand, place them side-by-side with the problems in my current situation and see how the lessons they shared hold true in life outside the boundaries of Pine Ridge. Their unbelievable insight and the amazing practices they shared . . . I learn from them still today. (Barnaby O., program participant, 2013)

Notes

1. This approach is also aligned with cultural relativism and the emic approach to research.
2. The concrete service we engage in begins with bringing 20,000 pounds of food from the Denver metro area (collected by Conscious Alliance) to the Conscious Alliance food bank on the Hands' property. We unload, sort, and sometimes distribute the food. We build fences and gardens for elders and contribute to the construction of community buildings. The exact nature of our daily service activities varies and is always directed by the Hands.
3. While Cultural Psychology is a senior-level course, I have occasionally invited sophomores to complete a related independent study that includes traveling with the Cultural Psychology course to Pine Ridge. The intention is that the independent study students will return their senior year as student-leaders in Cultural Psychology. For this role, they are trained to lead reflections and assist the faculty in decision making and maintaining positive group dynamics. The student quoted here is one such student.
4. I use the word *embodied* to demarcate the intention and depth of the experience. When we "embody" cultural practices the goal is to engage holistically and allow the perceptual, somatosensory, and motor systems to inform the cognitive and emotional responses.
5. As it has been explained to me, a spirit plate is an offering of food and gratitude to the ancestors. It is created before every meal. Prior to serving the meal, a small amount of each type of food prepared for the meal is placed on the spirit plate. The person who offers a prayer of gratitude for the ancestors and nourishment prays while holding the spirit plate. It is also an acknowledgment of how all things alive and deceased are inter-related.
6. Some students become distressed during the experience. As Natalie Hand suggested in an earlier quote, conversations that reveal power and privilege differences can be challenging, especially to those who have not thought about it before. But the work is necessary for intercultural healing and understanding. To assist the group, we have multiple trained leaders who consistently observe and communicate with students to ensure that they feel safe while acknowledging that they are outside of their comfort zones.

References

American Psychological Association, Board of Educational Affairs Task Force on Psychology Major Competencies. (2013, August). *APA guidelines for the undergraduate psychology major* (Version 2.0). Retrieved from http://www.apa.org/ed/precollege/about/psymajor-guidelines.pdf

Bringle, R. G., & Hatcher, J. A. (2011). International service learning. In R. G. Bringle, J. A. Hatcher, & S. G. Jones (Eds.), *International service learning: Conceptual frameworks and research* (pp. 3–28). Sterling, VA: Stylus.

D'Arlach, L., Sánchez, B., & Feuer, R. (2009). Voices from the community: A case for reciprocity in service-learning. *Michigan Journal of Community Service Learning, 16*(1), 5–16.

Green, M. F. (2012, January). Global citizenship: What are we talking about and why does it matter? [Web log post] Retrieved from https://globalhighered.files.wordpress.com/2012/03/ti_global_citizen.pdf

Hand, F. (1998). *Learning journey on the red road.* Pine Ridge, SD: Author. Jones, S. G., & Steinberg, K. S. (2011). An analysis of international service learning programs. In R. G. Bringle, J. A. Hatcher, & S. Jones (Eds.), *International service learning: Conceptual frameworks and research* (pp. 89–112). Sterling, VA: Stylus.

Kahn, H. E. (2011). Overcoming the challenges of international service learning: A visual approach to sharing authority, community development, and global learning. In R. G. Bringle, J. A. Hatcher, & S. G. Jones (Eds.), *International service learning: Conceptual frameworks and research* (pp. 113–124). Sterling, VA: Stylus.

Kiely, R. (2004). A chameleon with a complex: Searching for transformation in international service-learning. *Michigan Journal of Community Service Learning, 10*(2), 5–20.

Longo, N. V., & Saltmarsh, J. (2011). New lines of inquiry in reframing international service learning into global service learning. In R. G. Bringle, J. A. Hatcher, & S. G. Jones (Eds.), *International service learning: Conceptual frameworks and research* (pp. 69–85). Sterling, VA: Stylus.

Plater, W. M. (2011). The context for international service learning: An invisible revolution is underway. In R. G. Bringle, J. A. Hatcher, & S. G. Jones (Eds.), *International service learning: Conceptual frameworks and research* (pp. 29–56). Sterling, VA: Stylus.

Rogoff, B. (2003). *The cultural nature of human development.* New York, NY: Oxford University Press.

Steinman, E. (2011). "Making space": Lessons from collaborations with tribal nations. *Michigan Journal of Community Service Learning, 18*(1), 5–18.

Whitney, B. C., & Clayton, P. H. (2011). Research on and through reflection in international service learning. In R. G. Bringle, J. A. Hatcher, & S. G. Jones (Eds.), *International service learning: Conceptual frameworks and research* (pp. 145–187). Sterling, VA: Stylus.

PART FOUR

CONSORTIUM PROGRAMS

16

IS PLACE THE THING?

Integrative Learning at The Philadelphia Center

Rosina S. Miller

A perk about going to college is the ability to study off campus for a semester. This could mean studying while tasting flavorful tapas in Spain or studying [while walking] through the gardens of Versailles. I could have chosen either of those for my semester off campus. Instead, I chose a program that would take me to places much further than across the Atlantic Ocean. I wanted to be a part of a program that would help me discover new ways to grow as a creative and critical thinker. (Marina R., College of Wooster, program participant, Fall 2013)

With the increasing "globalization" of college and university campuses, the massive resources directed toward study abroad, and even the increasing adoption of study abroad requirements for graduation, what does *place* have to do with the ability of students to achieve the broad-based learning outcomes that educators desire of global education and higher education in general? As we learned in the 2008 National Survey of Student Engagement (NSSE), and as Randy Bass (2012) points out in "Disrupting Ourselves," many of the college experiences that correlate to the most powerful learning outcomes happen outside of the formal curriculum, in the experiential learning of the cocurriculum, or in special curricular experiences: "Students' participation in one or more of these [high-impact] practices had the greatest impact on success, on retention, on graduation, on transfer, and on other measures of learning" (Bass, 2012, p. 26).[1]

Located outside of the formal curriculum, off-campus study is widely recognized as a high-impact practice that has the potential to foster deep learning and student development. Too often, however, undergraduate students choose, and perhaps faculty and administrators recommend, off-campus study programs based on location as the primary factor. In fact, programs are usually listed by location in off-campus study offices across the country. While legitimate rationale for these choices certainly exists, often decisions for approving or choosing off-campus programs rely on factors that privilege exotic destinations over transformative learning potential and underestimate the value of programs much closer to home.

Using The Philadelphia Center (TPC) as a case study, this chapter argues that the *model* and not the *location* of the program is the most important criterion for determining the depth and nature of the learning that takes place during study away. As Mark Salisbury (2012) recently noted, "One basic tenet of learning is that deep, sustainable development comes from a process that includes an experience of disequilibrium followed by [a] period of reflective meaning-making." TPC's model and programmatic requirements provide such structured processes and demonstrate that it is the *intentional pedagogical engagement with place*, wherever the program is located, not the location itself, that ultimately provides for the development of the integrative personal and cross-cultural learning outcomes that are the promise of global education.

A Brief History

The Philadelphia Center's off-campus study program was founded in 1967 by the Great Lakes Colleges Association (GLCA) at a time when cities were in crisis.[2] Riots and protests against decaying urban conditions, racism, and police brutality, among other things, motivated the presidents of this consortium to consider opening a program to give students from their bucolic, homogeneous campuses in the Midwest an opportunity to experience and address pressing urban issues. Originally called the Philadelphia Urban Semester, TPC first brought GLCA students to the city through a connection between Antioch College's president and the president of the School Board of Philadelphia to work with youth in different capacities because, according to former TPC director Stevens Brooks (interview with author, July 3, 2008), vibrant experiments in education were happening in the city at that time.

Therefore, from the beginning, the sense of the city of Philadelphia as a place was tightly woven into the fabric of the program. The city was not to be just a "container" where students gained work experience, but rather Philadelphia itself was envisioned as the catalyst for learning and transformation. Student interests quickly expanded beyond working with youth to all sorts of workplaces, but the idea of attending to student experiences *in the city* in all forms was important from the beginning and was formalized by the City Seminar and critical reflection model developed shortly after the program began. By the early 1970s, faculty members were called *learning process consultants* and focused on integrating student experiences in work and the city through the seminars.

Forty-seven years later, elements of the program have been tweaked and improved, but the basic structure remains the same. Students, predominantly from the GLCA schools and similar small liberal arts colleges, attend TPC for either a fall or spring semester and engage in the following activities: they live independently in housing they find through a guided process during the first week; research and choose an internship, again through a unique process in the first few weeks of the semester, and then work 32 hours per week for the remainder of the semester; take a City Seminar with a full-time faculty member who also advises them throughout the internship; take an Elective Seminar in the evening, usually with a practicing professional in the field; and earn 16 semester hours for their participation.[3]

Sensing Place

> I arrived in Philadelphia scared, worried, and confused. I was scared of living in a big city. I was worried about starting my internships and fitting in. Lastly, I was confused on what to do first. (Jessica P., College of Wooster, program participant, Fall 2011)

At TPC, it all begins with housing. When students arrive in Philadelphia to participate in the fall or spring semester program, they (usually) don't know the city, often don't have any substantial experience living or spending any significant time in a big city, and definitely don't yet know where they are going to live for the semester. Shelter being a basic human need, students engage this challenging experience for different reasons: often because they are eager to get out of the "bubble" of small campus life, they are ready to gain some independence, or they simply trust their friends and the program that this is a rewarding, educative experience.

For the first week of the program, students live in a hotel around the corner from the Center's offices while they engage in orientation activities that include guided city walks and rides on public transportation; sessions that discuss city living, city smarts, and the housing process; and an introduction to materials such as housing search tools, guides, listings, and other resources. The act of walking itself is an important part of the process. As Jeff Speck argues in *Walkable City* (2012), walkability is what makes cities thrive, and Philadelphia is a very walkable city. Crisscrossing Center City Philadelphia and the neighborhoods that surround it to investigate as many housing options as possible in the first few days of the semester, TPC students turn the unknown spaces of the city into meaningful places in a very short period of time. For if space is the more abstract concept, a realm without meaning, then "when humans invest meaning in a portion of space and then become attached to it in some way (naming is one such way) it becomes a place" (Cresswell, 2004, p. 10). As Aaron B., a student from Earlham College (program participant, Spring 2011) noted, "Walking in the city helped me learn just how unique Philadelphia is."

The first week is disorienting for students, and no doubt produces the experience of disequilibrium of which Mark Salisbury writes (2012). For some students, like Jessica, quoted earlier, successfully navigating a big city is hard enough for them to imagine; for others, the big city is a welcome change from their small campuses, but the effort of getting to know it quickly, making new friends, choosing housemates (often from other colleges), and finding housing for the semester in a few short days can be challenging but also invigorating. As Fall 2010 student Shannon M. (Whitman College) writes, "After looking at 15 apartments in two days, my three housemates and I decided to rent a bi-level above an art gallery on South Street. I have never felt as engaged and alive as I did living in Center City—Philly became home in just four short months."

The disequilibrium continues, however, with the placement process. Reading placement descriptions and student evaluations of the organizations that interest them in our database of more than 800 options, students must select a minimum of three places to interview before choosing their internships.[4] Disconcerting because they don't yet know where they are going to work, this process also produces great learning: students begin to understand what exactly is involved in different types of roles, positions, and work, and how different organizations have different cultures (from corporate to nonprofit, small to large, but also the idiosyncrasies of individual organizations); they also continue to crisscross the city as they venture even farther out of the center for their interviews.

Critical reflection and meaning-making are core activities that students are taught from the beginning of orientation, as they are introduced to experiential education and our structured process for their semester's learning.

So while the housing and placement processes produce disequilibrium, they also contain requirements for reflection and articulation of learning, through development of a learning plan and a portfolio. In the learning plan, students articulate what they want to learn at work, in the city, and through their courses, in the form of knowledge, skills, and values/attitude objectives. This document becomes the road map for students' learning and also serves to inspire supervisors and workplace colleagues to create opportunities for growth and development. Throughout the semester students reflect on their learning objectives that become formalized in outcomes articulated in a portfolio, which thoroughly demonstrates student accomplishments through evidence, reflection, and assessment.

Over the process of the semester, with the guidance of our faculty advisers, these tools for experiential learning produce deep, sustainable development. As Mara R. (Kalamazoo College, program participant, Fall 2012) wrote:

> Further, because of my semester with TPC, my passion for the city of Philadelphia has truly come alive. I never knew it was possible to fall in love with a location as much as I have. I found five fellow roommates, and we decided to live in Chinatown, an area of only ten percent non-Asian inhabitants. Being the minority, I took my location as a personal opportunity to learn from the citizens of the area. Our pizza place downstairs and our landlord became more than my friends, but also my family. Also, due to my apartment's close proximity to Center City, I was able to better experience everything Philadelphia has to offer. In the end, after three months of positive ambiance and experiences, I was so amazed at the difference this program has made in my life, both academically and personally. I finally have more of an understanding of my personal identity as well as where I hope to venture to next in life.

Jessica, who admitted earlier to being afraid at the beginning of the semester, reveals how she felt at the end: "After a semester of living in Philly, I am proud to say that I am no longer scared, worried or confused about anything."

Inspired by the elegant insights of anthropologist Keith Basso on the "sense of place," I therefore contend that these first several intense weeks of the program are pedagogically intentional processes that, along with the program's model, make the city of Philadelphia an "object of awareness." As Basso (1996) reflects, "It is at times such as these, when individuals step back from the flow of everyday experience and attend self-consciously to places—when, we may say, they pause to actively sense them—that their relationships to geographical space are most richly lived and surely felt" (pp. 106–107).

This self-conscious act of sensing place, I believe, is essential to any true engagement with a place, and is especially important to move students from the position of visitor/tourist to citizen-participant in off-campus experiences. Because TPC students are living in their own apartments and because they are interning in their own organizations, they are participating in the city in meaningful ways. As a classroom and a resource, the city becomes the catalyst for their reflections on their experiences, what they are doing and learning, and what they want for themselves in the future. Basso argues: "Hence, as numerous writers have noted, places possess a marked capacity for triggering acts of self-reflection, inspiring thoughts about who one presently is, or memories of who one used to be, or musings on who one might become" (1996, p. 107).

One TPC assignment that attempts to reinforce this link between identity and place is our Self & the City project. In the first month of the semester, we ask students to submit photographs of themselves taken in a place in Philadelphia that holds special significance to them and that represents their experience of Philadelphia so far. In workshops in each seminar, we then show the photographs and discuss notions of home and qualities of place, ways places become meaningful to us and how this is happening in Philadelphia, and move toward Edward Casey's notion that "where we are—the place we occupy, however briefly—has everything to do with what and who we are" (1993, p. 8). At the end of the semester, during Final Assembly, we discuss the ways they and their relationships to the city have changed from that first photo.

Engaging Difference, Integrative Learning, and the Essential Learning Outcomes

> Embrace difference. If I could give advice to anyone who wants to come to Philadelphia it would be to embrace difference. Philadelphia offers a diverse population and countless experiences you will never forget. . . . I walked everywhere in Center City. It was a good walk because whether I was going to work, the Center, Olde City, South Street, or Rittenhouse Square, I would find new things. There were times when I walked to University City and ended on Penn's Campus. I encourage everyone to explore different parts of Philly and outside of Philly. . . . Enjoy Philadelphia. Live it up. Meet new people. Venture throughout the city and other parts of Pennsylvania. It's okay to be nervous. It's okay to be a little afraid. But remember the faculty, staff, students, supervisors, and many other people are there to help. Eat a cheesesteak, grab some frozen yogurt, head out to the pub, and explore! But remember to embrace difference. (Kimberly T., Alma College, program participant, Fall 2012)

Though many of the Essential Learning Outcomes of AAC&U's LEAP initiative are relevant to TPC and other off-campus study programs, I will focus on two of them for the remainder of this chapter: intercultural knowledge and competence, and integrative learning.[5]

On the AAC&U VALUE rubrics tied to these outcomes, *intercultural knowledge and competence* is defined as "a set of cognitive, affective, and behavior skills and characteristics that support effective and appropriate interaction in a variety of cultural contexts" (Bennett, 2008). Rubric categories for this outcome include knowledge of cultural self-awareness and cultural worldview frameworks, skills of empathy and verbal and nonverbal communication, and curious and open attitudes.

Philadelphia is a city of immense cultural diversity. It has, for example, long-standing Italian, African American, Irish, Puerto Rican, and German communities; it has vibrant newer immigrant communities from Mexico, Vietnam, West Africa, and many other places. It has active and visible lesbian, gay, bisexual, transgender, and queer communities, along with diverse communities of faith, including Quakers, Jews, Muslims, and Buddhists. It has visible economic stratification and segregation, and also richly rendered places of "civility and cultural convergence," what Elijah Anderson (2011) calls the "cosmopolitan canopy," using Philadelphia's Reading Terminal Market as a prime example.

Because of the foundation upon which our student experiences of the city are built, the attention to place, the subject matter and experiential practices of the City Seminars, along with the program's objectives and programmatic standards (see Figure 16.1), TPC believes that our students are well poised to reflect and engage difference in Philadelphia and are provided ample opportunities to practice and develop the skills crucial to successful intercultural interaction. For example, with a genuine interest in diverse populations, Meagan J. (Hope College, program participant, Spring 2012) chose the Nationalities Service Center (NSC) as her field placement. The NSC is a nonprofit organization that provides social, educational, and legal services to refugees and asylees in the Greater Philadelphia area. Since NSC's founding in 1921, it has helped 4,000 individuals from over 90 countries to participate fully in American society. Working alongside her supervisor, a resettlement case manager, Meagan learned about the processes involved with helping refugees and immigrants find housing, obtain a Social Security card, and pursue work along with various other issues related to assisting refugees with assimilating to life in the United States. Meagan says, "My internship allowed me to have a substantial learning experience by giving me a brief glimpse into the lives of a multitude of cultures that consider Philadelphia their home." Because of the objectives on her learning plan, she also chose to gain knowledge about various subfields within the larger structure of supporting immigrants and refugees.

But even without choosing such a specific internationally focused internship, students have the potential to engage difference every day, in their neighborhoods, on public transportation, on the streets, at work, and with their peers. They build relationships with neighbors, coworkers, housemates, and TPC faculty and staff. They invest in these relationships, contribute, and are stretched and changed in significant ways, creating transactional and

Figure 16.1 The Philadelphia Center's Objectives and Programmatic Standards

The Philadelphia Center Objectives

- To introduce students to the theory and practice of experiential learning through the process of designing a plan of action in which they document their learning from experience, develop learning objectives with their faculty advisers and field supervisors, and competently perform, engage in, and master coursework, fieldwork, and independent city living
- To help students develop knowledge in fields of work
- To encourage students to examine stereotypes and question assumptions about differences in age, class, ethnicity, religion, race, sex, gender, culture, sexuality, and so on, as well as to help students interact with people who they perceive as having different values and lifestyles
- To explore with students various career options and to help them develop strategies and skills for professional growth
- To guide students in seeking knowledge that is necessary for them to become more informed participants in the social and political processes by which cities, states, and the nation are governed
- To help students understand how a city is a site of learning, a resource in developing knowledge and skills, and a space which presents opportunities to examine one's values and attitudes
- To assist students in setting up housing, in managing resources, and in becoming competent in navigating and living in a city
- To demonstrate to students how to generalize and apply knowledge acquired through fieldwork, coursework, and city living, so that they can integrate this knowledge into their day-to-day lives

The Philadelphia Center Programmatic Standards

Students will be awarded academic credit only for college-level learning. This learning will demonstrate a conceptual as well as a practical grasp of the knowledge and/or skill acquired in the three learning contexts of field placement, city seminar, and city living, and will be applicable in other learning contexts as well. Students are expected to achieve the following:

- An understanding of experiential learning and the ability to apply academic subject matter to the field placement and city living experience
- An expanded sense of independence, competence, confidence, and resourcefulness; and a realization and appreciation of one's proactive role as a citizen-participant in relation to local and global communities
- A critical examination of one's prior experience, knowledge, attitudes, and values in relation to people who come from backgrounds and experiences that are different from one's own
- Knowledge of what an organization does in relation to its mission, how it achieves its goals, and how it functions in its economic, social, and/or political context
- The development and acquisition of work-based, city seminar, and personal skills, values, and knowledge

transformative experiences with the people and places they engage. This also happens, notably, in TPC classrooms, where students interact with participants from multiple campuses (largely from the Midwest, but from all over the country as well) and with the great diversity of majors that participate in the program each semester. In addition, our program has become popular with international students who are enrolled at our participating schools. Recently, it is not uncommon for one third of TPC students in any given semester to represent many different countries throughout the world. (For example, in the Spring of 2013, 36% of students represented 14 different countries, while the remaining 64% represented 19 different U.S. states and the District of Columbia.) This diverse participation in the program contributes still further to rich conversation and intercultural learning within the seminars themselves.

Recently, AAC&U made a commitment to support and further the emergent ideal of *integrative liberal learning*,[6] defined in the Essential Learning Outcomes as "an understanding and a disposition that a student builds across the curriculum and cocurriculum, from making simple connections among ideas and experiences to synthesizing and transferring learning to new, complex situations within and beyond the campus." TPC's model, in which a full-time faculty adviser teaches a seminar with course content that engages the city experientially and oversees the student's learning in the internship and city, provides an exemplary method for integrating the learning happening during the semester. The model also attunes to the prior learning students bring with them from coursework and life experiences and how this semester's experience will influence what they do next. This reflection and meaning-making are accomplished and assessed through numerous formal and informal individual meetings with faculty throughout the semester; meetings at the field placement site with student, faculty, and supervisor; the writing and reflection involved in the development of the learning plan; and the articulation and demonstration of learning in the portfolio, with feedback being an integral part of the cycle. For example, as Amber M. (Albion College, program participant, Fall 2012) says,

> Through [my TPC] courses, I was able to expose myself to some of the hidden injustices in our society. The more I was able to integrate myself in these classes, [my internship,] and the city, the more I realized the importance of preserving the law. By the end of my time in Philadelphia, I had discovered my personal passions, and realized my career path was leading me to become a lawyer.

Finally, Tessa M. (Kalamazoo College, program participant, Fall 2012) began her portfolio this way:

Most of my days in Philadelphia started and ended with the long trip on the 23 bus to Germantown that took me to and from work. It is an incredibly interesting route, going through many varied neighborhoods. I would get on in the heart of Center City, venture into Chinatown, make my way through North Philly and Kensington, and get off in Germantown. I passed abandoned factories, play grounds, and row homes; murals, mosaics, and art galleries; houses with fenced, green lawns; Temple students hurrying to morning classes; and, ultimately, into the stretch of historic sites and buildings that make up Historic Germantown, "America's most historic square mile." Some days when I would look up from the reading I invariably filled my transit with, I would see a mural with the words of a Chinese proverb: "Tell me, I forget. Show me, I remember. Involve me, I understand." Perhaps if I had not been involved in a program proof positive of the truth of that saying, I would have stared blankly out of the window when I glanced up. Maybe if I had not been reading [for my City Seminar] about the systemic forces that created the disparity passing by the window, I would have missed its significance. It is altogether possible that if I had not spent hours attempting to discover the untold history of those behind the wealth and privilege of one Philadelphia family [for my internship at the historic site and house museum Cliveden], I would not have understood the true meaning of what it means to be a member of society.

Place Is the Thing

My semester in Philly was definitely the busiest and most fulfilling experience I've had in college, and I now realize that the value of my liberal arts education lies in what I do with the knowledge I've acquired. This experience has made me a firm believer in the power of real world situations to educate and motivate people, to create active and conscientious citizens, and to ultimately enact positive social change. (Shannon M., Whitman College, program participant, Fall 2010)

Hopefully, it is now clear that at TPC we believe place is essential to student learning outcomes. Attending intentionally to their experiences *in place* through critical reflection allows students to address issues of difference and self-understanding, among other things, and integrate that learning more fully into their lives. For as Basso concludes in the following passage, "Place-based thoughts about the self lead commonly to thoughts of other things— other places, other people, other times, whole networks of associations that ramify unaccountably within the expanding spheres of awareness that they themselves engender" (1996, p. 107).

Through our experience at TPC, we believe that attending to place is critical to student development and integrative learning. But the important essential learning outcomes (Figure 16.1) don't happen just because of the location of a program on the globe. A program without systematic attention to the place in which it's located, woven into the fabric of its model, could end up being just another trip, a tourism experience for so many students.

Notes

1. Bass reproduces the list of high-impact practices outlined in the LEAP initiative of the Association of American Colleges and Universities (AAC&U): first-year seminars and experiences, common intellectual experiences, learning communities, writing-intensive courses, collaborative assignments and projects, undergraduate research, diversity/global learning, service learning, community-based learning, internships, and capstone courses and projects (www.aacu.org/leap/hip.cfm).
2. The GLCA today consists of 13 small liberal arts colleges located in Indiana, Michigan, and Ohio, and one located in Western Pennsylvania.
3. TPC also offers an eight-week summer program. This program has a different model (e.g., housing and the internship are prearranged) and offers deep learning in many ways; however, for the purposes of this chapter, I am writing about the full semester experience (www.tpc.edu).
4. TPC offers substantial internship opportunities for almost any major, ranging from educational and cultural organizations, to scientific institutions, public agencies, social service organizations, and corporations of all sizes.
5. The Essential Learning Outcomes are those related to knowledge of human cultures and the physical and natural world, intellectual and practical skills (inquiry and analysis, critical and creative thinking, written and oral communication, quantitative literacy, information literacy, teamwork and problem solving), personal and social responsibility (civic knowledge and engagement—local and global, intercultural knowledge and competence, ethical reasoning and action, foundations and skills for lifelong learning), and integrative and applied learning. See www.aacu.org/leap/ for more information on these and the Authentic Assessments/VALUE rubrics.
6. "Principles and Practices of Integrative Liberal Learning," Association of American Colleges and Universities, draft statement e-mailed to preannual meeting symposium participants, January 2014.

References

Anderson, E. (2011). *The cosmopolitan canopy: Race and civility in everyday life.* New York, NY: W. W. Norton & Company.

Bass, R. (2012, March/April). Disrupting ourselves: The problem of learning in higher education. *Educause Review, 47*(2), 23–33.

Basso, K. H. (1996). *Wisdom sits in laces: Landscape and language among the western Apache.* Albuquerque: University of New Mexico Press.

Bennett, J. M. (2008). Transformative training: Designing programs for culture learning. In M. A. Moodian (Ed.), *Contemporary leadership and intercultural com-*

petence: Understanding and utilizing cultural diversity to build successful organizations (pp. 95–110). Thousand Oaks, CA: Sage.

Casey, E. S. (1993). *Getting back into place: Toward a renewed understanding of the place-world.* Bloomington: Indiana University Press.

Cresswell, T. (2004). *Place: An introduction.* Malden, MA: Blackwell.

Salisbury, M. (2012, July 30). We're muddying the message on study abroad. *The Chronicle of Higher Education.* Retrieved from http://chronicle.com/article/article-content/133211/

Speck, J. (2012). *Walkable city: How downtown can save America, one step at a time.* New York, NY: Farrar, Straus and Giroux.

17

LEARNING TO STAND ON SHIFTING GROUND

The New York Arts Program

Linda Earle

L earning to locate oneself in relationship to places, systems, and populations that are unfamiliar and complex is the catalytic substance of off-
campus education, and one of the core benefits of acquiring a "global"
perspective. Often considered to be the province of international study
programs, domestic programs—specifically those sited in diverse urban settings—also support this process of discovery by integrating the transformation of relationship to *place* with specific learning goals. This chapter looks
at the development of Ohio Wesleyan University's New York Arts Program
(NYAP) to consider how program design, curriculum, and assessment can be
aligned to incorporate enough pedagogical structure to support the articulation and accomplishment of learning goals, and enough flexibility to facilitate the invention and improvisation that result from true engagement with
both place and subject. Because of its long history of combining engagement
with the city as a laboratory for learning and personal development with
more traditional academic elements such as seminars, NYAP's example may
also provide some insights into institutional adaptation to civic and cultural
milieus that are, by their nature, constantly changing.

Founded in 1967, NYAP (then called the Great Lakes Colleges Association [GLCA] Program in New York) was devised in a climate of seismic
cultural, political, and academic change and responded to the moment in its

approach to preparing Midwestern liberal arts students for work in the arts.[1] The educational model reflected key elements of the widespread conversation among educators about reform—particularly the argument that experiential means be found to engage liberal arts students more actively in their own educations. One particularly influential document, "The New College Plan," based its prescriptive model on "the conviction that the average student entering one of the better colleges is capable of far more independence than he now demonstrates (and) he must be given proper training and proper opportunities" outside of traditional coursework to achieve it (Barber, Sheehan, Stoke, & McCune, 1958/1965, p. 4).

The program was conceived around the idea that "apprenticeships" were to be the primary educational vehicle. Students were taught and mentored by practicing artists and arts administrative professionals within their specific fields of interest—visual arts, theater, music, film, and writing. This was complemented with symposia led by a small faculty based in New York to contextualize their work and share ideas across disciplines. The acquisition of discipline-specific skills and knowledge was embedded within engagement with the location of the program. The connection was made between New York City's status as a hotbed of artistic innovation to its also being a crucible for defining racial, political, and civic issues of the day. The city itself was to be a laboratory in which students were expected to activate their liberal arts skills.

Painter and Ohio Wesleyan University art professor Richard Wengenroth served as the first director of the program and established learning partnerships with artists and institutions that reflected the excitement and breadth of New York's creative community at that moment: individual artists, writers, composers, and designers; galleries; museums; performing arts companies; and nascent artist-run exhibition spaces. Formative program correspondence and memos refer to the importance of integrating advanced experience in the artistic practice with developing an "understanding of the intentions, problems, and means of the arts as they are practiced in this urban, multicultural world" and creating catalytic relationships between the cultures of "heartland" campuses and the professional arts community (Wengenroth et al., n.d.). Wengenroth, who was also a part-time resident of the city, and his colleagues in the program had deep collegial and professional ties to the community of individuals and institutions who partnered the program. This set a course that remains an essential element in NYAP's operation.

Following the lead of international programs, NYAP staff offered slightly tongue-in-cheek guides to New York money and argot—which nonetheless recognized that New York was terra incognito for their students and offered many of the same challenges and benefits as overseas programs. The process of navigating the city; learning about its people, geography, and rhythms; and participating in the creative community were, and remain, mutually informative elements of the experience.

During these early days the program owned no administrative, instructional, or residential facilities. Most students lived on the Lower East Side and in SoHo when those neighborhoods still offered affordable live/work space for artists and upstart performance and exhibition groups. Students spent most of their time with professional artists and organizations—sharing their mentors' geographic and professional communities. They met in museums, artists' studios, and workplaces for on-site lectures and instruction and gathered in the lofts, studios, and apartments of faculty and mentors for seminars.

Over the years, the academic, cultural, and civic contexts in which the program is conducted have changed enormously. Though still an international center for art, New York is now one of many vibrant and sophisticated centers of artistic practice and consumption across the country. What New York and other large cities can offer students as a part of their engagement with their art practice continues to be the contexts of social diversity and the complex social and economic layers of urban life. At the same time, there has been a proliferation of off-campus study and internship requirements and experiential programs across the academic disciplines. The educational value of experiential education is now more broadly recognized and is embedded in students' expectations of career preparation as part of their liberal arts education (DiConti, 2004).

The current NYAP program structure and assessment tools have been shaped by a set of outcomes identified in collaboration with representative administrators and faculty who serve as the program's liaisons with sending colleges. They reflect the original mission of the program, but recognize contemporary student needs and aim to articulate, map, and assess the learning acquired off campus in ways that can be understood and incorporated by home campuses.

The overarching goal identified by the group is that through their experience students acquire a more expansive perspective on the practical application of their liberal arts education. The components of this expectation include that students demonstrate they

- have acquired skills from the culture of the workplace as well its practices, including professional behavior communication, and ethics;
- have an ability to articulate learning goals and develop models of how they can be achieved and implemented;

- gained and can reflect on perspectives from their living in an environment of diverse practices, cultures, circumstances, and values;
- achieved an enhanced level of creative, intellectual, and practical independence (NYAP, 2012).

The structure to support these outcomes includes an internship (formerly known as an apprenticeship); a seminar in one of four broad areas (visual arts, performing arts, media, and writing and publishing), each led by a core faculty member;[2] an independent capstone project; and a journal reflecting experiences and the ideas and practices the students encounter. These components are supported by individual advising by faculty; programmed events to encourage interdisciplinary discussion and present a comprehensive view of New York as a global cultural capital; and professional development workshops focused on practical, strategic, and financial skills.

Internships remain at the core of the program and occupy an average of 25 to 35 hours per week. They anchor the students' experience in the city, and give them access to mentors' practices, workplaces, neighborhoods, and professional communities. Because New York's cultural life is no longer concentrated in Manhattan, where the NYAP residence and offices are located, it is students' work, errands, and audience experiences that take them to a wider variety of neighborhoods across the boroughs. The placement process is part of individual advisement by NYAP faculty who maintain active creative practices and bring with them extensive and diverse networks of artists and cultural and media organizations. Internship sponsors/mentors are vetted to ensure their understanding of the educational purpose of the student's participation. Specific learning objectives are identified by the student in concert with the faculty adviser and internship sponsor, and incorporated into a written agreement that includes mutual expectations and a code of behavior. The document relates to the program outcomes in very specific ways. Adapted from an instrument used by Kalamazoo College's Career Center, the Learning Goals Agreement is a grid that lays out each goal, which tasks support it, and how it will be assessed. The brief example in Table 17.1 of a student assisting a mural painter demonstrates the ways in which the program outcomes are incorporated in structuring internships.

This format has proven valuable in helping students discern how their skills can be put into action, what new competencies they need to acquire to meet a goal, and the relevance of even the most mundane of their daily tasks. It has also been used by students to negotiate for more responsibility or, when needed, more supervision. These documents often change as the semester proceeds, particularly in terms of the refinement of goals. The revisions map growth and integration of knowledge and experience.

TABLE 17.1
Learning Goals Agreement

Learning Objectives	Tasks	Evaluation
What you want to learn	How you're going to learn it	How my sponsor, adviser, and I will determine which learning goals have been accomplished
I want to learn techniques for making murals and other large-scale work.	I observe and assist my sponsor on-site by tracing the design, preparing the palette and other materials, and preparing the painting surfaces. (I will supplement this with research.)	I have supported the execution of a mural by maintaining the materials in good order, and preparing materials and surfaces accurately. In my journal I will document the effect this has had on my understanding of the materials and practices used to produce the work.
I will learn about the organizational side of creating public artworks and develop my thinking about the role of public art.	I will help my sponsor draw up work schedules, handle correspondence, research and document the site, track contracts related to the project, and communicate with the community liaisons about the project.	I have communicated to all parties in a way that supports the goals of the project and keeps the project on schedule. I maintain well-organized records and documentation. In my journal I will document the processes and articulate the aims and challenges involved.

The faculty seminars are organized around specific subject areas but encourage all students to bring their perspectives and interests to the discussion to explore interdisciplinary connections—creative and practical. They focus on contemporary practice and use the city as an active resource through site visits, performances, and guest speakers. The seminars are structured along a graduate seminar model and assume students' ongoing involvement with relevant lines of inquiry. For example, as part of their work in her seminar Art Worlds of New York: Critical Thinking in Contemporary Art, artist and NYAP core faculty member Emilie Clarke has students consider case studies of how artists have constructed their communities and networks, and how these relate to various exhibition platforms and institutions. The seminar incorporates extensive studio, gallery, and museum visits in New York's various art districts with their diverse economic, geographic, and demographic characteristics. This fieldwork is complemented by art, critical and historic readings, and guest talks by curators and historians to provide a context in which students begin to form a critical and conceptual foundation for their own studio or curatorial practice.

In addition to faculty seminars, the program brings in guest speakers to encourage interdisciplinary dialogue that relates to aspects of contemporary cultural life in New York. One such speaker recently used excerpts from two texts, Jane Jacobs's *The Death and Life of Great American Cities* (1961/1989) and Harold Skramstad's "An Agenda for American Museums in the Twenty-First Century" (1999), to explore with students the urban concept of "turf" as it is expressed by cultural institutions in their setting, design, and signage; what these elements signal to potential audiences; and how they affect public interaction with institutions. Students were asked to reflect on their New York workplaces as well as their audience experiences.

At midsemester, seminars are generally replaced by individual tutorial sessions in which students hone ideas for an independent project. Some students devise ideas that deepen their knowledge and experience in their primary field; others explore a collateral or divergent interest. In addition to this ongoing dialogue with their faculty adviser, students can choose to present for critique their ideas to their seminar cohort. The projects are essentially creative and exploratory but must be focused so that they are manageable within the time available and can be used as a resource for further thought and work when the student returns to campus. Most students have taken a direct approach to incorporating their new city experience. Projects have included choreography drawn from observing patterns of body language among commuters; interviews with New York City cultural figures; and short stories, films, and essays reflecting a newly acquired sense of "turf." One journalism student produced a video report on how GPS apps affect her fellow students' physical sense of the city. Her subjects were challenged to use conventional maps or landmarks to find unfamiliar addresses. What successful capstone projects like these have in common is that the exploration of a very specific aspect of experience contains the kernel of future work that can be developed more broadly as students move forward.

The required journal also gleans from internships, experiences at work, seminars, and explorations of the city. In this way it serves as a document of the journey traveled during the semester. In addition to being a means of self-reflection and instruction, it helps frame faculty's assessment of student progress and is reviewed and discussed during the semester. The writing is expected to be of a level that reflects the core skills students have developed through their liberal arts education: the ability to synthesize diverse elements of experience including unexpected benefits and challenges, and to analyze information and sort through the ways in which new experience has reordered or reinforced their thinking and goals. Some of the richest benefits of off-campus study can be drawn from anecdotal accounts of the small struggles and discoveries students experience in the course of their day; thus, the journal is valuable not only for recording eureka moments, but also as a document that students can look back on to perceive patterns and connections unavailable to them in the midst of the experience.

The most recent addition to the structure of the program is a partnership with Creative Capital—a national foundation based in New York. Creative Capital supports artists with grants and professional advisement to help them develop sustainable practices. The foundation has worked with NYAP in adapting its curriculum of professional development workshops to the needs of our students as emerging artists. Sessions focused on strategy and financial basics are aimed at giving students a taste of professional life and encouraging independence and invention. Writing and presentational exercises are used to develop students' ability to identify and express themselves—to define goals and give them practical tools to implement them. NYAP staff do not participate in these sessions so that students can sort through the processes of setting personal priorities without considering perceived expectations and judgment. Artists affiliated with Creative Capital's grants program, who are trained in this work, facilitate the sessions and share guidance from their own experiences, providing still another layer of mentorship. The ongoing partnership with a multidisciplinary arts organization that has national and international influence also extends NYAP's professional community and helps broaden our embrace of current cultural practice.

In addition to the curricular aspect of the program, the facility itself plays a key role in supporting program outcomes. It is also a lens through which to consider the challenges that international and domestic programs have in common. Darren Kelly (2009) observes that the experience of American students studying abroad can be buffered and, to some extent, neutralized by their tendency to create and maintain "physical and cultural comfort zones" (p.21) or "nested environments" (p. 21) that distance them from the benefits of engagement with their surroundings. He found this to be the case even in Western English-speaking environments as well as those where language or cultural difference were the perceived obstacles to interaction. We also see this tendency among students attending domestic programs and have to work to counter it.

In the early days of the NYAP, the search for living space and the need to negotiate the travel between instructional sites, work, and home presented an opportunity for an authentic and exploratory engagement with the city and its people. Over the years the program offices and seminar space moved to different rental locations. During this period students had the option of lodging in nearby hotels. As New York City real estate values began spiraling upward in the 1980s, it became evident that the program needed a stable location for its administrative offices and a reliably affordable and secure housing option in order to ensure its future. Ohio Wesleyan University purchased the building NYAP currently occupies in Manhattan.

Today students live in a five-story brownstone in the Chelsea district that also houses faculty and administrative offices and common space. Though it features some of the comforts students have become used to on campus, it is not designed to be a refuge from engagement with the city. Living arrangements simulate those of most young professionals in New York who have to budget and improvise studio and work space. By design there is no meal plan, laundry service, or dedicated studio space, and student rooms are much smaller than on their home campus. At the same time, the program benefits from its location in a neighborhood that is a microcosm of the city's diversity. The district is a mix of residential dwellings ranging from low-income public housing to some of the most expensive retail and residential units in the city, as well as one of the largest commuter hubs in the country—Pennsylvania Station. The neighborhood is also home to a soup kitchen that serves over 1,000 meals a day to the poor and homeless.

New York is a city where diverse populations live and work in relatively close proximity. Many students find this to be one of the biggest challenges to their comfort and their sense of themselves as they navigate the city. Students who have participated in international and domestic service projects have a structured position within their host communities: they are there to help. Students attend New York to advance their own work. They must consider themselves as part of the mix, and it is a process—and a struggle—that has figured prominently in the journals and creative work of students over the years. One recent project that crystallized the perceptual shift that can occur as a result was a student's visual/text essay on difference and identity that was inspired by observing and interpreting various unspoken protocols of looking at and responding to homeless people in the neighborhood. In conversations about the project, the student interrogated her relative privilege, her fears, her curiosity, and the preconceived narratives that were part of her gaze. She grappled with sorting through and differentiating what she *felt*, what she *thought*, and what, if any, were the implications for her behavior and actions. Not all students attain the same level of insight, but all are confronted by the challenge to navigate class, racial, and social difference outside of the boundaries of a physical campus that separates them from the community and college governance that structures and mediates conflict.

Some of the most valuable experiences students have had in New York City have been shaped by things such as getting lost or miscommunicating across cultures and language. What domestic and international programs can offer students through a variety of means is a conceptual framework in which experience acquires meaning and value, and a discovery process that keeps unfolding to incorporate change, transformation, and growth.

Notes

1. Though originally designed to serve students from the original 12 colleges in the GLCA consortium, NYAP is now open to students from all accredited institutions. Today it draws most of its students from homes and colleges in the Midwest and Southwest.
2. The NYAP employs a group of core faculty: http://nyartsprogram.owu.edu/people.html

References

Barber, C. L., Sheehan, D., Stoke, S., & McCune, S. (1965). *The new college plan: A proposal for a major departure in higher education.* (Original work published 1958). Hampshire College digital archives. Retrieved from https://dspace.hampshire.edu/bitstream/10009/343/4/Proposal_Major_Departure.pdf

DiConti, V. D. (2004). Experiential education in a knowledge-based economy: Is it time to reexamine the liberal arts? *The Journal of General Education, 53*(3/4), 167–183. Retrieved from http://www.jstor.org/stable/27797990

Jacobs, J. (1989). *The death and life of great American cities.* New York, NY: Random House. (Original work published 1961).

Kelly, D. (2009). Lessons from geography: Mental maps and spatial narratives. In E. Brewer & K. Cunningham (Eds.), *Integrating study abroad into the curriculum: Theory and practice across the disciplines* (pp. 27–40). Sterling, VA: Stylus.

NYAP (NY Arts Program). (2012). *New York Arts Program handbook for campus representatives and faculty.* New York, NY: Author.

Skramstad, H. (1999). An agenda for American museums in the twenty-first century. *Daedalus, 128*(3), 109–128.

Wengenroth, R., et al. (n.d.). Memos and notes. New York Arts Program archive. New York, NY.

18

LIBRARY AND MUSEUM COLLECTIONS AS LABS FOR STUDENT LEARNING

The ACM Newberry Research Seminar in the Humanities

Joan Gillespie

M ayor Richard J. Daley of Chicago is said to have remarked, "What is Paris next to Chicago? Has Paris got Lake Michigan?" A quintessential Chicago booster, the first Mayor Daley was followed in office a few decades later by his son, Richard M. Daley, whose vision as mayor was to add Chicago to the short list of global cities through planned economic growth and development. His vision began to take shape through the city's longtime core strengths, among them a dynamic intellectual and cultural life, a wealth of resources grounded in the community life of neighborhoods, and a high standard for urban aesthetics, beginning with Chicago's greatest natural asset—Lake Michigan. He visited Paris with the mind-set of a student, open to what he might learn there, and his visits inspired him to see the greening of Chicago as part of his mission. He oversaw the planting of hundreds of thousands of trees, the hanging of abundant flower baskets from downtown bridges and lampposts, and introduced a bike-share program, ideas all borrowed from Paris. He spearheaded initiatives to conserve water and energy, building Chicago's reputation as a green city. A term of off-campus study here offers students place-based learning that is the center of off-campus study; they live among a diverse population, and experiences in and out of the classroom direct them to recognize and interpret the complexity of urban life in the past and present. These are lessons that they can apply to their studies on their home campus and to their lives after graduation.

The Newberry Library in Chicago presents such a learning opportunity and can serve as a model for research libraries, museums, archives, and cultural centers in other cities and towns. This important independent research library hosts a term-length research seminar for undergraduates in the liberal arts that complements its mission to support "research, teaching, publication, and life-long learning, as well as civic engagement" ("About the Newberry Library," 2014) through service to scholars and an active program in public humanities. The Associated Colleges of the Midwest (ACM) Newberry Seminar: Research in the Humanities draws faculty fellows from the ACM and Great Lakes Colleges Consortium (GLCA) to team-teach a topical seminar that draws on the Newberry collections and to advise and mentor students in a significant research paper based on material in the Newberry collections. Faculty and administrators in the ACM and GLCA consortia view the program, grounded in the liberal arts and committed to the process of thinking critically and addressing complexity and multiple perspectives, as an invaluable opportunity for their students to do original research at one of the top libraries in the country. Students are not only engaged in a rigorous and sustained intellectual project, but also come to understand the ethos of public humanities and public scholarship at cultural and educational institutions in the United States, in the context of a major city whose history, ethnic diversity, and thriving arts scene support students' explorations and learning.

The Newberry Library was established in 1887 through a gift to the city of Chicago, specified in the will of Walter Newberry, and quickly took a leading role in the cultural life of the rapidly growing city through public education. It became part of the new university extension system in Chicago, and it divided specialized collections with the Chicago Public Library and a third newly established library for the sciences. From the start, collectors for the Newberry focused on acquiring primary or original source material "for the study of European and Western Hemisphere history, literature, and culture since the late medieval period. The Newberry has also continued to build its collection of secondary books—including reference works, monographs, periodicals, and other serials—and more recently digitized reproductions to support the use of its original sources" ("Collection History," 2014). This initial goal developed over time into significant collections from South America, Native Americans, and minority populations in Chicago. In the 1970s, the library created four research centers to distinguish its collections: History of Cartography, American Indian and Indigenous Studies, the

Renaissance, and American History and Culture. Public education continues through lectures, symposia, and special exhibits drawn from the collection.

In this setting, the Newberry Research Seminar was created by the ACM and the Newberry Library, based on the idea that it be "something in the humanities akin to the Argonne National Laboratory project as envisioned by the sciences" (Murray, 1961); the program celebrates its 50th anniversary in 2015. Students are drawn to Chicago and the Newberry seminar because the curriculum will be directly integrated with their on-campus work, particularly if they are preparing for a required capstone project or senior thesis in their major. Here they are fully immersed in the urban environment through the coursework, site visits, internships, and housing, and the city itself becomes a laboratory for learning, the ideal for off-campus study.

Chicago as a place and the experience of the city is central to the program; exploring its neighborhoods and institutions and meeting people whose lives are entwined with the city are activities that are built into the coursework, not only for students who are researching a question about Chicago in the Newberry collections but also for students who are pursuing topics on the Great Lakes region and the Midwest. The seminar uses the city as a learning environment, beginning with events that may be organized for the group or self-guided. A mandatory excursion for recent seminars is the Chicago History Museum, a few blocks from the Newberry Library; the tour is led by a museum curator who himself is an alumnus of the Newberry Research Seminar. Other sites and events include architectural tours; visits to ethnic neighborhoods such as Pilsen and the Mexican Museum of Fine Arts; particular collections in the Art Institute of Chicago; historic locations such as Jane Addam's Hull House and the Pullman Historic District; and performances at the Chicago Civic Opera House, professional theaters, and the Chicago Humanities Festival, whose fall schedule coincides with the seminar.

Another level of community integration of students occurs through an internship program that places each student with one of the Newberry's departments or offices. Before students even arrive on-site, the list of job placements has been shared with them so they can begin to consider how best to match their interests with available placements. Danny Greene and Diane Dillon, from the Newberry's academic programs, see the internship as integral to the program. Dillon said,

> The internship makes students part of the culture, they learn a lot about the working world. It gives them a feeling of privilege, to see the institution in a way the public does not, to be immersed in the culture of the library. It's especially important if they work in the development office, they come to understand how the library works, how all the public events are funded,

for example. (D. Greene & D. Dillon, personal communication, January 28, 2014)

Recent placements have included organizing archival files and assisting with seminars and other programming administration for the Center for American Indian and Indigenous Studies research center; in the development office, performing various duties supporting annual giving and corporate and foundation relations; and in the Special Collections Reading Rooms, assisting with preparations and staffing of professional development seminars for Chicago-area secondary teachers. Elizabeth McKinley, an alumna of the 2011 seminar and now a program assistant in library services at the Newberry and enrolled in the University of Illinois, Urbana-Champaign master's program in library and information systems, was a page in Special Collections. She said,

> I had lots of interaction with outside scholars and the general public and enjoyed helping them because I knew what it was to be in their shoes, as a student in the seminar. As an intern, I got to go into the stacks, retrieving materials for researchers, which is what the librarians were doing for me and the other students. (E. McKinley, personal communication, May 30, 2014)

The final programming detail that supports the student community is the housing in furnished apartments only a few blocks from the Newberry Library, a convenience that allows students to focus on their work more easily than if they were commuting from another part of the city. This proximity also eases their transition to the city environment, as they quickly become familiar with the neighborhood as their home base. Once situated, students are free to discover the city on their own. For those who have spent little time in an urban setting, as well as for students who grew up in Chicago's suburbs, essential lessons are learning the grid layout of city streets and the Chicago Transit Authority's (CTA) train and bus routes. Students are provided with a monthly pass for the CTA, specifically because faculty advisers to the program want students to take advantage of the city's resources. Some students struggle with the urban environment, and some students learn that they do not like it. But this realization is also part of the learning experience. As the term progresses, students create their own itineraries based on their research topics: social activism in turn of the century Chicago, as represented in the first African American parish that continues as an active community, serving a diverse population; how the portrayal of Chicago's inner city in *A Raisin in the Sun* (Hansberry, 1959) compares to the work of Richard Wright; the intersection between art and a vision of social order at Jane Addam's Hull House; and the planned model industrial town of Pullman.

The advantage to students, many of whom come from small Midwestern towns or from campuses in rural communities, is the connection between their social and academic lives in ways that simply do not happen on a campus. A music major chose the program in part so she could continue violin with an instructor who had connections to music faculty at her home college, and for the program's reputation for academic rigor. During the program she found her way to concerts at Millennium Park in downtown Chicago, which included a performance by singers from the Chicago Lyric Opera. "Even as a musician, I don't have many chances to see such high quality performances, so I loved being in Chicago" (Elizabeth C., Luther College, program participant, 2013). Faculty fellows likewise benefit from exploring the city, particularly if their campus life is distinct from urban life. William Davis (Colorado College, Comparative Literature) taught the Fall 2013 seminar with his colleague Eric Perramond (Colorado College, Geography). He said, "The cultural advantage to being in a big city can't be overstated, and Chicago is really interesting, with music and theatre" (W. Davis, personal communication, May 29, 2014).

The Newberry stands in the midst of Chicago's multiple communities—intellectual, social, and cultural, one being the community of scholars. Students' integration into this community is articulated as a learning goal of the program: "To develop an understanding of how a major research library operates through job placements and by participating in the community of scholars at the Newberry" ("Newberry Seminar: Research in the Humanities Learning Outcomes," 2014). Should students have any question about their status in this community before they arrive, it is answered at orientation, when they are asked to sign an agreement regarding library policies governing the reserve space and the use of the information systems as "fellows and scholars" and are provided with a list of the titles and e-mail addresses of the Newberry research staff, which include the reference librarians, curators, directors of programs and centers within the library, and even the president of the library.

The Newberry itself creates the substance of the academics and directs how students conduct their research. It is akin to a museum or an archive in terms of mission—to protect its collections for the visiting public and for researchers and to actively support research through scholar services. For students in the Newberry seminar, this goal translates into the individual experience of confronting an object—be it textual or graphic—and exploring it from a number of perspectives, depending on what one already knows and what one learns during the research process. This direct encounter with material culture—texture, true color, size, smell, whether document or object, the sounds of early audio recordings or film—represents the core of the Newberry seminar. The Newberry collections celebrate this materiality, and undergraduate students interested in conducting primary research through such sources are as eager—and careful—as archaeologists examining their finds from a dig site, in search of a story, or possible new connection. Dillon said, "It's very exciting for students to be working with the material culture of research. They can only get so far with digital resources. The Newberry research gives them a chance to unwrap the onion and learn all that's available by looking at manuscripts, letters, and photographs" (D. Dillon, personal communication, January 28, 2014). This hands-on experience with archival resources distinguishes the program as a lab for students in the humanities.

Students' experience with material culture occurs in the program's two overlapping segments: a six- to eight-week seminar that is topic based and draws from the Newberry collections, and an extended independent research paper. The seminar is team-taught by faculty fellows who are tenured or in tenure-track positions at one of the ACM or GLCA member colleges. The seminar has two purposes: to build common interests and knowledge among students by examining a particular set of questions, and to develop students' familiarity with the library holdings. In order to run the seminar, the faculty fellows must already be familiar with the Newberry, either through their own research, as part of a summer seminar sponsored by the National Endowment for the Humanities, or through a scouting mission that gives them time to explore the collections. Equally important is the faculty fellows' commitment to undergraduate research, given the necessity of creating scaffolding assignments that help students build toward their final paper and advising them through the multiple necessary steps of sound research, writing, and rewriting. Professor Davis said, "The seminar made me think about the different types of research papers that students can write." He supervises senior research projects at Colorado College and said, "I gained insights on working with students to set up a plan, including check-ins for a long paper" (W. Davis, personal communication, May 29, 2014).

A cross-disciplinary approach is the organizing premise of the six- to eight-week seminar, a framework that is supported by the Newberry's four research centers and is an intrinsic value of the program to students. For the purposes of this program, *cross-disciplinary work* is defined as looking at an issue from the perspective of more than one discipline. Seminar topics are purposely broad, given the range of interests of enrolled students whose majors and minors include American studies, anthropology, art history, history, literature, music, psychology, sociology, and self-designed programs.

Their themes raise questions that students can begin to answer using maps, texts, and images found in the collections. The description of the fall 2013 seminar (Representing the Other in Image, Text, and Landscape) takes this approach, building on the Newberry's collections across centuries and peoples:

> In the Old World, European philosophers and literary writers found novel ways of encountering both themselves and radical otherness in the "new world" through a variety of texts. . . . Columbus's voyage, Galileo's cosmos, Luther's threat to papal control—along with the rise of technologies such as the printing press—left many Europeans wondering exactly where in the universe they now belonged. New maps—both literal and figurative—were needed to orient people. . . . How did these new images, maps, texts, and landscapes transform both Old and New World ideas about human diversity, divinities, and cultural discourses? . . . To work toward answers to these questions, we will draw on the unique resources of the Newberry Library in Chicago, resources that will help you conduct substantive research in both humanistic and social-scientific aspects of this complex of historical and contemporary issues. (Perramond & Davis, 2013)

Elizabeth C. enrolled in the program intending to research Baroque music. In searching through sheet music, she came upon a box marked "Indian" with cover art in a late Romantic style and discovered her topic: the stylized representation of Native American themes in American classical music in the early decades of the twentieth century. She said, "My paper continued the discussion from the seminar of mixing the cultures of the Old and New Worlds, of influences and systems of thinking" (Luther College, program participant, 2013).

The 2012 seminar, Wild Cities: Chicago, Buenos Aires, and the Nature of the Modern Metropolis, similarly crossed disciplines. Brian Bockelman (Ripon College, History) and David Miller (Allegheny College, American Studies) wrote the following course description:

> What about its relationship to the wilderness beyond or the wildness within makes a city modern? . . . Is it a new way of experiencing and responding to the chaos, inequality, and creative potential at stake in such a breathtaking convergence of human dreams, struggles, and desires? . . . These are basic humanistic questions. (Bockelman & Miller, 2012)

While the seminar topic needs to be broad so students can incorporate what they have read and discussed into their papers, conversely, the student's research topic can expand the seminar. Professor Davis pointed out this breadth as one of the challenges of teaching the seminar. "Students work in such divergent fields. What they find in the library to research is sometimes chance." Elizabeth C.'s project is an example. As supervisor of this project, Davis articulated what instructors agree is one of the reasons they teach: "I learned so much from her project—the influence of Europeans on creating a pseudo-Native American music" (W. Davis, personal communication, May 29, 2014). A psychology student enrolled in the 2012 seminar wanted to research the trauma that resulted from the Chicago fire in 1872. Since no psychologist works on the Newberry professional staff, Professor Miller worked with the student to closely read textual material in the collections, as a student of literature learns to do.

The seminar in the first six weeks of the program takes students through the early steps of the research project and challenges them to structure their work and manage their time so they are prepared for the final six weeks of the program, when their independent study begins in earnest. Program administrators and faculty fellows break the project into research, writing, and analysis, skills that students learn individually then coordinate in interdependent motion, as swimmers coordinate breathing, stroking, and kicking. Program learning objectives describe this interdependence: "to develop abilities as researchers—formulating interesting and researchable questions; successfully locating, understanding, critically evaluating, and synthesizing materials from the rich Newberry collections; and effectively creating a substantial, well-written and documented research paper" ("Newberry Seminar," 2014). As with past seminars, the 2013 syllabus expands on this goal:

> Our primary focus will be developing you into a crew of independent critical thinkers and researchers, able to tackle and answer difficult questions with no easy solutions. You should expect to leave the Newberry with both a substantial written paper and experience of what graduate seminars entail through continued meetings and close readings of texts across the disciplines. (Perramond & Davis, 2013)

A basic question raised by this program model in the digital age is the existence of the archive itself in the historical context of the book. The Newberry Library has digitized some of its holdings, in keeping with the principle of democratizing access to them and to support the research process by permitting scholars and students to check online resources and plan a research strategy before they enter the building. The challenge of working with traditional-age college students who do not know the world without the Web is not to separate them from the resources with which they are familiar but to teach them to use digital tools in a new way, combining research with original artifacts and digitized material. For the Newberry program the solution lies both in the subjects that students research and in the questions they ask about them. For example, a student investigating a topic of current interest in the late nineteenth or early twentieth century can read the *Chicago Tribune* in digitized version, but seven other Chicago newspapers from the nineteenth and twentieth centuries are not digitized, requiring the student to investigate the archival holdings for a complete picture of how the press represented the topic. Elizabeth C. discovered the limitations of digital material in her research; while the music she studied had been digitized, the covers on the sheet music had not, and she found that this art romanticized Native American culture along with the music.

Faculty fellows build research exercises into the seminar with short assignments in the early weeks when students focus on the selection of their topic. Students explore the collections and choose specific texts or objects to examine—materials that might have been based on a presentation made by Newberry professional staff or that may build on a student's previous work in a course taken on their home campus. Students may be asked to propose two or three topics based on their explorations, one of which can serve as a backup in case the most favored topic does not prove feasible. The critical point is that the student's topic grows out of the collections with reference to the seminar theme. As students narrow their search for a topic, they practice research skills and simultaneously draw on different disciplinary methodologies. One successful strategy for learning how to structure the research process is to complete assignments that serve as building blocks for the long paper, such as analyzing documents through close reading, searching for secondary sources, and developing arguments. These early research and writing exercises also serve another purpose, to relieve student anxiety about a single grade for the final research paper.

Once students select a topic and articulate a research question, they are assigned to one of the two faculty fellows as a principal adviser and also are paired with one of several Newberry senior scholars from one of the four research centers who provides specialized advice about bibliographic resources. Students' access to the professional staff is embodied in Newberry's mission. As academic program staff note, "Service to scholars and students is at the center of the Newberry ethos," and the resident fellows and librarians enact this ethos by "enabling scholarship" not only for the PhD candidates and postdoctoral fellows but also for the undergraduates (D. Greene, personal communication, January 28, 2014). "Their job is to introduce undergraduates to the library and to the rigors and excitement of scholarship. And they see the reward in students examining the collections and developing their projects" (D. Dillon, personal communication, January 28, 2014). This community also provides another compelling reason to work with the Newberry collections directly, rather than conduct research by accessing digital sources, namely that students can examine the archival documents with an expert at their side. "I agree wholeheartedly with the idea of the Newberry being a community of scholars. It's a very welcoming group, everyone is very approachable, maybe because the collection draws so much on Chicago history and we're here, in Chicago. And Diane Dillon assigns students to the absolute best person to work with on their topic" (E. McKinley, personal communication, May 30, 2014). The intersecting communities of the Newberry and Chicago also benefit the faculty fellows who teach the seminar. As a faculty fellow, Professor Davis found it equally valuable to talk to other researchers at the library about their work and to use the collections for his own work.

Faculty fellows create peer groups, in part as an additional venue for students to receive feedback, in part to demonstrate the collaborative potential of academic research to counter students' perceptions of it as a highly solitary enterprise. The 2013 syllabus described this goal: "to develop skills as members of a research community, capable of discussing complex texts in an open-ended seminar setting; sharing the results of research and writing with peers; and offering, receiving, and using suggestions for revisions" (Perramond & Davis, 2013). Groups of three or four participants may be formed around a topic or a set of similar challenges and typically meet weekly to discuss the status of their individual work and report on each other's weekly progress to the faculty fellows. McKinley said of this approach, "I learned how to work in a group, and how to share ideas with people working on very different projects, which helped my listening skills. I have been able to apply (the experience) to my work and graduate school in a way I never had imagined" (E. McKinley, personal communication, May 30, 2014). Another successful model has been an afternoon workshop planned by each group to present and discuss a common practical problem, such as time management or editing one's work. Faculty fellows are also deliberate in working with students on their writing as part of the research enterprise. They might run a workshop on the writing process, starting with the elements of an introduction, and assign small writing tasks of only two or three pages.

The intellectual value of the term-length program is that it allows students time to rewrite—and rethink—their work. According to Newberry Library's Greene, "Not a lot of academic programs allow this much time any more. What students are doing takes time—ideas have to simmer. Students see something develop slowly, steadily" (personal communication, January 28, 2014). A further intellectual complexity of the writing and analysis, introduced through the lens of cross-disciplinarity, is entertaining or understanding the legitimacy of two conflicting ideas, a sign of intellectual and personal development. He continued, "They develop a point of view and can claim intellectual ownership of their idea" (personal communication, January 28, 2014). The writing ultimately works toward analysis. "The intellectual growth is for students to move from being consumers of knowledge to producers of knowledge," he said (D. Greene, personal communication, January 28, 2014).

Support for this program comes from the professional staff of the Newberry Library, faculty advisers to the program from ACM and GLCA colleges, and the consortial staff whose offices are in Chicago. Faculty fellows single out the central importance of the library staff to the success of the program, a point that cannot be overemphasized in the success of this model. The two faculty fellows from the 2011 program, Diane Lichtenstein (Beloit College, English and Women & Gender Studies) and Linda Sturtz (Beloit College, History), wrote in their final report, "The generosity and expertise of the Newberry Library staff are among the greatest strengths of the program. We and the students benefited in countless ways from the enthusiastic dedication of the reference and circulation librarians as well as from the directors of Centers" (Lichtenstein & Sturtz, 2012). The relationship between the faculty fellows and librarians begins when faculty make an early visit to the collections as they write their seminar proposals and continues through the admissions process when Newberry professional staff read student applications, then coordinate all details of the seminar and student research.

For the faculty fellows, opportunity for development extends beyond the life of the program. Many of them return to campus and become faculty advisers, committed to the program goals and dogged in identifying potential students for the program and advising them about it. They also form the program's institutional memory and are forthcoming in sharing their experiences with incoming faculty fellows about successes and challenges. The group meets at the Newberry while the program is in its final weeks to engage in discussions immediately relevant to the program. A recent meeting agenda topic, for example, focused on incorporating digital tools in applying quantitative methods through electronic sources to the humanities. Besides the opportunity to remain part of the Newberry community as faculty advisers to the program when they return to campus, faculty fellows realize other tangible benefits to their teaching and research. Professor Bockelman said, "I've made the Newberry part of my professional life, another base, there are all kinds of projects that I can do there," given the extensive collections on South America. Coteaching the Wild Cities seminar with Professor Miller, he realized parallels between Chicago and Buenos Aires that offer "long-term potential research." The term at the Newberry also made him more aware of resources in Chicago such as the University of Chicago, where he received a grant to conduct research, leading him to "re-envision my teaching and research as regional. The Newberry and the ACM work in tandem and connect to my best teaching experiences at Ripon [college]" (B. Bockelman, personal communication, June 2, 2014).

The Newberry Library program actively encourages students to think about their career options, since many students apply to the program with the thought of pursuing an academic career or work in a museum or library. It arranges brown-bag lunches with resident fellows and librarians to introduce students to a range of professionals in the humanities who arrive at the library via different routes. Faculty advisers see the research essay as a potential writing sample for graduate school or professional school, or an experience to discuss in a postgraduate scholarship or fellowship essay for awards such as Fulbright, Marshall, Rhodes, or Truman. The Newberry Library administrators see reciprocal benefit in hosting this program, because several students who were enrolled in the program have returned to work there. "They fall in love with the library and also are committed to working with students. They bring this ethos with them and communicate their enthusiasm to the other staff" (D. Greene, personal communication, January 28, 2014). The two students interviewed for this study found the Newberry of direct value when they completed their undergraduate degrees. In considering her experience, McKinley said, "I knew what I liked to study, history and French, but I wasn't sure how to apply it. Being at the Newberry, I learned what I wanted to do." Elizabeth C. is now enrolled in two master's degree programs at Indiana University, in musicology and library science, with the goal of working in a music library. The work that students complete in the Newberry Research Seminar extends beyond these career options: here, they learn to adapt to a new environment with new faculty mentors and peers, and they complete a major project of original research by working independently and in groups and by seeking advice from experts. These accomplishments, and the self-confidence that attends them, all represent transferable skills, and career options are open for a student who would bring such skills to his or her chosen work after college.

The key components of the Newberry Research Seminar that are articulated in the learning objectives and realized by committed staff and faculty might be emulated in different settings. The symbiotic relationship between the Newberry and the city of Chicago exists in other communities where a cultural resource is part and parcel of the locale. As the program itself was based on a prototype at the Argonne National Laboratory and translated for students in the humanities, so might other faculty and administrators seek out a partner that will provide the same benefits for their students. In summarizing the value of the seminar, Professor Davis noted, "For liberal arts students, time at an actual library is a very meaningful thing, and the experience of Chicago is eye-opening for them" (W. Davis, personal communication, May 29, 2014).

References

About the Newberry Library. (2014). Retrieved from http://www.newberry.org/about

Bockelman, B., & Miller, D. (2012). *Wild cities: Chicago, Buenos Aires, and the nature of the modern metropolis.* (2014). Retrieved from http://acm.edu/uploads.cms.document/newberry_syllabus_-fall2013_wild_cities.pdf

Collection history. (2014). Retrieved from http://www.newberry.org/collection-history

Hansberry, L. (1959). *A raisin in the sun.* New York, NY: Random House.

Lichtenstein, D., & Sturtz, L. (2012, February 7). Directors' Report, ACM Newberry Library Research Seminar 2011. Associated Colleges of the Midwest archives, Chicago.

Murray, J. (1961). Newberry research seminar (internal memo). Archives of the Newberry Library, Newberry Library, Chicago, IL.

Newberry Seminar: Research in the Humanities Learning Outcomes. (2014). Retrieved from http://acm.edu/programs/14/newberry/Academics.html

Perramond, E., & Davis, W. (2013). *Representing the other in image, text, and landscape.* Retrieved from http://acm.edu/uploads.cms.document/newberry_syllabus_-fall2013_representing_the_other.pdf

19

IMMERSING STUDENTS IN CONSERVATION AND COMMUNITY

Northwest Connections

Melanie Parker

Montana's Swan Valley is in the heart of the Crown of the Continent, an 18-million-acre ecosystem spanning the U.S.-Canada border and surrounding Glacier-Waterton International Peace Park. The Nature Conservancy considers it one of the top five intact ecosystems in the world. The Swan Valley is a forested gem, dotted with wetlands and teeming with wildlife such as grizzly bears, wolves, and lynx. It is surrounded on two sides by designated wilderness areas: the Bob Marshall Wilderness Area to the east and the Mission Mountains Wilderness to the west. The valley is home to a small community of residents and is the destination for many visitors who come to fish, hunt, hike, and explore. It is also adjacent to the Flathead Indian Reservation and is considered within the treaty territory of the Confederated Salish and Kootenai Tribes.[1]

Over the past 100 years, the Swan Valley has been characterized by a culture and economy tied to timber resources. By the 1980s, the Swan Valley was one of those iconic places where conflict over natural resources was high, and people found themselves on one side or the other of polarized environmental debates.[2]

In the 1990s, Northwest Connections, a nonprofit organization integrating conservation and education, was established. Many of the founding
board and staff members were practitioners in a growing movement toward
community-based conservation in the United States. We were among those
who had seen the environmental wars over spotted owls, salmon, timber,
water, and rangeland all across the West create deep rifts in civil society and
result in state and federal environmental policies that were locally resented
and likely not durable over time.

Through Northwest Connections, we initiated participatory science
projects to inform a more collaborative and long-lasting approach to conservation in our region of Montana. We noticed that most young professionals
arriving on the scene were not skilled in interdisciplinary thinking, sensitive
to rural culture, or experienced at navigating and collecting data outdoors.
We also noticed that the undergraduate students who were interested in finding common-ground solutions at the intersection of ecology and economy
were going overseas. It seemed that field programs existed in Southern Africa,
Central America, and Southeast Asia, but we could not find a field program
at that time that offered an immersion in community, collaboration, and
ecology here in the United States. We realized that a gap existed in field-
based education that we at Northwest Connections could help fill.

Northwest Connections began offering one-week winter-session courses
in 1997 through an agreement with the University of Montana.[3] As part of
the Winter Field Studies program, students learned about winter ecology,
animal tracking, and the conservation of rare carnivores. They spent much of
the week camping in the snow-covered mountains of Montana, and as part of
the course they participated in a long-term ecological monitoring project on
lynx, fisher, pine marten, and wolverine. Core to the curriculum was the
opportunity for students to spend time with local fur trappers, taxidermists,
and loggers, folks few students had ever met, much less spoken with. Often
students would discover that they had unexpected shared values with these
local residents. They met people who cared about the land and who valued
spending time outdoors. They were faced with the apparent contradiction of
people who saw consumption as a core part of stewardship and conservation.

A certain magic became evident. We would take students to meet with
local residents and biologists. At first these speakers were distrustful of our
motives and often came off as confrontational with students. Over time, we
noticed the residents warming up to the students, the academic world they
represented, and even new ways of thinking about conservation. In the students, we saw a rapid maturation: an expanded ability to accept complexity; a tolerance for views not their own; and a deeper appreciation for the

specifics of culture, history, and place. With the value of our field courses validated and students continuing to enroll, we resolved to grow the program.

In the year 2000, we planned and offered a full semester-length program titled Landscape and Livelihood.[4] We designed five different courses[5] and went about the project of weaving them together into a seamless immersion in ecology and community. Each of the courses had a formal academic introduction to the currently available ecological science, then progressed to readings and speakers highlighting environmental policy issues, and culminated in students going into the field to see examples of collaborative solutions that bridge science, policy, and community.

The pedagogy involved a full range of approaches. We typically began each day with a lecture, or what we call a "chalk talk," on the academic underpinnings of the day's lesson. We then would do one of two things: involve students in participatory science projects that help them understand the key natural science concepts, or engage students with regional experts to cement their grasp of the social science issues. The latter almost always included local residents with no formal training, but with experience and insight into the issue at hand. We also inserted a number of service-learning opportunities, such as the community firewood day where students cut and deliver heating wood to elderly residents.

We recruited for Landscape and Livelihood on campuses across the country, securing students from places as diverse as Lewis and Clark College, Purdue University, Texas A&M, University of Vermont, and University of Montana.

It became evident that living on our 80-acre rustic homestead in the heart of Montana's Swan Valley for two months had an amplifying effect. Now the students were not just short-term visitors but part of a learning community that brought them into contact with undergraduates from all over the country. They cooked together. They did chores together. They discussed issues together. They taught each other.

Finally, we instituted a homestay experience. Each student was pulled from the group and placed with a local family. While the duration of this homestay was only one weekend, it became one of the signature aspects of our program. It is often true that alumni come back 10 years later not to visit Northwest Connections, but to visit their homestay family.

Around the coffee table, or while out splitting wood or traveling to community events, students and families spent their homestay time confronting each other's preconceptions. Often students were uncomfortably stereotyped as hippies or environmental radicals. We asked them to listen first, not be defensive, not preach, and try to understand their homestay family's experience. The students found it challenging, but reported learning better discursive and analytical skills.

Toward the end of the Landscape and Livelihood field semester, we wrap up one of the individual courses, Forests and Communities, with a role-play where students are asked to represent the opinions of a diversity of stakeholders and develop a collective plan of action. Invariably, their homestay experience shines through as they demonstrate the ability to understand different worldviews. In the debrief, students report that the combination of meeting people with diverse perspectives and having to represent some of the views with which they are least comfortable has better equipped them to be collaborative problem solvers.

One of the hallmarks of Northwest Connections is that we work hard not to promote one particular perspective. Students often beg staff to tell them their own personal opinions, and we do our best to resist. Instead we challenge students to think for themselves. We expose them to as many divergent worldviews as we can and then ask them to reflect on how best to find common ground that meets the needs of both land and people.

> Being immersed in real world learning situations has been the most amazing, educational, and satisfying experience of my life. . . . I learned how to be an active, engaged citizen and community member and to always think critically. This has changed the rest of my life. (Will B., University of Vermont, program participant, 2009)

Recently, we developed a new program that returns us more to our roots in engaging students in outdoor fieldwork, and learning about the relative importance of science and local knowledge in conservation. Our new program, Wildlife in the West, has been running since 2011. This is a nine-credit course that lasts five weeks in May and June and looks specifically at the conservation of threatened and endangered wildlife. Since wildlife is the basis of so much of the controversy and policy tension in natural resource management, we think it is a great lens through which to study community and collaboration.

Students coming to Wildlife in the West are more often than not coming from land-grant colleges: institutions such as Iowa State and Virginia Tech. Exit interviews show that students gain tangible field skills, knowledge of plant and animal ecology, as well as a deeper understanding of the complexities in wildlife management. Seasoned biologists often tell the students that they went into school thinking their jobs would involve managing animals, and now realize that the bulk of their job is managing people. Our intent is to prepare undergraduates for this reality in wildlife and natural resource management.

> I gained extensive experience in animal tracking, plant identification, and habitat management practices, as well as enhanced my skills in radio telemetry, map and compass reading, and wilderness survival. My understanding of wildlife management and conservation is forever changed. I am a better student, scientist and person. (Andria D., Humboldt State University, program participant, 2012)

Conservation practices have undergone a dramatic shift over the past two decades. The trend in key landscapes across the world has been more toward a focus on people, a focus on economy, and an integration of science and local knowledge. The new conservation paradigm suggests that young professionals need new skills, new knowledge, and an increased appreciation for the relationship between humans and their environment. At Northwest Connections, we feel strongly that undergraduate students can benefit from immersing themselves in certain aspects of culture and experience here in the United States and learn something just as valuable as they might with an overseas program. Community-based conservation is just as instructive in Montana as it is in Kenya, Nepal, or Costa Rica—and the lessons learned might just be more transferable.

After 17 years of offering field-based courses in the United States, this is what we've learned.

The Case Study Approach Works

All of Northwest Connections' programs use Montana's Swan Valley and the surrounding communities in the Blackfoot and Mission Valleys as case studies. Students go deep into the specifics of the history and ecology of these places, and the complexities that have produced the environmental controversies here in Western Montana. But the impact of their learning reaches well beyond this localized geography.

Most students report that field-based courses at Northwest Connections give them a template for understanding other places. They reenter their college environment, or their home environment, eager to study the specific science and politics there. They exit our programs appreciating that context matters, and they apply that wherever they go on to live, work, or travel. "Place based education has provided me with essential skills that I can apply to pressing global issues" (Cody D., University of Montana, program participant, 2013).

Field-Based Education Is Relevant to Career Development and Professional Success

Students are able to use Northwest Connections' programs on their resumes and often use their experiences with us as work-related references. Because field courses involve so much time developing hands-on skills, and because we get to see them in a 24/7 situation, living and working with peers, we are uniquely positioned to offer students a scaffolding that bridges academia and work experience.

> The mentoring and experiences I was provided by the people at Northwest Connections was instrumental in shaping my awareness of natural resources, a factor which has contributed to much of my professional success and personal fulfillment. (Casey J., Wildlands Volunteer Corps, 1999)

Furthermore, once employed, several alumni report that Northwest Connections' programs contributed to their success. One student worked for the Bureau of Land Management in Nevada and reported that our courses helped him approach the difficult task of working with cattle ranchers to restore degraded rangelands. Another student reported that she learned the skills to be a better field biologist dealing with wolves and ranchers in Montana's Madison Valley. "I learned to be respectful of the people who live on the landscape, the multi-generational knowledge and love they have for their lands" (Julie F., Montana State University, program participant, 1998).

Community Members Benefit From Hosting Field Programs

Joanna Tenny was a 2002 program participant from Arkansas. After completing the program, she returned to Northwest Connections as a graduate student and Ford Foundation Fellow researching the impacts of our program. By interviewing community speakers and homestay families, she was able to document that these local participants in our program gained much from their involvement. Community members particularly appreciated being asked questions, not told facts, and discovering that students wanted to understand their perspectives.

> The students coming down to the ranch to work is a message, "Welcome to reality." I think it's great. Who thought this up? It's amazing. Students want to come here and listen to us and learn? The fact that they're here, wanting to talk to us, I mean, wow, that's amazing. (Tenny, 2006)

Further, they reported learning things about wildlife and ecology that they hadn't known before.

> What I gain and others do is the opportunity of a broader dialogue that you just wouldn't have if you weren't set up to think about it. When the students are here, you're thinking about what you're saying to them. I have to think harder about what is really happening on the land, so that what you're saying expresses as many of the truths as possible because what happens on the landscape we have is so complicated and we need to see them all together and weigh them. Without the students we would be more inclined to be lazy with our thought processes, and not think about it as a whole. (Tenny, 2006)

Currently, Northwest Connections is working to broaden its internship program. We welcome alumni back to serve for three- to six-month internships. Our goal is to further bridge undergraduates' studies to their future careers. We have interns managing the farm that produces fresh food for our students and the local community. We have interns doing media and communications work including producing short documentary films. Still other interns are assisting with courses and fieldwork. To us, this is just another way that students can further their apprenticeship in community-based conservation.

Domestic field study programs like those at Northwest Connections provide an important opportunity for undergraduates in the United States to better understand aspects of their own country that by virtue of their background they would otherwise never understand.

> Although the semester is very focused on the Swan Valley area the knowledge gained while here is transferable to any part of the county and globe. I am so grateful for this opportunity to get to know a place and its people. (Celeste M., University of Montana, program participant, 2009)

Notes

1. Treaty of Hellgate, 1855. Retrieved from www.cskt.org/documents/gov/helgatetreaty.pdf.
2. See, for example, Manning (1991).
3. Academic credit for all Northwest Connections courses is through the University of Montana's School of Extended and Lifelong Learning, which students transfer to their home institution.
4. Landscape and Livelihood is a 16-semester, credit program, running from late August through early November.

5. The five courses that make up Landscape and Livelihood are Biogeography of Northwest Montana (Geography 391); Forests and Communities (Natural Resource Science and Management 346); Watershed Dynamics (Natural Resource Science and Management 345); Sustainability and Agriculture (Geography 391); Community Conservation Research Project (Environmental Studies 395).

References

Manning, R. (1991). *Last stand.* Layton, UT: Peregrine Smith Books.

Tenny, J. E. (2006). *Community forestry education in the Swan Valley, Montana: Contributions of Northwest Connections' field program* (Unpublished doctoral thesis). University of Montana, Missoula.

20

"NO SUCH THING AS AWAY"

Urban Immersion in the Upper Midwest— and Around the World

Sarah Pradt

innesota in general, and the Twin Cities metropolitan area of Minneapolis and Saint Paul in particular, have long been identified as places that trouble notions of "the Heartland" as socially and economically conservative, clannish, insular, and complacent. Instead, Minnesota's past and present reveal many habits, policies, and movements that have been radical, focused on the broad social good, engaged with the world, and earnest in a desire to make change. The Minnesota mosaic of analyses of societal problems and solutions to them has come from many sources. Before Europeans arrived, the indigenous people who lived in a land of beauty and relative plenty had developed elaborate cultural traditions with care for others (family, the elderly, allies) at the core (Treuer, 2010; Westerman & White, 2012). Later, European and other immigrants also brought ideas about the obligations people have to care for one another. Newcomers in the nineteenth and twentieth centuries included Yankee elites who moved west with lumber and other extractive industries; Lutheran immigrants from Scandinavia and Germany; Catholic immigrants from Ireland, Eastern Europe, and Germany; African Americans in the two great northward migrations; and Latinos from Mexico and Texas. Toward the end of the twentieth century, Hmong refugees came from Laos and Vietnam, and East Africans came from Somalia, Ethiopia, and Eritrea.

Many explanations of the respective cultural contributions of indigenous Minnesotans and newcomers can be found—some verging on caricature (think Garrison Keillor). One apt description comes from Mark Ritchie, the current secretary of state of Minnesota, who has also served as president of the Institute for Agriculture and Trade Policy, a nonprofit organization that "works locally and globally at the intersection of policy and practice to ensure fair and sustainable food, farm and trade systems" (IATP, 2014). Ritchie has suggested that the legacy of past Minnesotans includes being conscious of the gifts of the land's beauty and diversity, caring for others in the community, providing for those less fortunate or with different abilities, caring for the nation by volunteering for military and other types of national service, investing generously in the arts, and participating in public life (Ritchie, 2008). Concrete early expressions of Minnesotans' values included the first child labor laws in the nation and one of the most active labor movements in the United States; settlement houses that served immigrants from Europe and African American migrants from southern states; radical agrarian movements; cooperative movements led by farmers and small processors to contest corporations' control of shipping and markets; early investment in public schools, a land-grant university, and numerous private colleges; and land set aside in extensive urban park systems (Adams, 2000, p. 109; Pratt & Spencer, 2001).

Higher education in Minnesota has a similarly progressive history, and off-campus study has developed in that spirit. In 1968, responding to the turmoil in Minnesota and around the world after the assassination of Dr. Martin Luther King Jr., several faculty members and administrators at colleges and universities in Minneapolis and Saint Paul sought to bring relevance to curricula by involving students directly in analyzing and acting on the "pressing urban issues of the day"—poverty and racial injustice. At the same time, some institutions of higher education in Minneapolis also began to try to tap the potential for learning in their urban locations, seeking to involve students in the extensive social service and advocacy networks in that city. Together, 12 institutions in Minnesota, Iowa, and North Dakota collaborated on a program they called "Crisis Colony," and so began what is now the Higher Education Consortium for Urban Affairs (HECUA). Crisis Colony, described as an "experimental project for academic credit" and a "live-in," brought students into Minneapolis neighborhoods struggling with high concentrations of poverty, unemployment, and deteriorated housing. Students remained enrolled in their home campuses but lived, learned, and worked in those neighborhoods. Over a period of two academic years, Crisis Colony brought undergraduates to different neighborhoods in Minneapolis, including a predominantly African American neighborhood and a neighborhood with the largest urban population of Native Americans in the United States. The Crisis Colony program reserved student places for each of the 12 campuses, and the program offered an "urban seminar" taught by residents and activists working in that particular neighborhood, an independent study project supervised by a home campus faculty member, and a "program of participant observation in community life" that involved significant time working at an agency or organization dedicated to social change.

The curricular design and teaching in that program had a number of deep and interrelated influences, ranging from progressive educational theory to theology to Marxism. The act of taking students out of the classroom and into the world was tied to the Scandinavian folk-school movement, which was also the initial inspiration for Myles Horton and the movement for popular education he built at the Highlander School in Tennessee, another deep influence on HECUA (Horton, 2003a). Going off campus also owed much to John Dewey's insistence on education as "reconstructed or reorganized experience," and to Dewey's confidence in the power of education to reshape society (Dewey, 1916, pp. 79, 99). The structure of the program and the deep involvement of neighborhood residents and advocates reflected Paulo Freire's ideas about community education and Dewey's redefinition of the teacher's role (Dewey, 1998, p. 65; Freire, 1998, p. 117). Similarly, the HECUA enterprise sought to enact Myles Horton's intertwining of movements for racial justice and for popular education (Horton, 2003b, p. 8). The program's connections to labor movements and to Lutheran activism both on and off campus embodied the early work of theologian Reinhold Niebuhr on the social gospel of Jesus.

The teaching did not always explicitly identify and explore each of those influences, but animated them in its extensive reflection, structured measuring of theory against practice, broad expansion of the notion of who was qualified to be a "teacher," and hands-on participation in civic life. In 1970 the Crisis Colony program was renamed "Metro Urban Studies Term." It had become a core component in the curriculum on some campuses and was offered every semester. The following year, the HECUA consortium was incorporated as a 501(c)(3) nonprofit to manage the finances, enrollment, and extensive community partnership work of the program. HECUA has offered the Metro Urban Studies Term continuously ever since, renaming it in 2012 as "Inequality in America."

Despite the longevity of Crisis Colony/Metro Urban Studies Term/Inequality in America, HECUA has been restless in its development of new off-campus programming, driven by the interests of faculty and students on consortium campuses, societal change, and a persistent interest in how people seek to solve social problems in other places, using other tools.

Robert White has described Minnesota culture as "simultaneously insular and worldly-wise" (White, 2000, p. 307). Minnesotans may be physically distant from both coasts, but maintain a focus beyond the borders of the nation (White, 2000). Before about 1990, Minnesotans looked to Northern Europe, where many had ancestral ties, and toward Mexico, Latin America, and Southeast Asia, from where many of the new Minnesotans of the twentieth century had come.

Thus, it was no surprise that in the 1970s HECUA moved beyond the United States, and it was natural for HECUA to move into Scandinavia and Latin America, home of thinkers and movements that had been so influential. A key leader of the Crisis Colony program was Joel Torstenson, a sociologist at Augsburg College (Minneapolis). In 1970 Torstenson was on sabbatical in Scandinavia, and the following year he led the HECUA co sortium in developing a study abroad program in Scandinavia. The "Scandinavian Urban Studies Term" was meant to complement the Metro Urban Studies Term, and offered comparative study of urban systems of politics, education, and planning in the United States and in the Scandinavian welfare states. Students were based in Oslo and spent time in Stockholm and Copenhagen. Like the Metro Urban Studies Term students in Minneapolis, they practiced reflection, tested theory against practice, and engaged first-hand with policymakers and planners.

With a growth of interest in engaged and community-based learning, in the mid-1970s Latin Americanists on the various campuses found the HECUA programs' Freirean approach appealing, and their students were seeking firsthand understanding of Latin American popular movements. The consortium developed a program that took students to Bogotá, Colombia, with field study in Peru and Guatemala. "South American Urban Semester" brought students into contact with pressing issues in Latin America—poverty, colonialism, indigenous rights, economic exploitation—and with the ideologies and movements that had emerged to resolve those issues. HECUA soon offered additional programs in Guatemala, Cuba, and Ecuador, and by the late 1990s had offered simultaneously or sequentially seven different programs in Latin America with a variety of core themes, including urban studies, art, literature, economics, and the environment.

As HECUA matured as an organization, there began to be an articulation of "the HECUA model." Faculty in the Twin Cities and Latin American programs met regularly and circulated position papers and reflections on teaching. The faculty in Latin America and the Latin Americanists on the campuses who supported the programs deepened HECUA's pedagogical methods and political analyses, particularly Marxist and Freirean, and these analyses sharpened all programs' focuses on systems, oppression, community education, and the role of popular movements in solving social inequalities. Across the programs, those who taught were also practitioners: organizers, artists, and board members and staff at nonprofit organizations. By the end of the 1980s, the faculty, staff, and board had developed a set of principles and practices for HECUA pedagogy, codified in a manual and in trainings for those teaching in the programs. Faculty, staff, and board members asserted the value of *practical knowledge*, which they defined as "gained through experience," and stressed the importance of the sociopolitical and cultural contexts in which knowledge is understood. Their commitment to experiential learning grew from an understanding of knowledge as multidimensional (social, emotional, and spiritual, as well as cognitive), and from a belief that experiential learning, with its constant attention to the intersection of theory and practice, is the best way for all involved in the educational process to see and acknowledge that multidimensionality.

The HECUA model laid out specific practices to help students see the constructed nature of knowledge and to cocreate through

- attentiveness to the learning environment and the quality and dynamics of relationships among learners and with the instructor;
- a collaborative, self-reflective process that asks students to become conscious of their own worldviews;
- involvement in the real world, not simply to "test theory" but to help students develop critical thinking skills within ethical parameters in order to make responsible, conscious choices; and
- the assumption that students are teachers as well as learners, with an invitation to students to become cobuilders of knowledge.

Finally, they articulated a clear goal of HECUA teaching: Programs in the United States and abroad are meant to help students "address the inequalities and social challenges in our society." Students who go abroad "develop skills in cross-cultural learning," but "a primary goal" is to help them "use the experience to analyze and address issues in their home communities" (HECUA, n.d.). It is not clear if HECUA's leaders in the late 1980s understood "home communities" to be global communities, but a fundamental assumption of the HECUA project today is that U.S. and global contexts are intimately linked.

Building Programs in a Local-Global World

Ongoing program building and teaching has engaged with that intimate connection of the local and global. In the 1980s and 1990s HECUA's semester-long programming in Minneapolis and Saint Paul expanded to explore the role of art and culture in social transformation, which often included the artistic responses of newer Minnesotans to challenges of racism and discrimination. In 1999 a faculty member on the Hamline University campus connected HECUA with his colleagues in Bangladesh to build a January-term program that not only taps into students' interest in international development but also questions assumptions about who and what international development efforts are for. In 2000 HECUA began a program that connects students to people working in Northern Ireland's postconflict transition to democracy. HECUA staff met with U.S. and Northern Ireland staff at Public Achievement, a youth civic-organizing program created at the University of Minnesota and now housed at Augsburg College. Public Achievement had recently begun working in Northern Ireland, encouraging young people to be "co-creators of the democratic way of life in their schools, neighborhoods and the larger society and world" (Boyte, 2002, p. 26). HECUA students in the Twin Cities had been interns in Public Achievement's work with East African, Latino, and Hmong residents in Saint Paul, and the consonance of programming in the Twin Cities and Belfast and Derry/Londonderry helped program development move swiftly.

In 2003 HECUA initiated a program in the Twin Cities focusing on environmental sustainability, with a focus on the social dimensions of environmental change, particularly climate change. In 2011 HECUA developed a fall semester program in New Zealand that explores Māori and European-heritage frameworks for managing that beautiful and fragile island environment.

No Such Thing as Away: The Proximity of the Local and the Global

The population of Minnesota has changed greatly since HECUA began its work in 1968. Minnesota now has the second-largest population of Hmong in the United States, and the largest population of Somalis outside of Africa. Between 1982 and 2008 more than a million immigrants from 182 nations passed through Minnesota seeking new homes; a third have remained (Owen, Meyerson, Otteson, Minneapolis Foundation, & Wilder Research Center, 2010, p. 2). During the 1990s the population of foreign-born residents in Minnesota grew by more than 130%, compared to a national increase of 57% (Owen et al., 2010, p. 1). Students in the Minneapolis and Saint Paul public schools speak more than 100 different languages (Minneapolis Public Schools, 2014; Saint Paul Public Schools, 2014). Latino, Asian, and East African residents bring many values and habits that closely resemble those of the European immigrants who preceded them—hard work, entrepreneurship, and loyalty to family and community. In the last four decades Minnesota residents new and old have created workers' centers, asylee organizations, and cultural centers; vibrant cultures of storytelling, including theater, hip-hop, and spoken word; new voices and perspectives in elected office and public discussion; training programs for immigrant farmers; and collaborative and innovative initiatives in welfare reform, health care, housing, transit, public art, development, and environmental conservation. Of course, much remains imperfect in Minnesota. Native Americans have been shoved out and left out, and the state's sesquicentennial came and went without a meaningful public conversation about the plunder and genocide experienced by the Dakota and Ojibwe.

To the many changes in Minnesota and the world, HECUA has responded as educators and allies, as organizers of connections between communities and the academy, and as facilitators of the creation of knowledge and the building of movements. Cross-fertilization among HECUA programs occurs in many ways. Two faculty who have taught the Twin Cities program on sustainability, for example, have also accompanied students to Bangladesh on that January-term program. Those faculty made links with Bangladeshi advocates for food justice and climate change action in the United States, involved U.S. and Bangladeshi students in the climate change movement in Dhaka, and have connected other students who could not travel across the world to a Bangladeshi who is a leader in food justice networks in the Twin Cities. More than a decade ago, the economist who has been teaching the Inequality in America program in Minnesota taught the Scandinavian Urban Studies Term, working with Norwegian colleagues to renew the curriculum and develop a meaningful internship component in a place where internships were virtually unknown. Similarly, the political scientist who has long been teaching the Race in America program in the U.S. South taught for a semester in Norway, examining with students the culturally and racially fraught project of Norway's relationship to the European Union. The program on inequality in the United States has used human rights frameworks developed by colleagues in Northern Ireland to examine realities in Minneapolis and Saint Paul.

HECUA has changed too. Where once there was a manual for how to teach according to "the HECUA model," there are now retreats in which all faculty and staff meet as a community of practice, sharing the joy and challenge of our dual tasks of seeing and naming injustices and oppressions *and* imagining and building, along with passionate students, alternatives to the status quo. So much of what HECUA has accomplished, as well as the potential for its future, stems from HECUA's peculiar location as being of the consortium institutions but not in them. It is that marginal location that allows HECUA great freedom to take intellectual risks. Since the original Crisis Colony, HECUA has sought to do more than bring students into transformative encounters with those different from themselves; HECUA has sought to involve students in transformation of the world. While faculty on campus may often need to move carefully and deliberately, helping their students to excavate the thought and action of others before students leap into action themselves, HECUA both benefits from and is beholden to its immediate and intimate connections with those working in real time to change the systems and patterns that currently dominate our world. Our colleagues, partners, and communities ask us very tough questions, and they insist that HECUA engage students in those questions and in the work of answering them. Usually those questions are disruptive, disturbing, and disorienting. This chapter's title, "No Such Thing as Away," borrowed from the Zero Waste movement, invokes that disrupting and disorienting mind-set. Zero Waste activists remind us that when living on the surface of a sphere, it is not really possible to throw anything truly "away" (Meyer, 2009). HECUA's domestic and international programs assume analogously that there is no such thing as studying "away," that there is no real "away" to contrast with the "here" we inhabit. And as international educator Richard Slimbach suggested at a study abroad conference in 2012, there's no such thing as "home," either, because whatever away does exist is always and increasingly close.

So with our students we ask questions that bring here and away together, again and again. With our students, colleagues, and villagers in Bangladesh, we ask what the millions of dollars in international aid mean to those described as their recipients. With students, colleagues, and partners in Mississippi, we ask what functions "untold truths" serve, and in Northern Ireland, we learn about the stories that can't be told. With students and environmental activists in rural Minnesota, we ask if we have the courage to intervene in the system—at the terrifying points that are the only ones that will be effective at this moment of peril for the planet. With our students, colleagues, and partners in Northern Ireland, we ask how it is possible to live together with those who've wronged you, or whom you've wronged. With HECUA's former executive director Nadinne Cruz, who visited recently, we ask how we can engage in a democratic epistemology, how we can find and learn from those whose ways of knowing contain the hints for the new paradigms that will keep us all from sliding into the abyss. With students and school change advocates in Saint Paul, we ask if disinvesting in our increasingly brown schools means that Minnesota does not want 60% of its population to succeed. With students and Minneapolis theater artist Meena Natarajan (2008), we also look at Minnesota's changing demographics and ask if we can understand globalization as something other than transactional global economics: What stories can we tell together that will provoke new ways of telling?

References

Adams, J. S. (2000). Minnesota: A work in progress shaping the landscape and the people. *Daedalus: Proceedings of the American Academy of Arts and Sciences, 129*(3), 101.

Boyte, H. C. (2002, November 1). A different kind of politics: John Dewey and the meaning of citizenship in the 21st century. Dewey Lecture, University of Michigan.

Dewey, J. (1916). *Democracy in education: An introduction to the philosophy of education.* New York, NY: Macmillan.

Dewey, J. (1998). Traditional vs. progressive education. *Experience and education: The 60th anniversary edition* (pp. 1–11). West Lafayette, IN: Kappa Delta Pi.

Freire, P. (1998). Pedagogy in process. In P. Freire, A. M. A. Freire, & D. P. Macedo, (Eds.), *The Paulo Freire reader* (pp. 111–162). New York, NY: Continuum.

HECUA. (n.d.). *HECUA program director's manual.* Saint Paul, MN: Author.

Horton, M. (2003a). Educational theory. In M. Horton & D. Jacobs (Eds.), *The Myles Horton reader: Education for social change* (pp. 211–216). Knoxville: University of Tennessee Press.

Horton, M. (2003b). The roots of southern radicalism. In M. Horton & D. Jacobs (Eds.), *The Myles Horton reader: Education for social change* (pp. 7–11). Knoxville: University of Tennessee Press.

IATP (Institute for Agricultural and Trade Policy). (2014). About IATP: Mission statement. Retrieved from http://www.iatp.org/about

Meyer, K. (2009, August 2). No such thing as away. Sermon delivered at Unity Church Unitarian, Saint Paul, MN. Retrieved from http://unityunitarian.libsyn.com/webpage/2009/08

Minneapolis Public Schools. (2014). Demographics of the Minneapolis Public Schools. Retrieved from http://multilingual.mpls.k12.mn.us/demographics

Natarajan, M. (2008, April 26). *What is the future of Minnesota?* (unpublished Samuel Morgan Lecture). Saint Paul, MN: Unity Church Unitarian.

Owen, G., Meyerson, J., Otteson, C., Minneapolis Foundation, & Wilder Research Center. (2010). *A new age of immigrants: Making immigration work for Minnesota: Summary of key findings.* Minneapolis, MN: The Minneapolis Foundation.

Pratt, J., & Spencer, E. W. (2001). Dynamics of corporate philanthropy in Minnesota. In S. R. Graubard (Ed.), *Minnesota, real & imagined: Essays on the state and its culture.* St. Paul: Minnesota Historical Society Press.

Ritchie, M. (2008, April 26). *What is the future of Minnesota?* (unpublished Samuel Morgan Lecture). Saint Paul, MN: Unity Church Unitarian.

Saint Paul Public Schools. (2014). About us: Strong schools, strong communities. Retrieved from http://www.spps.org/aboutus

Slimbach, R. (2012). *The fate of civilization and the future of education abroad: From doorstep to planet.* Carlisle, PA: The Forum on Education Abroad.

Treuer, A. (2010). *Ojibwe in Minnesota.* St. Paul: Minnesota Historical Society Press.

Westerman, G., & White, B. M. (2012). *Mni sota makoce: The land of the Dakota.* St. Paul: Minnesota Historical Society Press.

White, R. J. (2000). Minnesota and the world abroad. *Daedalus: Proceedings of the American Academy of Arts and Sciences, 129*(3), 307.

PART FIVE

COMMUNITY ENGAGEMENT AND DOMESTIC STUDY AWAY

21

LIBERAL EDUCATION AND SERVICE-LEARNING AS A HIGH-IMPACT PRACTICE

Rachel Tomas Morgan and Paul Kollman

What matters today in U.S. higher education?

The state of higher education in the United States has increasingly come under attack and scrutiny. Most high school students aspire to attend college but, despite popular belief that college is no longer reserved for a privileged few, those who enroll and attain a degree are still largely influenced by factors of race and income. Students these days face increasing pressure and competition and thus apply to more schools today than ever before. As a result, in the 2014–2015 academic year, the nation's top elite universities admitted the lowest percentage of students than ever before (Pérez-Peña, 2014). Our colleges and universities are graduating students with levels of debt higher than we have seen in history. Americans have long valued college education for their economic prosperity but grow skeptical when a weak U.S. economy means fewer high-quality jobs when they graduate. With such context, it comes as no surprise that the value of a college education more broadly, and of certain disciplines in particular, comes under deep scrutiny. The stakes are high for U.S. colleges and universities and especially targeted have been the traditional liberal arts associated with the humanities, fine arts, languages, and social sciences. Many students and their parents are unsurprisingly asking the value of a college education.

Educators, policymakers, and employers have been openly debating similar questions in order to articulate the kinds of learning, knowledge, and skills our graduates need and what we should expect from their colleges. Taking stock of concerns about higher education and the rapidly shifting landscape of American life amid the global economy, in 2005 the Association of American Colleges and Universities (AAC&U) launched Liberal Education and America's Promise (LEAP), a national advocacy, campus action, and research initiative that championed the importance of liberal education for the twenty-first century. Since then, the AAC&U's work through LEAP has sought to respond to the changing demands for more college-educated workers and engaged and informed citizens by helping schools focus on what really matters in college (Liberal Education and America's Promise, 2014).

Summarizing years of research and collaborative effort, the LEAP vision for college-level learning has advocated the following "essential learning outcomes" needed by all university and college graduates to navigate and face the demands of an increasingly complex and volatile twenty-first-century global economy (Association of American Colleges and Universities, 2007):

- broad knowledge of human cultures and the physical and natural world through study that focuses on engagement with big questions, contemporary and enduring
- intellectual and practical skills fostered through practices pursued extensively across the curriculum and in the context of progressively more challenging problems, projects, and standards for performance
- personal and social responsibility, anchored through active involvement with diverse communities and real-world challenges
- integrative and applied learning demonstrated through the application of knowledge, skills, and responsibilities to new settings and complex problems

This set of learning outcomes, developed by hundreds of colleges and universities across the country, not only articulates the essential aims and outcomes desired by presidents of a liberal education in the twenty-first century, but also replicates more recent research on what employers seek when they hire (i.e., graduates with knowledge and skills intuitively related to a strong liberal education). Data from a 2013 survey taken by the AAC&U reveal that "regardless of a student's chosen field of study," employers "strongly agree" or "somewhat agree" that every student should attain proficiency in problem-solving in diverse settings (91%); awareness of ethical issues and public debates important in their field (87%); and civic knowledge, skills, and judgment essential for contributing to the community and to our democratic society (82%)—all of which are learning outcomes related to personal and social responsibility. In addition, employers also value direct experiences with community problem-solving (86%), a learning outcome related to integrative and applied learning (Humphreys & Carnevale, 2013). As part of LEAP's framework for fulfilling these outcomes, it has identified certain "high-impact" practices that, within a comprehensive curriculum, help to achieve these outcomes and build real-world capabilities within our students (Kuh, 2008).

This chapter discusses attempts made by one institution to better pre-pare students for these twenty-first-century challenges through one of those high-impact practices: service-learning, now more commonly called community-based learning. We will describe strategies employed by the Center for Social Concerns (the Center) at the University of Notre Dame, and explore the kinds of educational attainments that can occur through the pedagogy, learning goals, and models of globally minded and locally focused civic engagement linked to a liberal education at a faith-based university.

We will focus on assessment the Center has undertaken with students who engage our programming. Such research, still ongoing, suggests to us that combining ethical reasoning and action (through Catholic social teaching, theological reflection, and social analysis), exposure to cultural and ethnic diversity, and global learning allows community-based learning and service-learning to become powerfully integrative avenues for our students. We will argue that combining global learning with civic engagement through community-based learning and service-learning can achieve important learning outcomes and also serve to defend the relevance and restore the vibrancy of liberal education for the twenty-first century.

The Center for Social Concerns at the University of Notre Dame

Founded in 1983, in its efforts to foster moral vision and practice for the kind of learning it hoped to instill in its students, the Center for Social Concerns has closely aligned itself with the university's mission, which includes as a stated goal

> to cultivate in its students not only an appreciation for the great achievements of human beings, but also a disciplined sensibility to the poverty, injustice, and oppression that burden the lives of so many. The aim is to create a sense of human solidarity and concern for the common good that will bear fruit as learning becomes service to justice. (University of Notre Dame, n.d.)

The Center has sought to fulfill core values of the university's mission by providing academic courses shaped by community-based learning, community-based research, and service-learning (Center for Social Concerns, n.d.). Over the past 30 years, the Center has grown to offer hundreds of community-based courses that allow students and faculty to better understand and respond to poverty and injustice with the resources of a research institution and the Catholic social tradition[1] that animates its educational mission. In addition, it has pursued research about how its programming affects students who participate, and research on how it affects communities that are engaged.

The Center employs a multitude of courses and program models. Engaging with local communities in its home in South Bend, Indiana, and with communities across the nation and around the world, the Center offers, supports, and facilitates over 180 academic community-based learning courses and service-learning[2] programs for over 4,400 students annually, working in collaboration with faculty, staff, and community partners.

The Center's "signature" courses and programs—that is, those that are run directly from the Center itself—include 25 offerings for over 1,000 students annually. These include courses and programs in two broad categories—shorter term social concerns seminars and Summer Service Learning Programs—and both types occur in local, national, and international contexts. Such courses offer between one and four academic credits, with class meeting time and coursework occurring before, during, and after the immersion experience, culminating in a final paper or project. Course and program fees are nominal. Most seminar expenses are subsidized through the Center, and summer programs provide additional travel stipends and tuition scholarships to minimize any socioeconomic barriers to participation. Most of the Center's signature courses and programs are oversubscribed, receiving more applications than positions and funding available, and having to turn students away each year.

Over 700 students annually participate in the Center's social concerns seminars, one-credit courses addressing a social issue. Seminars differ in length of community immersion, forms of engagement (direct service or intellectual experiential contact), location (urban or more rural), and religious focus (working with faith-based versus secular organizations). They feature course-specific learning goals and integrate classroom instruction before and after an experiential or service-learning immersion of two to seven days taking place over the university's one-week fall and spring breaks, or the three-week-long winter break. Amid the diversity, all share certain goals, practices, and structures. Students examine social issues connected to poverty and other forms of marginalization from multiple perspectives, study the Catholic social tradition, and take an active role in building a learning community. In addition, all participate in pre- and postimmersion classes, complete readings, and submit a final paper or project.

One of 20 seminars offered, the Appalachia Seminar, with over 400 students participating annually, is most popular with first- and second-year students. It serves as one of the Center's introductory experiential learning courses exposing students to rural poverty in the United States and issues of environmental sustainability. Offered in both fall and spring semesters, students spend their midterm break on a service-learning immersion with one of 16 community partners in the Appalachia region. In addition, for six class sessions before and after the program students learn about the communities and cultures in this region and the challenges they face and hopes they possess.

Other social concerns seminars are focused on topics and locations that range from community-organizing initiatives in Chicago; Mexico-U.S. border and immigration issues; U.S. health care policy in Washington, DC; and learning about the church and social action efforts in 30 cities across the nation. The seminar structure allows flexibility in developing new seminars responsive to emerging social issues and student interest, as well as venues for collaboration with other academic and nonacademic units across the university.

Each year, approximately 225 students participate in the Center's Summer Service Learning Program (SSLP), a three-credit service-learning course in theology with an eight-week immersion working with and learning from persons who are marginalized in society. A unique design within the SSLP is the close collaboration with Notre Dame's extensive alumni network of local clubs, formalized through the Notre Dame Alumni Association and located in over 100 U.S. regions and cities. The local Notre Dame clubs financially sponsor and mentor SSLP students in their geographic location.

The SSLP's goals include inviting students into the process of theological reflection and method of social analysis as a means of interpreting their experience of service in order to gain an understanding of broader social structures, privilege, race, and class, and to deepen a sense of social responsibility in light of Catholic social teaching. Students attend three orientation classes in the spring semester, complete readings and submit writing assignments throughout the summer immersion experience, participate in either a day-long workshop or three follow-up classes when they return to campus in the fall semester, and submit a final integrative paper or project.

Beginning in 1998 the Center has also granted opportunities for students to pursue similar goals within a global context through the International Summer Service-Learning Program (ISSLP).[3] The ISSLP receives over 300 applications for the 50–60 fully funded positions and places students by pairs in 8-week service-learning settings across 26 site locations, working in partnership with 38 site organizations, in 17 developing countries around the world.

Building off the SSLP, the ISSLP was developed specifically to challenge students who already had domestic service-learning experiences to examine causes of global poverty and injustice in order to create links of solidarity across borders. The program articulates three learning goals, hoping students will gain the following: (a) an understanding of the multidimensionality of poverty in the developing world by analyzing root causes and identifying strategies for social development and poverty alleviation; (b) an awareness of global social issues in light of Catholic social teaching, specifically through the themes of solidarity and the preferential option for the poor;[4] and (c) increased cross-cultural competency.

Structured similarly to the SSLP, the ISSLP adds enhanced components to address geographic and cultural study and the complexity of international travel to nontraditional study abroad countries. In recognition that participants earn four credits, it further incorporates a one-credit Global Issues course with 90-minute classes meeting weekly during the entire spring semester as the required predeparture course. Additional components include geographic area and cultural study, a cross-cultural training and weekend retreat, and additional training based on the population and scope of work. Like the SSLP, the ISSLP has students completing readings and writing assignments during the summer immersion, and during the fall semester adds a reentry retreat, additional class sessions, and a presentation in addition to an academic journal and final integrative paper or project.

Outside of the signature courses and programs, the Center also facilitates and supports faculty across the university, in all the colleges, to offer academic community-based learning courses within their disciplines and departments. Over 180 such engaged courses are published annually in the Center's "Community-Based Learning Course Guide" (n.d.), which is designed to help faculty promote and help students to find courses that address social issues and incorporate experiential learning, community-based learning, or community-based research pedagogy. The Center offers an annual institute, which provides faculty new to community-based learning the tools and resources for engaged teaching.

The majority of these community-based learning courses occur in the local South Bend community. For example, in a Spanish-language course taught by a faculty member in the Department of Romance Languages and cross-listed with the departments of Africana Studies and Latin American Studies, students examine key issues of race and ethnicity in U.S. Latina/o literary production, particularly in the works of Afro-Latina/o, Andean-Latina/o (and other Latinos of indigenous descent), and Asian-Latina/o authors. The range of races, ethnicities, and nationalities of the established and emerging authors studied in the course enhances the students' understanding of the complexity and heterogeneity of that group that we call "Latinos." The course, conducted entirely in Spanish, incorporates a service-learning component where students are required to spend two hours per week volunteering in South Bend's Hispanic community center, Casa de Amistad. Participation, frequent short essays, a journal, a midterm, a final exam, and a final paper determine the final grade.

The Center also provides leadership, training, guidance, and resources to support community-based research, linking local organizations with undergraduates, graduate students, and faculty interested in working collaboratively to address the community organizations' research needs, while furthering their academic agendas. The Center additionally organizes lectures and other events that serve to educate and to encourage advocacy on behalf of justice and peace; advises students considering postgraduate service programs such as the Peace Corps, Teach for America, and the Alliance for Catholic Education, among many others; works with and supports the activities of Notre Dame's student social action and service clubs; and links students and faculty to organizations in the South Bend community for volunteer community service.

Educational Attainments of Service-Learning as a High-Impact Practice

We have described thus far structures and courses that chart the geography of global-learning and civic-engagement opportunities that exist at the Center for Social Concerns. But what is happening within students themselves?

Recently, the Center conducted research to assess the kinds of learning that our seminar and SSLP models instill in their participants.[5] This particular study examined constructs that our researchers identified as salient in community-based learning and particularly relevant to learning goals across all the Center's courses and programs, building upon the field's existing research on student learning outcomes by considering intentionality of course model and structure, and the integration of academic content with sustained community immersion experience.

Utilizing seven separate scales to measure student learning, these outcome measures constituted a related set of attitudes and values pertaining to the recognition and denunciation of societal inequality, the importance placed on helping others, and beliefs about justice (Bowman et al., 2010a). The seven scales from various theoretical orientations in social science used to gauge student learning outcomes were the following:

1. *Situational attributions for poverty* (adapted from Feagin, 1971)
2. *Openness to diversity* (adapted from Pascarella, Edison, Nora, Hagedorn, & Terenzini, 1996)

3. *Responsibility for improving society* (adapted from Nelson Laird, Engberg, & Hurtads, 2005)
4. *Empowerment view of helping* (Michlitsch & Frankel, 1989)
5. *Belief in a just world* (Dalbert, Montada, & Schmitt, 1987; Furnham, 2003)
6. *Social dominance orientation* (Pratto, Sidanius, Stallworth & Malle, 1994)
7. *Self-generating view of helping* (Michlitsch & Frankel, 1989)[6]

The results found that participants in the Center's signature programs as a whole showed significant gains in all seven measures. Participation in seminar (one-credit service-learning) and summer service-learning (three- and four-credit service-learning) courses with a sustained immersion appears to have a positive impact on college student learning and development that captures a broad set of attitudes and values related to diversity, poverty, justice, social change, and inequality.

Among the results were also findings that showed some interesting points of similarity and differences between seminar students on the one hand and summer service-learning students on the other, which merit further attention. While seminar and summer service-learning students showed similar gains across the three measures related to diversity (*openness to diversity*) and views of helping (*empowerment view of helping* and *self-generating view of helping*), they differed among the other four measures. Seminar students showed statistically significant gains in *situational attributions for poverty* and *responsibility for improving society*, while the summer service-learning students did not show statistically significant gains, likely as a result of a smaller sample of students who took the three-credit courses, since the mean differences in both measures were positive and at least as large as those for students who took one-credit courses.

Maybe more compelling are the significant and desired changes of the summer service-learning students on measures of *belief in a just world* and *social dominance orientation* that the seminar students did not exhibit.[7] *Belief in a just world* identifies the extent to which one believes that the world, as it is, is a just place, that people deserve their lot in life—in general, good things happen to good people, and bad things happen to bad people (Dalbert et al., 1987). *Social dominance orientation* conveys one's acceptance of, and even preference for, inequality among social groups, that is, for hierarchy within a social system and group-based dominance in general (Prato et al., 1994).

According to Bowman et al. (2010b), both are widely employed in psychological research; considered to be worldviews that are highly stable over time among samples of college students; and viewed as personality traits or individual characteristics that gauge deeply felt worldviews and assumptions, rather than developmental outcomes. While students in the three-credit courses showed the desired change, reductions in both these measures, students in the one-credit courses changed in the opposite direction on *social dominance orientation*, demonstrating more acceptance of group inequality after their service-learning, and no significant change occurring for *belief in a just world*. Given that *social dominance orientation* and *belief in a just world* are considered to be deeply held worldviews and assumptions, Bowman et al. (2010b) conclude that while a one-credit seminar may not be sufficient to yield significant changes, the changes observed among our three-credit summer service-learners convey the potential in these three-credit courses to influence deep-rooted beliefs and feelings about world order and justice.

Further consideration of duration (eight weeks of sustained immersion versus one week), frequency of class sessions (number of pre- and postclasses), course design features (additional training), and academic and reflective components (lectures, assignments, and readings) is warranted before one can precisely attribute the factors contributing to the desired changes among our summer service-learning students with regard to these two measures.

The Center's research suggests rather significant changes in service-learners' orientations relevant to social justice and represents a significant finding about what needs to occur in service-learning courses for students to gain further insight into issues of social justice and inequality (Kollman & Tomas Morgan, 2014). The changes that indicate transformation in participants' perspectives signal the kind of worldview transformation that many proponents of service-learning and community-based learning seek. Furthermore, the findings provide helpful evidence of the potential efficacy for service-learning as a high-impact practice to foster LEAP's essential learning outcomes with respect to personal and social responsibility.

Conclusion

As we reflect on the three decades of work done by the Center for Social Concerns, we celebrate and continue to consider the ways that our institute, on behalf of the university, has pioneered creative educational practices and pedagogies that link the academy and communities, raised the level of quality while growing in scale and increasing inclusivity, connected college learning with the wider society, and instilled in our students a greater capacity for compassion, diversity, and justice. The hallmarks of the Center's community-based learning and service-learning courses and programs have been visible in its commitment to high quality as demonstrated in the intentionality of design, implementation, and continuous improvement; to assessing impact and research; and to equity and access of opportunity for all students.

In retrospect, it might seem that the practices and pedagogies employed by the Center over the past 30 years have been striving for precisely the essential learning outcomes that the LEAP vision for college learning wants to see. Giving students the opportunity to engage directly with the issues they are studying, with ongoing efforts to analyze and help solve real-world problems in and with diverse communities here and abroad, cultivates high-level intellectual and practical skills, encourages students to integrate and apply their learning, and fosters an active commitment to personal and social responsibility. Integrating the service with communities in academic courses and content, through study in the sciences, humanities, social sciences, languages, and arts, students gain knowledge about human cultures and the physical and natural world by direct engagement with questions that have endured throughout history and continue to be relevant today.

Other institutions that claim that their commitment to liberal education is one that empowers and prepares individuals to deal with complexity, diversity, and change; provides students with broad knowledge of the wider world as well as in-depth study in a specific area of interest; and helps students develop a sense of social responsibility, as well as strong and transferable intellectual and practical skills such as communication, analytical and problem-solving skills, and a demonstrated ability to apply knowledge and skills in real-world settings,[8] might look more closely within their own institutional walls and find eager supporters, already on the front lines of this work. By providing greater institutional support for high-impact practices, such as service-learning and community-based learning, that are focused on diversity, global and civic learning, and social responsibility, and by linking them more closely with the essential aims of a liberal education,

> institutions can overcome the mistaken view that liberal education is only "learning for learning's sake," disconnected from the practical skills and needs of work. On the contrary, they will demonstrate that a contemporary liberal education attends to work life, civic life, and personal life in a dynamically shifting, globally integrated environment. (Hovland, 2009, p. 4)

Academic service-learning and community-based learning institutes like the Center for Social Concerns, that have decades of experience, best practice, research, and expertise driving creative, effective educational practices and supporting student success, can help the broader university to achieve essential learning outcomes in its students, but it may also serve to restore the relevancy and vibrancy of its mission for liberal education in the twenty-first century.

Notes

1. For more understanding of the Catholic social tradition and the papal and episcopal documents that make up the body of teachings, see O'Brien and Shannon (1992).
2. The Center draws on a definition of *academic service-learning* as the intersection of relevant and meaningful service with the community, purposeful civic learning, and enhanced academic learning (Howard, 2001).
3. Both authors are involved in the ISSLP. Tomas Morgan developed the program and continues to oversee it. Paul Kollman has served in a key advisory capacity and taught sections devoted to theology and mission. Both are coinstructors of the courses.
4. For more understanding of the Catholic social teaching's principle of "preferential option for the poor," see Henriot (2004) and Gutierrez (1973).
5. Principal investigators of the project are Nick Bowman and Jay Brandenberger. For a presentation on the research findings specific to summer service-learning students, see Bowman, Brandenberger, Smith Shappell, and Tomas Morgan (2010). For publication on the research findings focused mainly on short-term seminar students, see Bowman, Brandenberger, Mick, and Toms Smedley (2010).
6. For more description of the measures used in the study, see Bowman et al. (2010).
7. For more on the Center's research findings differentiating between summer service-learning and short-term seminar results, see Kollman and Tomas Morgan (in press).
8. For AAC&U's definition of a *21st-century liberal education*, see www.aacu.org/leap/What_is_liberal_education.cfm

References

Association of American Colleges and Universities. (2007). *College learning for the new global century: A report from the National Leadership Council for Liberal Education & America's Promise*. Retrieved from http://www.aacu.org/leap/documents/GlobalCentury_final.pdf

Association of American Colleges and Universities. (n.d.). Liberal education and America's promise (LEAP). Retrieved from http://www.aacu.org/leap/

Bowman, N., and Brandenberger, J. (2012). Experiencing the unexpected: Toward a model of college diversity experiences and attitude change. *The Review of Higher Education, 35*(2), 179–205.

Bowman, N., Brandenberger, J., Mick, C., & Toms Smedley, C. (2010a). Sustained immersion experiences and student orientations toward equality, justice, and social responsibility: The role of short-term community-based learning. *Michigan Journal of Community Service Learning, 16*(3), 20–31.

Bowman, N., Brandenberger, J., Smith Shappell, A., & Tomas Morgan, R. (2010b). *Social justice outcomes on service-learning*. Indianapolis, IN: International Association of Research on Service Learning and Civic Engagement.

Center for Social Concerns, University of Notre Dame. (n.d.). Retrieved from http://www.centerforsocialconcerns.nd.edu

Center for Social Concerns, University of Notre Dame. (n.d.). Community-based learning course guide. Retrieved from http://socialconcerns.nd.edu/faculty/cblcourses.shtml

Dalbert, C., Montada, L., & Schmitt, M. (1987). Glaube an die gerechte Welt als Motiv: Validnering Zweier Skalen. *Psychologische Beitrage, 29,* 596–615.

Feagin, J. R. (1971). Poverty: We still believe that God helps those who help themselves. *Psychology Today, 6*(6), 101–110, 129.

Furnham, A. (2003). Belief in a just world: Research progress over the past decade. *Personality and Individual Differences, 34,* 795–817.

Gutierrez, G. (1973). *A theology of liberation.* Maryknoll, NY: Orbis Books.

Henriot, P. (2004). *Opting for the poor.* Washington, DC: Center of Concern.

Hovland, K. (2009). Global learning: What is it? Who is responsible for it? *Peer Review, 11*(4), 4–7.

Howard, J. (2001). *Michigan Journal of Community Service Learning: Service-learning course design workbook.* Ann Arbor, MI: OCSL Press.

Humphreys, D., & Carnevale, A. (2013). *The economic value of liberal education.* Washington, DC: Association of American Colleges and Universities.

Kollman, P., & Tomas Morgan, R. (2014). International service-learning in faith-based contexts. In P. Green & M. Johnson (Eds.), *Crossing boundaries: Tension and transformation in international service-learning* (pp. 190–214). Sterling, VA: Stylus.

Kuh, G. (2008). *High-impact educational practices: What they are, who has access to them, and why they matter.* Washington, DC: Association of American Colleges and Universities.

Michlitsch, J. F., & Frankel, S. (1989). Helping orientations: Four dimensions. *Perceptual and Motor Skills, 69,* 1371–1378.

Nelson Laird, T. F., Engberg, M. E., & Hurtado, S. (2005). Modeling accentuation effects: Enrolling in a diversity course and the importance of social engagement. *The Journal of Higher Education, 76,* 448–476.

O'Brien, D. J., & Shannon, T. A. (1992). *Catholic social thought: The documentary heritage.* Maryknoll, NY: Orbis Books.

Pascarella, E., Edison, M., Nora, A., Hagedorn, L., & Terenzini, P. (1996). Influences on students' openness to diversity and challenge in the first year of college. *The Journal of Higher Education, 67,* 174–195.

Pérez-Peña, R. (2014, April 8). Best, brightest, and rejected: Elite colleges turn away up to 95%. *New York Times.* Retrieved from http://www.nytimes.com/2014/04/09/us/led-by-stanfords-5-top-colleges-acceptance-rates-hit-new-lows.html?_r=0

Pratto, F., Sidanius, J., Stallworth, L. M., & Malle, B. F. (1994). Social dominance orientation: A personality variable predicting social and political attitudes. *Journal of Personality and Social Psychology, 67,* 741–763.

University of Notre Dame, Notre Dame, IN. (n.d.). Mission statement. Retrieved from www.nd.edu/aboutnd/mission-statement

22

FACULTY DEVELOPMENT AND OWNERSHIP OF COMMUNITY-ENGAGED TEACHING AND LEARNING

Celestina Castillo, Regina Freer, Felisa Guillén, and Donna Maeda

O ccidental College's location within the city of Los Angeles provides students and faculty with the opportunity to engage with an array of communities, where a number of different languages are spoken and cultural histories are deeply rooted. Like many major cities, Los Angeles is made up of a collection of local neighborhoods, including numerous ethnic enclaves. According to the 2010 U.S. Census, over 60% of households in Los Angeles speak a language other than English at home and 39% of the population is foreign born. One of the main goals of the Center for Community Based Learning (CCBL) at Occidental College (fondly referred to as "Oxy") is to guide faculty and students on how to interact with people and organizations in these communities in a respectful and reciprocal manner.

The role of faculty in community-based learning is crucial to its success on any campus. The CCBL has paid particular attention to the role of faculty in community-based learning, not only in using community-based learning as a teaching pedagogy, but also in developing and sustaining long-term, reciprocal relationships with community partners. The founding of the CCBL and the creation of a unique model of connecting community engagement to the curriculum emphasized faculty ownership of the approach and a commitment to ongoing faculty development and support. The process and form of writing this chapter mirror the approach to community-based learning at Oxy in that it is collaborative and reflective. The sometimes lengthy quotes that follow are excerpted directly from three reflective narratives by faculty members, which demonstrate how they have incorporated the philosophy and principles of the CCBL into their teaching. They also provide examples of how students develop a sense of social responsibility through their work in and with communities in Los Angeles. These three faculty members—Regina Freer, Donna Maeda, and Felisa Guillén—have been deeply involved in the creation, development, sustainability, and leadership of the CCBL.

The CCBL was founded in 2001 by a group of faculty and then-president Dr. Theodore Mitchell. The CCBL was charged with connecting community engagement to the curriculum, with a clear intention to expand relationships with local communities surrounding the campus, and shifting from a focus on volunteerism to developing long-term, reciprocal relationships and opportunities to share and create knowledge together. Prior to the creation of the CCBL, a Center for Volunteerism and Community Service (CVCS) existed as a resource for students interested in volunteering in the local community, but their work was not intentionally connected to the curriculum or the faculty. When reflecting on the founding of the CCBL, Regina Freer, professor of politics and one of the founding members of the CCBL, recalls:

> When I first arrived at Occidental College I knew that I wanted to develop connections between my classes and my community work and so I sought out institutional support for such efforts. I was vaguely aware of the field of service-learning, and had a skepticism of its reinforcement of the hierarchy that privileged the academy as a "savior" for the "needy" community. The field seemed fraught with language that reinforced this privilege and in fact Occidental's own approach to working with community seemed to be imbued with this perspective. Talk of students "using Los Angeles as a laboratory" and "serving poor communities" was immediately off-putting to me because I thought it seemed to disrespect the integrity of communities beyond the campus as being producers of knowledge with interests that may or may not align with those of Oxy. . . . In addition to the language of privilege, efforts to connect with community seemed to be relegated to student service.

The interest and concerns of Dr. Freer and a number of other faculty members led to the creation of the CCBL and a shift in focus from providing volunteer opportunities for students to supporting faculty in developing partnerships with community organizations for mutually beneficial work that could be connected to their courses and scholarship.

The founding director of the CCBL, Dr. Maria Avila, developed a model of civic and community engagement that is strongly influenced by community-organizing principles and practices. It continues to be used today (Avila, 2010). The model emphasizes developing ownership of the pedagogy with and by all the stakeholders of community-based learning and research—faculty, students, and community partners. It is faculty ownership and leadership that have been critical to the success and sustainability of the CCBL. This sense of ownership is developed by identifying and connecting to each group's and individual's motivation (in community-organizing terms, their "self-interest") for utilizing or engaging with the pedagogy. All of the key stakeholders are involved in the decision-making process when developing projects together. Each stakeholder defines what he or she wants out of a partnership in order to ensure that any work done together truly benefits all who are involved. Ensuring that each stakeholder is clear about what he or she hopes to gain through the partnership is foundational for developing long-term reciprocal relationships.

The intertwined core values of reciprocity, shared ownership, and respecting community knowledge guide the work of the CCBL. Dr. Freer's relationship with the Southern California Library, a nonprofit archival institution located in South Los Angeles, is an example of a long-term relationship built on reciprocity. Housing a collection of materials documenting the history of progressive and radical grassroots politics in Los Angeles, the Southern California Library is a one-of-a-kind institution. While its collections rival those of much more established institutions like the Huntington Library or archives at UCLA and USC, it is distinguished by its commitment to accessibility and community engagement. Likewise, it has a much smaller funding base and a tiny staff. Dr. Freer approached the library staff with the possibility of collaborating to teach a class on the archives. They expressed interest and through a series of meetings facilitated by the CCBL, the curriculum for a course was developed that would take students to the library, teach them archival methodology, have them produce finding aids for unprocessed archival collections, and then give community presentations to encourage young people in South LA to explore and use the collections. The class syllabus represented a negotiation of Dr. Freer's and the library's varied and shared interests. The course was ultimately a success, but it offered a number of lessons in the practice of community-based pedagogy. Dr. Freer noted:

> Constant communication was critical for making mid-stream adjustments when we realized that our goals were not being adequately met. For example, I had to adjust my expectation of the amount of time the staff could devote to guiding the students, and the SCL [Southern California Library]

staff had to adjust their expectation of the level of historical knowledge the students brought. There were also a number of logistical challenges involved in transporting students a significant distance from Oxy to South LA.

Also, the students in this course recognized that their learning stretched beyond the formal instruction in archival methodology and this was only possible because they directly engaged with members of the South LA community. As an example, when they confidently presented their "expertise" on the collections with an audience of local residents, they were pleased with the enthusiasm it generated, but shocked when community members challenged their findings and added their own analyses. The students realized they had more work to do and were humbled by the local expertise that greeted them. It would be a huge challenge to replicate this type of lesson within the bounds of a traditional classroom.

These types of reciprocal relationships enable faculty to demonstrate and lead students in their work with community partners and to challenge the assumption that knowledge is solely created in the academy. In her reflections on working with the CCBL, Dr. Donna Maeda, professor of critical theory and social justice and longtime member of various faculty committees on academic community engagement, notes that the CCBL's emphasis on processes in which mutually beneficial partnerships can develop has enabled her to connect students with communities in a way that pays attention to power differentials and students' attitudes to neighborhoods outside the college. Additionally, this challenged her to think further about the relationship between the humanities and community-engaged classes and knowledge production in the humanities.

> While academia focuses on participating in intellectual communities in which prior academic research must be drawn from (the scholar must show knowledge of current literature and debates), community-based research brings community knowledge to the forefront. Far from romanticizing perspectives from abstract communities, community-based research forces students (and me) to understand how work within communities produces knowledge in ways that are often invisible within academic institutions. While academic work is legitimized through academic knowledge-production institutions such as journals and presses who publish work and institutional review processes such as tenure and promotion, community knowledge is built through actual work and engagement of community members around issues that they identify and shape.

Maeda's community partner Evelyn Yoshimura, the community organizing director for the Little Tokyo Service Center (LTSC), describes her community as a "multicultural Japanese American community" (personal communication, 2013). As students hear about her work, they learn that they must unravel complex layers of the community in order to understand this seemingly simple description. Yoshimura's decades of community building in the face of pressures from different waves of development shape her detailed knowledge of Little Tokyo. She has worked to understand the needs and interests of community members, which include not only ethnically and nationally diverse business owners, members of community organizations, and residents of low-income and increasingly expensive condominiums, but also Japanese Americans from across the nation who continue to hold a relationship across generations to Little Tokyo, one of three remaining "Japantowns" in the United States. Yoshimura's knowledge of community is based on action—her work to sustain Little Tokyo—rather than the academically legitimized approach of building upon prior theorizing about the meaning of community.

Critical reflection, as demonstrated through the excerpts in this chapter, is not only for students. As an important piece of the CCBL model, faculty, students, and community partners are all encouraged to reflect on their experience working together. What have they learned from the experience? Why is the work important to them? Should it continue? Critical reflection allows stakeholders to make sure that the work they are doing with others is still connected to their self-interest and to their personal, professional, and/or educational goals. When done collectively, respectfully, and honestly—and after individual reflection—critical reflection can deepen the trust between faculty members and community partners, strengthen the working relationship, and allow for a truly reciprocal relationship.

Through various workshops and campus–community gatherings, the CCBL introduces and reiterates its philosophy and guiding principles to faculty, students, and community partners. Each summer, the CCBL hosts a faculty workshop focused on how to incorporate community-based learning into a course—from developing community partnership to managing logistics. Through experience and ongoing review of literature on community-based learning, the CCBL has developed key points of advice for faculty. For example, faculty must never compromise academic rigor when incorporating community-based learning into their courses (Howard, 2001). Additionally, faculty should always be clear how a community-based learning or research project meets course learning objectives, enhances student learning, and helps students understand and analyze readings and concepts presented in class. Faculty who are new to community-based learning are encouraged to begin slowly. For example, we may suggest they begin by organizing a panel of community leaders or incorporating visits to local organizations they are interested in partnering with in the future. Such contacts can provide an initial foundation on which to build a potential relationship with community partners. At the onset, teaching a community-based learning course can be difficult. As Felisa Guillén, professor of Spanish and longtime member of the CCBL faculty committee, noted:

> After so many years of individual work, it wasn't easy having to change my previous model and relinquish some of the control that I used to have over my classes and activities. For instance, I had to learn to work collaboratively, taking into account the student's input; relying on other people's expertise, such as the director and staff from the CCBL; and making room for the community in the teaching and learning process.

The initial changes and adjustments required to embrace community-based learning as a teaching methodology can yield many positive results. Dr. Guillén outlines important benefits in terms of teaching effectiveness, professional development, and community engagement:

> I believe that I have become a better teacher and mentor, creating more effective student-centered projects that promote not only language development but also community involvement. I have also expanded my research interests, going beyond my original expertise in literary studies and writing articles in collaboration with students and colleagues within the fields of sociolinguistics and the scholarship of engagement. Finally, I have greatly increased my connections with the local community, gaining a better understanding of their needs and also of their important role in the production of knowledge.

The CCBL provides ongoing support while the courses are being taught. The director is always available for individual consultations and is often very involved with the planning and implementation of courses. Additionally, student facilitators are hired by the CCBL to assist faculty teaching community-based learning and research courses and participate in a program called Education in Action. The program aims to challenge and encourage students to be engaged in facilitating and supporting their peers and faculty in community-based learning and research. Through the program, facilitators expand their role as students, build leadership skills, and further develop their understanding of social justice and responsibility. Student facilitators are selected by the faculty member they will work with and the CCBL's director. The role of the facilitator varies depending on the project. Facilitators have assisted with the development of the course syllabus and the community-based learning/research project, led trainings and workshops to prepare students to engage with off-campus community members, led reflection discussions, and assisted students in the course with research projects.

Facilitators also assist with the logistics of the community-based learning or community-based research project. Students are paid and expected to work 10 to 15 hours per week with a faculty member, the CCBL, community partners, and students in a course. The facilitators meet regularly as a group with the CCBL's director to learn about the history and pedagogy of community-based learning; to discuss projects and ask for guidance in the planning and implementation as needed; and to reflect on what they are learning through their role as a facilitator. Students submit written reflection papers twice per semester to share what they are learning. These reflection papers often demonstrate how the program is impacting their educational experience at Oxy. A rising senior who has been a student facilitator for three semesters titled one of her reflection essays "Growth and Reciprocity" and noted:

> My work as an EIA facilitator for CSP 50S: "Living Los Angeles" taught by Professors Maeda, Matsuoka, Freer, and Neti has exposed me to ways of initiating thoughtful and effective community-based research. . . . I have gained an increasingly developed sense of social responsibility and change. . . . While the nature of the CBR [community-based research] projects proved challenging and I continue to grapple with privilege and power, my experience has been extremely rewarding and I am thankful for the opportunity to engage in community-based learning. (Benyapa B., 2013)

At the end of each year, all the students, faculty, and community partners who have worked together are invited to an event to present their projects. These types of gatherings have been key to developing and maintaining community partnerships and for faculty development. Faculty and staff of the CCBL share responsibility for faculty development. Experienced faculty members are often asked to publicly share their experience and learning with others on campus. Dr. Freer also spoke about this in her reflection:

> One of the hallmarks of the CCBL's approach has been the development of faculty capacity to conceive of and do this work. Some of this has come through the staff's own engagement with the field through scholarly journals and publications, attending professional conferences, and by bringing experts to campus. But it has also come through the creation of space for faculty and community partners to share experiences. As an example, the CCBL used my experience with the SCL [Southern California Library] as a tool for building its capacity to support other faculty developing their own classes. At faculty development workshops I, along with SCL staff, presented my course as a case study, highlighting what worked and what didn't. I recall one lesson involved the need to formally integrate reflection

into course development. As a result of my experience of realizing that the hour's drive (!) to and from the SCL offered a rich opportunity for reflection that I didn't formally tap, the CCBL worked to encourage faculty to explicitly build reflection into community-based learning courses.

In order to address larger institutional systems and structures needed to support faculty, the CCBL works with a formally recognized faculty committee. The committee provides guidance on faculty development needs and examines and makes recommendations for policies related to community-based learning to the dean and the faculty council, the governing body of the faculty. Currently the committee is focused on integrating language that recognizes community-based learning and research for insertion into the faculty handbook's guidelines for tenure and promotion.

Supporting faculty in preparing students to engage with community partners and residents is another important role of the CCBL. Faculty will usually assign readings about the history of a local neighborhood or social issues students may encounter during their project. Faculty are also encouraged to spend time with students "checking" the assumptions they may have about the community, which may be similar to or different from their own, by having students first reflect on their own lived experiences to understand the perspective they bring to a project. For example, asking faculty to have students reflect on their own sense of "home" before engaging in a project that includes a lot of interaction with residents helps them first and foremost to think about the communities they are working in as people's homes. Another critical component to preparing students to engage with Los Angeles communities is to help students and faculty recognize the power and privilege they have of being part of an institution of higher education, particularly when Oxy is located in an area of Los Angeles that is predominantly low income and where college graduation rates are low.

An example of a course in which students were well prepared by faculty to engage with local communities was a team-taught community-based research course entitled Living Los Angeles, which focused on gentrification and development in four Los Angeles neighborhoods. The course was taught by Dr. Freer and Dr. Maeda, along with faculty from the departments of Urban and Environmental Policy and English and Comparative Literary Studies. The course was developed with four community partners: Avenue 50 Studio, a gallery and community arts space in Highland Park; and three community development corporations: East LA Community Corporation (ELACC) in Boyle Heights, Community Development Technologies (CD Tech) in South LA, and LTSC in Little Tokyo. After reading and discussing a number of academic articles on gentrification, conducting community-based participatory research, and the histories of each of the local neighborhoods, students were trained in conducting respectful interviews and working with community partners. A group of students was assigned to each community partner to conduct research and interviews with residents and business owners determined by the partner organization. The research was presented to the organizations at the end of the semester and incorporated into community-organizing campaigns to address displacement occurring within all four neighborhoods. The final presentation also served as an opportunity for each organization to hear more about each other's work. The course also offered students the opportunity to place the city of Los Angeles in different frameworks, from the very local to the global. Dr. Maeda notes:

> The class challenged students to re-think what is considered to be "good" and "bad" . . . [and] enabled students to see national and global contexts that shape the city and its communities. As the course examined shifting and overlapping communities, students learned about historical and political contexts that shape who lives in what parts of the city. Both the community-based research projects and course readings provided material for students to understand how shifts in Los Angeles communities are shaped by global and local dynamics, as these are shaped by complex historical forces, laws and policies, and ideologies around "difference." Students learned that shifts and changes in communities are not simply inevitable or random. Rather, the complex global and local dynamics affect different communities differently; communities have different levels of access to power.

Oxy is encompassed by predominantly Latino neighborhoods, with large Spanish-speaking populations. Given continually increasing enrollments in Spanish classes at Oxy and the needs of the local population, the department has developed relationships with a variety of organizations to create opportunities for meaningful and mutually rewarding interactions between students and the community. Over the years, Dr. Guillén has established partnerships with local schools, law centers, literacy programs, museums, and hospitals. Through her courses, Occidental students have engaged with the community in numerous ways: tutoring and mentoring bilingual children, translating important documents from English into Spanish, and attending parent–teacher conferences and other events. In her reflection she identified some of the learning outcomes based on her own assessment as well as the students' reflections:

> By becoming mediators between the institutions and the people, Occidental students have the opportunity of using their Spanish in a productive

way, while learning from and about the surrounding community. Some of the most evident advantages for our students were an immediate improvement in their communication skills, an increase in their confidence, and a new awareness of the community as a provider of linguistic and cultural knowledge. One could say that these learning outcomes are very similar to those achieved in a study abroad experience. In fact, many students mentioned in their written reflections that they felt better prepared to spend a semester in a Spanish-speaking country because of the level of language proficiency and cultural sensitivity that they have achieved thanks to their participation in the CBL component of the class.

Planning and preparation for these courses took at least six months and required ongoing meetings with the CCBL, students, and community partners throughout the summer and semester. However, when partnerships are well planned, they can be the most fruitful.

The work of the CCBL has expanded the types of relationships that Occidental College has with Los Angeles communities. We believe that it has moved faculty and students to see themselves as part of the broader Los Angeles community and to develop or strengthen a sense of responsibility for the community, as individuals and as part of an institution that has a tremendous amount of power and prestige. The experience and skills faculty and students gain through community-based learning and research can help them engage in and develop reciprocal relationships with diverse communities in Los Angeles and many other places in the world.

References

Avila, M. (2010). Community organizing practices in academia: A model, and stories of partnerships. *Journal of Higher Education Outreach and Engagement, 14*(2), 37–66.

Howard, J. (2001). *Michigan journal of community service learning: Service-learning course design workbook*. Ann Arbor, MI: OCSL Press.

U.S. Census Bureau. (2010). State & county QuickFacts. Retrieved from http://quickfacts.census.gov/qfd/states/06/0644000.html

23

THE WORLD IS AT THE CAMPUS DOORSTEP FOR PUTTING THE LOCAL IN GLOBAL EDUCATION

Kent Koth

O ver the course of the past three decades, hundreds of colleges and universities have developed community-engagement programs in their local communities. With the goal of providing hands-on experiential learning opportunities, these programs typically mobilize students to serve and learn at an organization for a quarter or semester, through a course or as a volunteer.

During this same period of time, colleges and universities from throughout the United States have also dramatically expanded their study abroad programs. Educators have promoted these international experiences, which can range from a week to a year, as a means for students to learn about another country and see themselves and their culture from another context.

Often, these domestic community engagement and international study abroad experiences are viewed as separate and distinct. Sometimes the experiences are even presented as polarities—either local or global. But this seems to be faulty logic. The homeless shelter, the public school, and the health clinic may be only a few blocks from the college campus, but frequently they are a "world apart" from the typical student experience. Sometimes, we need not board a plane to experience a different world—it might be just outside our window.

This chapter explores how students can experience "global education" through community engagement in their local university context. I begin by presenting the benefits of pursuing global learning through local community engagement. I subsequently present specific examples, from my own institution, of how colleges and universities can pursue global education by connecting their classrooms, campus, and their local communities. I conclude by offering several recommendations for institutions wanting to expand and deepen the use of local engagement to pursue global education.

Global Learning Through Local Community-Engagement Experiences

Any short list of skills for success in the twenty-first century would include the ability to understand, engage, and lead across cultures. Indeed, the continuing demographic shifts in the United States as well as the increasingly globalized nature of the workplace make these skills essential. Colleges and universities frequently see study abroad as a central strategy in helping students develop these skills. Yet, while significant, international study does not have to be the only strategy. Local engagement through service-learning courses, volunteer experiences, internships, and community service work-study can provide opportunities for intercultural learning. Colleges and universities that engage in and with communities near campus can bring significant benefits to their students, faculty, institutions, and partner communities.

The Benefit for Students

For years, studying in another country has been a means for college students to further explore their values and ideas. Yet the increasingly diverse college-going population in the United States, which includes thousands of first-generation and nontraditional students, calls for many more varied approaches to engage students in transformative learning experiences. For this reason, universities should strongly consider offering students deep learning opportunities in both international and local contexts. Deep learning involves engaging students in learning processes that combine direct real-world experiences with carefully structured reflection and analysis (Millis, 2010).

In some cases the local and the global experiences can offer complementary learning. For example, before studying in Ethiopia, a student might benefit significantly from volunteering with an organization near campus that serves East African immigrants. The skills and knowledge developed would likely significantly enhance the student's on-the-ground learning in Ethiopia. In other situations, engaging in the community near campus might take the place of the traditional international experience. For example, a student who is unable to study internationally because of finances, family responsibilities, or other issues might have a deep cross-cultural learning experience through a yearlong service-learning project with an organization that serves individuals who are culturally or ethnically different.

The Benefit for Faculty

Frequently, faculty who teach study abroad experiences draw upon the cultural and language skills they developed through their doctoral studies or ongoing research agenda. Many of these experiences occur in other countries. Yet the daily work of most faculty occurs on a campus in the United States. Given teaching loads, departmental expectations, and the economic realities of their students, it is difficult for these faculty to frequently take their students to the countries where they have expertise and knowledge. This can lead to dissonance and frustration for faculty. Developing a local community-based teaching and research agenda that complements their international interests can lead to greater integration and congruency with their teaching and scholarship.

For example, a faculty member with significant experience in China can engage her students in service-learning projects that assist the local Chinese American and Chinese immigrant communities. Students could engage in direct service like assisting with activities at a local center for Chinese American elders or in project-based experiences like researching and documenting the Chinese immigrant experience in the local community. These types of service-learning activities allow faculty members to draw upon their cultural awareness and language skills to offer strong learning experiences to their students and a service to the local community.

The Benefit to the University

Pursuing global learning by developing a significant local engagement program has several significant positive impacts on universities. First and probably foremost, a local community-engagement program enables the university to learn more about and better serve its immediate neighbors. This can lead to better relationships with the local neighborhood and region as a whole. Second, local community-engagement projects often require far fewer resources than international programs, enabling the campus to scale up and engage more and more students in cross-cultural learning experiences. Third, compared with international experiences, local immersion experiences may be more permanent because it is easier to develop longer term ongoing relationships between the campus and the local community.

Benefits to the Community

Universities that develop robust and coherent engagement efforts encompassing local programs can significantly contribute to the communities where their faculty and students serve and learn. By engaging more consistently and over a longer period of time, students are more likely to develop stronger skills in cultural competency, which can lead to more positive interactions with residents in the local communities. A well-crafted local engagement effort will enable faculty to become more skilled at bridging the campus and community, making it easier for community partners to forge positive relationships with the campus. Finally, if universities form solid long-term partnerships with local organizations, residents and community leaders will begin to see the university as an ongoing partner in making the community a vibrant place to live for all residents.

Connecting the Classroom, Campus, and Community for Global Learning: An Example

There are many strategies that colleges and universities can pursue to provide students with a global education through community engagement in neighborhoods near their campus. Seattle University (SU), with a nationally recognized community-engagement program, provides a case study of global learning in a local environment. The university's mission, location, and specific community-engagement strategies provide many lessons for pursuing global learning in a local context.

Inspired by its Jesuit Catholic roots, SU's mission statement and core values speak to its service to society and commitment to social justice. The many neighborhoods of Seattle provide an opportunity for students to learn about themselves and the world.

While historically Seattle has not been a very diverse city, in recent decades this has begun to change. According to the 2010 U.S. Census, one in three Seattle residents is a person of color and 17% of Seattle's population is foreign born (City of Seattle, n.d.). The neighborhoods immediately adjacent to the Seattle University campus are some of the most diverse in the city. Seattle's International District, the historic home to the city's Chinese, Filipino, and Japanese communities, is within walking distance of campus, as is the Little Saigon neighborhood, which is the commercial district for the city's Vietnamese community. In addition, Seattle's Central District stretches to the east of campus and is the center of Seattle's Black community. In more recent years a significant population of East Africans has also settled in the neighborhoods near campus.

For many years the university has drawn upon its mission and its geographic location to engage students in academic service-learning, volunteer activities, internships, practica, and other forms of community engagement. All of these activities are driven by university learning objectives that call for students to be

- prepared to encounter the world
- adept in their discipline
- empowered to make a difference
- self-reflective in their pursuit of meaning and purpose
- committed to justice and ethical action

SU's success in engaging students in the local neighborhood arises from the development of a number of strong practices that mobilize faculty to connect their teaching, research, and service to the local community. The university's success also stems from centralized coordination of community partnerships and a university-wide initiative that focuses on engaging college students in multiple service experiences in a neighborhood adjacent to campus.

Academic Service-Learning

One of SU's central strategies for engaging students in the local neighborhood is to infuse service-learning into academic courses. For over 20 years faculty at SU have utilized academic service-learning as a pedagogical tool to engage students in deep learning experiences. Adapted from Bringle and Hatcher's (1996) work, Seattle University defines *academic service-learning* as

> a credit-bearing educational experience in which students participate in an organized activity that meets community needs and reflects on the service activity in such a way as to gain further understanding of the course content while enhancing their personal development and leadership skills needed to work for social justice.

SU faculty learn how to connect their courses to the community through the Academic Service-Learning Faculty Fellows program.[1] In this yearlong program, faculty learn the theory and practice of how best to utilize service experiences as a pedagogical tool in their courses. Fellows receive a modest stipend and curriculum resources. Through regular meetings, workshops, and discussions, faculty engage in a process of revising a course syllabus to include service-learning, teaching the revised course, and conducting an action research project in which they collect data to answer a research question related to the student learning or community-impact aspects of their new course.

Faculty Immersions

While experiencing success in expanding the use of service-learning among faculty, SU has found it essential to also focus on the quality of the service-learning process. This focus on quality is often what positions SU students for more profound learning experiences in the community and equips them with skills to navigate in multicultural contexts.

One essential factor in attaining this high level of quality is the ability of faculty to facilitate the complex and sometimes messy service-learning process. Like most institutions of higher education, particularly those located in larger urban environments, the faculty who teach at SU do not necessarily live in the local neighborhood. In addition, the ethnic and cultural backgrounds of the majority of SU's faculty do not reflect the demographics of residents living in the neighborhoods adjacent to campus. These factors could lead faculty to struggle to effectively lead their students in local engagement activities. These factors also could lead faculty to make significant mistakes in navigating across cultures to form trusting partnerships.

Recognizing the need for trusting relationships based upon reciprocity, understanding, and respect, SU has developed neighborhood immersions for faculty. Ranging from one to three days, the immersions are designed for faculty to

- deep their experience of and commitment to the university's mission
- learn more about the assets and needs of the local neighborhood in order to develop ethical and respectful long-term partnerships
- strengthen the capacity to engage in cross-cultural partnerships
- develop new ideas for service-learning courses, community-based research activities, or other community-engagement activities

In pursing these goals, organizers utilize a process of disorientation—placing participants in settings that stretch their comfort zones and challenge them to see and understand other perspectives. Faculty engage in activities that directly connect with the lived experience of the many diverse communities within walking distance of campus. These activities are accompanied by meetings with local leaders in order for faculty to contextualize their experiences and connect theory with practice. Faculty also participate in reflection discussions during the immersions and are invited to attend a follow-up lunch several weeks after each experience.

An example of a local immersion is the three-day exploration of the Little Saigon neighborhood. Just a short walk from the campus, for three decades the neighborhood has served as the economic and cultural hub for a community of over 60,000 Vietnamese and Vietnamese Americans in the Seattle area. The 11 faculty and staff who participated in this immersion conversed with monks at several Vietnamese Buddhist temples, attended mass at a Vietnamese Catholic church, visited several nonprofit organizations and businesses in the Little Saigon neighborhood, and met with Vietnamese American Jesuits whose families immigrated to Seattle. The immersion ended with a celebration at a farm owned and operated by a Vietnamese American family.

Community and faculty leaders who are more familiar with the local community often serve as the leaders of the immersion experiences. This minimizes the possibility of tokenizing or trivializing the diverse communities that the faculty encounter and allows faculty to better understand the realities of the wider community. For example, the Little Saigon experience was cofacilitated by a Vietnamese American psychology professor. He provided leadership in conceptualizing the overall idea and purpose for the immersion as well as connecting with community organizations, assisting with interpretation during community visits, and bridging the cultural divisions between participants and the community. Frequently, community leaders craft portions of the immersion experiences, including presenting on historical and current community issues and introducing the university participants to local business owners, civic leaders, and residents. In this way, community leaders often develop new relationships with university faculty interested in contributing their time and expertise.

The lessons faculty learn through the immersions contribute significantly to their ability to create and facilitate high-quality service-learning experiences for their students. Based upon their immersion experiences, many faculty have made adjustments to their courses to deepen student learning and enhance the community impact of the students' service. A number of faculty have commented that the immersions put them in the context that they often place their students, which has led to a stronger ability to facilitate the students' service-learning experiences.

Centralized Coordination

Centralized coordination and support for faculty is critical to the success of the service-learning process. The Seattle University Center for Service and Community Engagement serves as the focal point for faculty wanting to connect their courses to the community. Center staff meet with faculty who are interested in developing a service-learning course and assist faculty with connections to community agencies. In some cases the center arranges community placements for students in service-learning courses. In other cases the center will work with faculty and community agencies to develop appropriate projects, research initiatives, or internships for students. Finally, center staff have worked in partnership with SU's counsel to establish policies, procedures, and guidelines for minimizing risk in university-sponsored service experiences.

The Faculty Fellows program and centralized support from the Center for Service and Community Engagement have contributed to the widespread use of service-learning at SU. Every year over 100 faculty from more than 30 disciplines teach over 250 courses engaging upward of 3,000 students in service-learning experiences. Many of the service components embedded in these courses include opportunities for students to learn across cultures and to stretch their comfort zones. Examples of such courses include the following:

- Urban studies students study the importance of urban art by partnering with a public development authority to research and make recommendations for the future site and structure of an official gateway to Seattle's Chinatown.
- Sociology students study race and class by conducting interviews and focus groups with residents of a central Seattle neighborhood with the goal of documenting the gentrification process that is negatively impacting communities of color.
- Fine arts students learn drawing by creating a mural at a local elementary school that depicts the history, culture, and prominent historic figures of the local neighborhood.
- Psychology students learn about issues of growth and development in multicultural settings by tutoring in an after-school program at one of Seattle's most ethnically diverse schools.
- Finance majors are confronted with the negative impact of predatory lending by organizing and offering workshops on financial literacy for low-income families.
- Biology students lead ecology activities for children at a local community garden in a multiethnic neighborhood in central Seattle.

University-Wide Engagement

Individual faculty use of service-learning is a powerful tool to engage students in cross-cultural learning that leads to increased skill, competency, and self-understanding. Yet an even more powerful way to engage students in these deep learning opportunities is for the entire institution to develop a comprehensive local-engagement strategy that offers numerous opportunities for student involvement and learning.

In 2007, recognizing the university's growing commitment to community engagement, SU's president, Stephen Sundborg, SJ, asked the campus two simple questions:

1. If Seattle University were to focus its community-engagement efforts on a particular topic, neighborhood, or issue, could it make more of a measurable impact on the community?
2. If it pursued such a strategy, could university students learn in deeper and more powerful ways?

President Sundborg's initial questions led to a three-year planning effort that engaged hundreds of campus and community members in a process that moved from vague idea to a specific plan focusing on the crisis of educational inequality. Inspired by programs such as the Harlem Children's Zone, in February 2011 the university launched the Seattle University Youth Initiative, the largest and most comprehensive community-engagement project in the university's history.

The initiative focuses on a two-square-mile neighborhood immediately south of the university. Over 20,000 people live in the neighborhood, and over half of the residents are people of color. The neighborhood is also Seattle's historic and current cultural home to the African American, Chinese American, Filipino American, Japanese American, and Vietnamese American communities. More recently, immigrants from East Africa and Latin America have also moved into the neighborhood.

Children and families living in this neighborhood face significant challenges. The percentage of neighborhood children living in poverty and the rates of youth violence and juvenile incarceration are among the highest in Seattle. In addition, many neighborhood youth encounter major academic challenges throughout their K–12 experience, barriers to graduating from high school, and lack of access to higher education. The rising cost of housing is also putting extreme pressure on the neighborhood's low-income residents.

The Youth Initiative strives to directly address these challenges. The first goal of the Youth Initiative is to dramatically improve the academic achievement of 1,000 low-income neighborhood students. The university is pursuing this goal by partnering with the city of Seattle, Seattle Public Schools, Seattle Housing Authority, and over 30 nonprofit organizations to create a "cradle-through-college" pipeline of educational resources for neighborhood children and their families.

The second goal of the Youth Initiative is to transform the education of SU students by further mobilizing them to serve and learn through academic service-learning, community-based research, internships, practica, work-study, and volunteer activities.

Through the Youth Initiative the university has pursued a community–school strategy with Bailey Gatzert Elementary, the neighborhood elementary school. SU has led an effort to extend the learning day by two hours for 180 Gatzert students. Each week through the program, over 100 university students lead recreation activities and provide individualized academic support to the children. An additional 100 Seattle University students serve as classroom assistants and tutors during the regular school day. Still more SU students are supporting a new summer-learning program for Gatzert children and engaging the parents of Gatzert schoolchildren through cultural outings, conversation circles, and workshops on parenting.

While Gatzert has been an initial focal point for Youth Initiative activities, it is not the only element of the effort. Dozens of faculty and students have partnered on other neighborhood projects including providing free tax assistance to neighborhood residents, assisting with health screening and referrals, offering tutoring to neighborhood residents studying to become U.S. citizens, and responding to the research and evaluation needs of neighborhood community partners. The efforts to respond to research questions can range from students conducting literature reviews for organizations on promising practices to faculty partnering with organizations to conduct formal research studies involving the Institutional Review Board and control groups. In 2012 the university also partnered with Seattle Public Schools to open a small public high school on the SU campus.

This intensive partnership with Gatzert and the myriad additional projects and partnerships that fall within the Youth Initiative are showing promising initial results—two years ago Gatzert children had the greatest academic growth of any school in Seattle. Last year, academic growth continued with significant progress in science and math, a particular emphasis of the university–school partnership. Attendance rates at the elementary, middle, and high school level are all on the rise.

The Youth Initiative is also having a profound impact on the university students who serve and learn at Gatzert and in other neighborhood locations. Whereas students in an individual service-learning course might have one quarter-long experience in the community, the Youth Initiative provides a series of experiences for students to engage in throughout their time at the university, increasing the likelihood that students are able to refine and enhance their ability to work and lead in situations outside of their ethnic and cultural contexts. The number of students making a yearlong commitment to serve in the neighborhood (a good indicator of the depth of student learning) has grown from 88 to 260 in only two years. Last year SU began to see a pattern among some students: they chose to come to SU because of the Youth Initiative. These results demonstrate the university's progress in expanding and deepening global learning opportunities for SU students in communities near campus.

Recommendations for Going Deeper

SU's experience mobilizing students to serve and learn in the culturally diverse communities near its campus provides many lessons for other institutions interested in doing the same. While not prescriptive, the following recommendations may assist universities wanting to deepen and expand global learning experiences through local community engagement.

1. *Develop a comprehensive vision.* As described previously in this chapter, it does not make sense to view student learning experiences in international and local contexts as separate and distinct. Therefore, institutions that are serious about leveraging the learning experiences arising from local community-engagement activities should create a comprehensive vision for student learning that bridges local and international contexts. This vision will allow faculty to avoid having to choose to engage students in either a local or international context, leading to much more holistic experiences for faculty and students. This comprehensive vision may also provide cost-saving opportunities in areas of risk management, preparation for service and study away, and travel expenses. Institutions may want to reinvest these cost savings in incentives for faculty to develop both local *and* international experiences for students.

2. *Create a plan.* The long-term success of local community-engagement programs that contribute to global learning outcomes often depends on how much forethought and planning occurred at the beginning of the process. Building strong campus–community partnerships takes time and intentionality. For example, in creating its university-wide Youth Initiative, SU took almost three years to move the initial idea from conception to implementation. While lengthy, the thoroughness of the planning process, based on community- and campus-organizing practices, led to significant ownership by many partners. As a result, this has made it much easier to move quickly and attain success in the initial implementation phase.

3. *Balance the goal of student learning with the goal of community impact.* Reciprocity is essential in developing a strong local community-engagement effort. If the university places too much emphasis on the learning experience

of its students, then the community will become disillusioned, question the university's motives, and eventually cease to participate in partnerships. Conversely, if the university overemphasizes the external focus on creating positive social change in the neighborhood, university leaders may question why the institution should be involved at all. Success depends on how these two goals dovetail and complement each other.

4. *Make trusting relationships a key to success.* The power imbalances that arise from differences in class, culture, race, religion, gender, and nationality are a central challenge to universities hoping to build campus–community partnerships that provide students with deep learning opportunities. Strong partnerships often require the university to question its assumptions about the community, enhance its overall cultural competency, and listen deeply before acting. Doing this well fosters trusting relationships between campus and community that form the foundation for all ensuing success. Moving with forethought and intentionality into the often messy issues arising from the complexities of race, class, gender, and national origin also provides students with incredibly powerful learning opportunities that are at the heart of the global learning experience.

The World Is at the Campus Doorstep

Throughout this chapter I have presented the benefits, specific examples, and recommendations for pursuing global education through local community engagement. My intention has not been to downplay the power of students studying and serving in other countries; this should remain an important strategy for universities wanting to promote cross-cultural learning that places students in contexts that stretch their comfort zones. In laying out an argument for how local community engagement can provide global education, my hope is to foster creative new thinking that might significantly enhance student learning and contribute to a more globalized society.

Increasingly, our institutions of higher education find themselves in communities that are becoming more and more ethnically and culturally diverse. We should take this opportunity to engage the world that is at our campus doorstep; in opening this door we will find significant new opportunities for attaining the goals we have for our students, our institutions, and ourselves.

Note

1. More information about the Faculty Fellows program can be found at www.seattleu.edu/csce/teaching/scholarship/sl-fellows/

References

Bringle, R. G., & Hatcher, J. A. (1996). Implementing service learning in higher education. *The Journal of Higher Education, 67*(2): 221–239.

City of Seattle. (n.d.). Race and ethnicity quick statistics. Retrieved from http://www.seattle.gov/dpd/cityplanning/populationdemographics/aboutseattle/raceethnicity/default.htm

Millis, B. J. (2010). *Promoting deep learning* (IDEA Paper No. 47). Manhattan, KS: The IDEA Center. Retrieved from ideaedu.org/sites/default/files/IDEA_Paper_47.pdf

24

THE POWER OF PLACE

University–Community Partnership in the Development
of an Urban Immersion Semester

JoDee Keller, Rose McKenney, Kathy Russell, and Joel Zylstra

Tacoma, Washington, otherwise known as the City of Destiny and the Gritty City, is home to a large port, an active manufacturing sector, several higher education institutions, and a history of blue-collar jobs (Mortland, 2001) through the region's logging history. The city's ethos continues to exhibit a strong emphasis on the arts, broad socioeconomic representation, and wide ethnic diversity (Table 24.1). Because Tacoma has seen wave after wave of immigrants and refugees, the community itself is a prime example of the blurring of boundaries between global and local. Located in the Pacific Northwest, Tacoma represents a myriad of cultural perspectives informed by proximity to the Asian Pacific, global trade influence from the Port of Tacoma, and one of the nation's largest Immigration and Customs Enforcement Detention Centers.

Pacific Lutheran University (PLU) is a small liberal arts university located in Parkland, Washington, a small, unincorporated area seven miles south of Tacoma. PLU has several programs that connect the university community with Parkland, a wonderfully diverse yet economically depressed community. Several dynamic influences including an adjacent military base, 68% free- and reduced-lunch rate in the surrounding schools, and a 50% renter-occupied rate in local housing create a stark contrast between the campus and local community.

TABLE 24.1
Selected Racial, Ethnic, Language, and Economic Characteristics
of the Tacoma and Washington State Populations (Data From
U.S. Census Bureau, 2014)

Demographic Characteristic (2010 unless otherwise noted)	Tacoma	Washington State
White alone (a)	64.90%	77.30%
Black or African American alone (a)	11.20%	3.60%
American Indian and Alaska Native alone (a)	1.80%	1.50%
Asian alone (a)	8.20%	7.20%
Native Hawaiian and Other Pacific Islander alone (a)	1.20%	0.60%
Two or More Races	8.10%	4.70%
Hispanic or Latino (b)	11.30%	11.20%
White alone, not Hispanic or Latino	60.50%	72.50%
Foreign born persons, 2008–2012	13.50%	13.00%
Language other than English spoken at home, age 5+, 2008–2012	19.00%	18.20%
Persons below poverty level, 2008–2012	17.60%	12.90%

Note. (a) Includes persons reporting only one race. (b) Hispanics may be of any race so also are included in applicable race categories.

Source. U.S. Census Bureau: State and County QuickFacts. (2014). Data derived from Population Estimates, American Community Survey, Census of Population and Housing, County Business Patterns, Economic Census, Survey of Business Owners, Building Permits, Census of Governments. Retrieved from http://quickfacts.census.gov/qfd/states/53/5370000.html.

This chapter describes the process through which the university is developing a local urban semester study away program that in many ways exemplifies a study away experience because of the variety of opportunities to participate in and learn from a range of diverse communities. Beginning with the context of the university in the community, a history of uneven relations, and questions about how to find synergy between global education and local engagement, we delineate our plan and rationale for involving community members and leaders from the inception of the program. We describe our plan for the academic structure of the semester, including the cocurricular aspects of the program. We outline the pedagogical strategies and philosophies that underlie this structure as well as our plans to assess and continuously utilize assessment data to strengthen this program and keep its goals compatible with current student, faculty, and community needs. This chapter also addresses the process of developing the program, consistent with the vision of the university and the interests of the community. We seek to bring clarity around how the local and global interact in multiple dimensions in this community and articulate how this urban semester exemplifies a study away experience. We identify challenges we have faced as well as moments of grace.

History of the Relationship Between University and Community

The university and larger community in which we live and work have had an uneven relationship over the years. Though individual faculty and staff have worked hard to respect the integrity of the community, some relationships were exploitive or paternalistic. Recognizing that community leaders and members are vitally important in student learning, providing insight and experiences that students cannot access through traditional classes on campus, and realizing the importance of collaboration and the strengths that all parties bring to the table, we seek to establish mutually beneficial relationships in the development and implementation of this urban semester program.

Currently, students and faculty alike recognize the important learning that takes place in collaboration with community residents, leaders, organizations, and programs. During their time at PLU, 71% of students volunteer while 31% of students take courses that include a community-engaged service or research component. PLU seeks to align with best practices in community engagement by defining mutual benefit through a shared purpose, vision, and set of values, recognizing community and organizational strengths as well as opportunities to build capacity, and implementing continual feedback processes that build on previous experiences (Community-Campus Partnerships for Health [CCPH]). Establishing a new program allows us to adopt these practices from the start rather than having to mend previous engagement strategies.

Local/Global in This Community

Due to our focus on immersing students in the community through intentional living while learning in depth about aspects of the community from community members and faculty, we envision this urban intensive program as a study away experience in the same way that a semester abroad might be conceptualized. The boundaries between local and global are becoming blurred in our world. We live in an increasingly diverse society, where migration and immigration have an impact on nearly every community. Instant and sometimes constant communication makes the world a small place. Despite global connectedness, many people are unaware of, or uncomfortable with, different cultural practices ranging from gender roles to use of sacred spaces. Some who are aware of differences are uncertain of how to interact respectfully with others. In order to become engaged citizens, our students need to be comfortable with and versed in relating with diverse populations in the United States as well as on the global stage. A local study away program provides students with the opportunity to learn deeply about a community that also wrestles with social, economic, and environmental issues, and consider how community strategies relate to solutions to similar issues around the globe. The program also may serve as a landing pad for students who have studied abroad during previous semesters, looking to reacclimate into a local community. It may be more affordable than studying abroad and leads to better informed students who stay involved with the local community and compel other students to do the same when returning to campus.

Years in the Making

In many ways, this urban semester has been a work in progress, with many different strands finally coming together. For a number of years, various faculty, staff, and students have been involved in at least three different neighborhoods in the larger Tacoma community—a public housing development that serves waves of immigrants, a downtown area with a high concentration of social services, and the unincorporated area that surrounds the university. All three are among areas with the highest concentration of poverty in the county. Involvement has included a range of community-based learning for coursework, internships, voluntary community engagement, and service.

In addition to community-based learning and service, a residential component has been incorporated at a few different times and locations. These efforts were not sustained for a variety of reasons, including limited institutional support and disappearance of the housing (demolition as part of community redevelopment). Along the way, we learned the importance of broad institutional support, as even these modest projects required involvement of the provost's office, risk management, student life, facilities, deans, and other administrative areas. We discovered that integrating course credit with the residential experience clarified academic expectations and accountability for students.[1]

Although PLU has a long history of domestic study away programs during the January term, the institutional support for developing a semester-long study away program emerged from "Educating for a Just, Healthy, Sustainable, and Peaceful World: A Strategic Plan for Global Education at PLU" (PLU, 2004). Subsequently, a faculty member penned a white paper, "Some Considerations in Developing a Puget Sound Gateway (PLU, n.d.)"[2] to structure discussions about adding this program to the existing set of university study away opportunities. This study examined the possibility of the local program from multiple perspectives, including (a) alignment with PLU mission, (b) institutional commitment to the "global/local dialectic" and to moving beyond "the artificial parameters of the intercultural/international divide" (Brusco, 2006, p.1), (c) Tacoma as a multicultural and urban site, (d) existing community ties and networks, and (e) existing related curricular offerings. Thus, this local study away program is envisioned as a balance and complement to PLU's robust study abroad offerings.

Proposing a Local Study Away Program

We also based our program in the "PLU 2020" aspiration to create "a diverse, just and sustainable learning community with a commitment to local, regional, national and global outreach and an ongoing commitment to a diverse learning community of faculty, staff and students" (PLU, 2013). We articulated this learning community commitment as an academic emphasis on the history and presence of the local area's rich multicultural *diversity*, complicated and painful histories that intersect with ongoing *social justice* issues (e.g., Mortland, 2001; Taylor, 1979; Treaty of Medicine Creek, 1854), and commitment to the *sustainability* of the region's natural resources.

Under the direction of the university's Center for Global Education and with support from the provost, funding was secured and a leadership team identified to develop a study away program in Puget Sound. To be rooted in *best practices in community engagement, partnership,* and *advocacy,* the program is to reflect both the guiding principles of those who have been engaged in the community for many years and the goals of the university's Center for Community Engagement and Service (CCPH Board of Directors, 2013; Cipolle, 2010; Jacoby & Associates, 2003; Stoeker & Tryon, 2009). Community members were involved from the program's inception, as we sought a true partnership in which the community and the university worked together to define strengths, opportunities for community study and service, and goals that were rooted in common values of both communities. We also intentionally includ people who have lived in the community who offer vitally important insights from a grassroots perspective as well as the "movers and shakers"—those people who are in clearly defined leadership positions in known community organizations.

Program Components and Pedagogy

Through several workshops with community leaders, we identified the key components of what came to be called the Tacoma Urban Immersion

Program: academic coursework, internship with an integrative component, and intentional living.

The *academic coursework* consists of four four-semester-hour credit courses, which is a full semester's academic load at PLU. All students will take Tacoma: The Power of Place, a foundation course that is focused on the history of the city as well as current challenges and resources, and requires significant experiential learning. Additionally, students will take a course that will change to match the theme of the particular semester and that meets a core university general education requirement.[3]

All students will also participate in an individual credit-bearing *internship or research project* with a community agency along with an accompanying integrative seminar. The fourth course may be a research project, a more extensive internship, or an independent study on a relevant topic.

Intentional living involves living in a community with other students and becoming aware of the neighborhood and one's impact on the social and physical environment. Although students could easily commute from campus to Tacoma's urban core, we intend to create an intentional living community that is a part of a Tacoma neighborhood. Similar to a semester abroad, students will live, serve, and study in the community without returning regularly to campus. This off-campus living experience is envisioned as a route through which students learn to engage the community. The engagement may include meals and informal discussions with neighbors as a way of generating more insight into what's happening in the community. Our goal is that students will learn to look within Tacoma for their own support systems as well as for solutions to community issues.

This entire experience is intended to provide the basis for students' post-college engagement in, learning about, and leadership of communities of which they become a part.

Learning Objectives and Assessment Plan

As we discussed assessment, we noted both student outcomes and program outcomes. We also talked about the partnership with the community and the different forms it could take, including rotating "sponsorship" with various agencies or having an advisory board made up of community members, PLU members, and PLU alumni. From this developed a set of learning objectives. Students will

- understand and explain the city of Tacoma as a complex urban community that responds to interaction among cultures, societal structures, and the physical environment;

- describe and analyze the city of Tacoma as a diverse community striving for equity and sustainability, and assess the steps it is undertaking to achieve this;
- evaluate the assumptions that underpin diversity, justice, and sustainability in the context of an urban setting;
- respond to the challenges and opportunities that arise from tensions and compatibilities among diversity, justice, and sustainability through intensive experiential learning (community research or internship);
- articulate the value of learning in, from, and about a community as a path to civic engagement and lifelong participation as responsible global citizens; and
- demonstrate the ability to integrate academic knowledge with professional workplace behaviors, in collaboration with professionals in the community. (Program Proposal to Educational Policies Committee, 2013)

These objectives will be assessed through products and activities embedded in the program. Part of the evaluation will use student academic products.[4] We also will assess internships and the living and learning community through student reflection and feedback from community partners. We plan to incorporate a sense of vocation into the internship seminar and explore how students exit the semester reflecting upon what aspects of this experience will inform their lives.

Shaping the Vision, Valuing Partnership

We realized that it was important to engage both the local and university communities, and chose to do so through a series of planning workshops. We intentionally included a small number of community leaders in our first workshop for frank conversations around the strengths and challenges of the Tacoma community, the university, and our past relationship. Participants identified unmet needs within the community, including a large number of concerns that are not limited to one geographic or demographic area. Further fostering this partnership, we explored ways in which PLU's and Tacoma's strengths complement each other and frame unmet needs, including education, employment, poverty, and pervasive environmental concerns, all intertwined with ethnic, class, and other dimensions of diversity.

Continuing the partnership, a second workshop with a broader range of community and university participants focused on developing program components. We determined that necessary elements included a shared vision for community engagement and advocacy; disciplinary and interdisciplinary research potential; and related coursework, cocurricular components, and residential and experiential living/learning components. To achieve buy-in from both communities, we recognized the need for combining the expertise and applied knowledge of community members with faculty research and consultation interests and abilities. We identified values that would anchor the partnership, including transparency, clear communication, strong mentoring relationships, and accountability. The structure of the partnership needed to incorporate assessment and feedback, foster cultural inclusivity and awareness, work with appropriate organizations, and consider potential roles for those in the neighborhood. For our specific purposes, we sought to identify those issues that would be appropriate for a study away semester and that would hold potential for study and student engagement. Identified

TABLE 24.2
Foundation Course

Theme	Questions to Be Answered/Course Activities
Racial/Ethnic History of Tacoma	Which individuals and organizations are helpful in understanding history?
History of Tacoma	What can we learn about earliest indigenous residents? Subsequent waves of immigrants? Roles of social services and grassroots organizations?
City Government	What can we learn from attending city council, school board, and other meetings? Interviews with past mayors and city officials?
Environment	What are the key environmental groups in the region? Issues surrounding port, water rights, Native American rights, smelter, Commencement Bay Superfund site, urbanization?
Poverty	What does poverty look like? Where is it located? What role has wealth played? What agencies are seeking to address poverty?
Educational System	What are the challenges and accomplishments of public schools? The connections between schools and city's economy? The changing demographics and changing educational strategies?
Religion	What are the specific religious traditions associated with immigrants? Role of religion and civil rights movement? Effects of living in the "none zone"?
Other Unique Dimensions	What are the effects of military presence? Correctional system?

issues included immigration, youth homelessness, arts, education, and social justice and diversity.

We partnered with community residents to elaborate on program design and development. We affirmed the mission and values of the program, and brainstormed ways in which the city becomes the text for learning. We developed goals, learning objectives, thematic foci, coursework, experiential components, and possible locations. Participants provided a range of suggestions for the foundation course, many of which were incorporated into a draft syllabus. Participants suggested the underlying theme, that students learn to appreciate others whom they may have avoided, ignored, or simply were not previously aware of. As an example of content areas and specific activities to be included in a foundation course, Table 24.2 summarizes what our community and university partners developed.

Outcomes

Through this workshop process, we began to establish a shared vision for building a fruitful partnership between PLU and the broader community in this stand-alone semester program. This partnership will support this program that incorporates the community and surrounding area as part of course pedagogy. The base of the partnership is shared values that were identified by community members and university members early in the process. We used these values to craft a working mission statement for the program:

> Tacoma Urban Immersion Program (TUIP) is an educational program grounded in a dynamic and inclusive partnership between the Puget Sound Community and Pacific Lutheran University that seeks to promote a deep and nuanced understanding of how thoughtful inquiry, service, leadership and care foster collaborative engagement in the ongoing development of a diverse, just, and sustainable community. (Program Proposal to Educational Policies Committee, 2013)

We made a point of requesting input on themes and values that should be included in the mission statement, then vetted this statement among members of the university and local community, incorporating revisions as necessary to ensure compatibility with stakeholders. Early identification of shared values led to broad buy-in.

Lessons Learned

Development of this program takes advantage of a history of individuals from the university engaging with the community. These existing relationships tie the university to the community and provided a foundation of trust during initial meetings. Individuals from the university who have been historically engaged in the community have been leading the university in building this collaborative partnership.

Further, the program also opens the door to new partnerships and exchanges—community members assisting in teaching classes, and faculty members participating in research and consultation. It also may enhance visibility of the university in the community, having benefits on multiple levels. The university has sought to increase the ethnic diversity of its own student population. While the Tacoma Public Schools are culturally diverse, many high school students erroneously consider this private university out of reach when thinking of financing their education. Many others do not even consider college at all. This urban semester could increase the likelihood of local youth considering university attendance and more specifically attendance at our university. Despite this encouraging beginning, we must be aware of the challenge of creating and maintaining long-term relationships between PLU and community partners while celebrating and supporting Tacoma's cultural diversity.

We identified other challenges: A one-semester internship may not be as effective as a yearlong internship or meet the agency's needs. Agencies and the university may hold differing visions of the format of the internship—total time, how time is distributed throughout the semester, and responsibilities and tasks of students and supervisors. Additionally, various community and university partners may have differing visions of program location and necessary planning timeline. Some workshop participants wanted a clearer mission and recommended a longer preparatory timeline. As a result, we asked participants to identify key components for TUIP's mission statement. We weighed the concern about the timeline with the interest of our community partners as well as the anecdotal interest from students, seeking to launch the program with adequate preparation, while not losing momentum.

Working collaboratively with community partners to establish a program that will ultimately be administered through a university poses its own set of challenges. Holding tension with the pace, bureaucracy, and integrity of long-standing institutions can be a tiring process. Seeking community input takes considerable time when community leaders inevitably face pressing issues that make an educational program peripheral. Turnover from the initial workshops to subsequent workshops allowed broader participation while also creating a need to "start over" with new representatives. Additionally, some organizations are more comfortable participating in a university program than others, creating a temptation to partner closely with certain organizations, which might exclude other partners from the process.

Program logistics present their own set of dilemmas with decisions on specific location, adequate housing for students, and anticipating unforeseen problems with managing a facility located away from the university's main campus. While studying away locally should prove more affordable than studying abroad, we also face the challenge of keeping students immersed in the program. Should they be prevented from taking advantage of opportunities on campus, accepting local jobs, and meeting familial obligations? One option that we have considered is to not allow students to return to the campus nor have visitors from campus during the first month of the program in order to reflect a true immersion program.

Conclusion

The Tacoma Urban Immersion Program reflects purposeful movement from service-learning toward community-engaged learning. This shift reinforces with students and faculty that the community is not a resource to be mined, but is instead the context in which engagement, living, and learning become the hallmark of local and global citizenship (Pompa, 2005). It weaves community and university more tightly together, strengthening each in turn and moving us toward more effective collaboration. Increasingly, we are realizing benefits to the university that extend beyond the TUIP. Additional workshop and training opportunities are of interest to faculty, broadly, whether or not they ever participate in the semester program. Such workshops offer strategies for using the city/community as text and training in structured immersion into the community. Thus, the benefits of this program extend beyond the program itself in terms of providing opportunities for faculty development, familiarizing faculty with the community, and utilizing community partners as the experts that they are, all resulting in a program that is sustainable and valued by the university and broader community.

Notes

1. One iteration of the residential living/learning community served as a reentry opportunity for a small group of students (four to five each year) returning from a semester away at a university program in Trinidad and Tobago. Faculty had observed that students struggled with returning to life on a sheltered college campus after living in a very diverse community and being exposed to a range of challenges and circumstances. In housing provided by the local housing authority, students resided in a multiethnic low-income community, and were expected to participate in community service in exchange for rent. Later, an academic component was implemented, with the goal of integrating service, readings, community voices, and student experiences in the community.

2. Gateway programs are PLU-administered, semester-long academic study away programs that incorporate local educational, cultural, and logistical resources. These Gateways offer programs in diverse areas of study, from multicultural heritage in Trinidad and Tobago to alpine ecology in Telemark, Norway to the intersection of development, culture, and social change in Oaxaca, Mexico. The term *gateway* evokes the idea of exchange, similar to a gate that swings in two directions.

3. The elective course will change each semester as different on-campus faculty will be recruited to teach each semester. The course will meet a general education requirement, and faculty in wide-ranging disciplines (e.g., religion, political science, languages, literature) are prepared to offer courses. Additionally, we anticipate that semesters will have themes and intend to match the elective course with a given theme (e.g., environmental challenges, indigenous history, poverty and social justice, contemporary urban challenges).

4. Academic products may include a research project, final reflection, or papers, linked to the learning objectives. For example, we may ask students to write a paper on the city of Tacoma and how it is working toward equity and sustainability or to reflect on the value of learning within and from a community and how this will inform their future civic and global engagement. We also will use the assessment tools used with other Gateway programs (PLU's own and the Global Perspective Inventory [GPI]) and compare aggregate data to see if the local study away yields comparable results.

References

CCPH Board of Directors. (2013). Position statement on authentic partnerships. Community-Campus Partnerships for Health. Retrieved from https://ccph .memberclicks.net/principles-of-partnership

Cipolle, S. B. (2010). *Service-learning and social justice: Engaging students in social change.* Plymouth, UK: Rowman & Littlefield.

Jacoby, B., & Associates. (2003). *Building partnerships for service-learning.* San Francisco, CA: Jossey-Bass.

Mortland, C. A. (2001). Tacoma, Washington: Cambodian adaptation and community response. In D. W. Haines & C. A. Mortland (Eds.), *Manifest destinies: Americanizing immigrants and internationalizing Americans* (pp. 71–88), Westport, CT: Praeger.

PLU. (n.d.). *Some considerations in developing a Puget Sound gateway* (internal document). Tacoma, WA: Author.

PLU. (2004). *Educating for a just, healthy, sustainable, and peaceful world: A Strategic Plan for Global Education at PLU 2004.* Retrieved from http://www.plu.edu/ wang-center/wp-content/uploads/sites/227/2014/11/global-ed-plan.pdf

PLU. (2013). PLU 2020: Affirming our commitments, shaping our future. Retrieved from http://issuu.com/pacific.lutheran.university/docs/plu-2020?e= 1067239/2651397

Pompa, L. (2005). Service learning as crucible: Reflections on immersion, context, power and transformation. In D. Butin (Ed.), *Service-learning in higher education* (pp. 173–192). New York, NY: Palgrave Macmillan.

Stoeker, R., & Tryon, E. (2009). *The unheard voices: Community organizations and service learning*. Philadelphia, PA: Temple University Press.

Taylor, Q. (1979). The emergence of black communities in the Pacific Northwest: 1865–1910. *The Journal of Negro History, 64*(4), 342–354.

Treaty of Medicine Creek, U.S.–Nisqually-Puyallup – Sa-heh–wamish-S'Homamish–Squawskin—Squi-aitl–Stehchass–T'Peeksin (1854, December 26). 10 Stat. 1132.

U.S. Census Bureau. (2014). State and county QuickFacts. Data derived from Population Estimates, American Community Survey, Census of Population and Housing, County Business Patterns, Economic Census, Survey of Business Owners, Building Permits, Census of Governments. Retrieved from http://quickfacts.census.gov/qfd/states/53/5370000.html

AFTERWORD

Larry Braskamp

In his introduction to this book, Neal Sobania writes, "The most recent cause du jour is 'global learning,' but what does this mean and must a student always go overseas to be a global learner?" (p. 2).

This book has provided me with some very useful and insightful answers to this fundamental question. First, what do we mean by global learning and, by extension, global learner? Kevin Hovland (2014) has recently provided us with an excellent starting point in helping us make sense of the current emphasis on preparing students for the twenty-first century. He writes, "Focusing on global learners—who they are and what they can do—may help those conversations become more concrete and productive as they progress" (p. 10). He recognizes the importance of being—affective, sense of self, noncognitive elements—and the behavioral dimensions as well as the cognitive dimension in defining what we want students to be and become as future citizens of this pluralistic and global society.

I like this focus on the global learner because it means that we are to educate learners—students, human beings. It acknowledges the complexity of global learning and the human element. To me this has always meant that students learn and develop holistically. To me life and learning go together; they are inseparable. Or as I like to stress, we as learners are living using our head, heart, and hands.

If we think of global learning and the current way to think of holistic student learning and development—educating the whole student—the focus can mirror an education in the liberal arts, albeit a more contemporary view and approach to what a liberal education can entail.

I have stressed this theme of a holistic view of student learning and development throughout my entire career since it focuses on the whole student. Kegan (1994) and King and Baxter-Magolda (2005), leading theorists on human development, stress that we as humans do not learn just intellectually or cognitively, but holistically, integrating our cognitive, intrapersonal, and interpersonal dimensions. Magolda and King use the term *intercultural maturity* to describe this holistic view within a global context. In our work we refer to it as a *global perspective* (Braskamp & Engberg, 2011; Braskamp, Braskamp, & Engberg, 2014).

Thus, as students learn and develop, they are doing more than acquiring knowledge and understanding or engaging in complex abstract thinking. Students are being challenged to grow not just intellectually but also in ways that reflect social, spiritual, affective, personal, and behavioral dimensions. When students develop they acquire not only the awareness of cultural differences and values, but also the skills and competencies to function in different cultures. It is based on a constructive developmental approach to understanding how persons learn and develop in their lives.[1] I also like this focus because students as learners now live in a pluralistic and global society. Thus, we as educators have additional responsibilities in educating students. We must help students develop as workers and citizens in a global world.

I like the image of a journey to describe student learning, as Sobania presents in chapter 1, since it helps me wrestle with the second part of the question, "Must students always go overseas to be a global learner?" I have often used the image of journey to describe student and human development because it signifies movement and change but also detours, hurdles, pain, and achievement. No journey in life is an easy straight path to a destination. Moreover, both implicitly and figuratively the journey is now global because globalization is now a part of our life. Global interdependence is now present going beyond any national, regional, ethnic, racial, political, and economic boundaries. Thus, we in higher education must prepare students to interact, lead, and flourish in a world that is interdependent.

We accomplish this goal through our academic offerings, but also through the cocurricular activities and the ethos of the campus. We can visualize a journey in life, especially that of students during their collegiate days, as one of continually stopping at places along the way, sometimes by design and sometimes as a part of life over which students have no control. But at these places they visit and meet others, including those unlike them, and learn and develop skills, engage in new behaviors, enhance their cognitive reasoning, form new relationships, and develop their sense of self and identity. Some places more profoundly influence student learning and development—the dimensions of head, heart, and hands, as a way to summarize the cognitive, intrapersonal, and interpersonal dimensions of global holistic learning. We know from the research on student learning that environmental influences are an important element in understanding how students learn and develop as human beings (Braskamp & Engberg, 2011). This book clearly highlights the importance of the environment in a student's journey by focusing on the value of study away in the life of students (Sobania & Braskamp, 2009). When Sobania and I wrote the 2009 article "Study Abroad or Study Away: It's not Merely Semantics," I did not realize as I do now the value and potential of study away as a pedagogical strategy.

Sobania, in his introduction, and the authors of a wide range of study away domestic academic programs in this volume provide a convincing argument that a student's journey should be diverse and inclusive. Sobania recognizes that a student's journey occurs in classrooms, in residence halls, on athletic fields, through participation in social media, as well as in engagement in programs that exist in domestic and foreign places. He presents three over-lapping domains—study abroad, domestic study programs, and engage-ment in the community and service-learning—to portray the major places outside the campus walls in the journey of students, while recognizing that the third element can also be an aspect of overseas or domestic off-campus programs.

To me, what is important and powerful is that all these places can pro-vide encounters with difference. Encounters with difference are important in student development, because they challenge the students' thinking, being, and doing or their head, heart, and hands. Encounters are more than experiences, because encounters create challenges, cognitive dis-sonance, unsettling moments, and require changes in the way we think about ourselves and interact with others (Terenzini & Reason, 2010). As Sobania points out, in the past we have equated opportunities for encoun-ters with difference to be primarily or even completely embedded in places in a foreign country. In our history in American higher education, some have argued at least implicitly that students will acquire competencies for effective living in a global society most effectively through immersion and exposure to a culture in a foreign country, preferably also being required to become proficient in the language of the host country. Based on research, we can conclude that study abroad programs do influence students holisti-cally and globally (Braskamp & Engberg, 2011; Engberg & Jourian, in press). Study abroad is recognized as a "high-impact" pedagogical strategy (Kuh, 2008).

But today we take a more inclusive pedagogical stance, asking ourselves if study abroad is the only place of such learning. Study away domestic pro-grams can also influence student global perspective thinking as one indica-tor of global learning (Engberg, 2013). The most compelling argument of this book is that many places—in this case domestic programs—can also be effective and powerful places that provide encounters with difference. The chapters present persuasive evidence that students can become global learn-ers at many different locations, some quite close to home.[2] With advances in technology and social interactions with others in our growing pluralistic society in the United States, students now have and will continue to have sufficient opportunities for encounters with difference here in the United States like never before.

As more and more students want to be and must become educated in an increasingly diverse and pluralistic global society, we need to become more creative, practical, and cost-sensitive in educating all of our students; that is, provide encounters of differences in many settings not far from a campus. This book provides not only an argument but also a multitude of examples, interventions, programs, policies, and practices for others to adapt on their home campus. *Putting the Local in Global Education* will become an important catalyst for discussions and planning among educators in all types of institutions. What will the readers learn from this book? What are some lessons that they can take away? I offer five thoughts that are intended to enhance the usefulness of this book for professionals with responsibility for curriculum and cocurricular initiatives, faculty, and researchers interested and committed to making global learning a goal of a college education.

First, what study away programs exist? I suggest that you take an inventory of pedagogical places that now exist in your department, college, and/or campus that are intended to promote global learning and development. In doing so, ask some additional, more probing questions. What types of encounters of difference that now exist in these study away programs are most likely to influence which dimensions of global learning? Are they intended to effect cognitive learning and cultural understanding, to encourage acquisition of skills to more successfully interact with others unlike themselves, instill and provide motivation for engagement in global issues, to provide insights into one's sense of self, to encourage more social and personal responsibility prompt concern about civic engagement, and so on?

Second, what features of study away in the form of domestic programs on your campus highlight and provide (or could be developed to highlight and provide) encounters with difference? What types of people are engaged; do real-life situations exist; and do the problems and issues identified require input and problem solving from participants with different skills, talents, and perspectives such as ethnic, economic, and life study cultural backgrounds? Many of the examples in this book highlight the centrality of problem solving in diverse settings. In almost every program, "hands-on" experiences are present and problem solving is an expectation. This experiential learning pedagogical strategy puts the human face in the learning environment. It is pragmatic rather than abstract. In short, what features of the domestic programs best promote global learning?

Third, how are these study away programs integrated into the journey of the students at your campus? Who participates? Are the programs intended and designed for all students or primarily for those who can afford the time and have the resources? How do these programs fulfill requirements in the major or integrate with courses taught on campus or online? Do students perceive their journey through multiple places as connected or disjointed?

Fourth, are students both challenged and supported in the places they visit and in which they participate? The principle of balancing challenge and support in a student's journey has existed for nearly half a century (Sanford, 1966) but its relevance in providing places for encounters of difference is perhaps more important today than ever before. Our global society has additional challenges and complexities, and a wider range of students are now enrolled in college. Balancing challenge and support will differ with each student since each student needs to find his or her unique balance between challenge and support when engaged in encounters with difference. However, if the domestic programs can offer experiences that motivate students to be holistically engaged, that is, to use their head, heart, and hands, students are more likely to grow and change without becoming overwhelmed. Thus, what pedagogical strategies are employed for optimal learning?

Fifth, how do you know that your domestic places for encounters with difference are fulfilling your goals? What types of evidence are you collecting and using to gauge your successes and identify issues, concerns, and problems in both what and how students as global learners are learning and developing? As Astin (1993) argues, we need to learn as much as we can about the environmental conditions so we can most effectively develop the talent of our young people. Thus, an assessment is most useful if it connects the experiences of students with their global learning (the wide array of learning outcomes presented in this book). Do you collect evidence about what students experience and what they learn, and how they mature as global learners?

Conclusion

Putting the Local in Global Education provides an important marker in the pursuit of higher education adopting new pedagogical strategies for global learning, the desired inclusive student learning outcome that is now emerging as one of the most significant outcomes in a twenty-first-century education of our students. It highlights that study away grounded in domestic experiential learning can be a powerful pathway to influence *global learning*, which when broadly defined includes civic responsibility, personal and social responsibility, thinking more complexly, and functioning in a diverse and pluralistic global society. If we think of education as providing encounters of difference that make a difference, then we are free to explore, plan, and implement a variety of interventions, that can include all sorts of stops along the way. The potential for expanding study away opportunities is indeed very promising.

Notes

1. This view of development is based on a constructive–developmental tradition of human development. That is, as we develop we are engaged in meaning-making, or making sense of our journey in life. Making sense of the world in which we live is not just an intellectual pursuit, since as we develop, most of us become more complex and integrated in our thinking, feeling, and behaving. Robert Kegan (1994) has argued that three major dimensions of human development—cognitive, intrapersonal, and interpersonal—need to be taken into account when humans make sense of their experiences. Patricia King and Marcia Baxter Magolda (2005) refined these dimensions in describing students in their social–cultural development during their college years. Students need to acquire *intercultural maturity*, a term that describes how human beings strive and struggle in forming their beliefs about what is truth and what makes the most sense to them, their identity, and their relationships with others. We now live in a global world in which multiple worldviews and salient cultural traditions have lasting influences on how we think, feel, and relate to others. We need to understand and empathize with persons who differ dramatically in national origin, ethnicity, and religious and spiritual orientations as well as in race, gender, and sexual orientation.

    In our pluralistic and global society today, this developmental journey has become so much more complex. Encounters with differences in a pluralistic society mean more than having diversity, as Sobania argues in his introduction. Pluralism means engaging in differences that will create productive and respectful relationships but still allow individuals to be able to keep and develop their unique identity. These encounters in a pluralistic society can occur within a country as well as among nations, but they require dialogue with others (hands); an understanding of the world and cultural, ethnic, and racial differences (head); and a commitment to become mature as unique persons within a community (heart). Thus, each of us needs to develop a global perspective in our journey in life (Braskamp & Engberg, 2011).

2. *Service-learning*, one of the three major strategies described by Sobania in this book, has been defined as a "teaching and learning strategy that integrates meaningful community service with instruction and reflection to enrich the learning experiences, teach civic responsibility and strengthen communities" (Engberg & Fox, 2011, p. 255). If viewed holistically, it is more than a set of programs on civic engagement, since it is grounded in experiential learning and is an integral part of a college's mission to "make a difference in our democracy" (Saltmarsh & Hartley, 2011, p. 291).

    Service-learning, one of the terms used to describe civic engagement, community-based research and problem solving, and experiential learning, has been shown to be an effective pedagogical strategy in fostering student learning such as social responsibility, working with others, and moral development, including global learning (Engberg & Fox, 2011; Finley, 2012; The National Task Force on Civic Learning and Democratic Engagement, 2012). It is one of the "high-impact" initiatives often promoted as ways to enhance student deep learning (Kuh, 2008).

References

Astin, A. (1993). *Assessment for excellence: The philosophy and practice of assessment and evaluation in higher education.* Washington, DC: Oryx Press.

Braskamp, L. A., Braskamp, D. C., & Engberg, M. E. (2014). *Global perspective inventory*. Retrieved from https://gpi.central.edu/supportDocs/manual.pdf

Braskamp, L. A., & Engberg, M. E. (2011, Summer/Fall). How colleges can influence the development of a global perspective. *Liberal Education, 97*(3–4), 34–39.

Engberg, M. E. (2013). The influence of study away experiences on global perspective-taking. *Journal of College Student Development, 54*(5), 466–480.

Engberg, M. E., & Fox, K. (2011). Service participation and the development of a global perspective. *Journal of Student Affairs Research and Practice, 48*(1), 85–105.

Engberg, M. E., & Jourian, T. J. (in press). Intercultural wonderment and study abroad. *Frontiers.*

Finley, A. (2012). *Making progress? What we know about the achievement of liberal education.* Washington, DC: Association of American Colleges and Universities.

Hovland, K. (2014). What can learners do? *Democracy & Diversity, 17*, 8–11.

Kegan, R. (1994). *In over our heads: The mental demands of modern life.* Cambridge, MA: Harvard University Press.

King, P., & Baxter Magolda, M. (2005). A developmental model of intercultural maturity. *Journal of College Student Development, 46*(6), 571–592.

Kuh, G. D. (2008). *High-impact educational practices: What they are, who has access to them, and why they matter.* Washington, DC: Association of American Colleges and Universities.

The National Task Force on Civic Learning and Democratic Engagement. (2012). *A crucible moment: College learning and democracy's future.* Washington, DC: Association of American Colleges and Universities.

Saltmarsh, J., and Hartley, M. (2011). *To serve a larger purpose: Engagement for democracy and the transformation of higher education.* Philadelphia, PA: Temple University Press.

Sanford, N. (1966). *Self and society.* New York, NY: Atherton Press.

Sobania, N., & Braskamp, L. A. (2009, Winter). Study abroad or study away: It's not merely semantics. *Peer Review, 11*, 17–20.

Terenzini, P. T., & Reason, R. D. (2010, June). *Toward a more comprehensive understanding of college effects on student learning.* Paper presented at the meeting of the Consortium of Higher Education Researchers, Oslo, Norway.

ABOUT THE CONTRIBUTORS

Jennifer L. Benning is an Assistant Professor in the Department of Civil and Environmental Engineering at the South Dakota School of Mines and Technology (SOSM&I) and the Creator and Program Director of the minor in Sustainable Engineering. She serves as a Coprincipal Investigator on a National Science Foundation program, Oglala Lakota College/South Dakota State University/South Dakota School of Mines and Technology Pre-Engineering Education Collaboration, which helps to support her and SDSM&T students' involvement in the Native American Sustainable Housing Initiative project; its primary focus is on increasing Native American participation in engineering fields. Her research expertise is in contaminant transport and indoor air quality. She obtained her BS in Civil Engineering at Rutgers University, her MS in Environmental Engineering at Virginia Tech, and her PhD in Environmental Engineering at the University of Alaska Fairbanks.

Jacquelyn Benton is a faculty member in the Department of Africana Studies at Metropolitan State University of Denver, where she has taught for several years. Courses that she has written for the department include African Authors, Black Women Writers, The African Diaspora, The New Negro Movement of the 1920s, and The Gullah Experience. Over the years, her interest in the African continent and African retention in the Americas has taken her to East Africa, Brazil, and Belize. More recently, she has begun to explore the transatlantic slave trade from the other side of the Atlantic. That interest has taken her to the United Kingdom in order to tour the permanent gallery on "London, Sugar, & Slavery," and the International Slavery Museum, located in London and Liverpool, respectively. Her passion, however, remains Gullah/Geechee culture in the Sea Islands of South Carolina and Georgia, where she has led six study tours to date.

Connie Ledoux Book came to Elon University in 1999 as a faculty member in the School of Communications to provide instruction in broadcast journalism and new media adoption. Since earning promotion to Professor, she has served as Associate Provost for Academic Affairs. Dr. Book's primary responsibilities include providing leadership for general education, the Elon experience (student engagement), academic advising, and career services. She earned her doctorate from the University of Georgia and publishes in the area of digital television.

Larry Braskamp graduated from Central College (Pella, Iowa) and earned his PhD from the University of Iowa, with a dual focus on Student Learning and Development and Statistics. He was a faculty member at the University of Nebraska–Lincoln, and held administrative positions as Dean of Applied Life Studies at the University of Illinois at Urbana–Champaign and Dean of Education at the University of Illinois at Chicago. He served as the Senior Vice President for Academic Affairs at Loyola University Chicago. He is a coauthor of numerous publications and seven books, including *Assessing Faculty Work and Putting Students First: How Colleges Develop Students Purposefully* (Jossey-Bass, 1994) and the survey instrument Global Perspective Inventory. Currently he is President of the Global Perspective Institute and consults with a number of colleges, universities, and other organizations that are committed to assisting students in becoming global learners and citizens.

Phil Brick is Miles C. Moore Professor of Politics and Director of Environmental Studies at Whitman College, an independent liberal arts college located in Walla Walla, Washington. His scholarly work focuses on environmental politics and natural resource policy on the nation's public lands, which constitute a third of the landmass of the United States. Most recently, his interests have moved to the impacts of climate change and to documentary film. He is codirector and producer of *The Beaver Believers*, a film about climate change, watershed restoration, and effective environmental activism in the Anthropocene. He is Founding Director of Whitman College Semester in the West, an experiential field program in environmental studies described in this volume. Brick earned his MA and PhD in Political Science at the University of California, Berkeley, and his BA in Government, summa cum laude, from Lawrence University in Appleton, Wisconsin.

Kathryn Burleson is a Psychology Professor at Warren Wilson College in Asheville, North Carolina. She earned an MA in Psychology from Humboldt State University in California in 1999 and a PhD in Developmental Psychology from the University of California, Santa Cruz in 2004. She is an active proponent of service-learning and utilizes the pedagogy in her courses covering child, adolescent, and adult development; cultural psychology; and psychology of creativity. Her continued dedication to service-learning was honored in 2011 when she was awarded the Andrew Summers Award for Faculty Leadership in Service. As the Director of General Education for Warren Wilson College, she coordinated the full revision of the general education program, championing the inclusion of "engaged citizenship" as one of the college's three overall educational outcomes. Her areas of interest include nurturing the transformation of students from service-learning participants to civically active leaders and building robust, ethical, and balanced relationships with community partners. Through her work, she seeks to promote collaboration, social justice, and intercultural learning.

Celestina Castillo is the Director of the Center for Community Based Learning (CCBL) at Occidental College. Prior to joining the CCBL, she was a community partner for over five years, primarily through the CCBL-founded Northeast Education Strategy Group, and as a supervisor and mentor for Occidental students regarding community projects. Castillo earned her BA in History at Pomona College, and an MS in Urban Policy Analysis and Management at New School University in New York. She has worked with a wide range of community-based organizations focused on education, workforce development, advocacy, and organizing. At the Los Angeles County Children's Planning Council she worked with a number of community-based service organizations, schools, and county departments to integrate community-organizing principles and practices into service-delivery models.

Lisa M. Davidson is a PhD student and research assistant in Loyola University Chicago's Higher Education program. She earned her master's degree in Counseling at DePaul University, where she has also served as an adjunct faculty member teaching undergraduate and graduate courses in liberal studies and college student development, respectively. Davidson's additional higher education experience spans enrollment management, career counseling, and academic advising, where she has focused on the role of academic support services in student learning. Her current research interests include examining the intersection of faculty identities and its relation to the learning environments and evaluative approaches employed by faculty. Davidson is also interested in examining effective practices to recruit and retain diverse faculty and the ways in which various aspects of diversity are conceptualized and assessed in postsecondary curricula.

Christina Dinges has served as a Higher Education Administrator in International Education for more than eight years, first at the University of North Carolina Exchange Program and the University of North Carolina at Greensboro. Dinges is currently the Study Away Advisor and Program Director of Cross-Cultural Programs in New Orleans and Cyprus for the Global Opportunities Program (GO) at Susquehanna University. She is an active NAFSA mentor to young professionals in Education Abroad and has presented on various related topics in International Education nationally and internationally, including the importance of cross-cultural competency and postexperiential programs for returning study away students. Dinges holds an MA in Liberal and Global Studies from University of North Carolina at Greensboro. She studied abroad in Germany at Mannheim University and has lived in, worked in, or visited more than 15 countries across the globe.

Linda Earle is the Executive Director of the New York Arts Program, an off-campus study program for undergraduate and postbaccalaureate students in the visual, performing, and media arts; writing; and journalism managed by Ohio Wesleyan University. Before joining NYAP she served as the Executive Director of Program for the Skowhegan School of Painting and Sculpture, one of the nation's leading organizations for emerging visual artists. She was a Senior Program Director at the New York State Council on the Arts, where the multidisciplinary Individual Artists Program was founded under her direction. She has taught film and cultural studies at Mason Gross School of the Arts, Rutgers University, Hunter College, and Barnard College and has served on numerous grants and commissioning panels and artist advocacy groups. Earle has worked on independent film, theatre, and film and visual arts curatorial projects over the years. As a writer, she has had residencies at Hedgebrook and NYC's Writers Room. She holds an MFA in Film from Columbia University and a BA in Film Culture from Hampshire College. She serves on the boards of Poets House, Art Matters, Inclusion in the Arts, and the Alliance of Artists Communities.

Michael Edmondson is the Associate Vice President for Career Development at Augustana College in Rock Island, Illinois. Previously he was a faculty member and Director of Marketing and Recruiting at The Philadelphia Center (TPC), an off-campus program founded in 1967 by the Great Lakes Colleges Association and managed by Hope College in Holland, Michigan. In 2013–2014, Dr. Edmondson was one of the 26 members of the 2013–2014 Senior Leadership Academy (cosponsored by The Council of Independent Colleges and American Academic Leadership Institute) that prepares mid-level administrators of higher education for vice presidencies. He graduated from Cabrini College (BA in History) in Radnor, Pennsylvania; Villanova University (MA in History) in Villanova, Pennsylvania, and Temple University (PhD in History) in Philadelphia, Pennsylvania. He has been the Keynote Speaker at the Minnesota Re-entry Conference and has presented at conferences hosted by the Accreditation Council for Business Schools & Programs, the Southern Regional Institute & Educational Technology and Training Center, Richard Stockton College of New Jersey, the

National Association of Experiential Education, and the National Business Incubator Association, to name a few.

Mark E. Engberg is Associate Professor and Chair of the Higher Education program at Loyola University Chicago. He earned his doctoral degree in Education from the University of Michigan and received his master's degree in Counseling Psychology from Northwestern University. Dr. Engberg's research investigates the educational benefits of diversity, with specific attention to how different college interventions can be used to prepare students for the diversity and global challenges of the twenty-first century. He also examines individual and organizational factors that underlie the college choice process, with a particular focus on improving access and opportunity for underserved populations. Engberg has published his work in a number of journals including *Review of Educational Research, TC Record, The Journal of Higher Education, The Review of Higher Education,* and *Research in Higher Education.*

Amanda E. Feller is an Associate Professor in the School of Arts and Communication at Pacific Lutheran University. Her teaching, scholarship, and practitioner work sits at the intersection of communication theory, conflict management, and pedagogy. She particularly focuses on the method of dialogue in learning and peace building. She works extensively with the Transformative Learning Association as well as with nongovernmental organizations using dialogue and transformative learning to create community in divided societies. Her publications and invited lectures address conceptual frameworks and skill-specific techniques related to communication efficacy, dialogue, and transformative pedagogy. Amanda's scholarship in experiential and transformative pedagogy is rooted in her work with students: taking students on the road every other weekend for speaking competitions, managing student internships, engaging in off-campus faculty–student research, and leading study away programs. She leads short-term off-campus courses in and about locations that have included London, Macedonia, Northern Ireland, Norway, and Serbia. She holds a BA from the University of Denver, an MS from Portland State University, and an MA and a PhD from the California Institute of Integral Studies. Her first teachers and study away facilitators were Don and Mary Feller, with whom she shares passions for travel, education, and gardening.

Regina Freer joined the faculty of Occidental College in 1996, after receiving her BA from UC Berkeley and PhD in Political Science from the University of Michigan. She is a Professor in the Politics Department. Her research and teaching interests include race and politics, demographic change, urban politics, and the intersection of all three in Los Angeles in particular. Dr. Freer has published widely in these areas and is coauthor of *The Next Los Angeles: The Struggle for a Livable City* (University of California Press, 2006). She is currently working on a study of Black community organizing in the Obama era and a biography of Charlotta Bass, an LA-based African American newspaper editor and activist who ran for vice president of the United States in 1952. She serves on a number of boards of LA-based community organizations and recently stepped down after eight years on the Los Angeles City Planning Commission, where she served as Vice President.

Joan Gillespie is Vice President and Director of Off-Campus Study Programs at the Associated Colleges of the Midwest (ACM), a consortium of 14 liberal arts colleges located in Illinois, Iowa, Minnesota, Wisconsin, and Colorado. She serves as a member of The Forum on Education Abroad Council and is Vice Chair of the Forum's Curriculum Development and Academic Design Committee. She was the Chair of the working group of the Forum's Standards Committee that developed guidelines for undergraduate research abroad. Joan also is an Instructor at Northwestern University School of Education and Social Policy in the graduate program in Higher Education Administration and Policy, where she teaches comparative higher education. She has authored articles and made presentations on quality standards and evaluation in international settings, assessment of student learning and development, and community-based student research. Prior to joining ACM, Joan served as Associate Vice President for Academic Affairs and Assessment and Program Dean at IES Abroad, with responsibilities for developing and managing programs of education abroad, initiating curricular innovations, and creating and implementing program quality standards and assessment guidelines. She holds an MA and a PhD in English Literature from Northwestern University, with a specialty in Anglophone literature and postcolonial theory, and a BA in History from Vassar College.

Felisa Guillén, Professor of Spanish at Occidental College, teaches courses in Spanish and on Spanish medieval, Renaissance, and Baroque literature. She publishes regularly on seventeenth-century narratives and their connections with the visual arts. Lately she has been expanding her research interests into the fields of heritage language learning and sociolinguistics as well as the scholarship of engagement. Her more recent publications explore different ways of including Latino communities in the teaching and learning process by developing long-lasting and mutually beneficial collaborations. A native of Madrid, Spain, Dr. Guillén holds a BA and an MA from Universidad Complutense and a PhD from the University of California Santa Barbara.

David R. Huelsbeck is Professor of Anthropology and Dean of Social Sciences at Pacific Lutheran University. Dave received his MA and PhD in Anthropology at Washington State University. He was part of the Ozette Archaeological Project, a collaboration between the Makah Tribe and Washington State University. Huelsbeck's research examines the frequency and distribution of faunal remains from different species and different cuts within a species to answer questions about socioeconomic status and social relations among people in prehistoric and historic contexts. His work ranges from the late prehistoric Northwest Coast to Gold Rush and post-Gold Rush sites in Skagway, Alaska, with prehistoric Native American and historic logging and mining sites in the Washington Cascades. As an anthropological archaeologist he strives to help students ask and answer good questions about the past and to understand the importance of collaborating with living descendent communities of the people being investigated. He belives that getting students into the field to do anthropology is the best way to teach anthropology.

JoDee Keller is Professor of Social Work and Chair of the Global Studies Program at Pacific Lutheran University. After attending Hope College and participating in the Great Lakes Colleges Association's Philadelphia Urban Semester, she earned her MA from the School of Social Service Administration, University of Chicago, and her PhD from Jane Addams College of Social Work, University of Illinois at Chicago, and has worked and consulted as a social worker primarily in public school settings. She teaches courses in direct social work practice and first-year experience programs, but also has taught short-term domestic and abroad off-campus courses. Her current research interests are in the area of public housing and immigrant communities as well as program evaluation. Most recent publications focus on challenges and strengths of public housing residents, development of community in public and mixed-housing developments, student learning and growth in study away experiences, and teaching strategies for social work.

Paul Kollman is an Associate Professor of Theology at the University of Notre Dame, where he has been on the faculty since 2001. He became the third director of Notre Dame's Center for Social Concerns in July 2012. Kollman is a fellow of the Kellogg Institute for International Studies, the Kroc Institute for International Peace Studies, and the Nanovic Institute for European Studies, all at Notre Dame. His academic interests include African Christianity, world Christianity, and international service-learning. He has taught in eastern Africa, and pursued research there and in Nigeria, South Africa, as well as in archives in Europe and the United States. Kollman received his BA and MDiv degrees from the University of Notre Dame and his doctorate from the University of Chicago Divinity School.

Kent Koth is the Founding Director of the Seattle University Center for Service and Community Engagement, where he has overseen a rapid expansion of campus–community partnerships that have received national recognition. Since 2009, Kent has also directed the Seattle University Youth Initiative, a long-term commitment by Seattle University faculty, staff, and students from all disciplines to join with parents, the Seattle School District, the city of Seattle, foundations, and more than 30 community organizations to help children of Seattle succeed in school and life. Kent is an adjunct faculty member in Seattle University's Liberal Studies program and has written several articles and book chapters related to service-learning and university–community partnerships. Earlier in his career, Kent worked as Executive Director of a nonprofit K–12 community-service organization and also served as Program Director of the Haas Center for Public Service at Stanford University. He received his BA from Grinnell College and his MA from the Pacific School of Religion.

Patty Lamson is the Director of International Programs at Earlham College, an institution that has developed an award-winning model for community-based study away programming and that is committed to creating a global learning community on campus. She collaborates closely with faculty and students in all facets of creating intentional, integrated learning experiences, including semester programs in Jordan, Nicaragua, Tanzania, Northern Ireland, Dharamsala in Northern India, Spain, France, England, Germany, and the U.S.-Mexico border; and May term immersion programs in various locations around the world. She also oversees advising of international students; the Thematic Studies Abroad Program, an exchange program with Waseda University in Tokyo, Japan, based at Earlham; and the English language program on campus. She and her husband created the Border Studies program in 1997 with support from the Great Lakes Colleges Association and co-led the program in 1998. They have also led many off-campus programs to Mexico and Spain. Lamson holds a BA from Ohio Wesleyan University, an MS and MA from Indiana University, and a PhD from Ball State University.

Leonard Lone Hill is an enrolled member of the Oglala Sioux Tribe, has been an instructor in the Oglala Lakota College Applied Science Department since 2006, and is the Construction Director for the Native American Sustainable Housing Initiative collaboration on Pine Ridge. Leonard has more than 20 years of experience working on tribal housing projects and his research interests include sustainable construction and traditional Lakota life-ways.

Donna Maeda is a Professor in the Department of Critical Theory and Social Justice at Occidental College in Los Angeles. She teaches courses about the politics of cultural representation; meanings of community; and critical studies in race, gender, culture, and law. She has served as a Cochair of Occidental's Community Engagement Working Group and Special Assistant to the President on issues of diversity and equity. Donna holds a PhD in Social Ethics from the University of Southern California and a JD from the University of California, Berkeley, School of Law (Boalt Hall).

Scott Manning is Dean of Global Programs and Associate Professor of French at Susquehanna University, where he has taught French, Italian, and Gender Studies. He has a PhD in French from the University of Kansas and has written and presented on French Literature and sexual orientation issues. More recently, he is the founding director of the Global Opportunities (GO) Program, an Andrew Heiskell award-winning cross-cultural experience and reflection requirement, through which every Susquehanna graduate must complete a study away immersion experience abroad or in the United States. He currently teaches Global Citizenship, a postexperience reflection course in the program, and has codirected short-term study away programs in France, Italy, and New Zealand. Scott has presented on a range of international education topics, including program assessment, student choices, and sexual orientation issues. His most recent work involves the development, with his partner, of a strengths-based approach to study abroad.

Oumatie Marajh is the Director of Study Abroad/Study Away and International Internship Programs in the College of Social Science at Michigan State University. She has more than 25 years of work experience with coordinating and managing study abroad programs. Her current position involves meeting with faculty on the design and development of new programs, creating and managing the international internship programs, and overseeing the portfolio of over 70 study abroad and study away programs in the college. She also supports the Dean and Associate Dean in providing leadership for new international education initiatives.

Rose McKenney teaches Geology courses in surficial processes, resource conservation, and spatial analysis; and coordinates interdisciplinary environmental studies courses at Pacific Lutheran University in Tacoma, Washington. She has also taught Environmental Geology at Minot State University (Minot, North Dakota) and Environmental Studies at Franklin College (Lugano, Switzerland). After receiving her undergraduate degree in geology at Oregon State University, she taught high school science at Tupou College while serving in the Peace Corps in the Kingdom of Tonga. She received her MS and her PhD in Geosciences from the Pennsylvania State University. Her field research has taken her to diverse environments from Florida swamps to upper Midwest prairies to rivers in the Yukon Territory. Her background in field geology; service, work, and travel abroad; and subsequent interdisciplinary teaching have led to a deep interest in pedagogies that combine service, inquiry into place, and interdisciplinary integration.

J. McMerty is the Founding Director of the Elon University in Los Angeles program. Based in Los Angeles, Professor McMerty provides oversight of the operations of the program and teaches courses in digital production. McMerty earned his MFA from the University of North Carolina at Greensboro in Film Production and his BA in Communications from Elon College. He is currently working on a documentary about artist Betty Gold's remarkable career that will be released in 2015.

Riley Merline is the Resident Director of the Earlham College Border Studies program. As part of his responsibilities in guiding the development of this community-based integrated program in Tucson, Arizona, he teaches a course on the historical and structural causes of undocumented migration from Mexico and Central America to the United States and the consequences for individuals and communities as a result of that migration. He is particularly interested in exploring with students the ethical implications of border restrictions in the twenty-first century. Before joining the Border Studies program, Riley worked on the Witness for Peace International Team in Colombia leading educational delegations and investigating the effects of Plan Colombia's military aid and antinarcotics programs on human rights and development efforts. After moving to Tucson, he worked for BorderLinks, leading experiential education seminars along the U.S.-Mexico border with a focus on migration and immigration policy, free trade, international debt, cross-border economies, labor issues, and human rights. Over the years Riley has also made work and study visits to Cuba, Puerto Rico, Venezuela, Nicaragua, and Chile. Riley holds an MA in Latin American Studies from the University of Arizona, where he focused on the history of U.S.–Latin American relations.

Rosina S. Miller is the Founding Director of Stanford in New York City. When this chapter was written, she was serving as the Executive Director (2007–2014) of The Philadelphia Center (TPC), an off-campus study program founded in 1967 by the Great Lakes Colleges Association (GLCA) and managed by Hope College. A longtime employee of TPC, she previously served as a faculty adviser, researching, teaching, and publishing in areas of urban culture, art and performance, and experiential education. As Executive Director, Rosina established the TPC Institute for Collaborative Urban Research to engage GLCA faculty in urban scholarship with the resources and opportunities available through TPC. She is also a cofounder and former member of the Board of Trustees of the Independence Charter School, a community-oriented elementary school that offers an internationally focused curriculum and the city's first Spanish immersion program. Miller holds an MA and a PhD in Folklore and Folklife from the University of Pennsylvania; an interdisciplinary MLA in Performance Studies, also from the University of Pennsylvania; and a BA in English from Temple University.

Esther Onaga is an Associate Professor in the Department of Human Development and Family Studies. Her doctorate is in Ecological Community Psychology from Michigan State University. She has conducted the Hawai'i Study Program for over 15 years in collaboration with the University of Hawai'i, utilizing service-learning as a mechanism to help students engage with Hawaiian and South Pacific cultures. She has worked with advocacy groups on policies related to children and youth with disabilities since 1985, and since 2002 she has coordinated the Michigan Family Impact Seminar for state policymakers. Her research program has been examining employment outcomes for people with disabilities. She has received funding from the Office of Special Education Programs and the National Institutes for Disability and Rehabilitation Research as well as from the Michigan Department of Community Health. Her teaching includes courses on introduction to human services, families of children with disabilities, ethnic minority families, family policy, and program design and evaluation. She has used service-learning in many of her courses to support students' education about taking the perspective of the "other." Her courses offered in the summer in Hawai'i in large part included service-learning.

Melanie Parker is Cofounder of Northwest Connections and serves as its Executive Director. Melanie is an award-winning educator who has developed and taught a number of field-based ecology courses. She is also known for her ability to bring diverse people together to accomplish large-scale projects. Parker was the primary catalyst behind the Montana Legacy Project, an effort to permanently protect 310,000 acres of corporate timberland. She graduated with honors from the University of California at Santa Cruz in 1988 with a bachelor's degree in Environmental Studies. She then completed a master's in Education combined with a Secondary Education Teaching Credential at UCSC in 1990. Melanie attained a master's of science degree in Environmental Studies from the University of Montana in 1997. Melanie is on the steering committee for the Rural Voices for Conservation Coalition, serves on the Forest Stewardship Council U.S. Board of Directors, and has been the chair of the local school board for over 10 years.

Sarah Pradt is Director of Programs at the Higher Education Consortium for Urban Affairs (HECUA), a consortium of about 20 institutions with a shared dedication to off-campus study that prepares students with the tools and skills for making social change. At HECUA, Sarah is responsible for the design and quality of 14 immersive off-campus study programs that focus on social justice. These programs immerse undergraduates in analysis and action in the Twin Cities of Minneapolis/Saint Paul and in rural Minnesota; in Jackson, Mississippi; and in Bangladesh, Ecuador, New Zealand, Northern Ireland, and Norway. The programs take up issues like poverty, inequality, climate change, food justice, racism, international development, indigenous rights, conflict and peace, immigration, and globalization. Sarah has degrees in English and East Asian Literature from Cornell University, and has held faculty positions in modern Japanese literature and film. She taught and wrote about representations of AIDS/HIV in Japan, the persistence of the image of the geisha in Japan and the United States, and communist and pro-gressive writers in wartime Japan. She serves on the board of AdopSource, a nonprofit dedicated to meaningful integration of culture and life experience for transracial adoptees.

Rob Pyatt is a Senior Instructor and Research Associate, has been in the Environmental Design Program at the University of Colorado Boulder since 2008, and is the Director of the Native American Sustainable Housing Ini-tiative. He has extensive experience in design-build and community-based research projects focused in rural and tribal communities. His research inter-ests include affordable housing design, tribal housing, housing design edu-cation, sustainable technologies, and alternative materials and methods of construction. He obtained his bachelor of environmental design (BEnvd) at the University of Colorado Boulder and a professional master of architecture (MArch) at the University of Colorado Denver.

Kathy Russell is Chair and Assistant Professor in the Department of Social Work at Pacific Lutheran University, where she teaches policy and macro social work practice classes. Kathy came to PLU from the University of Nebraska at Kearney, where she was Director of the Social Work Program, and from her private macro social work practice, Great Plains Consulting, where she specialized in large-group dispute resolution, training, and congre-gational and organizational development. She earned her BSW from Lock

Haven University, and her MSW and PhD from the University of North Carolina at Chapel Hill.

Mark Salisbury is Assistant Dean and Director of Institutional Research and Assessment at Augustana College in Rock Island, Illinois. His research has explored the predictors of participation and the learning outcomes of study abroad. He is a coauthor of the Association for the Study of Higher Education monograph *Study Abroad in a New Global Century*. His work has been featured in *The Chronicle of Higher Education, Inside Higher Ed*, and on NPR. More recently, his writing focuses on the nature of learning outcomes assessment and its role in spurring institutional improvement. In addition, Mark writes *Delicious Ambiguity*, a weekly blog that explores how Augustana College uses evidence to improve the quality of student learning (www.augustana.edu/blogs/ir).

Neal W. Sobania has been involved in global education for more than 30 years, initially as the Director of the Fried Center at Hope College (Holland, Michigan) and then the Executive Director of the Wang Center for Global Education at Pacific Lutheran University (Tacoma, Washington). As a U.S. Peace Corps Volunteer he taught ESL and served as a staff member in Ethiopia, worked in Kenya as a consultant on arid land projects for Unesco and the Federal Republic of Germany, and has held visiting appointments at Meiji Gakuin University (Tokyo) and the University of Michigan. During his career in international education he served as the Chair of the Conference for IES and Chair of the Academic Consortium Board for CIEE, was a National Consultant with NAFSA, and served on numerous committees, all the while also maintaining his standing as a recognized scholar. In his other identity, he is an Africanist who regularly researches, writes, and publishes on Ethiopia and Kenya, visual culture, and photographs as historical documents. He holds a PhD in History from the University of London (School of Oriental and African Studies) and an MA in International Affairs from Ohio University. His BA is from Hope College, where as an undergraduate he studied abroad in Yugoslavia. He is Professor of History at Pacific Lutheran University.

Jeff Thaler is the University of Maine's first Visiting Professor of Energy Policy, Law and Ethics, and Assistant University Counsel for environmental, energy, and sustainability projects. He graduated magna cum laude from Williams College and from Yale Law School. He has developed and taught multidisciplinary courses at Maine Law School and UMaine to law, graduate, and undergraduate students on renewable energy, climate change, and energy economics issues, as well as administrative law at Maine Law. In 2006–2007

Professor Thaler created, and has directed annually since, a nationally unique program for Williams College students entitled Resettling Refugees in Maine, where the students each live for a month with a refugee or immigrant family and work with school and public health service providers in Portland, Maine. He also helped start, and currently chairs for the third time, a fund at Williams College that promotes innovative experiential education programming on and off campus, and has frequently presented on pedagogies that encourage students' uncomfortable learning and active, deep self-reflection. Before joining the university, Professor Thaler developed over several decades a wide-ranging legal practice focusing upon environmental and energy matters, as well as litigation for a wide range of clients.

Nick Tilsen is an enrolled member of the Oglala Sioux Tribe and the Founding Executive Director of the Thunder Valley Community Development Corporation on the Pine Ridge Indian Reservation. Nick has over 11 years of experience in working with nonprofit organizations and tribal nations on projects that have a social mission. Nick is also currently the Project Director for Oyate Omnicye, funded by the Department of Housing and Urban Development's Office of Sustainable Housing & Communities to create a reservation-wide plan for sustainable development for the Oglala Lakota Nation. President Barack Obama at the 2012 White House Tribal Nations Conference recognized Nick's community service in support of the Pine Ridge community.

Charles Jason Tinant is a faculty member at Oglala Lakota College (OLC) and Principal Investigator for the pre-engineering collaborative among OLC, South Dakota School of Mines and Technology, and South Dakota State University. Tinant teaches coursework in civil engineering and earth science using a project-based service-learning approach. Tinant's formal and informal background in service-learning and stakeholder development includes a watershed survey in Haiti as part of a project to replace the existing water collection and distribution system for Hospital Albert Schweitzer, seven months at the Darkhan branch of the Mongolian University of Science and Technology as a visiting water resources instructor and researcher, and a two-year internship as a natural resources specialist through a joint appointment with the Environmental Careers Organization and the Bureau of Livestock Management to develop adaptive management approaches for threatened and endangered species in Off-Highway Vehicle use areas. At OLC, Tinant collaborates with students, academic collaborators, and Tribal Agencies to address sustainability issues involving surface and ground water resources, stream health, and housing on the Pine Ridge reservation.

Rachel Tomas Morgan is Assistant Director of the Center for Social Concerns and Director of International Engagement, where she oversees the international engagement efforts of the Center and works with the Center's justice education programming. Tomas Morgan designed, implemented, and directs the Center's International Summer Service Learning Program and works with other Center colleagues on international service-learning and community-based learning abroad. As a concurrent assistant professional specialist faculty in the Department of Theology, she teaches courses associated with the Center's international programs. She also works with faculty across the university interested in developing courses that include an international experiential or community-based learning component and consults on international related initiatives across the university. She served on the working group for international volunteerism with the Brookings Institute and presents and writes in the fields of international education, service-learning, and global learning. Tomas Morgan received her MA in the area of Systematic Theology from the University of Notre Dame. She has previously worked in international development and natural disaster assistance, religious studies in secondary education, and faith-based social outreach.

William Webb is an Associate Professor of Performing Arts and the founding director of the Elon University in New York City program. In addition to his teaching responsibilities, Professor Webb serves as the Lighting Designer and Production Manager for Performing Arts. A native western New Yorker, Webb earned his MFA from the University of North Carolina School of the Arts and his BA from Alfred University. Professor Webb's scholarly work is in theatrical design and production and he has worked with companies such as Cirque du Soleil, Arkansas Repertory Theatre, Bungalow Scenic Studios, and I. Weiss Inc.

Adam Weinberg is President of Denison University. Previous to this he was President and CEO of World Learning, an international nonprofit that provides exchange and development programs in more than 60 countries, and before that he was Vice President and Dean of the college at Colgate University, where he was a member of the Sociology Department. At Colgate he gained national prominence for his work on increasing the level of civic engagement at colleges and universities, and founded a number of organizations, including the Center for Outreach, Volunteerism, and Education (COVE) and the Partnership for Community Development. He holds a BA from Bowdoin College, and studied at Cambridge University before earning his MA and PhD in Sociology from Northwestern University. He has coauthored two books, Urban Recycling and the Search for Sustainable Development and Local Environmental Struggles (Princeton University Press, 2000), and has published in a range of academic journals as well as articles in The Washington Quarterly, The Chronicle of Higher Education, Inside Higher Education, and Peer Review. He is a member of the Council on Foreign Relations and of the Higher Education Working Group on Global Issues.

Joel Zylstra serves as the Director of the Center for Community Engagement and Service at Pacific Lutheran University, located in Tacoma, Washington. He received his master's degree in Educational Leadership from Miami University and has taught multicultural education and sociocultural foundations of education at the undergraduate level. Joel was instrumental in developing a Master of Arts in Global Urban Leadership program, which served leaders living and serving in informal settlements in Nairobi, Kenya. His scholarly interests include K–12/higher education intersections, college access, and place-based university community engagement.

INDEX

Also available from Stylus Publishing

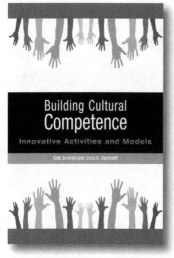

Building Cultural Competence

Innovative Activities and Models

Edited by Kate Berardo and Darla K. Deardorff

Foreword by Fons Trompenaars

For HR directors, corporate trainers, college administrators, diversity trainers, and study abroad educators, this book provides a cutting-edge framework and an innovative collection of ready-to-use tools and activities to help build cultural competence—from the basics of understanding core concepts of culture to the complex work of negotiating identity and resolving cultural differences.

Building Cultural Competence presents the latest work in the intercultural field and provides step-by-step instructions for how to effectively work with the new models, frameworks, and exercises for building learners' cultural competence. Featuring fresh activities and tools from experienced coaches, trainers, and facilitators from around the globe, this collection of over 50 easy-to-use activities and models has been used successfully worldwide in settings that range from Fortune 500 corporations to the World Bank, non-profits, and universities.

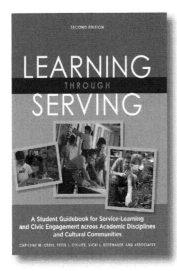

Learning Through Serving

A Student Guidebook for Service-Learning and Civic Engagement Across Academic Disciplines and Cultural Communities

Second Edition

Christine M. Cress, Peter J. Collier, and Vicki L. Reitenauer

Reviews of the first edition

"[This] is a self-directed guide for college students engaged in service-learning. The purpose of the book is to walk the reader through elements of learning and serving by focusing on how students can 'best provide meaningful service to a community agency or organization while simultaneously gaining new skills, knowledge, and understanding as an integrated aspect of the [student's] academic program.' [The authors] bring their expertise to the pages of this helpful and practical guide for college students engaged in service-learning. Intended as a textbook, this work reads like a conversation between the authors and the college student learner. The publication is student-friendly, comprehensive, easy to follow, and full of helpful activities."

—Journal of College Student Development

"Finally, a companion reader for students in service-learning courses! It is filled with meaningful exercises to help students make sense of their service experience and relate it to the course content. This is an important contribution to the field of service learning and faculty should utilize this book to help students understand and make the most of their service-learning experience."

—Elaine K. Ikeda, Executive Director, California Campus Compact

Working Side by Side

Creating Alternative Breaks as Catalysts for Global Learning, Student Leadership, and Social Change

Shoshanna Sumka, Melody Christine Porter, and Jill Piacitelli

This book constitutes a guide for student and staff leaders in alternative break (and other community engagement, both domestic and international) programs, offering practical advice, outlining effective program components and practices, and presenting the underlying community engagement and global learning theory.

The authors address student leadership development; issue-focused education; questions of power, privilege, and diversity; and the challenges of working in reciprocal partnerships with community organizations. They offer guidance on fund-raising, budget management, student recruitment, program structures, the nuts and bolts of planning a trip, risk management, health and safety, and assessment and evaluation. They address the complexities of international service-learning and developing partnerships with grassroots community groups, nongovernmental and nonprofit organizations, and intermediary organizations.

For new programs, this book provides a starting point and resource to return to with each stage of development. For established programs, it offers a theoretical framework to reflect on and renew practices for creating active citizens and working for justice.

22883 Quicksilver Drive
Sterling, VA 20166-2102   Subscribe to our e-mail alerts: www.Styluspub.com